D1226848

Probability and Certainty in Seventeenth-Century England

Barbara J. Shapiro

Probability and Certainty in Seventeenth-Century England

A STUDY OF THE RELATIONSHIPS BETWEEN NATURAL SCIENCE, RELIGION, HISTORY, LAW, AND LITERATURE

PRINCETON UNIVERSITY PRESS

Princeton, New Jersey

Copyright © 1983 by Princeton University Press
Published by Princeton University Press, 41 William Street, Princeton, New Jersey
In the United Kingdom: Princeton University Press, Guildford, Surrey

Publication of this book has been aided by a grant from the Paul Mellon Fund
of Princeton University Press

This book has been composed in Linotron Baskerville

Clothbound editions of Princeton University Press books are printed on acid-free
paper, and binding materials are chosen for strength and durability

Printed in the United States of America by Princeton University Press,
Princeton, New Jersey

To Martin and Eve

CONTENTS

	Acknowledgments	ix
I	Introduction	3
II	Natural Philosophy and Experimental Science	15
III	Religion	74
IV	History	119
V	Law	163
VI	Witchcraft	194
VII	Language, Communication, and Literature	227
VIII	Conclusion	267
	Notes	273
	Index	333

ACKNOWLEDGMENTS

IN A VERY REAL sense the origins of this book can be traced to the undergraduate teaching of Professors Mark Curtis and Trygve Tholfsen, then of U.C.L.A., who introduced me to intellectual history and to the intriguing but elusive relationship between religion and science.

I was fortunate enough to do a good deal of research at the William Andrews Clark Memorial Library, the Huntington Library, the Los Angeles County Law Library, the British Library, and the Bodleian Library, whose librarians were unfailingly helpful. All scholars engaged in Tudor and Stuart intellectual history are deeply indebted to the microfilm projects that have made available such a large proportion of the works printed in early modern England. I spent many happy hours comfortably ensconsed in the well-equipped microfilm reading facilities of the History Department of the University of California, San Diego.

I have dispensed with a bibliography both because the notes are so numerous and because the chapter divisions should make it relatively easy to locate references on a given topic. The spelling and punctuation in most quotations from contemporary sources have been modernized.

My research was aided by a University of California, San Diego, summer research grant. A fellowship from the National Endowment for the Humanities in 1980-1981 enabled me to complete the manuscript. The Research Committee of the University of California, Berkeley, the Abigail Hodgen Publication Fund, the Center for Studies in Higher Education and the Yale Law School, defrayed most of the typing costs. I would especially like to thank typists Lorrie McCracken and Wanda Mulcahy, who patiently struggled with my difficult-to-decipher drafts and footnotes, and the "galley slaves" Jonathan Bielak, Wanda Mulcahy, and Marilyn Raff.

A number of colleagues at the University of California, San Diego and the University of California, Berkeley, have discussed various aspects of the project with me. Professors Art Quinn and Tom Sloan read portions of an earlier version of the manuscript and saved me from at least some errors. I would also like to thank my colleagues in the Department of Rhetoric for broadening my intellectual horizons and introducing me to the richness of the rhetorical tradition.

The scholarly journals in which several of the book's themes were initially explored have generously permitted me to draw on those materials. Portions of Chapter III initially appeared in "Latitudinarianism and Science in Seventeenth Century England," *Past and Present*, No. 40 (July 1968) World Copyright, the Past and Present Society. An earlier version of part of Chapter V appeared as "Law and Science in Seventeenth Century England," *Stanford Law Reveiw* 21 (1969). A substantial portion of Chapter IV draws on "History and Natural History in Sixteenth and Seventeenth Century England: An Essay on the Relationship between Humanism and Science," which was delivered to the William Andrews Clark Library Seminar, February 5, 1977; and subsequently published in their Seminar Series as part of *English Scientific Virtuosi in the 16th and 17th Centuries* (University of California, Los Angeles, 1979).

I want to thank Martin Shapiro for many many hours of copyediting. I also owe a great deal to the patience of my daughter Eve, who usually, if not always, accepted with good grace the fact that I was often more occupied with the seventeenth than the twentieth century.

June 1982   B.J.S.

Probability and Certainty in Seventeenth-Century England

I

Introduction

WITH A FEW notable exceptions, scholars dealing with seventeenth-century intellectual history have devoted themselves to studies dealing with a single aspect of English thought. While this specialized scholarly effort has enormously deepened our knowledge of natural science, religion, history, law, and literature, it has not lent itself to looking at the broader continuities and changes that characterized English intellectual life. When the various facets of that life are examined together, a set of common concerns emerges that binds together most of those who thought and wrote about natural, spiritual, and social truth. Above all, there is a common set of assumptions about the nature of truth, the methods for attaining it, and the degree of probability or certainty that might be attributed to the findings produced by those methods.

These common methodological concerns were the consequence of the modification and eventual breakdown of a centuries-old tradition that divided "science," "knowledge," "certainty," and "philosophy" on the one hand, from "opinion," "probability," "appearance," and "rhetoric" on the other. It was the erosion of this scheme, derived from the ancient Greeks and Romans and revived by early Renaissance humanists, that subtly altered the way in which research and investigation in many fields was pursued and made possible a more intimate relationship between empirical, natural philosophy and religious, historical, legal, and even literary thought.

The breakdown of this dichotomized vision of human knowledge involved rethinking a family of concepts and ideas, none of which was entirely new. Included in this family were "certitude," "demonstration," "probability," "evidence," "matters of fact," "hypothesis," and "conjecture"—all of them related to fundamental issues of the nature of truth and man's ability to apprehend it. It was the reshaping of relationships among these concepts that modified the

3

way many seventeenth-century English intellectuals approached theoretical problems relating to the nature of knowledge. By the end of the seventeenth century, most English thinkers, no matter what their field of inquiry, had ceased to believe that their labors would produce the certitude or "science" that had for centuries been the goal of the philosopher.

As the natural scientists became more empirical and more concerned with matters of fact, and as those in other fields became more sensitive to issues relating to evidence and proof, knowledge in all fact-related fields was seen to fall along a continuum. The lower reaches of this continuum were characterized as "fiction," "mere opinion," and "conjecture"; its middle and high ranges as "probable" and "highly probable"; and its apex as "morally certain." "Knowledge" was no longer reserved for the logically demonstrable products of mathematical and syllogistic "science." The morally certain was also a form of knowledge, and the highly probable came close to being another.

Although the terms, as well as the categories, of demonstrable science and of probability were the legacy of the ancient world, the work of seventeenth-century intellectuals was not simply a recombination of earlier views, but rather an innovative development of important new directions in modern thought. Traditional concepts were employed to create a new pattern of thought.

The reshaping of science, opinion, and belief produced a satisfying, if not certain, natural philosophy; and this development in turn made possible a closer relationship between science and fields once thought to be evaluated by entirely different standards. Experience, conjecture, and opinion, which once had little or no role in philosophy or physics, and probability, belief, and credibility, once the possession of the rhetorician, theologian, and lawyer, now became relevant and even crucial categories for natural scientists and philosophers. Indeed, much of the "new philosophy" was recognized as incapable of the certainty traditionally expected of science. Investigators of natural and social phenomena now encountered similar, if not identical, methodological problems. The knowledge derived from these investigations involved an enormous expansion of the realm of the probable and a contraction of the certain. This enormous expansion of the "factual", together with reduced expectations of the certainty of results, gave English thought its special character.

The quest for certitude was not abandoned, but it soon became evident that only mathematics and a few logical and metaphysical principles were capable of demonstration in the strict sense. Most English intellectuals were deeply concerned with matters empirical, and they concluded that neither the syllogism nor mathematical reasoning was an appropriate vehicle for ordering the data they were collecting. Larger and larger portions of intellectual endeavor that once had been expected to attain the status of science by achieving demonstrative truth were now relegated to the domain of one level or another of probability. A fundamental problem, then, was to work out standards for well-founded, reasonable, highly probable, but noncertain, belief.

In the course of establishing such standards, one issue that became crucial was that of fallibility—both the fallibility of the senses, which threatened empirical observation, and the fallibility of the understanding, which threatened conclusions derived from that observation. One important aspect of this fallibility was individual and cultural bias, for which various antidotes were suggested; but beyond the concern for bias lay a vivid appreciation of the fundamental limits of the human condition. The result was a tension between skepticism and inquiry that was partially resolved by the assertion that cooperative, collective efforts by many investigators, over time, would achieve relatively error-free findings that, if not "certain" in the old sense, would at least attain to the highest level of the probable. By the end of the seventeenth century, most English thinkers found considerable satisfaction in a highly probabilistic knowledge. A willingness to accept the notion that very little in this world was capable of "science" had become an accustomed feature of English intellectual life.

Because one of the key features in this acceptance of the probable was a new relationship between the two ancient traditions of logic and rhetoric, we must briefly trace those traditions. The goal of philosophy in the ancient world was knowledge or science. Its model tended to be logical demonstration, which produced a certitude in the mind that was compelled. Although natural philosophers might consider sense data, they sought to establish immutable, causal relations in physics and to apprehend the nature of reality itself. Philosophy, with its goal of demonstrative certitude and apprehension of the forms or being of nature, was contrasted with the fluctuating realm of sense impression, common experience, and opinion—the realm of ordinary perception and ordinary life. If the master of the "truth" and "science" was the philosopher, the master of the commonplace world of appearance and the world of affairs came to be the rhetorician, whose function was to persuade popular audiences about matters of common interest. The rhetorician, or orator, might sway or convince his audience to one or another desired opinion by means of his skill with words and arguments and by playing on the emotions, biases, or commonly held views of his audience. In the ancient world, then, philosophy was associated with truth, logic, compelled assent, and an intellectual elite, while rhetoric was associated with opinion, experience, probability, the active life, choice, and popular appeal.

This basic dichotomy continued until the sixteenth century, although it had necessarily been modified in important ways to include the "truth" of Christianity, which must be "believed." Christianity required belief or faith in a truth that was not acquired by philosophical or logical means. It was a truth that involved choice, not compelled assent, and was accessible to ordinary and nonphilosophically trained individuals. It was also a truth based on the acceptance of a set of historical events.

Especially after the revival of Aristotle's work, the medieval period employed the dichotomized tradition of knowledge and opinion with an overlay of Christianity. From the thirteenth to the sixteenth centuries, philosophy or "science" was dominated by Aristotelian logic and Aristotelian natural philosophy. Although Aristotle had not neglected empirical investigation, neither he nor his medieval successors were able to bridge the gap between contingent sense experience and the certitude of principles on which it was agreed that demonstrative science must rest. However much the Aristotelians might refer to sense data, in the end they required an intuitive recognition of principles. Scholastic philosophers and theologians also developed a science of opinion, which they called dialectic. On the whole, dialectic tended to follow the pattern of logic. There was a general conflation of logic and dialectic, and later thinkers tended to think of them as essentially the same method. A self-conscious, rhetorical tradition was largely, if not completely, eclipsed during the medieval era.[1]

RENAISSANCE HUMANISM

Humanism, the most dynamic and influential intellectual movement of the Renaissance, played a significant though ambivalent role in the development of an empirical and probabilistic approach to human knowledge. On the one hand, the humanists retained and gave new importance to the dichotomy between philosophy and rhetoric. They expressed a good deal of hostility toward logic, formal philosophy, and the natural sciences, which, at least initially, they placed firmly in the realm of logical demonstration. On the other hand, they revived an intellectual interest in experience of the ordinary, everyday variety. Most humanists concentrated on moral philosophy, history, and literature very broadly defined. Employing and developing the skills and tools of ancient orators, they dealt with the world of common experience in terms of the probable, the likely, and the verisimilar. They concerned themselves little, or not at all, with the formal systematic search for abstract truth. If the humanists did not entirely relinquish all claims to wisdom which necessarily involved philosophy, their passion for rhetoric provided their basic intellectual identity.[2] Although the ideal of combining rhetoric and philosophy was voiced from time to time, efforts to link them were almost always entirely directed toward capturing the wisdom provided by moral philosophy not natural philosophy or metaphysics. By the beginning of the sixteenth century, the humanists had not only created a worldly, active intellectual style but had contributed substantially to the declining reputation of scholastic philosophy, with its disputational forms, inelegant technical vocabulary, and metaphysical concerns.

The sixteenth century produced several shifts in humanist thought which had a substantial, if indirect, impact on the development of natural philosophy and empirical research. After the middle of the fifteenth century, some humanists turned in the direction of philosophy, toward which they had previously expressed disinterest or distaste. There was renewed study of Plato, and then of the ancient skeptics, epicureans, atomists, and others.

If the humanists did not become extremely involved in the natural sciences, which were still dominated by Aristotelian physics, their expressions of hostility to the study of nature became less common and less sharp.[3] This change in tone may in part be related to a growing sense of self-confidence and self-esteem, and in part to the changing intellectual environment. The expansion of factual knowledge of the Old and New Worlds made a great impression on humanists and nonhumanists alike. Not only were the new facts interesting in and of themselves, but they seemed to suggest that the ancient world was not the repository of all knowledge. An orientation toward the future became possible. Indeed, some sixteenth-century humanists began to treat politics and history in a more matter-of-fact, less moralistic, and less rhetorical manner. If the humanists remained readily distinguishable from academic, scholastic philosophers and Aristotelian scientists, they were becoming less distinguishable from natural philosophers and naturalists. This convergence became even more clear as the emphasis on experience and considerations of utility, long of interest to the humanists, began to pervade those arts and sciences oriented toward nature and technology. Humanists like Acontio and Vives stressed the importance of artisans and practical men. These themes would be developed further by Bacon and the Royal Society.

The beginnings of a breakdown or, at least, an erosion of the boundary between demonstrative certainty and probability that had once marked off the rival territories of philosophers and humanists can be seen in the writings of Vives. He not only introduced a kind of empiricism but suggested that it was often necessary to be content with probabilities where rigorous proofs were not possible. Vives signals the new humanist interest in natural observation, the practical arts, and the utility of knowledge; there is, in addition, a hint that probability might become relevant to philosophy.[4] On the whole, however, both Aristotelians and anti-Aristotelians like Campanella and Telesio, who stressed the importance of the senses, were still striving for certain universal principles.[5]

The wall that for centuries had separated philosophy from rhetoric, reason from experience, and certainty from probability crumbled still further as a number of humanists attempted to develop unified arts of discourse that rearranged and combined elements of logic, dialectic, and rhetoric.[6] These efforts, the best known being that of Ramus, blurred once separate and distinct intellectual modes at the very time that Aristotelian philosophy and scholastic logic were losing prestige. In the process, particular subject matters and disciplines lost their definitive moorings in rhetoric or philosophy. It became increasingly unclear which kinds of proofs, evidence, language, or appeals were appropriate to which subject matters.

Yet the movement was clearly not all in one direction. The sixteenth century also brought with it a renewal of the demonstrative model of science based on mathematics. The new interest in mathematics did much to revitalize the traditional division between science and nonscience. Indeed, the mathematical model began to edge out logic, and particularly the syllogism, as the model for demonstration. On the whole, it was Continental rather than English thinkers who were attracted to and developed the new model of demonstrative certainty joined to a causal physics associated with and dependent on mathematics. This approach, even more fully developed in the seventeenth century, retained the ancient distinction between the realms of demonstrative science and probable opinion and experience.

During the sixteenth century, too, one wing of the humanist, rhetorical tradition was increasingly preoccupied with poetics and aesthetics, so much so that at times it is difficult to distinguish rhetorical from poetic theory. Poetry and literary humanism were thus becoming more involved with the imagination and with fictional literary creations and aesthetic criticism. Those deeply committed to this kind of aesthetic concern expressed relatively little interest in experimental science.

Thus, by the end of the sixteenth century, the categories philosopher, humanist, and scientist no longer quite fit the persons to whom we wish to apply them, and it was not clear in what direction the developments of the century would lead. Remarkably few sixteenth-century intellectuals claimed to be philosophers or consciously practiced philosophy. If the next generation of natural philosophers adopted the mathematical, demonstrative mode, and if rhetoric continued to merge with poetry and fictive literature, the traditional dichtomy of logic and rhetoric might well continue to flourish, and the realms of knowledge and opinion presumably would remain as separate as they had been for centuries. If, however, the number of humanists with interests in the natural world continued to increase, and if experience, appearance, and probability came to have philosophical and scientific relevance, much of the traditional division between knowledge and opinion, between certitude and probability, would erode, and the possibility would arise of creating a new philosophy on an experiential base. Although both of these tendencies continued in play, this book will argue that the development of a family of ideas that breached the epistemological barrier between logic and rhetoric, or knowledge and opinion, created a distinct intellectual style that marked the endeavors of nearly all seventeenth-century Englishmen engaged in philosophy, the investigation of nature, religion, history, law, and even literature.

We will first focus on the reorientation of scientific thought that occurred as empiricism became more central to scientific endeavor. Mathematics and those aspects of physics which continued their search for certainty will be contrasted with the empirically grounded sciences that examined the phenomena of nature. We will suggest that, while the Baconian model of scientific inquiry still aspired to certain knowledge, most members of the mid- and late seventeenth-century English scientific community[7] adopted a quite different approach to scientific knowledge, one that attributed moral certainty or a high degree of probability to any knowledge derived from observation of fact. A sketch of the research program of the Royal Society and its members will indicate tensions between the Baconian quest for certainty and the growing realization that products of empirical investigation could not be made to yield such certainty. An essentially Baconian research program was combined with a philosophy of science that substituted concepts of probability once associated with rhetoric for the demonstrative certainty traditionally associated with science and logic. With few exceptions, the dominant approach to English science became empirical and probabilistic.

Theologians and churchmen also were forced to reconsider the complex problems of certainty, knowledge, and belief. We will be particularly concerned with efforts to establish a rational foundation for the truths of natural religion and of scriptural Revelation, as well as with Protestant-Roman Catholic controversy over infallible religious knowledge. During this period, numerous groups claimed possession of religious truth, some on the basis of tradition, others on the basis of Scripture or divine illumination. Practical problems of Church government and of how to handle religious dissent were linked to theories of knowledge and the nature of religious belief. The seventeenth-century movements toward toleration and latitudinarianism were intimately related to changing theories of knowledge and new claims about the degrees of probability or certainty that might be assigned to religious doctrine. Over time, it seemed increasingly obvious to some Englishmen that religious persecution and enforced conformity made little sense if one had little confidence in the certainty of any given theological doctrine or in the divine authority of any particular religious practice or ceremony. Many seventeenth-century English religious controversies—polemical, theological, and ecclesiastical—were intimately related to problems of evidence and proof.

We then will survey historical thought, particularly the extent to which early modern English historians felt it possible to make true statements about events they could not have observed directly. Central to this problem were their modes of evaluating sources and their concern for the validity of testimony and authority. Here, again, we will discuss the degrees of probability and certainty that seventeenth-century Englishmen thought might be assigned to their findings. The treatment of history also emphasizes the linkages between seventeenth-century natural science and seventeenth-century historical thought. In particular, it will develop the parallelism between that branch of science called natural history and other sorts of history, and compare scientific and historical approaches to hypothesis, conjecture, and causal explanation. We will not argue that history is or ought to be particularly scientific, but rather that the reorientation of English natural philosophy, which gave a new prominence to experience and matters of fact, forced historians and naturalists into a closer relationship. When the natural sciences became more empirical, many seventeenth-century historians embraced the new scientific currents. They did so, however, without fully abandoning the literary, and even the moral, aspirations derived from the older association of history with rhetoric. Perhaps for the first time in European historiography, the historian experienced the contrary pulls of literature and science that he has experienced ever since.

The link between historical and religious thought will also be explored. Particular attention will be given to theologians and historians who explicitly applied the same approaches to establishing historical facts and the truth of Scripture and to those who argued that historical conviction and religious conviction involved the same intellectual processes.

The discussion of seventeenth-century legal thought which follows will again encounter assessments of probability and degrees of certainty, as well as the concept "beyond a reasonable doubt." We will be particularly concerned with problems of evidence and the changing roles of judges, juries, and witnesses in the truth-finding process. It is in this connection that we will see how changing views of the nature of human knowledge in the realms of science and religion were brought to bear on legal thinking about evidence.

Unlike earlier chapters, Chapter VI, which deals with witchcraft, does not examine a recognized type of scholarly endeavor but instead seeks to investigate a working arena in which the newer modes of evaluation of evidence encountered older belief systems. Changing attitudes toward evidence and proof seem to have been involved in both the decline of witch belief among educated elites and in the rapid seventeenth-century decline in prosecution and conviction for witchcraft. The problems associated with witchcraft also seemed to have helped to focus both religious and philosophical approaches to the inference of nonobservable forces from observable data. The issues connected with witchcraft were linked not only to epistemology, to religion, and to fact finding in general but also to the necessities of proving disputed facts at law.

Our discussion of seventeenth-century approaches to evidence then turns to the realm of language and literature. Here we will suggest that the breakdown of once distinct categories of philosophy and rhetoric modified notions of appropriate language and terminology. Attempts were made to bring words and the phenomena to which they referred into a closer relationship, and there were efforts to create a universal philosophical language.

These developments were at least partly responsible for the well-known seventeenth-century critiques of certain varieties of poetry and of traditional rhetoric and for the advocacy of a plain, unadorned style. Traditional rhetorical usage presented special problems to the experimental scientists of the Royal Society, who responded in part by attacking contemporary rhetoric and poetry, and in part by rethinking and re-examining the nature of language itself. Portions of the religious, historical, and legal communities were moving in similar directions, although they did not feel the need for precision with quite the same intensity.

We will briefly discuss the impact of the new emphasis on fact and observation on the development of the newspaper, and related efforts to produce accurate descriptions of places, things, people, and events. Precisely because some fiction writers were attempting a more realistic mode of presentation, the relationship between fact and fiction became a central literary problem.

Thus, the structure of this book is a field-by-field treatment of what today we would call the disciplines of natural science, theology, history, law, and literature. In the course of this march through the disciplines, a good deal may be shown about the particular development of each. The principal purpose of the enterprise is, however, to indicate the major linkages among them. Ultimately, what allowed both ideas and investigators to migrate freely between these various learned endeavors was the reorientation of all of them in the direction of empirical inquiry to establish matters of fact. There was a growing commonality of approach to matters of fact in terms of degrees of probability and certainty, as opposed to the traditional contrast between knowledge and opinion. This new approach to questions of evidence and proof permeated every aspect of intellectual life. Indeed, while it is not the only strand of seventeenth-century English intellectual life, this probabilistic empiricism became its most distinctive feature.

It must be admitted, of course, that even this emphasis on shared epistemological problems does not entirely overcome the anachronism of treating seventeenth-century intellectual life as if it neatly divided into disciplines. The disciplinary approach is adopted here for the convenience of modern readers, who will notice that figures like Robert Boyle, John Wilkins, and John Locke reappear in one chapter after another. Seventeenth-century intellectuals were far less bound by disciplinary boundaries than their modern counterparts for a number of reasons. Many areas were less complex than they subsequently became, and amateurs could and did participate in a number of them simultaneously. For much of the seventeenth century, many aspects of natural science, history, and theology were not beyond the capabilities of the educated layman. Since clergymen, in particular, engaged in every conceivable variety of intellectual activity, we should not be surprised to find theological traces in many of these fields. The gentleman, lawyer, and physician too, might use their leisure, and sometimes a portion of their income, to participate in or patronize one or more varieties of intellectual enterprise. The English were more, and probably better, educated in the seventeenth century than they were in subsequent generations. A substantial number of professional men and gentlemen not only had passed through the grammar school but had spent some time at Oxford, Cambridge, or the Inns of Court.[8] The amateurism fostered by a common, but eclectic, education helped make cross-fertilization possible.

This overlap or interpenetration of disciplines must be borne in mind in assessing the traditional dichotomy between humanism and science. In a sense, this book challenges the commonly held view that the scientific revolution created or intensified the modern division between the humanities and the sciences. That division was conceptually quite sharp in the early Renaissance when rhetoric and philosophy were seen as pursuing different goals by different means, with the humanities firmly assigned to rhetoric and the sciences to philosophy. As some philosophers moved from logical to empirical modes of proof, and some humanists moved from the rhetorically plausible to the empirically probable, a common ground was created.

While we are not arguing that intellectual history should be viewed as a seamless web, we are suggesting that seams are much more difficult to detect than is often thought, and that they are often joined in rather unexpected places.

Before proceeding to that web and its seams, we should note some of the limits of this study. This book is intellectual history in a traditional sense, and little effort has been taken to link intellectual life with the large-scale changes occurring in social, economic, or

13

political arenas. The focus is on the problems that intellectuals perceived as central to their own endeavors, rather than on the grand historical forces that may in some way have set that agenda.

Nor have we attempted a comprehensive survey of English intellectual life, or even a summary of the crucial developments in each of the fields considered. For instance, the chapter on religion focuses primarily on the latitudinarians, and largely omits Puritanism and the religious strife that extended unremittingly throughout the century. It does so because the latitudinarians were peculiarly concerned with the development of rational proofs in the realm of religion. Similarly, our intention in the chapter dealing with natural science and philosophy is not to describe the scientific revolution or even the whole range of contributions of English scientists. Rather, it is to trace certain changes in the way English scientists thought about the problem of scientific knowledge. Each chapter, then, is a highly selective treatment of a discipline or type of inquiry focusing on questions of evidence and proof.

Although our temporal boundaries will stretch from roughly 1500 or 1550 to 1700, our primary focus will be on the period from 1630 to 1690, the period of the generation or two that followed Baconian and Cartesian efforts to reconstitute knowledge on a basis of certainty. England is the center of this study. Our brief efforts to place English thought in the context of Continental developments may help toward some understanding of the extent to which the intellectual and scholarly changes described should be viewed as part of a larger European culture. On the whole, however, we will be suggesting that, while English thinkers shared a great deal with their Continental counterparts, their attraction to a fundamentally empirical rather than mathematical natural science, and their many-pronged efforts to maintain a scriptural, Protestant, and yet rational Christianity led them to a distinctively probabilistic approach to knowledge that culminated in John Locke, perhaps the most English of English philosophers.

II

Natural Philosophy and Experimental Science

INTRODUCTION

IN THIS CHAPTER, we will trace the development of a distinctively English philosophy of science which was worked out in the context of a commitment to both an empirical and experimental science and the mathematically oriented physics of Descartes and Galileo. We will be looking primarily at the generation spanned by Bacon and Locke, a generation whose problems and concerns led it away from the traditional philosophical norm of the demonstrably certain toward a more probabilistic view of human knowledge and natural science. The result was a new pattern of natural knowledge in which a more central role was assigned to experience, probability, and degrees of certitude, and primary, though not exclusive, emphasis was placed on the acquisition and analysis of empirical data.

These developments grew out of an increasing dissatisfaction with the traditional pattern that distinguished science or knowledge from opinion. It built on the erosion of that distinction which had resulted from some of the new directions taken by sixteenth-century humanism. Experience, that is, the realm of probability, had come to be valued more highly in the sixteenth century, when humanists were at the peak of their influence and prestige. This reassessment of experience took place in the context of growing dissatisfaction with Aristotelian science and logic, and considerable confusion about the boundaries between logic and rhetoric. Although the early-seventeenth-century efforts of Bacon and Descartes to reconstitute philosophy, particularly natural philosophy, on a sounder basis reaffirmed traditional notions of a certain science and philosophy, doubts soon arose not only as to the validity of their respective philosophies and methods but also with a model of human knowledge that distinguished so sharply between certain science and probable opinion.

Francis Bacon was the first to proclaim widely and publicize the translation of experience from the realm of opinion to that of science. He prescribed a vast program of data collection and experiment, the results of which would be scrutinized according to his inductive procedure and then built into a new and certain natural philosophy. His successors in England adopted the Baconian research program, making it the major activity of the Royal Society, but rejected the Baconian assumption that a certain natural science based on experience was possible. In the process of re-examining the notion of certainty, seventeenth-century English virtuosi to a considerable extent abandoned the hope of achieving science in the traditional sense and came to feel that much of the new philosophy would never reach that status. In the process, the Baconian research program was severed from Baconian method and philosophy of science and anchored to an empirical, but essentially probabilistic conception of natural science.

With hindsight, we can see that the task of the mid-century virtuosi was to develop a philosophy of science that would combine a central role for mathematics with a commitment to empirical research. The new philosophy was fashioned from a reconsideration of what constituted science or knowledge, a re-evaluation of opinion and probability, and the creation of a new role for hypothesis.

The once simple dichotomy between knowledge and opinion gave way to considerations of the differing varieties of knowledge and the kinds of certainty one might attribute to each. These refinements resulted in distinguishing logical and mathematical demonstration from moral certitude, a concept borrowed from theology. Moral certainty became the highest certainty available where facts and experience were concerned. Though assent was not compelled, under optimum conditions the "reasonable man" might be certain of his experience. As a result, although mathematics and mathematical demonstration remained the surest kind of knowledge, empirically derived facts acquired a certainty once denied them.

At the same time that moral certainty acquired a status approaching that of mathematical demonstration, a new interest arose in probability, once of little interest to natural philosophy. The crucial development was the erosion of any firm boundary between moral certainty and probability. Natural knowledge, whether in the form of individual fact, generalization, or hypothesis, was increasingly seen to fall somewhere on a continuum running from "mere probability," through "high probability," to "moral certainty." For better or worse, most natural knowledge was probable, not mathematically demonstrable or even morally certain.

Complementing the addition of the morally certain and then the probable to the realm of scientific knowledge, there was a transformation of hypothesis from a "fictional" mathematical supposition to a powerful theoretical tool anchored in empirical data. Not only was scientific explanation and theory increasingly couched in terms of hypothesis, but awareness of degrees of probability associated with hypothesis pushed English scientific philosophy even further in a probabilistic direction. Although not universally favored, hypotheses came to play an important role in seventeenth-century empirical science. A family of related and overlapping concepts—experience, matter of fact, moral certainty, probability, and hypothesis—thus played a major role in shaping seventeenth-century English natural philosophy.

We will also see that the new science, whose findings were frequently expressed in probabilistic terms and relied heavily on hypothesis, created a new scientific style hostile to dogmatism, system-making, and assertions of authority. Changes in theories of knowledge, approved models of scientific research, and modes of scientific discussion created a new intellectual type—the open and inquiring natural scientist bent on investigation rather than the pronouncement of ultimate truth.

Our primary focus will be on the propagandists for and practitioners of this new science: John Wilkins, Thomas Sprat, Joseph Glanvill, Walter Charleton, Christopher Wren, Robert Boyle, Seth Ward, John Wallis, Isaac Barrow, John Ray, and Robert Hooke, most of whom were associated with the Royal Society and its predecessor, the 1650s Wadham College group at Oxford. We will be most concerned with the pre-Newtonian era in which Robert Boyle, the "Christian Virtuoso," and Robert Hooke typified and symbolized English science.

Newton and Locke, for quite different reasons, mark our terminal points. Newton's staggering scientific accomplishments resulted in a subtle but real change in the expectation of many English naturalists, and the Newtonian period represents a new phase in English science. Locke drew together many strands of thought explored by earlier virtuosi and put them into a more coherent and systematic philosophical form.

This chapter, then, will describe how the integration of empirical and experimental knowledge with logic and mathematical demonstration created a new pattern of what constituted natural philosophy.

BACON AND THE RESEARCH
PROGRAM OF THE ROYAL SOCIETY

The first step in creating an empirical philosophy of science and a program of empirical research was taken by Francis Bacon, a thinker who exemplifies the pitfalls of the humanist-scientist dichotomy of conventional scholarship. Those who have considered Bacon in the context of the history of science or of philosophy have too often ignored his many humanist concerns. His interest in law, history, and morality and his efforts to advise rulers immediately suggest a humanist orientation, as do his literary and linguistic concerns. It would be difficult to imagine anyone who more confounds our typology of early modern intellectuals. His emphasis on experience and on the usefulness and application of knowledge also suggests how humanist patterns of thought might imperceptibly merge with those of empirical science. Bacon's adoption of various humanist concepts and attitudes suggest that empirical philosophy may have owed a good deal more to humanists than is usually recognized.

Bacon's goals as a philosopher were quite traditional. He sought to restructure knowledge so as to create a new philosophy which would, using carefully analyzed and refined sense data and his inductive method, reach natural principles of scientific certitude. His *New Organon* would replace the old, and he, Bacon, would replace Aristotle as "The Philosopher." The novelty of his appeal to sense and experiment, his repudiation of scholastic logic and science, and his insistence that knowledge must be of practical benefit to mankind may not have been as great as he claimed, but he appeared to himself and to his contemporaries to represent a sharp break with the past. As much as any ancient philosopher, however, Bacon remained confident that his philosophy could attain a knowledge of the "forms" which existed behind the fluctuating world of experience. He was sure, as his successors would not be, that caution, proper procedure, and manipulation of empirical data would yield certain scientific knowledge. This is not to say that knowledge would come easily or quickly. Bacon's method was designed to prevent premature, overzealous assertions of truth.

18

If he readily admitted that the skeptics, "those who have decried certainty," had "some agreement with my way of proceeding at the first setting out," he explicitly "separated and opposed" his position from their assertion "that nothing could be known." While little could be known by employing the methods "now in use," his new method, which "rightly ordered" experience, would lead "by an unbroken route through the woods of experience to the open ground of axioms."[1]

The Baconian vision of a new philosophy based on observation and experiment proved to be extremely powerful. Indeed, the research program of the Royal Society, the primary locus of scientific activity in England from the date of its foundation in 1660, was Baconian. The Society was to devote its efforts to acquisition of empirical data, not discussion of metaphysical principles. Experience, facts or "matters of fact," as they were frequently called, henceforth became an essential feature of English science. The members of the Royal Society were no more interested in the contemplative ideal than were the humanists. Bacon and his followers insisted that knowledge must be useful and must be employed to improve man's estate. Knowledge was to be empirical and practical.

The facts and experience of the humanist were too vague, too inexact, and too related to common opinion and assertions of authority to provide the basis for a natural philosophy. Francis Bacon contributed more than any other single individual to the establishment of a research program that would both incorporate matters of fact and experience and refine the methods of distinguishing common experience and opinion from validated fact. From the time of Bacon onwards, "natural history," or "the phenomena of the Universe,"[2] and "experiment," a new and improved way of obtaining relevant, factual information about nature, became central features of English scientific philosophy and of the research program of the early Royal Society. Thomas Sprat, the Society's historian and defender, insisted "It is matter . . . visible and sensible matter, which is the object of their labors," and that the "Principal work" of the Society was to collect observable natural data and to perform experiments.[3]

Although observation of and experiment with "visible matter" were not the exclusive, or perhaps in the long run, even the most important scientific contribution of the Society, the members were united in stating that collection of matters of fact obtained directly by observation or indirectly by report was the fundamental task of the Society. The chief "intendment" of the Royal Society was to

19

"create a well-grounded Natural History."[4] The research program of the Society thus centered on the collection of an ever-expanding store of facts and the compilation of these findings into natural histories which would in turn provide the basis for the "real" or "experimental" philosophy.

Although natural history had a long tradition, it had never been central to natural philosophy. The natural history of the past, full of "pretty Tales, and fine monstrous Stories," and characterized as "Romance," was contrasted with the "solid Histories of Nature" being produced by the Society. These histories would include not only experimental data and results but natural data derived from intensive investigations of England, Europe, and the more recently explored parts of the world. The difficulty with the old natural history was not simply that the ancients had not known the newly explored lands, but that they lacked satisfactory criteria for evaluating facts. If the new philosophy was to have a sound basis, it needed facts that were "true," rather than those alleged by authority or derived from unverified opinion or unscrutinized and unexamined common experience.[5]

The Society thus embarked on a vast program of data collection requiring "many Heads and many Hands."[6] Although some of their collecting fever can be dismissed as naïve, the undramatic but systematic data collection and measurement that they pioneered remain a central feature of modern scientific activity; some of the most distinguished scientific work of the seventeenth century resulted from the patient efforts of John Ray, Francis Willughby, Martin Lister, and Nathaniel Grew, who systematically collected, sifted, and analyzed observations and reports dealing with an extraordinary variety of botanical and biological topics.[7]

The crucial term, "matter of fact," which now encompassed both the results of observing quiescent nature and experimental manipulation, was not itself new. It had traditionally been associated with the human facts of the historian or the law court. During the seventeenth century, "matter of fact," like "experience," would be assimilated into natural science. Standards for evaluating and judging the evidence of matters of fact brought before the scientific community now became essential. The Society's members preferred things amenable to their "own Touch and Sight," to second-hand report. They recognized, however, that they would frequently be "forced to trust the reports of others."[8] For Boyle, natural knowledge was described as the knowledge of matters of fact communicated to man by means of the senses and communicated to others by testimony. In this respect, he admitted it was no different than the matters of fact of the historian or law court.[9] The basis for experimental philosophy, like that of most other varieties of knowledge, was a mixture of "immediate" and "vicarious" experience.[10]

The scientific community adopted and further refined existing traditions for evaluating testimony and applied these to natural facts. Personal characteristics such as the probity, knowledge, and reputation for honesty of the original observer or experimenter had to be taken into account. It was necessary to consider the number of observers, their skill, the extent to which they might be biased by custom or education, or whether they might have a personal interest in the outcome. Since the Society was seeking information from all over the globe, assessments of the credibility and bias of the reporters were obviously essential. The reports of scientific observation and experiment were thus a special case of the more general problem of dealing with reports of events and matters of fact.[11]

There were special problems connected with employing testimony, for religious and rhetorical usage had linked credible testimony to authority. Although the scientific community relied on "vicarious" as well as direct experience, it refused to take anything on authority. It was necessary to employ testimony, eliminating "mere hearsay," fabulous traditions, and reports suspected of being fictitious, biased, or erroneous, without becoming so skeptical as to refuse to assent to all testimony. The best that could be done was to establish reasonable criteria on which to evaluate testimony.[12]

Experiments performed by the Society itself were obviously preferable to second-hand reports. Experiments could be repeated under varying conditions before a presumably well-qualified, impartial group of observers.[13] Sprat and Glanvill, both spokesmen for the Society,[14] felt confident that, though reports might sometimes prove unacceptable, and experiments occasionally be so inconclusive that one must suspend one's assent, it was nevertheless frequently possible to reach sound, valid conclusions. Such conclusions, however, were never reached until "the whole Company" was "fully satisfied" with the "certainty and constancy" of the experiment in question.[15] "Critical and reiterated scrutiny" of "things, which are the plain objects of their eyes," provided the best basis for assent. Repetition under differing conditions, observed by many, would eliminate error introduced by individual differences or the weakness of sense. The Society's judgments were based on the "concurring testimonies" of its sixty to one hundred members rather

21

than the mere two or three who typically made judgments in matters of "life, and estate. . . . Indeed in . . . all other matters of Belief, of Opinion, or of Science," except the mysteries of religion, "the assurance is nothing near so firm as this." Scientists could thus make sound judgments on the matters of fact and experiments, which were the chief business of the Society.[16]

The program of data collection envisioned first by Bacon, and then by the Royal Society, required a vast network of observers and collectors. Sailors, military men, traders, and native and foreign observers were recruited to contribute appropriate matters of fact. Natural history would thus be the work of many hands and eyes not only of the present but also of future generations.[17] Data collection also became more intensive. Scientific instruments such as the telescope and microscope made distant and minute observations possible. Following Bacon, the Society placed enormous faith in the capacity of scientific instruments to compensate for the frailty of human sense organs. In addition, "outward description" was to be supplemented with the "dissection of inward Parts" of many things and creatures.[18]

The Society acknowledged Aristotle's recognition of the importance of sense data but proclaimed its advance over scholastic scientists who had nevertheless neglected empirical investigation.[19] "He who dares indubitate the testimony of that first and Grand Criterion, Sense, in regard that all Natural Concretions fall under the perception of some one of the Senses," and attempts to "stagger the Certitude of Sense" would "subvert the Fundamentals of all Physical Science."[20] The skepticism so often voiced in French intellectual circles rarely was heard in England.

While faith in the reliability of the senses was to some degree essential to the advocates of the experimental philosophy, its proponents recognized that the senses were limited and frequently deceived. They had not only absorbed the arguments of ancient and more recent skeptics like Montaigne[21] but were aware that sense data would not provide adequate support for many positions they accepted as fundamentally correct. Copernicanism, for instance, depended only partially on the relevant telescopic observations and required that reason be employed to refute commonplace sense experience.[22] The interplay between the necessity of sense-derived data and the weakness of the senses was a frequently expressed theme. The remedy for the fallibility of sense, according to Charleton, Wilkins, Boyle, Hooke, and others, was to bring reason to bear on sense experience. Natural science, then, would involve the "Descent of Reason upon the short Testimony of Sense."[23]

Reason could assist in evaluating the testimony of sense so that one could gain "sufficient assent" that "our Judgment of any object occurring to our senses was concordant to the reality thereof."[24] Reason must be brought to bear on sense data to eliminate error and to fully organize sense perception. Although no unanimity existed as to the extent to which the reasoning faculties should be allowed to judge, theorize, and hypothesize about observed facts, virtually all would have agreed with Joseph Glanvill that the Royal Society dealt with the "plain objects of Sense."[25] The more deeply rooted skepticism of Montaigne and his disciples thus did not permeate English scientific thought although, as Bacon suggested, it did contribute a certain caution about both data and reason.

If the interpretation of sense data posed some problems, so did the data themselves. Massive data collection might simply end as "rude heaps of unpolish'd and unshap'd material."[26] The most elementary classification was the natural history of some specified place, thing, phenomenon, or technology. It was evident, however, that all the facts within separate natural histories could not simply be thrown together. Those who were most committed and involved with natural history and description contributed most fruitfully to the development of scientific classification, particularly John Ray, Francis Willughby, Martin Lister, Thomas Willis, and others who dealt with plant and animal life. Such classificatory impulses also led to library cataloguing projects, to a catalog of natural things for the museum of the Royal Society, to Christopher Merrett's work on a catalog of natural things, and to John Wilkins's ambitious scheme of cataloguing all things and concepts. The collection of data resulted in a variety of efforts to comprehend and handle that data. Natural history and classification thus were closely brigaded.

Another problem which arose from the new emphasis on facts and things related to appropriate nomenclature. There was a technical vocabulary to deal with relevant elements and concepts of scholastic science, but not with the plethora of things and facts of nature thrown up by the new empiricism. As we shall see in Chapter VI, efforts to refine and define the names of things went hand in hand with the new fact orientation of natural science.

Still another means of making at least some kinds of data less unwieldly was quantification or mathematical description. Quantification of observed phenomena interested some, though not all, seventeenth-century English scientists. They were unclear, however, whether such mathematical calculations, sometimes called "mixed mathematics," should be considered only a more precise, empirical description, or whether the qualities of mathematical certitude might be attributed to them. It is important to note the peculiar respect that English mathematicians had for empirical studies. Experimental science and empirical data were as important to mathematically oriented scientists, such as John Wallis, Seth Ward, Christopher Wren, Robert Hooke, Isaac Barrow, and Isaac Newton, as it was to nonmathematicians like Boyle and Ray. It would be difficult to find a mid- to late-seventeenth-century English mathematician who did not share in the empiricism proclaimed by the Royal Society or participate in its experimental program.

The most serious problem was not what to do with the storehouse of information gradually being organized, classified, and labeled, but the scientific and philosophical status of the collected data. Although the research program adopted by the Society was directed toward Baconian natural history and experiment, Bacon's successors soon came to doubt the viability of a fully Baconian philosophy of science.

Bacon had thought of knowledge as a pyramid whose base was natural history and its mid-level "physique." "Metaphysics" rose above physics and reached almost, but not quite, to the apex. At the apex, perhaps not attainable by men, was "the summary law of Nature."[27] Physics would deal with "causes," though not with the "fixed or constant causes" which belonged to metaphysics. Natural history would thus ascend from physics to metaphysics where dwelt the "Forms" which, "of all other parts of knowledge," were the "worthiest to be sought."[28] For Bacon, sense data would lead to the certitude of physics and eventually to the forms. Baconian science aimed for the certainty of mathematical demonstration via empirical data and proper scientific procedure.

Baconian optimism, however, faded, and with it the confidence that data collection and analysis would yield general axioms or the forms of nature. Metaphysical principles were rarely if ever discussed in the context of empirical science. Although the building metaphor, with its "strong foundation" and "firm base," was endlessly repeated, no one seemed willing or able to explain how substructure and structure were related, or the process by which natural history became natural philosophy. The Royal Society, to a very considerable extent, quietly abandoned Bacon's philosophy of science while continuing to pursue Baconian projects.

Sprat's *History of the Royal Society* suggests some of the difficulties the virtuosi encountered. Sprat asserts, in principle, that the investigation of nature would in time yield the principles of philosophy and be used "to raise axioms and the building of theory,"[29] but he is extremely vague about the process. Hooke, in some ways very much a Baconian, realized that "rude heaps of unpolish'd materials" would not automatically yield philosophical principles.[30] Yet it was not clear how such heaps, even well-classified heaps, could reach sound generalization. In the context of criticizing Cartesian philosophy, Isaac Barrow insisted that it was necessary to consult nature before reaching generalizations; but the character of that consultation was not specified.[31]

The experience of disagreement on alleged empirical principles and axioms no doubt led to recognition of the difficulties, since disagreement itself meant assent was not compelled or automatic. Indeed, the more the problem was considered, the more doubts arose as to whether certain natural knowledge was possible. In the process, the goal shifted from certain to probable truth, and well-supported hypotheses replaced axioms demonstrated to a certainty. Though the mood was not consistent, increasingly scientists were exhorted to be content with probabilities rather than certainties. Most of the virtuosi felt that experiment and observation of matters of fact must provide the basis for sound philosophy but were unsure how much data or precisely what kind of analysis were necessary to yield principles, and to what degree such principles would be certain. Complete induction of all particulars was obviously impossible. In some instances a single experiment was thought to be enough. But how much was enough to move uncertain or probable conjecture into the realm of "true theories" or "certain axioms"? The method outlined in Book II of Bacon's *New Organon* did not provide the answer to what has always been one of the most vexing problems for philosophers of science.

One way out of the problem was to avoid the issue entirely by concentrating on data collection, deferring the philosophical problems to a later generation. Although adopted by some, this route did not satisfy the more creative scientists who were unwilling to ignore explanations and causal analysis. The new science, as Hooke insisted, aimed at "Causes and Reasons" as well as natural history.[32] The Society's zeal for experiment did not lead it to avoid attempts at causal explanation and theory. The members did, however, refuse to assume that such theories necessarily followed from the data or would rise in the Baconian pyramidic structure if only they followed proper procedure. Indeed, they said virtually nothing of metaphysics, the search for "Forms," or the hope of discovering the underlying structure of nature itself. Increasingly, English experimentalists came to feel that their knowledge of the physical world, no matter how well acquired and analyzed, would be limited to the appearances themselves.

Sprat suggests their confidence about facts as well as their tentativeness about principles. "True Philosophy" begins with "a scrupulous and severe examination of particulars." Derived from these "there may be some general Rules, with great Caution drawn." Given "human frailty," it was wiser not to seek "universal Philosophy," but to concentrate on "particular Subjects." And even here, he voiced concern for those who were "too forward to conclude upon Axioms." Sprat also made it clear that there was no ideal experimental method. Experimentation must never become "a fix'd and settled Art," constrained "by constant Rules." There must be no "standing precepts" in the experimental way.[33]

Sir Matthew Hale, a leading judge with scientific interests, expressed a similar view. While one could be quite certain of sense data, the attempt to derive universal and general conclusions or deductions from that data often led to failure. It was impossible, he thought, to perceive the "Forms of Things," the matter or substance which is the subject of nature. It was only possible to conjecture about the principles that Bacon visualized as the goal of natural philosophy.[34]

The Society, then, would not simply collect data for future natural philosphers, nor avoid causal explanations of observed phenomena. If they would not engage in the "general contemplations" of causes, which in the past had led to "error, False Lights, disguised Lies, [and] deceitful Fancies," the virtuosi did not avoid "conjecturing" on causes.[35] In speaking of explanation and causal analysis, however, the virtuosi quite deliberately discarded the language of certainty for that of conjecture, hypothesis, and probability.

Sprat repeatedly emphasized the importance of avoiding "over hasty, and precipitant concluding upon the Causes, before the Effects have been enough search'd into." He insisted that the Society's reluctance to "settle" principles or fix doctrines and the fact that the members were "not yet very daring in establishing conclusions" did not imply that they were so skeptical as to refuse to assign any causes. Sprat admitted that they might "perhaps be suspected" of being "a little too much inclin'd" to the "fault of Sceptical doubting," precisely because of their reluctance to settle principles or fix doctrine.[36] They refused to "own" any "hypothesis, system, or doctrine of natural philosophy," and would not "dogmatically define or fix axioms." The Society, which expressed such faith in its facts and experiments, thus expected much less in the way of agreed upon general principles or axioms. Explanations must be grounded in facts and experiments, but they were rarely expected to attain the status of "true axioms" or "true theories." Yet in some ill-defined sense, the members still hoped to build "a solid system of philosophy fit to explain the true causes of natural phenomena . . . on the basis of observation and experiments frequently and accurately performed."[37]

The transformation of the concepts of hypothesis and probability would allow the virtuosi to develop an empirical and experimentally based natural science in which conclusions, theories, and opinions could be offered, examined, and evaluated. In the process, however, the search for certain axioms was largely abandoned for probabilistic explanations and generalizations.

VARIETIES OF KNOWLEDGE AND LEVELS OF ASSENT

Members of the scientific community, in their combined roles as scientists, clergymen, and lay theologians, discussed and experimented with the categorization of different kinds of knowledge, the kinds of evidence and proofs appropriate for each, and the degrees of mental assent which might be accorded each. Henry Van Leeuwen, who has pointed out the non-Baconian character of this development, also perceptively suggests how these categorizations contributed to seventeenth-century philosophical development.[38]

The ancients, as we noted, had distinguished knowledge and truth from the transient, imperfect realm of opinion. Christianity viewed its doctrines as truth, not opinion, but Christian doctrine could not be apprehended or proved true by means of logical demonstration. Theologians and philosophers had long grappled for appropriate ways of establishing the truths of Christianity. This problem intensified as scholastic logic, dialectic, and the principle of authority were challenged, and as religious divisions growing out of the Reformation made more salient the issues of where religious truth resided and what means were appropriate to demonstrate one's possession of it. The newly enhanced claims of mathematics, too, challenged older notions of proof. The most common categorization remained that of the ancient world: science or knowledge on the one hand, and opinion, belief, or probability on the other. What is interesting for our purposes is that the efforts to define and refine the varieties of science or knowledge led to the gradual erosion of the distinction between knowledge and probability.

A great many English thinkers grappled with these problems between 1650 and 1690, seeking to reshape traditional categories to current needs. Among them were John Wilkins, Seth Ward, Walter Charleton, Matthew Hale, Joseph Glanvill, Robert Boyle, and John Locke. Two common themes run through all their work. The first is the attempt to establish a schema involving three or sometimes four categories or varieties of knowledge, each with its own kind and level of certainty. While the details of these schema differ, they exhibit certain commonalities. God's complete and perfect knowledge, attaining a level of absolute, infallible certainty, was placed above and beyond the three or four human categories. Opinion or probability was placed below them. The highest level of human knowledge attained a "conditional infallible certainty" compelling assent and consisted of the propositions of mathematics and certain axioms of metaphysics, both of which could be logically demonstrated. The lowest level of human knowledge attained moral certainty, and consisted of religious belief and much of our common conclusions about human affairs, including history and judicial decisions. The middle level consisted of immediate sense data which appeared to some to rise above the level of moral certainty. It is, however, the least stable element of the schema and tends to slip downward into the category below it, in part because the virtuosi knew that many direct sense observations, like that of the flatness of the earth, were incorrect. While most of the virtuosi invoke three levels, they are clearest in delineating a realm of moral certainty that does not attain to the level of mathematical certainty on the one hand, but clearly rises above the realm of mere opinion into that of real knowledge on the other.

The second common theme is the insistence that mathematical proofs, which had enjoyed so much prestige in the early seventeenth century, and immediate sense data were not the sole or even the appropriate modes of proof. To demand immediate sense data for a past event was as foolish as demanding a demonstration—logical or mathematical—of a long-past comet or Christ's Resurrection. Matters of fact, physical as well as historical, had to be handled very differently from mathematical propositions. There were, then, different kinds of knowledge which demanded differ-

FIGURE 1

Knowledge	Method	Certainty
God's knowledge	none (creation)	absolute, infallible certainty
Science A: mathematics, metaphysics (in part)	logic, mathematical demonstration	compelled assent
Science B: direct or intuitive knowledge	immediate sense experience, introspection	more than moral certainty
Belief (including science C), religious belief, history, & conclusions about everyday life	observation, analysis of reports of others of their observations	moral certainty at best
Opinion	gathering evidence including second-hand reports of sense observation & reports of other opinion	probability, "mere" probability, plausibility

ent kinds of proof, which in turn produced different kinds of certainty.

This complex of ideas can be rendered diagrammatically (Fig. 1). The principal value of the diagram is heuristic, as we shall see in examining the particular treatments of the matter by various contributors. It does bring out certain basic features of the movement as a whole. For instance, the juxtaposition of opinion with belief, a kind of real knowledge, would have momentous consequences for philosophy, particularly the philosophy of science. For if opinion about empirical matters rested on an evidentiary base, just as did belief in God, it became difficult to relegate empirical truths to the realm of "mere opinion" in which one man's views were as good as another's, without relegating religion to the same realm. And the virtuosi were certainly not prepared to do that. The uncertain place of "science" is also instructive. Science, in the traditional sense of demonstrable knowledge (labeled Science A), clearly belonged at the highest level. For some of the virtuosi, empirically based science attained a level of certainty higher than that of belief, and so fell in the middle tier (Science B). For others, aspects of the new science only attained a level of certainty that placed it above the realm of opinion (Science C).

The new categorizations of knowledge were first articulated in England by William Chillingworth, who distinguished knowledge from belief or faith, and both from opinion.[39] In the first, assent was compelled; in the second and third, it was determined by the relative weight of evidence. Significantly, he did not clarify the distinction between belief and opinion. Though he dealt with moral certainty largely in terms of religion, he also applied that term to judicial decisions and to those of daily life.[40]

John Tillotson, an Anglican clergyman in close touch with scientific circles, provided another list of categories. There was mathematical demonstration, capable of the clearest and strictest demonstration; natural philosophy, "derived from sufficient Induction of experiments"; moral certainty, attained by moral arguments and evidence; and matters of fact, proved by credible testimony.[41] Completely infallible knowledge was unavailable to fallible man. Although Tillotson listed demonstrative certainty and the certainty of the immediate sense perception, he was primarily concerned with moral certainty or "sufficient assurance" which was a matter of belief, not science, and might include error. He noted, however, that the term had several meanings:

tho moral certainty be sometimes taken for a high degree of probability which can only produce a doubtful assent, yet it is also frequently used for a firm and undoubted assent to a thing upon such grounds as are fully to satisfy a prudent man: and in this sense I have always used this Term.[42]

Moral certainty sometimes meant "a certainty as makes the cause alwaies work the same effect, though it take not away the absolute possibility of working otherwise." Others used the term to mean "a certainty as seldom fails, or such as human action is generally grounded on."[43] One thing that was clear, however, was that there were degrees of certainty to be determined by the capacity of the individuals making the assessment and the evidence brought to support it. Tillotson was particularly interested in the evidence for matters of fact. The senses provided the best evidence, experience (never defined) the next best, and testimony of witnesses was last.

The categorizations of Walter Charleton, who was considerably more involved in scientific affairs than Tillotson, also suggest that the boundaries between such categories as knowledge, belief, and probability were eroding. Mathematics might yield demonstrative or scientific knowledge, but much of what we would call natural science was, for Charleton and others, beginning to straddle the categories including those of belief, moral certainty, and even probability and opinion.[44]

There was relatively little disagreement that demonstration, particularly mathematical demonstration, was the most certain knowledge of all. There was also agreement that it was an inappropriate model for the natural sciences, history, law, or religion. Thus, most scientific analysis and discussion now fell into nondemonstrative knowledge or belief and probable opinion. John Wilkins, Robert Boyle, Sir Charles Wolseley, Joseph Glanvill, and John Locke continued to refine and develop these categories.

Wolseley distinguished mathematical certainty, moral certainty, and natural certainty, and suggested that all might employ sense data. He also identified two other categories—probability and mere probability—which were not to be considered knowledge.[45] Boyle's knowledge categories were the metaphysical, the physical, and the moral.[46] The moral, which involved cogent proof or a concurrence of probabilities, was the certainty of religion and natural science. Wilkins identified three kinds of knowledge or certainty: the mathematical, the physical, and the moral. Wilkins, somewhat atypically, felt that physical certainty, or the immediate perception of the internal and external senses, was a higher certainty than that of mathematics. Yet he was most interested in the moral certainty which existed when a reasonable man assented in cases where no reasonable doubt existed. This kind of assurance was to be found in a variety of situations—not only in morals and politics but in religion, history, and natural sciences. In all, evidence arising from testimony and experience, both personal and physical, was considered. Relevant evidence went beyond testimony and was derived from personal "observation and repeated trials." He concluded that many things in "Moral and Natural Philosophy" should be "as firmly believed as any Mathematical Principle or Conclusion can be."[47] Wilkins also retained the nonknowledge category, the realm of opinion or probability, where the evidence was insufficient to reach moral certainty.

Although the line of development is clear, there was not a great deal of uniformity. Wilkins rated physical certainty higher than the mathematical. But "physical certainty" to Wilkins referred to the immediate perception of the external and internal senses, while to Boyle it meant the knowledge of causes, given the certainty of physical principles. Wilkins's physical certainty is fairly close to Locke's sensitive knowledge and perhaps included what Locke called "intuition." What is important for us is the erosion of the traditional dichotomy of knowledge and opinion, and its replacement by a more complex schema which seemed to fit better with current epistemological views and with developments in the natural sciences. Individually, Chillingworth, Glanvill, or Wilkins may not have been impressive philosophers, but collectively they indicate a shift in direction which culminated in the formulations of John Locke. Though they might not agree with Locke in every particular, he nevertheless represents the culmination of a generation's attempt to devise a new theory of knowledge appropriate to the experimental science of the era.

Although the categories employed by mid-seventeenth-century virtuosi were not consistent, virtually all of them distinguished demonstration, particularly mathematical demonstration, from other proof, agreeing that the natural and moral sciences as well as religion were incapable of such rigorous demonstration, and that proofs in these areas were of a different character. In "pure mathematics," one "may be sure of the truth of a conclusion without consulting experience."[48] Mathematical demonstrations "built upon the impregnable foundation of geometry and arithmetic" were "the only truths that can sink into the mind of man, void of all uncertainty."[49] Mathematical demonstration compelled assent. Some confusion arose in connection with "mixed mathematics" which involved making mathematical calculations of natural phenomena, e.g., in physics, astronomy, and mechanics. While mathematical calculations which described the behavior of natural things became increasingly common, the extent to which these calculations partook of demonstration or were simply mathematically formulated descriptions was not often discussed.

Virtually all of these writers on epistemology included a category of moral certainty. Originally, moral certainty had focused on testimony. Increasingly, however, the testimony of the senses and therefore of natural facts was included. In this way much of the subject matter of experimental science might, under certain circumstances, reach moral certitude. Isaac Barrow explicitly rejected the "way of the schools" which limited "belief" to authority and testimony, replacing it with a notion of persuasion based on sense, reason, and testimony. In religion and natural science, belief rested on a variety of proofs—rational, sensible, and testimonial—and resulted in a "mind fully convinced and persuaded of the truth" of the proposition in question.[50] Usually, however, these men treated certitude about the observed facts themselves as the only certitude available in the natural sciences. Causal analyses of these facts were only hypotheses, which rarely were granted morally certain status.

Even prior to the inclusion of natural facts and experiment in the realm of knowledge, standards for evaluating the credibility of testimony had been developed. These were now applied and expanded to deal with physical as well as religious and historical events. The greater the number of direct witnesses to a phenomenon, the greater the likelihood of moral certitude, even if one admitted that the senses might be deceived, and that custom, bias, and interest were factors to take into account. If, having properly discounted such factors, the witness's testimony was sufficient to "satisfie a rational man," moral certitude was possible.[51] This was knowledge beyond a reasonable doubt.[52]

Natural facts thus were quite easily assimilated into "moral certainty." Statements about the facts of natural history could be assessed for credibility even more readily than those of history or law, for, in certain instances at least, they might be replicated. Assessing, judging, and evaluating physical facts and physical evidence became a fundamental aspect of seventeenth-century English science.

If there were several varieties of knowledge, each with their appropriate brand of certainty, there was also a realm of probability or opinion. Here one might have some evidence and reason for holding an opinion, but insufficient to consider it morally certain. This category, too, permitted gradations so that some statements might have high and some very low probability. At the high end, evidence might be sufficient almost to compel assent. At the low end, the observer would register his substantial doubt that the evidence offered sustained the opinion held. Where proofs were intermediate between these two levels, one might suspend one's assent.

What is interesting here is that the line between knowledge and opinion was becoming blurred. Where propositions attained moral certainty, they clearly passed over into the realm of knowledge. Particularly in the areas of empirical, natural science, however, propositions were being generated that, while not attaining the extremely demanding requirements of moral certainty, nevertheless reached a high level of probability that seemed to distinguish them from "mere opinion." More and more, natural knowledge seemed to fall somewhere between mere opinion and moral certainty. Wilkins, for example, suggested that most natural science belonged in that realm of probability in which the greater the evidence, the closer one came to the attainment of knowledge. So did Sir Matthew Hale, who, while distinguishing "Belief" from "Persuasion and Opinion," insisted that the concurrence and multiplicity of concurring arguments brought some aspects of natural philosophy to the "very next degree to Belief or Knowledge." For Hale, however, most natural and moral philosophy remained in the realm of persuasion and opinion.[53]

Robert Boyle's writings rather neatly illustrate how even the most rigorous skepticism toward the physical certainty of scientific findings might nonetheless lead to a promotion of natural science above the realm of mere opinion by brigading the probabilities of sciences with the moral certainty encountered in other kinds of study. Boyle says that little of the science of his day would pass his own test for physical certainty, that is, knowledge of causes deduced from certain physical principles. Most findings in the natural as well as the human sciences of law, religion, and history could at best have "moral assurances." The great difficulty in obtaining adequate experiments and the rigor required to build "an undoubted theory" meant that "many things in Physics that men presume they believe upon physical and cogent arguments," they really had only a moral assurance for. Given the "doubtfulness and incompleteness of natural philosophy," even "modern virtuosi" were "wont to fancy more of clearness and certainty in their physical theories, than a critical examiner will find."[54] In "physical inquiries," however, it was "often sufficient" that "determination should come very near the matter, though . . . short of a mathematical exactness."[55]

John Wallis agreed that the demonstrative arguments of mathematics and logic were unavailable in the natural sciences, but he did not for this reason desist from scientific endeavor. Instead, he accepted the task of rendering scientific findings as precisely as the circumstances permitted.[56] Walter Charleton is the most explicit defender of the empirical sciences against the claims of logic and mathematics. Demonstration was admittedly the most convincing kind of proof, but most physical problems, being of "so retired and abstruse a nature," could not be brought under the strict laws and rules of geometry. Nevertheless, it was possible to "acquire a competent certitude by well examining their Effects and constant Observations." For Charleton "substantive and satisfying Reasons" for a proposition in either the physical or moral realm were sufficient "to the full establishment of its Truth in the mind of a reasonable man."[57] Though there were no "infallible Theories" in physics, one could nevertheless acquire "a competent certitude" by examining the "Effects and constant Operation of Moral and Physical Things." "All the beams of the Light of Nature" did not "concentre only in Mathematical Demonstration." There was thus no reason to complain of or to reject the less than perfect knowledge of the natural world.[58]

Although we can discern a movement away from the Baconian position—that an improved induction would produce true and certain knowledge—toward one characterized by a more complex classification and analysis of knowledge and probability, it is not precisely clear where individuals fall. Robert Hooke sometimes appears to be an advocate and practitioner of the newer probabilistic science, and at others a Baconian who asserted that science "aimed at . . . a true and certain knowledge" of the works of nature. Hooke defined scientific knowledge as "a certainty of information of the Minds and Understanding founded upon true and undeniable Evidence" obtained "immediately by Sense without Fallacy, or mediately by a true Ratiocination from such Sense." "Sense without Fallacy," for Hooke, meant that the fallacy had been detected and that the evidence had been examined and "found to be free and clear of all such Fallacies." The limits of sense and the abstruseness of causes meant many inductions would be required to "raise exact definitions and general propositions." Yet Hooke tempers these statements by suggesting that, by comparing these inductions, one could arrive at sufficiently "great assurance" to "ground conjectures," and that one could often only arrive at negative, not positive, proofs. Using the language of moral certainty and belief, he then suggested that if one could not produce positive proofs, one could often arrive at proofs just "as cogent and undeniable," that is, proofs that "none but a willful or senseless Person will refuse his assent unto it." Hooke thus seems to aspire to Baconian certitude, but also employs the language of reasonable belief and moral certainty.[59] The line between universally true generalization derived by the Baconian method, and propositions that were so highly probable or morally certain that one should treat them as if they were universal generalizations, is thus not always easy to draw.

We can see something similar in Isaac Barrow's discussion of the differences between reasoning and proofs in mathematics and the physical sciences. Barrow, who later gave up his Professorship of Mathematics to Isaac Newton, insisted that demonstration dealt with universally true principles which compelled assent. Such demonstration was unavailable "in other Disciplines," because the "Things which they consider are of a Nature more recondite and abstracted from the Senses, more intricate and complex, and more dark and confused to the Apprehension." It was therefore extremely difficult to "imagine distinctly, and define exactly," what color was in physics, happiness in ethics, or the law of nations in politics. The natural and human sciences were thus too complex to attain the certitude of mathematics.[60]

Barrow went on to say that the "principles on which the superstructure" of these sciences were "to be raised" were all "weakened as to their Universality." One encountered contrary instances and was forced to make exceptions, limits, and distinctions. These sciences necessarily mixed the doubtful with the certain, and "Things taken upon Presumption with things solved by Experiment, Things obscure with such as are manifest, and true with things false." Conclusions reached did not force assent and typically required further confirmation or "prolix Explications." Induction simply could not provide the basis for universally true principles.[61]

Incomplete induction was useful, if not certain. When a proposition was "found agreeable to constant Experience . . . [and] pertains to their principal Properties and Intimate Constitution," it was "most safe and prudent to yield a ready assent to it." Using the language of probability and prudence, Barrow argued that one should assent to propositions consistent with constant experience, when our "Expectations [were] most accurately answered, after a thousand Researches." These were "sufficient to make us look upon any Proposition confirmed with frequent Experiments, as universally true." One might consider these findings "universally true," even though one did not have proof of universality.[62] Newton, who insisted that physics required exact description of phenomena couched in quantitative terms, also insisted that the natural sciences could not anticipate certain knowledge concerning the essence of things.[63]

The experimental science of the Royal Society might not yield universally true principles, but it might be expected at least occasionally to yield principles that were sufficiently true to be treated as such. This level of certainty typically was called "moral certainty." English virtuosi felt confident about, and even morally certain of, many if not all the matters of fact with which they dealt. Observations and experiments thus might yield morally certain natural histories, although of course not all the data currently available reached that exalted status. The findings upon which they agreed were not to be considered "as unalterable Demonstration," but as "present appearance." The general principles and explanations that dealt with these facts or were induced from them might or might not reach a moral certainty. More often than not, less certain propositions that dealt with matters of fact were labeled hypotheses and awarded the status of greater or lesser probability rather than moral certainty. The Royal Society absolutely refused to "bestow infallibility" on these hypotheses.[64]

Locke represents the culmination of the efforts to redefine and clarify the varieties of knowledge and certainty. For Locke, knowledge—the perception of the agreement or disagreement of ideas—was distinguished, albeit not sharply, from probability. The three varieties of knowledge were intuition, demonstration, and sensation. The last, essential to the experimental science Locke admired, resulted in a certainty less certain than the other two. Most findings about nature for Locke, however, did not achieve knowledge but only probability. A continuum existed in which probability would be graded according to the quality and quantity of the evidence. Only when the evidence was in every way impeccable could one speak of sensitive knowledge. Natural science, then, was for the most part probable. The category of opinion, once so clearly "nonknowledge" or nonscience, now merged with "knowledge" itself.[65]

The efforts at distinguishing varieties of knowledge and proof first led to a modification of traditional divisions of science and opinion. As these became the subject for philosophical analysis, it appeared to English virtuosi that little which related to experimental science belonged to "demonstrative science." As demonstration was increasingly recognized to be an unattainable goal, the natural sciences, as practiced in seventeenth-century England, were fitted somewhere into belief—a category first created for theological purposes—or were included in an emerging continuum that ranged from mere opinion or probability to the moral certainty which no reasonable man could doubt. In the process, much of science, history, religion, and law were promoted from the realm of mere opinion to a realm of greater or lesser probability, a realm in which the word probable was losing the negative connotations assigned to it by the traditional distinction between logic and rhetoric.

PROBABILITY

In the ancient world, probability had been associated with opinion and rhetoric and had, with the exception of Carneades, little philosophical significance.[66] During the medieval period, probability found a place in casuistry that dealt with moral choices under conditions of uncertainty, and in dialectic, a nondemonstrative form of reasoning used in argumentation that dealt with opinion. An important feature of both was the proper use of authority, and probability for many generations was associated as much with what was approved as with what was provable.[67] Although some seventeenth-century writers continued to use probability in this sense, scientific usage gradually changed as the realms of fact, experience, and even opinion became central elements in the natural sciences. Probability began to lose its association with authority, a principle little esteemed by seventeenth-century natural philosophers and experimental scientists.

Yet there was little in the early decades of the seventeenth century to suggest that probability would have a philosophical future. Neither Descartes nor Bacon had any interest in a probabilistic natural science, and Bacon used "probable" in the traditional, rhetorical sense. Galileo, however, did employ the term in connection with the natural sciences. Although his goal seems to have been certain demonstration, he also recognized the technique of increasing probability by means of experience and experiment, suggesting that this path would lead "almost to absolute demonstration."[68] From one point of view, Galileo appears the Platonizing mathematician; from another, the empirical scientist employing the new concept of probability.

Ian Hacking's study of the origins of mathematical probability suggests that newer notions of probability were linked to empiricism, and particularly to medicine and astrology, which made diagnoses, prognoses, and predictions on the basis of observable signs. For Hacking, signs play a particularly important part in the transformation from probability in the "low sciences" to mathematics. Because his primary concern is mathematics rather than philosophy or the natural sciences, and his focus is on the Continent rather than England, Hacking tends to slight the role of the Royal Society. Nevertheless, both Hacking, by emphasizing astrology and medicine, and Paolo Rossi, by emphasizing technology, have made important contributions to our understanding of how experience and probability of the "low sciences" made inroads into conceptions of scientific philosophy.[69] They help to show us that natural science not only was freeing itself from the unattainable goals of scientific demonstration but was helping to shape a new mathematics more suited to scientific inquiry.

Benjamin Nelson, however, has argued that the revolution in the philosophy of science involved the search for certitude which characterized the efforts of Bacon, Descartes, and Galileo. He therefore rejects a connection between the scientific revolution and probabilism, either in its older casuistic forms or the newer ones represented by Pierre Gassendi and the "Royal Society theologians."[70] Though correct for Descartes, the case, as we have seen, is less clear for Galileo, since historians remain divided on the question of whether he should be taken as representing the goal of a mathematically demonstrative certitude, or the new experimentalism and verification by means of sense data, or some elusive combination of the two. And while the work of Bacon demonstrates that empiricism need not have resulted in probabilism, empiricism, as preached by Gassendi and practiced by the virtuosi of the Royal Society, clearly moved in that direction. Unless we are somehow to read Gassendi and the Royal Society virtuosi entirely out of the scientific movement, it is going to be impossible to break the link between the new science and the new, positive treatment of probability.

Although we are concerned primarily with England, it would be impossible to trace the development of philosophical probabilism without mention of the French philosopher Pierre Gassendi, an opponent of both Aristotelianism and Cartesian "dogmatism." Believing that ideas derived from sense, Gassendi trod warily between a skepticism which claimed no knowledge was possible and dogmatisms—old or new—which claimed to have achieved certain knowledge. Knowledge was possible, though its results were probable rather than certain. Observation and experience could lead to a useful but less than perfect knowledge of phenomena. Natural knowledge was thus probable knowledge, not science. The once distinct division between knowledge and opinion was clearly breaking down. Although the transmission and absorption of Gassendi's thought has not yet been thoroughly studied, his views were favorably noted in England, beginning with Walter Charleton's efforts in the 1650s.[71]

Thomas Hobbes, writing about the same time as Gassendi, was moving in the same direction, or, rather, in two directions at once. While retaining, and indeed expanding, traditional notions of science as mathematical and demonstrative knowledge, and anticipating demonstrative natural and civil sciences, he also held a nominalist view of phenomena. The "signs" of experience were "conjectural." As these "often or seldom failed," so their assurance was "more or less; but never full and evident."[72] Hobbes, unlike Gassendi, however, had little interest in natural phenomena or experimental science. In Hobbes, then, we can see the early seventeenth-century efforts to develop demonstratively certain natural and civil sciences combined with a probabilistic phenomenalism.

In John Wilkins, an enemy of Hobbes and popularizer of Copernicus and Galileo, we can see the beginning of the shift from the rhetorical to the more scientific view of probability among the English virtuosi. Wilkins's first scientific work, an attempt to persuade a popular audience of the truth or probability of the Copernican hypothesis, and written before those of Hobbes, Gassendi, and Chillingworth, mixes the old and the new. He combines traditional notions of "good arguments," testimony, and authority with that of "good evidence," and at the same time denies the principle of authority. At some times, he insists that the evidence of the senses made his position more probable. At others, he insists that one follow reason, not the error-prone senses. He suggests that observations are similar to testimony and necessary to the process of making probable statements that one should accept as valid. The Copernican hypothesis, as presented by Galileo, was "most probable" because it was the simplest explanation most consistent with the observed data. Experiments and observations, that is, empirical data, increased the probability of Galileo's propositions. When Wilkins considered the possibility of lunar inhabitants, he indicated that there was as yet no evidence on which to build "a certainty" or even "good probability." One could only "guess," and "that very doubtfully." In this instance, there was "no ground wherein to build any probable opinion."[73]

Wilkins's later works were less vague and contradictory.[74] When unquestionable certainty was unavailable, we must be guided by the "most probable and likely." "Evidence" was more clearly distinguished from the citation of appropriate testimony and authority. The "testimony" of the senses and understanding had become critical. Repeated trials resulting in experimental evidence had clearly become the mode for establishing probabilistic truth. Here Wilkins was both guiding and echoing the program of empirical data collection of the Royal Society. The evidence of "effects" and "things" contributed both to moral certainty and probability.

We must now turn to the Royal Society itself in order to indicate the extent to which probability was of interest to those committed to the new philosophy. Sprat uses the term "probability" primarily in his treatment of the Society's discussion of causes, suggesting that the Society would indicate which "Opinion" or "Cause" was "more probable" than another after "full inspection." It was careful not to "bestow infallibility" on these probabilistic judgments.[75] Causal explanations and hypotheses could, according to Sprat, be no more than probable. Sprat's usage suggests that facts might be established with greater certainty than generalizations or hypotheses which incorporated those facts.

Robert Hooke used the concept of probability in a similar way when he indicated that it was "very probable" that the moon had a principle of gravitation. He, too, insisted that it was only "a probability," and "not a demonstration."[76] Scientific hypotheses and scientific explanations might range from mere opinion, or the barely probable, to the highly probable. Natural philosophy, as conceived and practiced by the Royal Society, typically dealt with degrees of probability, not certainty or demonstration.[77]

The fact that much of natural science involved probability and opinion did not prove to be too discouraging. Indeed, Glanvill suggests it was only the dogmatist who pretended to "perfect knowledge." Unlike the dogmatist, Glanvill would "proportion the degree of . . . belief to . . . evidence, without expecting the hopeless encouragement of a universal suffrage."[78] Philosophical inquiry no longer required "science." Probabilities and belief had become an integral part of natural science and natural philosophy.

A proposition or generalization might move from mere to high probability as a result of a number of confirming observations and experiments, although at times it was suggested that a single appropriate experiment might be sufficient.[79] The "concurrence of probabilities," too, was sometimes invoked. Boyle even suggested that one might reach moral certitude—something surer than high probability—by means of a concurrence of probabilities,[80] and Glanvill suggests something very similar:

After all, I cannot say that each of them is an absolute demonstration; or that the evidence of every one is impossible to be avoided: there are few proofs of that nature. But this I do, that all of them together, I think, will make a cord hardly to be broken. And these considerations in conjunction may amount to a moral demonstration, and have force enough to obtain assent from those that are not stupid or unreasonable.[81]

Since assessment of evidence was involved, some individuals might feel a proposition had reached moral certitude, while others would award it only the status of "high probability." While demonstrative science had compelled assent, a subjective element or choice was involved in probabilistic science.

Probability was also an important feature of Locke's theory of knowledge, and through his widely read works, it became integrated into English philosophical thought. For Locke, as for Wilkins, Glanvill, Boyle, and others, probability was distinguished from knowledge, which, as we have seen, was now divided into a number of different types. Probability, for Locke, involved proofs

whose connection is not constant or immutable, or at least is not perceived to be so, but is, or appears for the most part to be so, and is enough to induce the mind to judge the proposition to be true or false, rather than the contrary.[82]

The degree of probability rested on its conformity to previous experience and the testimony of others, which in turn was evaluated by a set of criteria which centered on "number and credibility." Assent to propositions was to be in accord with the evidence.[83]

Probability, however, varied "in things which were constant, which were usually constant and those which were variable, and where things are indeterminate":

The first therefore, and highest degree of probability, is, when the general consent of all men, with a man's constant and never failing experience in like cases, to confirm the truth of any particular matter of fact, attested by fair witnesses; such are the stated constitutions and properties of bodies, and the regular proceedings of causes and effects in the ordinary course of nature.[84]

The "best natural science" for Locke would thus fall into the highest degree of probability. Such probabilities, however, rose "so near to a certainty, that they govern our thoughts as absolutely, and influence all our actions as fully, as the most evident demonstration . . . we make little or no difference between them and certain knowledge."[85] Probability thus effectively became knowledge. For, if assent is as much compelled to the highest degree of probability as it is to demonstration, then the distinction between compelled and voluntary consent, which was crucial to the old boundary between demonstrated knowledge and probable opinion, has been obliterated.

There were also lesser levels of probability, for all men's experience rarely agreed. Lesser but still quite good levels of probability respectively produced "confidence" and "confident belief."[86] Each of these levels was proportioned to the weight of the evidence. These assessments of probability involved matters of fact. Locke considered assertions on nonobservable questions to be hypotheses and speculations. Like most of the Royal Society scientists, Locke felt that description and experiment, that is, matters of fact, rested on a surer basis than explanations and hypotheses which possessed a lesser level of probability. The experimental program of the Royal Society, as discussed by Sprat, would make perfect sense to Locke, for it concentrated on the more certain matters of fact, and moved from these to probable hypotheses. For Locke, the natural sciences, e.g., physics, chemistry, and biology, rested to one degree or another on probable grounds.[87]

The redefinition of probability and its direct application to the natural sciences received perhaps its clearest scientific statement from Christian Huygens, a Dutch scientist much admired by the English virtuosi.[88] A mathematically oriented physicist and avid experimentalist, he felt, with Glanvill and Locke, that physical principles and physical hypotheses could never be more than probable.[89] In nature, certainty was impossible. In natural philosophy,

tis a Glory to arrive at Probability. . . . But there are many degrees of Probable, some nearer Truth than others, in the determining of which lies the chief exercise of our judgment.[90]

"I do not believe we know anything with complete certainty, but everything probably and to different degrees of probability . . . as 100,000 to 1 as in geometrical demonstration."[91]

Though physical topics did not permit demonstrative certitude, it was possible

to attain . . . a degree of probability which very often is scarcely less than complete proof. To wit, when things which have been demonstrated by the Principles that have been assumed to correspond perfectly to the phenomena which experiment has brought under observation: especially when there is a great number of them, and further, principally, when one can imagine and forsee new phenomena which ought to follow from the hypothesis which one employs, and when one finds that therein the fact corresponds to our prevision. But if all these proofs of probability are met with in that which I propose to discuss, as it seems to me they are, this ought to be a very strong confirmation of the success of any inquiry.[92]

In Huygens, notions of probability, degrees of proof, hypotheses, and natural philosophy are securely joined.

Propositions or statements of fact dealing with the natural world might range from the possible, plausible, or merely probable on the low end of the scale, to the highly probable and even morally certain on the high end. Even those propositions enjoying the highest probability were not "necessary," but they provided no grounds for reasonable doubt. Thus conclusions about the natural world involved a subjective element and were closer to "belief" than "science" in the older sense. The result of this shifting, displacement, and elaboration of the traditional categories of knowledge and opinion was the evolution of an empirical philosophy of science dominated by probabilistic statements.

HYPOTHESIS

Modifications of the concepts of knowledge and probability allowed English virtuosi both to retain a place for mathematics and mathematical demonstration and to find a new and more valued place for empirical knowledge, which would range in certitude from the merely probable to the morally certain. These changes were accompanied by changes in the definition of, and prescription for the appropriate use of, hypothesis, and in a new association of hypothesis with empirical data and concepts of probability.

A crucial issue in the transition of hypothesis from an essentially mathematical tool to a more general one encompassing all the natural and some human sciences was the extent to which hypothesis could represent or approximate reality. New questions were raised about the appropriate standards for judging discrete and rival hypotheses. In the course of describing these developments, we will occasionally touch on the relationship between reason and the senses in the formulation of scientific generalization. Our discussion will also suggest how newly linked concepts of probability and hypothesis came to play an important role in creating a distinctively English science.

Hypothesis was no novelty in the seventeenth century, for early astronomers employed mathematical suppositions about the heavens. Geometrical hypotheses employing uniform circular movements had been offered to explain the apparently irregular motions of heavenly bodies, without any claim that such suppositions represented physical truth. Ptolemy's hypothesis came to be considered the best hypothesis of this type. Because it was unnecessary to assert that hypotheses of this type conformed to physical fact, they coexisted without difficulty with Aristotelian physics.[93]

The Copernican hypothesis was initially presented to the public as a fictional hypothesis of this variety,[94] though discontent with mathematical "fictions" was developing during the Copernican period. Copernicans increasingly took a "realist" position, asserting that Copernicus had discovered an objectively real system of the heavens capable of demonstration. Tycho Brahe asserted that astronomical hypotheses should state the real physical disposition and movements of heavenly bodies, and he substituted his own planetary system for those of Ptolemy and Copernicus.[95] The fictionalist position further eroded as telescopic evidence increased.

Further modification occurred when Johannes Kepler distinguished logical and mathematical hypotheses from astronomical ones, the latter requiring physical evidence and confirmation. Kepler's integration of Tycho Brahe's empirical data was a significant departure, for now a given mathematical framework of astronomy was to be accepted for empirical reasons. The nature of hypothesis was altered as astronomy became an empirical as well as theoretical science.[96] The growing union of physics and astronomy meant that hypotheses might now be employed in physics as well as astronomy. Nevertheless, there was little consensus on whether they were to be considered useful fictions, mathematical suppositions, or approximations of reality to be accepted or rejected on the basis of empirical data.

Early seventeenth-century intellectuals expressed a wide range of opinion on the nature, function, and usefulness of hypothesis, and consensus would be difficult to locate during the decades in which some sought new certainties, some clung steadfastly to the older ones, and some were beginning to harness a variety of traditional modes of thought to the new science.

Mid-century English scientists did not find the positions of either Bacon or Descartes congenial. Bacon was extremely hostile to hypothesis, associating even the Copernican hypothesis with fiction. Descartes did allow a role for hypothesis despite the fact that his method, too, was designed to establish demonstratively certain physical principles. Hypotheses were derived a priori from the principles of Cartesian physics. Experiments might help decide between alternate a priori ways of "deducing" the phenomenon to be explained, but the hypotheses themselves were not derived from experiment or observed data. Hypothesis came to play a sufficiently important role in Cartesian physics for some historians to call it a "hypothetical physics." For Cartesians, hypotheses were plausible or possible explanations which might be false. They were not offered as either approximations or exact statements of physical reality.[97]

Galileo, the most prestigious scientist of this era, illustrates the early seventeenth-century lack of clarity. On the one hand, he brought telescopic observations to bear on the validity of the Copernican hypothesis and emphasized the role of experiment in testing theories; yet he also viewed both earthly and heavenly motion in mathematical terms. All nature was in some sense geometrized for him, and geometry, as for Descartes, provided the model of science. His approach to scientific philosophy involved a complex and still unclear combination of rational thought, mathematics, and sense data. Galileo did not provide a consistent or easy-to-follow position on hypothesis or scientific philosophy.[98]

Early English popularizers of the Copernican hypothesis, as proved by Galileo, used a mixture of arguments and evidence to convince readers of its superiority. John Wilkins suggested its "Convenience" in "resolv[ing] the Motions and Appearances of the Heavens into more easy and natural Causes," as well as the notion that it depicted reality.[99] Wilkins's defense of Copernicanism, like his early treatment of probability, suggests a mixture of older and newer views.

There existed side by side in the early seventeenth century the traditional mathematical use of hypothesis, its rejection as fiction by Bacon, its adoption by Cartesian physicists as deductions from a priori principles, and the beginning of efforts to anchor and evaluate hypothesis to observable data. On the whole, English thinkers attempted to link hypothesis to experimental data, while Continental thinkers tended to follow the a priori and mathematicizing approach of Descartes and Galileo. Though English virtuosi were impressed with the achievements of Kepler, Galileo, and Descartes, they came to feel that hypothesis and theory construction must be securely grounded on the empirical data they believed would provide the foundation for natural philosophy. No English thinker of note was long attracted to the alleged certitude of Cartesian physics or its use of hypothesis.

The development of atomic and corpuscular theories, particularly during the 1650s and 1660s, enhanced the intellectual status of physical hypotheses, and those who participated in the revival of ancient atomic theories or who developed variants of their own were driven to utilizing hypothesis as a necessary part of scientific philosophy. Although the existence of atoms could not be empirically proved, the "atomical hypothesis" was widely adopted as that best able to link appearances, to describe the behavior of phenomena in mechanical laws, and to predict future observable events. These ideas, which initially were explored in the circle of Marin Mersenne and Gassendi in France, rapidly gained ground in England through the efforts of Walter Charleton and Robert Boyle. English scientists became largely, though never completely, committed to one or another version of atomism, and thus to hypothesis.[100]

If the English scientists were to employ hypotheses extensively, however, they had somehow to be linked securely to the Royal Society's experimental program and to the newer notions of certainty and probability that were in the process of coalescing. During the Restoration, hypothesis was increasingly employed in the context of physical and empirical data, where it began to merge with notions of conjecture, probability, and probable opinion, and was sometimes used in connection with, and sometimes interchangeably with, explanations and explications.

Thomas Sprat combined the Baconian research program with an un-Baconian, though somewhat ambivalent, approach to hypothesis, which he usually equated with scientific explanation. If, on some occasions, "hypothesis" and "conjecture" suggest an undesirable, fictional element for Sprat, on other occasions, they were considerably desirable if, and this was a crucial *if*, they were based on the empirical data of natural history and experiment.

Though the Society refused to deal with causes in general, such as the cause of motion, believing they involved at best only "a better sort of metaphysics," it was committed to "conjecturing on the causes" of natural phenomena. The Society permitted, and even encouraged, the use of hypothesis, but required great circumspection, modesty, and wariness so as to escape the "disguised Lies, deceitful fancies" which resulted from "catching at it too soon." Even when causal explanations were "found to hold good," it was necessary to continue experimentation to avoid "overhasty and precipitant concluding upon Causes." Though reluctant to settle "Principles" or fix doctrines, the virtuosi would indicate that one "Opinion" or "cause" was more probable than others. Their successors, with a greater store of empirical data, would do even better. "Solid speculation" would require time.[101] Yet there is no suggestion that the Society felt, as Bacon had, that "The End of our Foundation is the knowledge of Causes, and secret motions of things."[102]

Sprat presented and discussed a long list of hypotheses, making clear that speculation and theory building were an important part of the activities of the Royal Society.[103] Yet Sprat remained defensive. Aware that some of his readers, perhaps more committed Baconians, might feel hypothesis to be inconsistent with the primary tasks of gathering empirical data and experimentation, he admitted "Speculation and Principles" were not an "absolute end," but insisted they were an important aspect of the Society's work product.[104]

The model new philosopher that Sprat held up to his readers was thus not the indefatigable data collector, but the youthful Christopher Wren, whose "true Theories" were confirmed by "many hundreds of Experiments," and whose "Natural and easy Theory of Refraction . . . exactly answered every Experiment."[105] About the time Sprat wrote, Wren, then Gresham Professor of Astronomy, informed Hooke that "I have, I think, lighted upon a true hypothesis" concerning the path of comets, "which when it is riper and confirmed by your observations, I shall send you."[106] For Wren, hypotheses might be "confirmed" as "true." They were neither fictional constructions nor derivations from pre-established, a priori principles.

Glanvill, too, insisted that the "enlargement of the history of Nature" was necessary in hypothesis and theory building. Without it, hypotheses must remain "but Dreams," and our "Science mere conjecture and opinion." If "we frame Schemes of things, without consulting the Phenomena, we do but . . . describe an Imaginary World of our own making." The "advancement of natural Theory" and fruitful hypothesis were dependent on an ever-expanding knowledge of "events and sensible appearances." Presently, there was insufficient phenomena to make hypotheses, "much less, to fix certain Laws and prescribe Methods to Nature in her Actings."[107]

Glanvill also linked hypothesis to a conception of natural science that could never go beyond the knowledge of appearances. There was no "scientifical procedure" for dealing with causes. Everything was "but hypothesis, within the circle of which we may conclude many things, with security from Error."[108] Even constant repetition did not merit a finding of "science," and he argued that it was wrong to impute causality from concomitancy.[109] "Youthful Philosophers" in particular were advised not to "fix eternally" on theories "as establish'd and infallible Certainties," but to "consider them in the modest sense of Hypotheses."[110] Hypotheses might be well grounded, but never certain. Generalizations about the physical world were themselves hypotheses of a sort and must remain so. The "best Principles of Natural Knowledge," he insisted, were "but Hypotheses."[111]

On some occasions, Glanvill lost confidence even in such modest generalizations, noting:

all we can hope for, as yet, is but the History of Things as they are, but to say how they are, to arise general Axioms, and to make Hypotheses, must, I think, be the happy privilege of Succeeding Ages. . . . We have yet no such thing as Natural Philosophy; Natural History is all we can pretend to.[112]

He thus alternated between a hope for tentative generalizations or hypotheses based on natural history and the feeling that natural history was all that was possible.

Samuel Parker, another propagandist for the Society, also suggests something of Glanvill's hesitancy and ambivalence. Unlike Sprat, he felt the Society had appropriately discarded "all particular Hypotheses," "addicting" itself instead to "true and exact Histories." Yet he, too, thought that natural history eventually would "lay firm and solid foundations to erect Hypotheses." These, however, would never be certain. No matter how "exact and certain" the experimental data, "application" to any given hypothesis could "be fastned and cemented to it no other way but by conjecture and uncertain (though probable) applications."[113]

A brief examination of the writings of several leading scientists of the pre-Newtonian era suggests how the Baconian research program was forging an alliance with hypothetical reasoning and theoretical concerns, while rejecting the speculative, hypothetical physics associated with Cartesianism. John Wallis, known primarily for his mathematical contributions, was quite willing to entertain physical hypotheses. He expressed reluctance to assent to newly proposed hypotheses until arguments on all sides had been made, or "until the truth emerges through the very clearness of the thing," something that happened "not rarely with true hypotheses." New hypotheses which could "be proved neither by ocular inspection nor by certain demonstration" were particularly troublesome. Nevertheless, if "founded on true reasoning," they would "at last," after much wrangling, "find a place in the minds of those who philosophise freely." In the course of a critique of an hypothesis that Leibniz had offered to the Society, Wallis indicated that he considered many parts of it to have "great probability," if not certainty.[114] Wallis, then, exhibits the new emphasis on a combination of reasoning and empirical confirmation.

Isaac Barrow, like Wallis a mathematician with empirical interests, suggested that experiment might "establish a true Hypothesis, to form a true Definition and consequently to constitute true Principles."[115] Barrow's "true hypotheses" were obviously different from the Cartesian variety, but it is not clear in what sense they differed from generalization or from what some called "theory." Walter Charleton spoke of the "great evidence and certainty" of Harvey's "hypothesis" of circulation of the blood, noting that he was "well satisfied" with its "Verity." Hypotheses, in this instance, seem very close to, if not identical with, moral certainty. In discussing the superiority of the Copernican hypothesis over others, however, Charleton emphasized its "singular probability." It was accepted "upon grounds of as much certainty and clearness, as the sublime and remote nature of the subject seems capable of."[116] This statement, not as strong as the previous one, suggests the highly probable rather than the morally certain. It is interesting that Copernicanism was always labeled an hypothesis, never a theory, fact, or demonstration.

In Robert Hooke, we see the committed Baconian, dedicated experimenter, and ingenious designer of mechanical devices and experimental equipment. We also see the theoretically oriented physicist and astronomer who frequently presented mathematically sophisticated theories in hypothetical form. Hooke spelled out his position on hypothesis and theory in his *Micrographia* (1665), a pioneering work that described and illustrated microscopic observations and offered hypotheses on light and combustion. Typically, he praised the Society's refusal to espouse hypotheses insufficiently "grounded and confirm'd" by experiment, approved its effort to "correct all Hypotheses by Sense," and requested that his own hypotheses be considered "only as Conjectures and Quaeries." His conjectures on the "causes of the things" that he had observed must not be construed "as unquestionable Conclusions, or matters of unconfutable Science." He had produced nothing "with intent to bind" the "understanding to an implicit consent." The reader must therefore not expect "any Infallible Deductions, or certainty of Axioms."[117]

Hooke's vision of empirical science stressed the role of the reasoning faculty, which was to "order . . . the inferior services of the lower Faculties." The best scientific procedure began with observation, continued according to reason, and returned to the "Hands and Eyes" again by a "continual passage round from one Faculty to another" in a never-ending process. With an adequate supply of empirical data, a "storehouse" of "Thousands of Instances" to work on, the rational and deductive faculties might accomplish a great deal. Hypothesis and empiricism were closely linked, and Hooke was hopeful that "true hypotheses" would emerge.[118]

Hooke employed hypotheses in a variety of contexts, though not always consistently. In geology, he posed a number of alternative hypotheses which he then considered in the light of known geological evidence. He took a similar position in connection with his explanation of the "Original of Springs," in this instance substituting the word "theory" for hypothesis. Theories, like hypotheses, "signifie no further than right reasoning from accurate Observations and Experiments doth confirm and agree with them."[119]

Yet there were instances when Hooke offered as speculations hypotheses that could not be adequately "verified" or supported by empirical data. He offered an hypothesis on "animal Motion" which "no Man ever did or will be able to explicate either this or other Phenomenon in Nature's true way and Method." He had published his speculations, he said, because he felt Anton van Leeuwenhoek's microscopic observations had given his hypotheses "an appearance of reality."[120] His discussion on the nature of frozen figures were "conjectures." Though they might give a "satisfactory account of the cause of those creatures," they remained "probable," precisely because they were not sufficiently certified "by Observation . . . to conclude anything positive or negative concerning it."[121]

Hooke also employed hypothesis in the context of astronomy and physics. While working on a physical explanation for planetary motion in 1661, he suggested that the active influence of the central body might "give us a true hypothesis of their motion."[122] His discussions of the Copernican and Tychonic hypotheses were couched in terms of "possibility" and "probability," apparently because of the absence of the requisite empirical data. "Probable arguments" might be urged on both sides "to the worlds end, but there never was nor could have been any determination of the Controversies without some positive observations for determining whether there were a Parallax or no of the Orb of the earth."[123] Astronomical hypotheses obviously must be tested by empirical data. It was not clear in this context how one distinguished a true from a highly probable hypothesis.

In his "Cometa," Hooke addresses the question of how to deal with competing hypotheses in the absence of adequate data. He considered various means of "knowing the distance" of comets:

yet there are some other which seem more easie arising from the consideration of the motions, that may be thought to be concern'd in the producing the appearances. And though they be wholly hypothetical, and so need some other arguments to prove the ground and principles on which they are founded, yet since there are not very many considerables wanting to make the probable and rational, I shall here add somewhat of my inquiries after the distance, position, motion, magnitude . . . of these Comets by these means.[124]

Elsewhere in the work, he uses hypothesis in the sense of explanation:

This Explication . . . may be, with probability enough, supposed to be the true cause of the appearance, whilst there is nothing therein supposed which is not manifestly the method of Nature in other operations; and the supposition even of the Aether, may seem to be Chimera and groundless; yet Had I now time, I could by many very sensible and undeniable experiments, prove the existence and reality thereof, and that it doth actually produce not only as sensible effects as these I have named, but very much the same, and many others much more considerable, which by Philosophers have hitherto been ascribed to quite different causes.[125]

Though not yet sufficiently supported by the data, Hooke feels his hypothesis would be adequately supported when further observations were made. Here Hooke seems to come closer to the Continental use of hypothesis.

In Hooke, then, we can see a certain confusion, or at least vagueness, in connection with the concepts of probability and hypothesis. He insisted that the Royal Society rightly rejected the merely "plausible and discursive" for the "real and solid part of Philosophy."[126] He criticized an hypothesis offered by Descartes as being "a very plausible Explication of the Phenomenon," but one which nevertheless had been contradicted by experiment. "Plausibility" clearly was insufficient. Yet Hooke suggests that the Society could deal with the "probable," which at times he uses almost as a synonym for plausible. He also used the term "probable," indeed "very probable," to suggest that the "Moon had a principle of gravitation." His explanation, he confessed, was "but a probability, and not a demonstration," because of the current state of astronomical observations.[127]

Hooke, then, exhibited no reluctance to employ hypothesis and theory, insisting that hypotheses be tested and evaluated according to the best empirical and experimental data available. Sometimes, empirical testing might yield "true hypotheses," at other times, only "probable" ones. Yet his usage is not consistent and is on occasion closer to the Cartesian position than he cared to admit.

Robert Boyle, a far less theoretical scientist, also insisted that hypotheses be supported by and evaluated according to empirical data. Boyle, however, links this position more directly to man's inability to penetrate the essence of things. In Boyle, Baconian experimentation was combined with hypothesis, and both securely fastened to a fallibilist view of human knowledge and a probabilistic natural science. He suggests, as had Glanvill, that all generalizations in the natural sciences were in some sense hypotheses. Most "theorems and conclusions in philosophy" were hypotheses in the sense that they were not absolutely certain.[128] In this sense, hypothesis was not merely a scientific tool that might be selected or rejected at will, but a characteristic of knowledge itself.

Thus Boyle recognized that his "corpuscularian doctrine" was necessarily an hypothesis, though it rendered "intelligible" a vast number of effects "without crossing the laws of nature or other phenomena." Experiments might not constitute "direct proofs of the preferableness" of his doctrine, but they did serve "for confirmation."[129] Explanations, though not certain, might be proved beyond reasonable doubt.[130]

Boyle, no more than Hooke, desired merely the compilation of experimental data, and he, like Hooke, insisted that reason, which he set above sense, must be applied to the observations of the senses.[131] Reason judged what conclusions could and could not be "safely grounded on the information" of sense or testimony. It was sometimes "condusive to the discovery of truth, to permit the understanding to make an hypothesis." Hypothesis, however, must be used only to see "how far the phaenomena" were "capable of being solved by that hypothesis."[132]

Boyle willingly went beyond "bare description" and variously offered hypotheses, conjectures, explications, and theories in connection with his work. The "proofs" offered for these hypotheses were not of the mathematical variety that he thought some readers might expect. His experimental proofs, he readily admitted, would not yield the certainty of mathematics.[133]

Although Boyle was probably happier performing experiments which "enrich[ed] the History of Nature," and felt, given the state of the empirical data, that hypothesis and theory were often premature, he frequently ventured "Conjectures" of the "Causes of the Phenomena" he described.[134] All theories or "superstructions," even if well grounded, were to be considered temporary. Even the best should not be entirely "acquieced," either as "absolutely perfect" or incapable of improvement, for even well-substantiated theories might be "confuted" by new experimental data.[135]

Boyle's planned but never realized treatise on the philosophy of science included consideration of the "Requisites of a Good Hypothesis," and a description of an "excellent" one. The former must be intelligible, assume nothing impossible or demonstrably false, be sufficient to explicate the phenomena, be consistent with related phenomena, and not contradict any known phenomena. The "excellent Hypothesis" must not only be the simplest one to "Explicate the Phaenomena," but must also permit prediction of future phenomena.[136] With Boyle, we have a clearly formulated view of hypothesis. A modest yet positive view of hypothesis thus was characteristic of the English scientific community at least until Newton's more critical views were proclaimed.

We must beware of assuming that a favorable view of hypothesis was itself a guarantee of superior scientific work. Much of the most valuable work in natural history was devoid of theory, and many seventeenth-century hypotheses proved to be little more than idle speculation.[137] We must remind ourselves, too, of the enormous contributions of Continental scientists, with their greater commitment to rationalism, certainty, and mathematical demonstration. While it is not unfair to contrast the English position on hypothesis with that of the Continent, or to compare English reluctance to pronounce definitely on the principles of natural philosophy with a system-oriented Cartesianism, the contrast must not be drawn too sharply.[138]

The geological controversies initiated by Thomas Burnet's *Sacred Theory of the Earth* (1681) suggest the widespread use and the range of meanings given to concepts of theory and hypothesis in the late seventeenth century. In the process of justifying the doctrine of a universal deluge, Burnet suggested that theories were often considered philosophic romances without "Truth or reality." His notion of a proper theory involved deduction "in due order, and with connexion and consequence of one thing upon another." Theory demonstrated causes, and reason was its first guide. Recognizing, however, that "sensible arguments" would be required by most of his readers, he also provided evidence from the "Effects" of nature.[139] If the various bodies of evidence agreed with one another and with his theory, Burnet argued, he could "safely conclude" that he was dealing not with an "imaginary Idea" but a true piece of natural history.[140]

But how fully or easily soever these things may answer Nature, you will say, it may be, that all this is but an Hypothesis; that is, a kind of fiction or supposition that things were so and so at first, and by the coherence and agreement of the Effects with such a supposition, you would argue and prove that they were really so. This I confess is true, this is the method, and if we would know any thing in Nature further than our senses go, we can know it no otherwise than by an Hypothesis. When things are either too little for our senses, or too remote and inaccessible, we have no way to know the inward Nature, and the causes of their sensible properties, but by reasoning upon an Hypothesis . . . if that Hypothesis be easie and intelligible, and answers all the Phaenomena . . . , you have done as much as a Philosopher or as Humane reason can do.[141]

His theory rose "above the character of a bare Hypothesis." Though a well-supported hypothesis might be "morally certain," the "general parts" of his theory "must be given even more than a moral certitude."[142]

Astronomer William Whiston, however, rejected Burnet's theory as a "precarious and fanciful" hypothesis which relied on "no known Phenomena of Nature."[143] Another critic commented that theories and hypotheses were to be judged on the extent to which they conformed to the data "physically, mechanically, and experimentally," and that proper answers would be found by rational examination according to the laws of gravity and hydrostatics.[144] Baconian John Woodward thought Burnet's theory had "no real Foundation either in Nature or History." "Observations . . . carefully made, and faithfully related," were "the only sure Grounds whereon to build a lasting and substantial Philosophy." His own hypothesis was, he concluded, the sole "Hypothesis that answers Nature, and shows all the Phenomena observable on the Earth in an easy and Geometrical Manner."[145]

The rational deductions, observations, matters of fact, and moral certainties proposed by some natural philosophers were often attacked by others as fanciful conjectures. Thomas Robinson, who criticized Woodward and Burnet, contrasted the certainties obtained from experiment with "Hypothesis and Conjecture." Mathematician John Arbuthnot, who found Woodward's conclusions inconsistent with known physical laws, noted that far too many natural philosophers made everything "fit their darling Hypothesis."[146] Arbuthnot called for better observation and more caution in system building. In their correspondence, John Ray, Edward Lhuyd, and William Nicolson used the terms "conjecture" and "hypothesis" almost interchangeably, though conjecture implied a somewhat less well-substantiated position. Nicolson felt unsure whether "Dr. Burnet's roasted egg, Dr. Woodward's hasty pudding, or Mr. Whiston's snuff of a comet" would carry the day, but he agreed with Arbuthnot "that a successful theory must be built upon many nice enquiries, and not forwardly advanced on the encouragement of a few likely phenomena."[147] The issue for most, despite their disagreement, was the extent to which the quality and quantity of observed phenomena were consistent with the proposed hypotheses.

Late seventeenth-century terminology remained unclear. Theory, hypothesis, explication, and conjecture are often used interchangeably. Though theory typically suggested greater certainty than hypothesis, and hypothesis than conjecture, one man's theory was another's mere hypothesis, conjecture, or imaginary fiction.[148]

It is with this varied and somewhat inconsistent usage in mind that we should approach Newton's emphatic rejection of hypothesis. Newton's denunciations have puzzled historians of science. Some have felt he had a fundamentally different vision of science than that reflected in the various versions of hypothesis offered by Hooke, Boyle, and the Royal Society. Others have emphasized that, in spite of his rejection of their views on hypothesis, Newton shared with them the belief both that man could not penetrate the nature of things and that certainty was limited to describing the phenomena of nature. Still others emphasize his rejection of Cartesian hypothetical physics, but not all hypothesis.[149]

The fact that both Hooke and Newton sometimes have been described as Baconians suggests the complexity of the empirical tradition. Hooke obviously found hypothesis more useful than did Newton. To Newton, Hooke's hypotheses seemed dangerously close to the suspect "hypothetical physics" of the Cartesians. Yet Newton also engaged in hypothesis and theory building, though he might prefer to call it something else.

A number of historians have suggested that the acrimonious debate between Newton and Hooke, dating from the 1672 optical papers, exemplified two different approaches to the use of hypothesis and to more general questions of probability and certainty in natural science.[150] Newton wrote:

A naturalist would scarce expect to see the science of those [colors] become mathematical, and yet I dare that there is as much certainty in it as in any other part of optics. For what I shall tell concerning them is not an hypothesis but most rigid consequences, not conjecturing by barely inferring 'tis thus because not otherwise, or because it satisfies all the phenomena (the philosopher's universal topic) but evinced by the mediation of experiments concluding directly and without any suspicion of doubt.[151]

The dispute turned both on the substance of Newton's "hypothesis" and on Newton's seemingly dogmatic claims to certainty. Newton's affirmation that he was offering certainty, not an hypothesis, appeared inappropriate to Hooke, who felt that his own hypothesis explained the phenomenon equally well, that both were necessarily devoid of absolute proof, and that neither was falsified by experimental findings. Newton's theory, like his own, was therefore an hypothesis.[152] Yet in other moods, Hooke expressed the hope that "even physical and natural enquiries as well as mathematical and geometrical will be capable of demonstration."[153]

Newton insisted that conclusive experimental evidence supported his position. He had presented

nothing else than certain properties of light, which now discovered, I think easy to be proved, and which if I had not considered them as true, I would rather have them rejected as vain and empty speculation, than acknowledged as hypotheses.[154]

His "theory," then, was no "hypothesis." Misunderstanding of his position had no doubt resulted from the common practice of calling "whatever is explained in philosophy" an hypothesis.[155] Newton insisted:

it is to be observed that the doctrine which I explained concerning refraction and colours, consists only in certain properties of light, without regarding any hypotheses, by which those properties might be explained. For the best and safest method of philosophizing seems to be, first to inquire diligently into the properties of things, and establishing those properties by experiment, and then to proceed more slowly to hypotheses for the explanation of them.

For hypotheses should be subservient only in explaining the properties of things, but not assumed in determining them; unless so far as they may furnish experiments. For if the possibility of hypotheses is to be the test of truth and reality of things, I see not how certainty can be obtained in any science; since numerous hypotheses may be devised, which shall seem to overcome new difficulties.

Hence it has been here thought necessary to lay aside all hypotheses, as foreign to the purpose.[156]

Newton was even more emphatic in his *Mathematical Principles of Natural Philosophy* (1687), where he announced his famous "Hypothesis non fingo:"

I frame no hypotheses: for whatever is not deduced from the phenomena is to be called an hypothesis; and hypothesis . . . [has] no place in experimental philosophy. In this philosophy particular propositions are inferred from the phenomena, and afterwards rendered general by induction.[157]

Newton insisted he had established the existence of gravitational attraction and its mode of operation. Gravitation was no hypothesis.[158]

Although Newton was less sympathetic to hypothesis than were Hooke and Boyle, the thought of all three men was characterized by a fundamental commitment to empirical data and an insistence that facts and phenomena were the basis of natural philosophy.

We can only speculate as to why Newton deviated from the more favorable views of hypothesis expressed by Hooke, Boyle, and many other members of the Royal Society. Such speculation must include Newton's arrogance, his confidence in his own scientific work, and his obsession with the idea of rigor.[159] It must also include the persistence in Newton of a Baconian vision of certain natural truth attained by means of experiment and induction, his commitment to the centuries-old tradition of the classical demonstrative sciences and the powerful appeal of the mathematical model of science.[160] One must also take account of neo-Platonic and hermetic elements in Newton's thought.[161] Newton then does stand somewhat apart not only in accomplishment but also in his philosophy of science. The examples of Boyle and Hooke on the one hand and Newton on the other suggest that the late seventeenth-century scientific community comprehended, as their propagandists claimed, not only different points of view on specific scientific issues but also different conceptions of the proper nature of scientific investigation.

The Newtonian era differed from its predecessor, and many of his contemporaries felt that the divinely inspired Newton had discovered something more than a highly probable account of nature's operation. Newton's *Principia* soon became the reigning orthodoxy among English natural philosophers. Admirers and disciples, such as Edmund Halley, emphasized the demonstrative, mathematical character of his discoveries, suggesting that Newton had revealed the true system of the universe.[162] Either Newton was no ordinary mortal or greater certainty was possible than his predecessors had thought.

English philosophers, however, did not renounce their more limited view of natural knowledge. Indeed, in the hands of John Locke, it received its fullest and best known statement. The eighteenth century was to be the century of both Locke and Newton. Locke was no stranger to the Restoration scientific scene or to the Royal Society. He not only was a close friend and associate of Boyle but was an active experimenter and, from 1668, a member of the Society. Locke, like Boyle, insisted "science" was not a reachable goal in natural philosophy, and like most empiricists, he thought it important to avoid speculative systems.[163]

Although Locke, like Boyle, was more comfortable with experiment, observation, and natural history which had a basis in experience, he also allowed some room for hypothesis, theory, and explanation. His limited use of hypothesis must, however, be put into a more general context. After asserting that the foundation of natural and civil knowledge was "matter of fact," he noted that two important defects must be avoided. The first was to heap up facts, the second, to draw general conclusions and raise axioms from insufficient particulars. Echoing Bacon, Sprat, and others, Locke noted that the mind often ran "too fast into general observations and conclusions" without "sufficient examination of particulars." The too common result was "ill grounded theories."[164] Most "general maxims, precarious principles, and hypotheses" were "laid down at pleasure," and did not promote "true knowledge." "General observations drawn from particulars" were the "jewels of knowledge," and one must take extraordinary care to distinguish the counterfeit from the true.[165] Hypotheses must be built "on matter of fact" and made "out by sensible experience." Matters of fact must not be presumed on the basis of one's hypothesis. One could, nevertheless, make good use of hypotheses in explaining natural phenomenon if one carefully examined the particulars and performed experiments. It was always necessary to remind oneself not to take for "unquestioned truth" what was at best "doubtful conjecture," "such as are most (I had almost said all) of the hypotheses in natural philosophy."[166]

Locke also linked hypothesis to probability. Evaluations of probability were appropriate in two scientific contexts. The first concerned matters of fact and things "Capable of observation and testimony"; the second, "Opinions with variety of assent," incapable of sense or testimony. These "opinions" included conclusions on the "existence, nature, and operation of finite immaterial being," life on other planets, and nature's "manner of operation," where one might observe sensible effects without comprehending the causes or modes of operation. Causes were "more or less probable," as they "more or less agree to truths that are established in our minds, and as they hold proportion to other parts of our knowledge and observation." "This sort of probability" was useful in "the rise of hypothesis."[167] Locke's view of hypothesis, like that of the Royal Society, was hesitant and cautious, but he recognized, as did the Society, the need for hypotheses built on and tested by observation of natural phenomenon. Such hypotheses might never be certain, but they could be highly probable and very useful.

Indeed, there were several hypotheses or theories which Locke felt were true or very probably true. The first was the corpuscular theory of the nature of matter.[168] The second was the Copernican hypothesis,[169] and the third was Newton's theory of gravitation. Newton's discovery of gravitation and the Christian doctrine of loving one's neighbor as oneself figured among the few "fundamental truths."[170]

In Newton, however, Locke encountered something of a dilemma, for he seemed to have attained what Locke insisted was unattainable:

Though the systems of physics that I have met with afford little encouragement to look for certainty, or science . . . yet the incomparable Mr. Newton has shown, how far mathematics, applied to some parts of nature, may, upon principles that matter of fact can justify, carry us in the knowledge of some, as I may so call them, particular provinces of the incomprehensible universe.[171]

If other scientists "could give us so good and clear an account of other parts of nature . . . we might in time hope to be furnished with more true and certain knowledge . . . than hitherto we could have expected."[172] With the "incomparable Mr. Newton," probability might become certainty. With Newton, Locke leaves the language of the probable, and even the morally certain, for that of demonstration and certitude.

As we have seen, English scientific intellectuals tended to be ambivalent about hypothesis and theory. Purely mental constructions or fictions were dangerous, leading to the dogmatic system of Descartes or the verbal abstraction of the scholastics. Baconian empiricism was modified to allow a modest, if important, role for theory and hypothesis. These hypotheses, however, must be presented as tentative suggestions, not certain truths. They must be tested against the empirical data and experiments. The more empirical evidence that seemed to support them, the better the hypothesis was thought to be, and the nearer it might be said to approximate truth and reality. If for Newton even these empirically supported hypotheses were still far too uncertain, most scientific intellectuals working between about 1650 and 1690 regarded them as a central feature of natural science.

THE STYLE OF SCIENCE AND THE FALLIBILITY OF MAN

The new philosophy of science dictated a distinctive style of scientific discussion and analysis. The most important ingredient of the new philosophical style was an acute sense of human fallibility, which was in part the legacy of Augustinian Christianity, now channeled into Protestantism and the skeptical revival, which had so recently undercut the foundations of all knowledge. Bacon's "Idols," which describe the weaknesses of intellect and sense, were heavily influenced by the skeptical critique, particularly that of Montaigne, and had a considerable impact on English thought. In England, however, the skeptical critique tended to be used to emphasize the fallibility of human knowledge and to inspire reluctance to make claims of certitude rather than to repudiate all claims to knowledge.

The Baconian Idols represented "the deepest fallacies of the human mind."[173] Though the Idols of the Theater—the "corrupt theories or systems of philosophy" and the perverted rules of demonstration—might be eliminated by re-education, the Idols of the Tribe, Cave, and Marketplace were innate, and all that could be done was to guard prudently against them. The Idols of the Tribe resulted from the tendency to press one's own ideas of order and reality on nature. The natural inclination to note confirming instances and ignore contradictory ones resulted in imposing "a greater uniformity" on nature "than really is." The deceptiveness and deficiencies of the senses were among these Idols. The Idols of the Cave, or defects of individuals, had their source in custom and education, while those of the Marketplace, for Bacon the most troublesome of all, were due to the deception of words.[174]

Though Bacon suggests the permanent effect of the Idols, he also suggested they might "be renounced and put away," and that one could, under proper conditions, enter Bacon's "Kingdom of man, founded on the sciences," as some would enter the Kingdom of Heaven.[175] If later virtuosi did not feel that Bacon's *New Organon* provided entry to that kingdom, they nevertheless cited, echoed, and paraphrased Bacon's catalogue of human weakness. The senses, though fallible, could at least partly be corrected, sometimes by scientific instruments and sometimes by reason,[176] which in turn could often be corrected again by the senses. The interplay between fallible reason and fallible senses was a characteristic subject. The imperfections of sense and reason and the detrimental effects of passion, interest, and party became constant themes, and the repetition itself contributed to the belief that absolute truth could rarely be achieved. Human knowledge did exist, but it, like those who produced it, must necessarily partake of imperfection.

This increasing sense that man should not anticipate a completely certain and demonstrative knowledge of all of nature is most clearly exhibited in the writings of Joseph Glanvill, who emphasized the necessity of treading a careful course between skepticism and dogmatism. Though we could not "fix certain Laws and prescribe methods to Nature," and our best principles were "but hypotheses," one could nevertheless conclude many things in nature with reasonable security from error.[177] This position, sometimes called "constructive skepticism,"[178] insisted that imperfect knowledge did not mean no knowledge. If there were many things which man did not know, and probably would never know, there was still a great deal that he could know with reasonable certainty or a sufficiently high level of probability.

This position was espoused by most leading figures in the Royal Society circle. Charleton noted the "Obscurity of Nature and Dimness and imperfection of our Understanding and the Irregularity of our Curiosity," and suggested that man would probably never know the essence of things or the "intimate nature of objects."[179] Sir Matthew Hale felt that the "forms of Things, the matter or substance, which is the subject of Nature," might be conjectured upon, but not known.[180] For Boyle, too, there were many things which were not understood, though some might be believed, if not understood.[181] The virtuosi frequently took the position that certain phenomena might be described adequately, but the causes of phenomena must remain unknown. In some instances, hypotheses might be offered; in others it was assumed the causes could never be known. Men might "fancy themselves Eagles," but they were "grovelling Moles incessantly labouring for light."[182]

The appropriate response was a combination of humility and strenuous effort. Though many things were unknown and others were unknowable, that did not mean men could know nothing. The senses and reason, though limited and prone to error, must be laboriously employed even though the result would be less than perfect knowledge. Isaac Barrow thus insisted:

Our business is to find Truth: the which . . . is not easily to be discovered; being (as a vein of silver, encompassed with earth, and mixed with dross) deeply laid in the obscurity of things, wrapt up in false appearances, entangled in objections and perplexed with debates; being therefore not readily discoverable; especially by minds clouded by prejudices, lusts, passions, partial affections, appetites of honour and interest; whence to decry it requireth the most curious observations, and solicitous circumspection that can be; together with great pains in the preparation and purgation of our minds toward inquiry of it.[183]

The fact that the "works of nature . . . operate by ways, too far surpassing our faculties to discover, or capacities to conceive," and could not "be brought into a science" must "not deter . . . one from the study of nature." Natural philosophy, that is, the "principles, properties and the operations of things," might be beyond human knowledge, but men might achieve probabilities with respect to them.[184]

The post-Baconian generation thus took to heart Bacon's Idols but no longer believed that his *New Organon* or any other method would result in certain natural knowledge. The essentialist search for real essences and ultimate causes or the reality behind appearances was largely abandoned.[185]

This adoption of the nonessential position, which culminated in the writings of Locke, also reshaped attitudes on how science ought to be conducted. Skepticism in England undercut confidence and the expectation of certitude but not the hope of improvement or the commitment to concerted effort. One frequently expressed theme was the expectation of constant revision and refinement. More and better observed matters of fact were anticipated. New hypotheses, too, might be anticipated, though they must never be considered "unquestionable conclusions or matters of unconfutable science," since "Future . . . experiments" might well prove them erroneous.[186] The ability to alter one's conclusions as new evidence presented itself was critical.[187] Natural science was viewed as an ongoing process of continual improvements. If the present was brighter than the past, the future promised even more. But the process would be slow and laborious.

The emphasis on scientific progress, first associated with technology and the arts, was thus extended to experimental knowledge and natural philosophy.[188] Truth, as Bacon and so many others noted, was the "daughter of time." Time had not only "revealed unto us many things which our Ancestors were ignorant of" but would "manifest to our posterity that which we now desire and cannot know."[189]

This position was inconsistent with a veneration of ancient authority or indeed any authority.[190] The ancients, being human, were necessarily subject to the same frailties as their modern counterparts. Typically Aristotle was praised, but his followers were condemned for dogmatically following his every word. Aristotle would undoubtedly have changed his mind on many questions had he had the opportunity to reconsider them in light of current knowledge. Ancient natural philosophers presented a twofold problem. First, they were more interested in metaphysics than natural science. Second, each "Philosophical Master" presented himself as "the Principal Secretary of Nature" whose disciples were expected to consider him as the "Grand Oracle . . . and the infallible Dictator of Scientifical Maxims." The new philosophers would permit no "infallible dictator," and considered most, if not all, claims of "Scientifical Maxims" suspect.[191]

No new oracles must be permitted to replace the old. Descartes was felt to be the potential purveyor of a new dogmatism. No ancient or modern master would be permitted to assume the mantle of authority. It behooved

everyone in the search for truth, always to preserve a Philosophical Liberty, not to be enslav'd to the Opinion of any Man as to think whatever he says to be infallible. We must labour to find out what things are in themselves, by our own Experience, and a thorough Examination of their Natures, not what another says of them.[192]

Philosophical liberty was thus contrasted with the "dishonourable tyranny of that Usurper Authority."[193] The virtuosi must be willing "to follow the banner of Truth by whomsoever it shall be lifted up."[194]

A sense of fallibility also led to emphasis on cooperation. Though individuals might begin carefully enough, they soon became overly "confident of the certainty of their knowledge." The Royal Society, which exposed opinions and evidence to many and had to satisfy a "multitude of judges," was more likely to examine theories "indifferently." The members were therefore appropriate "Umpires" of competing theories and hypotheses. Collective "wariness and coldness of thinking, and rigorous examination," so necessary for the "solid assent" and "lasting conclusions," was superior to anything "any single mind" could comprehend.[195] There was clearly an anti-elitist thrust to the Royal Society.[196]

It was assumed that there was, and always would be, diversity of opinion.[197] What was required, given this diversity, was a nonimperious, nondogmatic, noncontentious mode of discussion and presentation.[198] If the virtuosi had been dealing primarily with things capable of demonstration, that is, those which compelled assent, there would have been no need to take such a tentative stance or to reexamine or reconsider alternatives. Their antidogmatic stance, then, was linked to their philosophy of science.[199]

The same sense of fallibility led to a preference for nondogmatic and nonassertive language and modes of presentation. The Royal Society insisted on modest and tentative modes of expression and the avoidance of peremptory opinions. English virtuosi were advised to preface their conclusions with the language " 'tis probable that . . ." and to state their views in "a wary and becoming language."[200] They should employ expressions "as argue a diffidence of the truth of the opinions" adhered to. The "difficulties in search into the cause and manner of things" and the inability to "surmount these difficulties" made Boyle reluctant to "speak confidently and positively," except in cases of "matters of fact."[201] "Rigid Censoring" was clearly inappropriate behavior in the "perfect Virtuoso." Philosophical discussions were "Enquiries," not final determinations.[202] Glanvill even claimed it was "a Law" that the Royal Society repudiate assertive language.[203]

The fact that one can point to instances of scientific rivalry and acrimony does not reduce the importance of the ideal. Indeed, it is possible to view one of the most acrimonious scientific disputes of the late seventeenth century, that between Hooke and Newton over optical theory, as a conflict between different philosophies of science, and therefore of scientific presentation. Newton's mathematization of scientific argument and his emphasis on certainty contrasts with the tentativeness and modesty proclaimed by the early Royal Society, with its unwillingness to attribute certainty and necessity to scientific findings. Newton's assertive and Hooke's cautious languages can perhaps be linked to their different approaches to science.[204]

The Society's hostility to dogmatism and system making were thus closely linked to its assumption of human fallibility and to its belief in the modest but real successes that would come from prolonged cooperative effort. In the seventeenth century, the word "scientist" would have suggested claims to certain knowledge that were consciously rejected. For this reason, the practitioners of experimentally based natural science variously called themselves "real," "experimental," mechanical, or free philosophers, who were seekers after truth, not its possessors.[205]

The model naturalist or virtuoso, at least before Newton, was not some super human who rationally comprehended the structure of nature via mathematics or induction. However much Descartes, Galileo, and Boyle were admired, the model scientist was the admittedly imperfect and fallible "reasonable man" who collected and examined data and the propositions and hypotheses derived from them as calmly and impartially as humanly possible. He employed his rational faculties to weigh, judge, and evaluate observed sense data, experiments, and testimony dealing with natural phenomena. He engaged in a certain amount of speculation and hypothesis construction, but was careful not to attribute certainty to his intellectual constructions. He was prepared calmly and judiciously to evaluate the contributions of others in terms of probability and degrees of certainty. He avoided both skepticism and dogmatism, and was, above all, open-minded. He expected diversity of opinion and the gradual improvement of natural knowledge. The "new philosopher" and natural scientist represent a new intellectual type that can be contrasted profitably with the ancient philosopher, as well as with his early seventeenth-century and Continental counterpart.

BACON AND HIS SUCCESSORS

Bacon's work has made repeated appearances in this chapter, and his influence on this period has been a subject of controversy among intellectual historians. Thus it might be well to summarize our findings about Bacon before moving on to more general conclusions. It should by now be apparent both that Baconian impulses were powerful in the Society and that its leadership was not consistently Baconian. Bacon was proclaimed as the Society's prophet. The Society's research program can and should be traced to Bacon, as should the vision of a practical, utilitarian science. The Baconian "Idols," which portrayed the weaknesses of contemporary philosophy, and the human mind more generally, exerted a powerful influence, as did his vision of scientific endeavor as a non-elitist and cooperative enterprise. We thus would be wrong to underestimate the role of Bacon as propagandist for the new, empirical science. The Baconian vision of scientific progress based on data collection and experiment was a powerful stimulant, and we must not dismiss Sprat's statement that Bacon was the "one great Man, who had the true Imagination of the whole extent of this Enterprize, as it is now set on foot."[206]

Yet, when one examines the kind of science practiced by Hooke and Boyle, and the views of the Society's propagandists and defenders, one is struck by a number of non-Baconian elements. Boyle, Hooke, Wilkins, Charleton, Sprat, and Glanvill were something more or something else than Baconian purists. Although they felt that the experiential data of natural history must provide the basis for natural philosophy, they were not only more aware of the difficulties in establishing the facts of nature but more aware that these facts might be established with varying levels of certitude. More general propositions were unlikely to attain the status of axioms, let alone the "forms" Bacon sought. The Baconian method and the search for ultimate forms of nature was largely abandoned for a description of natural phenomena. The "reality behind appearances" and an "understanding" of "true causes" were thought to be beyond man's capacity.

Bacon had felt confident that axioms would rise "by a gradual and unbroken assent . . . at the most general axioms last of all." This, for Bacon, was "the true way, but as yet untried."[207] Though his successors did not explicitly reject this true but untried way, described in Book II of the *New Organon*, most scientists found that the Baconian method did not prove practical or useful. The most productive scientists also found hypotheses, rejected by Bacon, to be extremely useful and sometimes necessary, insisting vehemently, however, that they must not be considered to possess the certainty of axioms. For Bacon, hypothesis was still too identified with fiction and with "mere supposal" to be scientifically useful. Hypothesis, in the hands of Boyle and Hooke, was a different kind of hypothesis, being based on or supported by empirical data. Nor was Bacon sympathetic to notions of probability which, to him, were still identified with rhetoric and opinion. Like natural philosophers for over a thousand years, Bacon sought scientific certitude. Perhaps Bacon's caution about actually announcing specific scientific truths may be viewed as a sort of spiritual ancestor of Boyle's and Hooke's fondness for hypothesis, but in the final analysis he rejected hypothesis and they did not.

On the whole then the Royal Society adopted a Baconian research program and took to heart Book I of the *New Organon*, which provided an extensive critique of traditional natural philosophy and scientific method. At the same time, it largely ignored Book II, which attempted to replace the old method based on scholastic logic with a new inductive method.[208] The legacy of Francis Bacon was thus very great, but it is only part of the story.

Any explanation of why Bacon's successors moved in different directions must recognize that the post-Baconian generation experienced a different philosophical environment. It was a generation that had witnessed and absorbed the achievements of Kepler and especially of Galileo, who impressively combined observation and experiment with theory and mathematics. Bacon had not appreciated the role mathematics would play, and his approach could not easily be made to incorporate the mathematization of physics that was taking place. The profound effects of mathematics and the new mechanical theories had altered the scientific environment.

An examination of the Wadham Group of experimental scientists at Oxford suggests how new problems and issues of the 1640s and 1650s helped shape the philosophy of the Royal Society. As a group, these men had strong mathematical and astronomical interests, as well as a commitment to experimentation. John Wallis, Seth Ward, Laurence Rooke, Christopher Wren, and Robert Hooke all served at one time or another as professors of astronomy and/or mathematics. Post-Baconian naturalists were becoming more familiar with elementary mathematics, and many incorporated the newer mathematical approach into their own work.

This generation, too, beginning with Wilkins, defended the Copernican hypothesis as the best hypothesis because it was best confirmed by the empirical data. Hypothesis became increasingly acceptable in the 1650s and 1660s as atomic and corpuscular theories were adopted. Many hypotheses—magnetical, atomic, Copernican—were readily debated by the Oxford scientists.[209]

This generation faced the challenge of Thomas Hobbes, whose vision of the sciences ran counter to the new experimentalism, and whose denial of immaterial substance seemed to deny the existence of God and the soul. The Hobbesian model appeared dangerous because of its attempt to apply the geometrical or demonstrative model of science to inappropriate subject matters and kinds of knowledge.

The promises and dangers of Cartesianism, too, were important, for it appeared that there might be new, as well as old dogmatisms to guard against. As we have seen, Aristotelianism and Cartesianism were linked, and both were rejected as dangerous systems. Bacon and Descartes might have accomplished more "if they had promised less." Their "high confidence" had become the "heat and scheme of party" rather than "sober philosophy."[210] The capacity for error extended to Bacon and Descartes, as well as Aristotle. Despite the insistence that Cartesianism as a system was fraught with dangers, various aspects of Cartesian science made an enormous impact on the English scientific community. Indeed it would be difficult to comprehend the development of English physical theory without taking account both of Cartesian mechanism and the particular issues explored by Descartes and his disciples. If those historians concerned with the development of astronomy and theoretical physics have tended to view the Baconian contribution as negligible and have instead stressed the role of Galileo and Descartes at the expense of Bacon, we must be aware that the mid-century scientific community strove to combine Baconian empiricism with Galilean physics and with at least some aspects of Cartesian science. A simple Baconianism could no longer suffice, but Baconianism was not entirely swept away by Continental influences.

The naïve Baconianism adopted by some radical religious and educational reformers in the 1640s and 1650s also may have prompted second thoughts about Bacon. Certainly the naïve notion that inductive logic could replace deductive was roundly rejected. There was no single method, and "Induction is ridiculously applied to Physics." It was in the context of these Interregnum conflicts that Seth Ward cited the limitations of the Baconian method, noting "It is a misfortune that my Lord Bacon was not skilled in Mathematicks, which made him jealous of their Assistance in all natural Enquiries."[211]

Religious dogmatism, a far greater problem during the civil war and Interregnum era than in Bacon's lifetime, also seemed a danger. The Wadham group recognized the practical need to exclude religious issues which were in the process of destroying both the university and the country. Antidogmatism, both scientific and religious, was increasingly perceived as essential. Changing conditions of intellectual life, then, contributed to the new scientific style.[212]

A significant number of the Oxford scientific circle were also theologically knowledgeable clerics. They were familiar with the concept of moral certainty, the probabilistic aspects of casuistry and contemporary discussions of the nature of belief. Since they, unlike Bacon, wished to unite religion and science, such categories and concepts were available for secular as well as religious use. It is possible, too, that their theological orientation made them particularly sensitive to the distance between human and divine knowledge and thus to the view that mere humans could not penetrate reality itself. The specifically religiously related contributions of

Ward, Wilkins, Wallis, Boyle, and Locke will be discussed in the next chapter.

The Oxford circle, the precursor of the Royal Society, thus did not commit itself exclusively to a program of Baconian observation and experiment, but was already in the process of moving away from a purely Baconian philosophy of science. After the foundation of the Royal Society, these tendencies became even more marked. Baconian experiment was combined with a non-Baconian willingness to entertain hypothesis, to employ mathematical tools, and to find satisfaction in a natural science that could not produce certainty.

The tension between Baconian and non-Baconian tendencies was not always resolved or even explicit. One meets occasional assertions that, in time, natural history and experiment would produce true philosophy and penetrate its nature and causes with the certainty of mathematical demonstration. Far more typical, however, were the assertions that fallible men could never do more than describe phenomenon and hypothesize about causes. In the course of the seventeenth century, English philosophy of science moved from a Baconian to a Lockean search for truth.[213]

CONCLUSION

At the outset of this chapter, we suggested that English science and scientific philosophy were transformed during the seventeenth century. The first step in the process was the re-evaluation of experience undertaken as Renaissance humanists emphasized the importance and value of everyday moral and political experience. For them, however, the world of experience and fact was contrasted with philosophy and science and was associated with rhetoric and the problems of daily life. The next step was that of making experience a more basic feature of philosophy, particularly natural philosophy. This was the contribution of Francis Bacon. Bacon made empirical data the centerpiece for a demonstratively certain natural philosophy. The generation between Bacon and Locke absorbed a great deal of Bacon's empiricism. It adopted his research program, which featured natural history and experiment, while moving away from, and sometimes denying, the possibility of a certain, inductive science of nature. The virtuosi abandoned the philosophical goal of comprehending the forms of nature for the more limited knowledge of appearance and phenomena. Phenomenal matters of fact derived from observation and experiment became a, if not the, central concern of English natural philosophers. Borrowing from fields such as history, law, and religion, which were long accustomed to dealing with matters of fact, the virtuosi could now rigorously examine factual findings for their probability and certainty. If the surest were morally certain and could not be doubted by a "reasonable man," many others had a more doubtful status. The status of facts might change as more and better information was provided. The scientific community thus could anticipate a changing and ever-expanding and more accurate collection of natural data.

Well-established facts became of fundamental concern to seventeenth-century English scientific philosophy and practice. Indeed, it is necessary to remind ourselves that this was not always so, and that natural and experimental data were not always considered fundamental, or even very important, to the establishment of physical truth. What we have described here, then, is both the creation of a new philosophy of science and a new research program.

Matters of fact established with moral certainty were not often available, and naturalists recognized they must often deal with the more or less probable. Indeed, one of the most significant changes in scientific philosophy was the erosion of the once sharply defined categories of probability and certainty. In the process of judging facts and theories on a continuum which ran from mere probability and mere opinion to high probability and moral certainty, the scientists and philosophers contributed to the further breakdown of the traditional philosophical categories of logic and knowledge on the one hand, and rhetoric and opinion on the other. A new family of ideas once associated with rhetoric, everyday affairs, and theology now became not only philosophically relevant but central to scientific endeavor.

This family of ideas was not limited to the assessment of matters of fact. English naturalists were interested in sound, if not certain, generalization based on facts, and were quite willing to conjecture, explain, and hypothesize about the causes of phenomena. Assessments of probability and degrees of certainty, however, were to rest on, or be judged by, primarily empirical data. Hypotheses were transformed from mathematical suppositions and astronomical fictions to propositions about and explanations of physical phenomenon to be evaluated according to established criteria for assessing the relative certainty of physical findings. Whether one was engaged in data collection or theory building, the physical sciences were

71

thought to deal with varying degrees of probability. Although some English virtuosi expressed a lingering hope for a certain physical science in some distant future, most scientifically oriented intellectuals believed that a probabilistic, natural science was all that might be expected. In one sense, the scientific knowledge of the seventeenth century was not considered "science" at all, since its principles and conclusions could not compel assent. The new knowledge was considered neither fixed nor perfect, and its proponents did not feel that they could capture truth or penetrate to the essence of things. Natural science would always contain elements of uncertainty and the possibility of progress.

Mathematics and mathematical demonstration, which now largely replaced syllogistic forms of logical demonstration, retained a great deal of prestige. Most virtuosi readily admitted to the greater certainty of mathematical than physical propositions. But mathematics was not practiced as widely or as deeply in England as on the Continent. Indeed, English mathematicians tended to be as deeply engaged in experimental endeavors as their nonmathematical counterparts. When Hooke, Wren, or others did turn to mathematical analysis of the physical world, they tended to speak in terms of probability rather than demonstration, and to insist on empirical verification or validation. At the end of the century, two great figures, Newton and Locke, consolidated the new philosophy and symbolized its continued tensions. Newton wholeheartedly adopted its empiricism, but strove to move beyond its probabilism to the generation of mathematically certain propositions of fact. Locke, whose writings consolidated and synthesized its empiricism and probabilism in a unified theory of knowledge, was forced to treat Newton as a special case, but nonetheless held firmly to probabilism. English scientific circles thus cultivated both empirical investigation and theoretical science, but the balance was generally tipped in the direction of the empirical, the experimental, and the probable.

The focus on the empirical and probable, rather than the certain and demonstrative, resulted in a philosophical style that strove to avoid dogmatic statements. System making, associated with dogmatism, was considered philosophically unsound and scientifically dangerous. An acute sense of human imperfection led the scientists to insist on "philosophical liberty," a moderate and tentative mode of discussion, and a rejection of authority. English epistemological thought was thus characterized by a mixture of optimism and pessimism—pessimism when one contemplated human frailty and capacity for delusion and error; optimism as one considered the

72

continued improvement in knowledge made possible by careful observation, experimentation, and collective effort and judgment.

The empirical bent of English science made it less elitist than Continental science. It was possible for the relatively unsophisticated to participate in the collection of natural data. This amateur element helps to explain the ease with which the educated Englishman absorbed scientific publications. Although the mathematically sophisticated theories of Hooke, Wren, and especially Newton commanded a narrower audience, the combination of what Thomas Kuhn has recently considered two quite different scientific traditions[214] not only gave English science its peculiar character but helped make science a socially sanctioned intellectual activity. Except for a tiny group of critics who poked fun at the virtuosi, there was no serious opposition to the new philosophy.[215]

The contrast between English and Continental science, however, should not be drawn too sharply. Gassendi's empirical phenomenalism, which exhibits considerable affinity with the pre-Lockean, English virtuosi, provided a counterweight to Cartesianism. Experimental science was not lacking in France, either before or after the foundation of the Academy of Sciences in 1666. Christian Huygens recommended a program of experimentation and natural history to Colbert in the planning stages of the Academy. Roger Hahn has pointed to the late seventeenth- or early eighteenth-century development of a phenomenological positivism and a vision of the gradual acquisition of scientific knowledge that was similar to that of the Royal Society. Though writing somewhat later than Sprat or Glanvill, Fontenelle emphasized the importance of fact gathering. He expressed both an antagonism toward premature system making and a willingness to conjecture on causes.[216] The character of English and French science was different largely because the balance between the empirical and the theoretical and exact sciences was somewhat different. Cartesian science was, and remained, a far more powerful force on the Continent. The English scientific community was committed to natural science, but rejected "scientism."

As a result of their new orientation toward matters of fact, experience, probability, and hypothesis, English intellectuals created a new philosophy of science that brought them into closer contact with intellectual endeavors once considered to belong to a totally different realm.

III

Religion

THE RELATIONSHIP between religion and science in seventeenth-century England has long been a matter for discussion. Early writers tended to assume that there was an inherent conflict between the two, and that religion was harmful to science. More recent writers, also assuming conflict, concluded that the damaged area was religion.[1] Beginning with Max Weber and culminating with Robert K. Merton and Christopher Hill, a school of historically oriented sociologists and Marxist oriented historians have suggested an affinity between Puritanism and the development of science. In current thinking generally, there is little doubt about the close relationship between religion and science, although very substantial differences of opinion exist concerning the precise nature of that relationship.[2]

Our purpose here is not to review this growing literature, but to discuss those aspects of the problem which relate to seventeenth-century theories of knowledge and the search for truth and, particularly, those religious writers whose approach either contributed to or ran parallel to the developments discussed in the last chapter. In general, we will find that scientists and Anglican theologians sought to defend their findings and conclusions both from claims of infallible authority and from a skepticism which denied that any form of truth or knowledge was possible. They defended reason as a tool for examining the natural and spiritual world, while at the same time denying that the reasoning faculty could yield what had traditionally been called science or absolute truth. By first employing, and then reshaping, traditional categories of science, faith, belief, and opinion, a group of Anglican theologians, many of whom were deeply involved in the study of natural phenomena, sought to create a rational defense for a set of religious beliefs and

74

practices that, in turn, could provide the basis for a reasonably broad ecclesiastical establishment.

Because this theology and the modes of thought associated with it sprang from problems and traditions that were not peculiarly English, it will be necessary to describe briefly some general sixteenth- and early seventeenth-century developments before turning to an examination of the ideas of this group of like-minded latitudinarian laymen and theologians. From at least the thirteenth century, Christian theologians had employed the most recent advances in philosophy. Indeed, it was the philosophic underpinnings of late medieval theology that were so heavily attacked by the humanists. Instead of a theology which they considered to be manmade, abstruse, and full of meaningless and barbarous terminology, Renaissance humanists offered a simple, nonphilosophical, ethically oriented Christianity. As a result, they did not become deeply involved in the epistemological questions that necessarily arise when philosophy or reason are brought to the aid of a religion based fundamentally on scriptural authority.

Issues of reason and authority resurfaced in the early years of the Reformation. Although the Protestant attack on papal authority was a crucial element in undermining respect for the principle of authority, most Protestants raised Scripture into a counterauthority without providing an unambiguous mode of scriptural interpretation. Diverse biblical interpretation created a proliferation of Protestant churches and sects, each of which viewed its rivals' creeds as erroneous or even heretical. With the exception of certain radicals who disavowed the need for any established church, those who claimed to possess religious truth were frequently willing, if given the opportunity, to persecute and punish those who would not conform.

Beginning with Erasmus, a few individuals sought a way out of these conflicts over religious belief. In his debate with Luther over freedom of the will, Erasmus not only introduced a line of thought which would emphasize religious peace over theological precision but also contributed to a new approach to religious knowledge and belief. Erasmus repeatedly employed the term "opinion" to characterize religious doctrine. While God's injunction that man follow a moral life was clear, theological questions, e.g., the nature of the will, were not fully knowable by men, whose capacity for knowledge was limited. Noting his "deep seated aversion to fighting" and his "dislike of assertions," Erasmus insisted "I merely want to analyze and not to judge, to inquire and not to dogmatize. I am ready to learn from anyone who advances something more accurate or more reliable."[3] This position, which perhaps owes something to late academic skepticism,[4] led Luther to denounce Erasmus for treating Christian doctrine "as nothing better than the opinions of philosophers and men." The Holy Spirit has written "no doubts or opinions" but "assertions, more certain and more firm than all human experience. . . . Not to delight in assertions is not the mark of a Christian heart."[5] Erasmus, however, still insisted that:

unless we define as little as possible, and in many things leave each one free to follow his own judgement, because there is great obscurity in many matters, and [mankind] suffers from this almost congenital disease that he will not give in once a controversy is started.[6]

Such questions were best settled at the time that one saw God face to face.[7]

Luther's emphasis on dogma and dogmatic assertion was elaborated by John Calvin, Theodore Beza, and others, who insisted that one could grasp the meaning of Scripture by means of illumination of the Holy Spirit. This illumination would yield an inner persuasion that what one understood was true. The tradition of certitude exemplified by Luther tended to prevail over Erasmian tentativeness. With the development of Calvinism, Zwinglianism, and the counter-Reformation, no European country escaped religious strife or governmental efforts to insure conformity to whatever the dominant group deemed to be true doctrine.

Peace-making efforts occurred from time to time. In France, the scene of a series of bloody civil wars, such proposals tended to be offered by politiques less concerned with the nature of religious truth and the degree to which it might be correctly ascertained than by the pressing need for public peace. Religious argument was particularly influenced by skepticism, which had become a more powerful intellectual force in France than elsewhere. Pyrhonnist doubt as to the possibility of all knowledge inspired a group of early seventeenth-century Jesuits to perfect what they thought to be "the perfect machine of war" against Protestants. Fideism, born of epistemological skepticism, became a special characteristic of French Catholic thought.[8]

A few scattered individuals, however, adopted the Erasmian preference for Christian living over doctrinal purity. Sébastien Castellio, responding to the Calvinists' burning of Michael Servetus, emphasized the obscurity and insignificance of the questions over which men killed each other. His *De Arte Dubitandi et Confidendi, Ignorandi et Scienti* distinguished between knowledge and belief. The former was dependent on sense experience or demonstration. The latter, based neither on evidence nor demonstration, depended on faith or an authority recognized by the believer. Religion was based on faith not knowledge. Castellio concluded that the Christian faith was comprehensible to all, and that the moral content of Scripture, rather than right opinion or dogma, was critical.[9]

This peace-making mentality also characterized Jacopo Acontio, an Italian Protestant whose *Satanae Stratagemata* (1565) became widely known in liberal English religious circles. In his discussion of heresy, this jurist, philosopher, and engineer emphasized the capacity for error and difference of opinion exhibited by even the wisest of men. Indeed, it was Satan who encouraged claims of infallible knowledge. To persecute others on the basis of an arrogant, subjective conviction was wrong. Mankind must continue to seek truth despite the fact that no individual could expect to achieve it. Acontio's distinction between fundamental articles of Christianity which everyone believed and the lesser doctrines about which dispute was acceptable became an important one for later English theologians. His approach influenced the religious moderates of the Great Tew Circle, the mid-seventeenth-century Independents who supported religious toleration, and the latitudinarian churchmen of the Restoration.[10]

Hugo Grotius's attempt to find a rational basis for Christianity, *The Truth of the Christian Religion* (1624), also assisted English theologians promoting Christian reunion. Noting Aristotle's dicta that different proofs were required for different things, and admitting that proof in matters of faith was not as powerful as mathematical demonstration or the immediacy of sensation, Grotius insisted that it was possible to reach sound conclusions in matters of faith and matters of fact. A reasonable person, that is, one without an excess of passion or prejudice, could reach sound conclusions as to Christian doctrine. Indeed, Christian texts must be evaluated by the same means as secular histories. This association of scriptural with historical texts, as we shall see later, provides one of the major links between religious and historical thought.[11]

Castellio and Acontio, and most clearly Grotius, represent an advance beyond the Erasmian position in their attempt to find a rational basis for the truths of religion without making claims to the kind of religious certitude that dogmatic theologians were making. Utilizing the traditional distinctions between science and opinion or knowledge and belief, their Continental and English successors attempted to forge a rationally based religious doctrine that could be defended against claims of certainty based on authority, "science," or spiritual intuition.

ENGLAND

Initially, the problems faced by Englishmen were not substantially different from those on the Continent. As England became Protestant, its theologians defended the English Church against Roman Catholicism and its claims of infallibility by relying upon Scripture as a counterauthority. In England, however, the development of Protestant groups which disagreed among themselves about the doctrine and the ecclesiastical model contained in Scripture led some churchmen to stress reason and tradition, rather than authority, in matters of religion. The Anglican solution was to promote a comprehensive, historically based Church that could be defended with some mixture of reason, history, tradition, and Scripture. In the process, Anglicans expanded the role of reason and developed the doctrine of *adiaphora*, or things indifferent, that is, the principle that certain doctrines and rituals cannot be proved essentials of Christian faith. Theologians bent on employing reason to provide the strongest possible intellectual defenses for their doctrinal positions necessarily were drawn into current philosophical speculations on the nature of reason, evidence, and proof. Neither English theologians nor philosophers, however, were much attracted to skepticism.

In England, then, theologians defended theological positions and ecclesiastical arrangements on rational grounds without jettisoning the primacy of Scripture. Richard Hooker employed traditional modes of rational thought, those developed primarily by Aquinas. His successors attempted to steer somewhere between infallible knowledge and the skeptical repudiation of all knowledge. At the same time, they increasingly dismissed or attempted to bypass scholastic philosophy, though they owed more to it than they often recognized. Those upon whom we will concentrate were attracted to natural religion, the rational defense of Protestantism, and a scripturally based Christianity. They attempted to develop a basis for religious knowledge that was, if not equivalent to science, at least morally certain. Particularly after 1650, a group of Anglicans with a special interest in natural science and in history sought epistemological solutions to religious problems almost identical to those being worked out by their associates and themselves in the realms of natural and historical knowledge.

The works of controversialists John Jewel and Richard Hooker outlined some of the basic issues, albeit in still traditional terms. Central to Jewel's argument against Roman Catholic claims to religious authority was the emphasis on human fallibility and the then typical Protestant insistence on the "very sure and infallible rule of Scripture."[12] Evading the issue of how to arrive at a true understanding of Scripture, he, like Calvin, felt Scripture somehow carried "its own evidence with it."[13] The best interpretations were to be found among the Church fathers whose authority was based on their general agreement and consent. Jewel, the first major apologist of the Anglican Church, stressed unity in essentials and argued that variety of beliefs about nonessentials was not harmful.[14]

Richard Hooker, whose *Of the Laws of Ecclesiastical Polity* was directed against Puritan dissenters, placed greater emphasis on both reason and experience. Repudiating claims to absolute truth based on individual interpretation of Scripture, he emphasized tradition and common consent without suggesting that they were in any way infallible. Scripture, reason, and tradition were all in some sense authoritative. Since churches were shaped by human reason and experience, and thus could not conform to a divinely ordained plan knowable to man, Hooker defended a broadly based, established church within which individuals, including Puritans, might differ on doctrines and ceremonies deemed indifferent.[15] While Hooker's concept of reason was traditional, his effort to support a Protestant church on the basis of history and reason was an important departure, for it required renewed attention to the nature and varieties of reason and reasoning.

Although one might expect Bacon to exert considerable influence, the relatively small role Bacon allotted to reason in matters of religion meant that natural theologians turned to non-Baconian sources and traditions.[16] The Baconian "Idols," however, did find their way into theological discussion. For if the adverse effects of education, upbringing, and prejudice could be minimized, the level of assertiveness in religious discourse might be reduced.

Although a calm, dispassionate temper was rarely to be found in religious discussion during the decades following Bacon's death, the Great Tew Circle, located on Viscount Falkland's estate near Oxford, provided as close an approximation as could be found in England during the acrimonious 1630s. Early seventeenth-century England was characterized by intra-Protestant controversies we now label Puritan and Anglican. On the whole, these controversies took place in the still dominant scholastic or Ramist format, and were relatively little concerned with philosophical and epistemological issues. A substantial exception, however, was the latitudinarian circle at Great Tew. Indeed, historians have often pointed to John Hales, Viscount Falkland, and William Chillingworth as models of rationality and calmness in a world increasingly characterized by religious conflict and dogmatism.

The group, whose most powerful intellect was William Chillingworth, was characterized by two major concerns which were both treated in such a way as to have consequences for philosophy. The first was the search for religious unity and charity. The second was the construction of a defense against the increasingly sophisticated attacks of Roman Catholic controversialists. The work of the Tew Circle in both these areas provided an important step toward the formulation of the concept of probabilistic knowledge that we have found so central to the development of English science.[17]

Although the inclination to exalt the authority of the early Church and the Church fathers as a makeweight against the authority of the Roman Church had become a characteristic element in some Anglican circles, the Great Tew Circle insisted that the Church fathers were as fallible as other men. Hales and Falkland insisted that the contemporary era was as good as the patristic age. Antiquity was simply "man's authority born some ages" earlier.[18] Traditions, particularly universal traditions, might be useful, but they were not authoritative. Dismayed by the increasing dogmatism of their countrymen, they advocated greater unity in the Church through emphasis on religious essentials and emphasized moral improvement as a substitute for doctrinal disputation.

The most important developments emerged from efforts to refute Roman Catholic claims to infallibility. Not only did Falkland insist that neither popes nor Church councils were infallible, but he rejected the idea that any religious principles were capable of demonstration. In religious questions, it was necessary to be satisfied with probabilities. Such probabilities were as suitable as guides in religion as in the affairs of daily life. Falkland, without elaborating, extended the scope of probability, insisting that there was little in nature capable of demonstration except "lines and numbers."[19]

It was Chillingworth, however, who developed these still quite traditional concepts in such a way as to shape the outlook of a whole generation of philosophically oriented theologians. Employing traditional scholastic distinctions, Chillingworth identifies two, or perhaps three, relevant epistemological categories: knowledge, faith, and opinion. Knowledge or science, which consisted of the demonstrations of mathematics and the axioms of metaphysics, is always true. In matters of faith, unlike those of knowledge, assent is not compelled but is dependent on evidence. Opinion is like faith, since it, too, invites rather than compels assent. While Chillingworth wished to distinguish opinion and faith, he was obviously unclear about the difference. While he did not wish to be open to the charge that faith and opinion were identical, he could suggest only that opinion required less evidence than faith, and that he would be willing to discard the term "opinion" in exchange for a better one.[20]

Chillingworth combined the categories of knowledge in the broader sense (that is, science, faith, and opinion) with categories of certitude. The first, "absolute infallibility," was available only to God. "Conditional infallibility," the best man might aspire to, could be found in mathematical demonstration and the axioms of metaphysics. A third, "moral certainty," involved what was believed but not known. Not only did this category cover the everyday conclusions of a reasonable and impartial man considering the relevant data, but it also included the kind of knowledge employed in the law courts, in travelers' reports, in history, in merchants' decisions, and in religion.

While there was always a possibility of error in the realm of faith, there were degrees of certainty that depended on the evidence. It was this kind of certainty that Chillingworth elaborated in connection with religion, whose truths could achieve moral certainty at best. His categories are utilized to show that God gave no man or institution an infallible guide. Indeed, it is erroneous to think that, in religion, one must have an infallible certainty or none at all. Using the analogy of courts, Chillingworth said Roman Catholics were like those who would insist either that judges must be infallible or that there be no lawsuits at all.[21]

Chillingworth's approach to Scripture greatly enhanced the role of reason. Even the assurance of scriptural truth consisted of only a reasonable certainty. Here again, there was no need for authoritative interpretation. The resulting lack of uniform belief would not be harmful since Scripture was not an oracle to settle disputes. Differing interpretations were merely matters of opinion. Disputes must be judged by individuals employing their reasoning faculties. Like all writings, Scripture was "deaf, dumb and inanimate." A judge hears, examines, and declares his mind to disagreeing parties and thus must be a living, reasoning man. Scripture could no more displace the act of human judgment in religion than the laws could in lawsuits. Scripture must be evaluated by the full use of man's reasoning faculties. Men were thus to employ their rational faculties in their search for religious truth. Echoing Baconian prescriptions for philosophical investigation, he argued for eschewing prejudice and passion and the influence of birth, education, authority, and prejudice. In the end, men would embrace those principles which seemed most credible to their reason. Honest error in religion was not disastrous. Indeed, Chillingworth assumed that individuals would reach differing conclusions. He distinguished between fundamentals of religion held with a high degree of certainty and nonfundamentals which presumably remained in the realm of opinion.[22]

Working in the tradition of Hooker, Acontio, and Grotius, and looking forward to that of Wilkins, Tillotson, and Locke, Chillingworth gave a new emphasis to the role of reason in religion. If Chillingworth exhibited no particular interest in the new philosophy, the categories he developed were assimilated and expanded by scientists and philosophers seeking religious support for the new science. They were also developed by a new generation of theologians still anxiously seeking to defeat the continuing assertions of Roman Catholic infallibility, and, as we have seen, by naturalists seeking to incorporate natural science into the realm of fallible knowledge.

Now that we have looked at the pre-civil war forerunners, we can turn to a series of related religious themes involving theories of knowledge that are prominent roughly from the civil war era to the end of the century. These themes, all of which involve the role of reason and the kinds of knowledge that may be arrived at in religion, were invoked in the attempt to construct a natural, that is, rational, theology and to place revealed theology on a rational basis. In addition, the Roman Catholic-Protestant debate over the "Rule of Faith" continued to provide a fruitful arena for discussion of epistemologically related religious questions. We must also consider the development of the latitudinarian movement, which developed a distinctive approach to problems of religious knowledge. The chapter will conclude with an effort to show the linkage between religious thought and the natural sciences.

NATURAL THEOLOGY

The quest for a natural theology became a dominant element of Restoration religious thought. This attempt to produce a set of religious beliefs founded on reason was a response to two mid-century movements. The first was the rise of anti-intellectual religious sects which denigrated the use of reason in religion. They emphasized the role of illumination, grace, and private revelation. The challenge of these "enthusiasts" was faced during the 1650s not only by traditional Puritans, but also by a new group of rational theologians. Beginning in the mid-1650s, John Wilkins and Seth Ward at Oxford, the Cambridge Platonists, and a number of others developed a rational or natural theology that repudiated the anti-intellectualism which characterized so many of the "enthusiasts."

The second stimulus, which, like the first, began in the 1650s and continued throughout the Restoration era, was a response to atheism. While it is difficult to find an atheistic movement, seventeenth-century rational theologians were convinced that both theoretical and practical atheism were at hand. The shadow atheism they perceived was concocted of bits of Hobbes, Aristotle, and the new atomism, mechanism, and materialism in science.

The first step in the attack on enthusiasts and atheists was to establish the basic principles of religion by means of the unaided reason. Although the lists of basic principles varied slightly, they usually included the existence of God and his attributes, the immortality of the soul, the existence of rewards and punishments after death, and the need to worship the deity and live a moral life. A large number of works dealt with one or more of these topics, and together they make up a not inconsiderable portion of the major theological writings of the era.

Before making the effort to establish these principles, many felt it necessary to show what kinds of reason and what methods were appropriate to their investigations. As a group, they were peculiarly sensitive to such matters, perhaps because so many of them were deeply involved in the scientific movement.

Virtually all those who dealt with natural religion went out of their way to refute opponents who allegedly insisted on "Geometrical," or "Mathematical," or direct sense demonstrations of the truths of religion.[23] Their opponents were rarely named. Henry More, however, did note his dissatisfaction with Cartesian proofs for the immortality of the soul as being "on this side of mathematical evidence."[24] Seth Ward, in one of the earliest treatments of natural religion, specifically identified Hobbes as the culprit, though Hobbes never attempted to find mathematical demonstration for religious belief. It was evidently Hobbes's association of all reasoning with reckoning, his desire to use the rigor of mathematical demonstration and to repudiate the role of experience and prudence in philosophy, that Ward considered so dangerous. Certainly the spate of natural theological publications that followed so soon after the publication of *Leviathan* in 1651 suggests that Hobbes was to be feared on this as well as other grounds. In any event, Ward specifically attacked Hobbes for claiming that his discourses would proceed mathematically and would achieve the certainty of demonstration, when in fact, the evidence he had presented was considerably short of the evidence which might properly be considered demonstrative. He also suggested that Hobbes's misunderstanding of mathematics injured mathematics and the "very name of Demonstration."[25] Similarly, most of the natural theologians felt that the principles of religion could not be proved by the external senses. God, being Spirit, was invisible. He might, however, be proved mediately from His effects or examples of His providence.[26]

If the principles of religion were not to be proved by demonstration or even the senses, but were, nonetheless, to be rationally derived, it became crucial to develop the distinction between demonstration and other types of acceptable proof.

Typically, the natural theologians began with three categories of knowledge. The first was mathematical demonstration, where assent was compelled. The second was physical knowledge based on sense data. The third, moral knowledge with its moral certainty, was the variety with which they were most concerned. If natural theologians were unanimous in insisting that mathematical demonstration had no place in religious matters, they were not always in agreement as to whether physical or moral categories yielded higher levels of proof. Indeed, not a few of them ended by blurring the distinctions between physical and moral knowledge. Despite frequent expressions of hostility to scholasticism and scholastic theology, most natural theologians more or less openly acknowledged that these categories were derived from the scholastic tradition.[27] Their indebtedness to the Thomist tradition was perhaps greater than is usually recognized. Despite slight differences of detail, all the natural theologians could agree that a reasonable man, that is, one capable of making judgments without being swayed by prejudice or passion, would conclude that there was no reasonable doubt about the principles of religion.

John Wilkins's popular *Principles and Duties of Natural Religion*, which would prove almost as significant for scientific as religious thought, suggests the directions that seventeenth-century religious thinkers were taking. Wilkins began with a categorization of evidence. Simple evidence was that derived either from the senses or the understanding. Mixed evidence was derived from a combination of the two. The understanding was described as the faculty which enabled men to apprehend the objects of knowledge, "Generals as well as particulars, Absent things as well as Present; and to judge of their Truth or Falsehood, Good or Evil." Evidence available to the understanding arose from "the Nature of things," that is, the "Congruity or Incongruity betwixt the Terms of a Proposition" or deductions from those propositions. Evidence would either "satisfie the mind" or leave it in doubt. The testimony of others was also evidence to be evaluated according to the authority and credit of the witness in question. Wilkins did not commit himself on the question of whether the senses or understanding provided better knowledge. In some instances the senses were superior, in others the understanding was to "correct the errors" of sense and imagination.[28]

Wilkins proposed two fundamental levels of certainty. The first, knowledge or certainty, was the "Assent arising from such plain and clear Evidence as doth not admit of any reasonable cause of doubting." The second he labeled opinion and probability. Knowledge was itself composed of three varieties: physical, mathematical, and moral. The first, derived from sense data, yielded "the highest kind of Evidence, of which humane nature is capable." It included evidence obtained from the inward as well as outward senses. Wilkins, it should be noted, tended to give higher valuation to physical certainty than some of his associates who gave priority of place to mathematical certainty. Mathematical certainty included certain matters of self-evidence, basic principles of logic, and deductions made from those principles.[29] John Tillotson had a very similar approach, though he suggests four categories of knowledge: mathematics; natural philosophy, whose "conclusions were proved by sufficient Induction of experiments"; moral things to be proved by moral arguments; and matters of fact, proved by credible testimony. Only mathematics was capable of "strict Demonstration." All the others were capable of "undoubted assurance," if based on the best arguments they could bear.[30]

It was the objects of moral certainty that most concerned Wilkins and other rational theologians: those

not capable of the same kind of Evidence . . . so as to necessitate every man's assent, . . . yet they may be so plain, that every man whose judgement is free from prejudice will consent to them. And though there be no natural necessity, that such things must be so, and that they cannot possibly be

85

otherwise, . . . yet may they be so certain as not to admit of any reasonable doubt concerning them.[31]

These theologians then considered the kind of certainty available in each area of knowledge. For Wilkins, who was typical, physical and mathematical knowledge yielded "infallible" certainty. This infallibility, however, was "conditional," because only God was "absolutely infallible." Moral investigations yielded "indubitable" certainty, which arose from evidence derived from both testimony and experience. It was from this variety of knowledge that a man free from passion and prejudice might derive the principles of a natural religion. Both testimony, which must be judged according to the "credit and authority" of witnesses, and Experience, which is never adequately defined, allowed one to be assured of the succession of night and day and to have no reason to believe that the house one was now standing in "shall this next minute fall upon me, or the earth open and swallow it."[32]

There were many instances, however, when one could not achieve even "indubitable certainty." When the proofs were good but still permitted reasonable doubt, it was appropriate to speak of "opinion" and "probability." The distinction between opinion and moral certitude lay in the quality of the proof.

Truths in all of these areas of knowledge were equally true even if not capable "of the same degree of Evidence." One must deal with the best evidence for a thing of which it is capable and not demand what is impossible. Wilkins thus disposed of the skeptical positions. That the contrary could not be ruled out completely was an insufficient reason to doubt good evidence. It was appropriate to suspend one's judgment only when the probabilities on each side were equal. The absence of mathematical demonstrations in fields where they were unavailable was no bar to truth.

All this was preliminary to Wilkins's major point. Religious principles belong to the realm of moral certainty. In that realm it was possible, at best, to reach knowledge that was "highly credible." The basic principles of natural religion might not achieve quite the same certainty as mathematics or immediate physical experience, but that was, to Wilkins as to other natural theologians, a positive element. For there could be no virtue in assenting to something that one could not help but believe. If assent was compelled, there could be no faith or ethical choice. What was emphasized by virtually all the natural theologians was that atheists and doubters who demanded a religion based on mathematical demonstration or the direct evidence of the senses were asking for the impossible.

Clearly the central principle to be proven was the existence of a deity. One could be assured of God's existence either by means of "an internal impression of the Notion of God upon our Minds, or else by such external and visible Effects as our Reason tells us must be attributed to some Cause." For Tillotson, the author of this statement, and most other natural divines, the route of reason was preferable, for they found difficulties in the argument from innate ideas.[33] Locke asserts that, although there were no truths which were "stamped" by God on the human mind, man had been provided with the faculties to discover what it was necessary for him to know. Locke thus proves the existence of God by a means "equal" to, though not the same as, mathematical certainty.[34]

Proofs for God's existence typically were followed by a discussion of His attributes.[35] Such discussions, which emphasized some attributes more than others, contributed to changes in the concept of the deity. Wilkins, like many others, emphasized God's goodness, noting that without it other divine attributes, such as knowledge and power, "would be but craft and violence."[36] The rationalists rejected the "frightful and overtimourous notion of the Deity," which presented Him as "austere and rigorous, easily provoked by every little circumstantial mistake." Unlike the Calvanists, they put little stress on God's justice. And while emphasizing the distance between man and God, they conceived of the deity as providing "the Rule and Measure" for man. Some of divine goodness was communicated to man.[37]

Avoiding discussion of predestination, grace, and original sin, they typically believed man to be naturally endowed with principles leading him to seek earthly happiness and salvation. In a sense, salvation was in man's own hands. Although none denied God's ability to intervene in the daily lives of men, they more often emphasized God's General Providence, which regulated the world through second causes. God became more distant as He became more benevolent.

Another crucial principle to be proved was the immortality of the soul.[38] Hobbes was the chief contemporary opponent, his *Leviathan* suggesting the materiality and mortality of the soul. Several difficult issues were addressed in these discussions. Could the concept of material substance and a physics based on matter in motion still allow belief in God and an immortal soul? These and other questions related to the issue of whether matter was inert and

87

devoid of a spiritual element were often discussed in the context of the immortality of the soul. One of two positions was typically taken. The first, typified by Robert Boyle, was that matter was devoid of spirituality, but the cosmos and matter had been created and ordered by God. Just how the soul was joined to the body was beyond the capacity of man to know. The other approach, typified by the Cambridge Platonists, was to find the spiritual principle in nature or matter itself. If the investigations of the "Boyle school" led to a concern for the mechanical principles established by God, the approach of More and the Platonists led to investigations of occult phenomenon and witchcraft, which involved the action of immaterial forces on material objects.

RATIONAL RELIGION AND NATURALISTIC ETHICS

It has been often suggested that the emphasis on natural theology and the related effort to develop a naturalistic ethics led away from Christian theology and Christian ethics, and eventually to deism and secularism. While this was no doubt true in the long run, seventeenth-century proponents considered their efforts preparatory to Christian Revelation and Christian ethics. Indeed, Christianity itself had a rational basis. Thus most ardent natural theologians emphatically insisted on the rationality of Revelation and the harmony between natural and revealed religion. Wilkins, Edward Stillingfleet, Boyle, Tillotson, and Locke were firm supporters of this position. It must be admitted, however, that as a group, the rationalists rarely discussed Christ. Their emphasis was on God, God the Creator, not the God who in His mercy gave His Son to man.

Efforts to establish the principles and duties of natural religion merged imperceptibly with efforts to develop a naturalistic ethics. There were two lines of development, both to a large extent a response to Hobbes. One featured innate moral principles which could be known and followed. A more complex effort was begun by Wilkins, Tillotson, and others in the process of showing how leading the good life in this world might contribute to gaining the good life in the next. Ethics was given a hedonistic basis in which the individual rationally calculated what was in his best interest.[39] Thus, Wilkins suggested that the moral was "discoverable by natural light." Although results did not follow inevitably and God was free to act as He would, Wilkins attempted to show in ways reminiscent of Aristotle and Thomist theology how religious and moral behavior contributed to happiness, producing such benefits as health, liberty, riches, and peace of mind. The "rational and prudent man" should "order his actions in favour of that way which appears to be most safe and advantageous for his own interest."[40] Given that man's dominant interest was happiness in the next life, and his secondary interest happiness in this life, the rational man, confronted with uncertainties about the ethical worth of a course of action that promised immediate benefits, would choose the more ethical path. John Tillotson's famous *Wisdom of Being Religious* (1664) contained the same kind of argument.

Though the assurance of future rewards and punishments based on one's behavior fell "short of the evidence of sense" or mathematical demonstration, there was enough evidence to inspire "a well grounded confidence" or "Moral demonstration." This moral demonstration was sufficient to persuade a reasonable man to believe. Wilkins was moving in the direction Hume would take when he indicated that, in their everyday existence, men acted on the basis of "moral assurance," not "mathematical demonstration," and acted to reduce their risk.[41]

These discussions were characterized by the insistence that "Demonstration," mathematical or logical, was inappropriate in moral and religious matters, and that the certainty being sought was moral certainty. This level of certainty involved the judgment of the "reasonable man" evaluating all the appropriate evidence. The character of this evidence was not strictly defined, but the most frequent proofs were those from "common consent," the effects of nature, and the providential order of the world.

Initially, the most common argument or proof was the argument from common consent, e.g., that men in all times and places had believed in a deity.[42] Universal consent, however, soon became immersed in the controversy over "common notions" and "Innate ideas."

INNATE IDEAS

Lord Herbert of Cherbury and others of an earlier generation had grounded the basic principles of religion on common notions or innate ideas. Many mid- and late-seventeenth-century natural theologians became uncomfortable with this approach. While Walter Charleton continued to use the concept of "common notions . . . engraved on our Minds," he also suggests that the engraving might be done in part by repeated sense impressions of external objects.[43] The erosion of arguments from common consent occurred at the same time that scientists were being forced to admit that common consent included a great deal of error and superstition. It was difficult for scientific virtuosi like Charleton to assert the value of long-held opinions in religion while denying the validity of traditional beliefs about the natural world. John Yolton has suggested that the standard solution to the increasingly problematic position of both innate ideas and common consent was to combine the two in a more sophisticated version of innate ideas.[44] Henry More, for example, argued that the innate idea was triggered by natural stimuli, the mind, thus awakened or jogged, offering immediate assent.[45]

Before John Locke rejected innate ideas entirely, Walter Charleton, John Wilkins, and others struggled to bring the doctrine of common consent and common notions, on which their natural theology was built, into a more intellectually satisfying relationship with current investigations of the nature of human knowledge. In the process, they undermined and eroded, without thoroughly rejecting, innate "common notions."[46]

Wilkins, whose treatment marks a kind of intellectual mid-point, provides an excellent illustration of how natural theologies might contribute to advancing theories of knowledge. Wilkins begins quite traditionally with the Ciceronian pronouncement that common consent is valid because time weeds out the fiction of "Opinion" and eliminates "ungrounded persuasion."[47] Wilkins, however, was hardly in a position to stop there for he had earlier, in a work defending the Copernican astronomy, argued that the length of time an opinion had been held was not an appropriate means of determining its validity. Indeed, this had been a central argument for rejecting the Ptolemaic geocentric universe.

Noting contemporary disagreement on the "rise and original" of "common notions," Wilkins felt it essential to compare the "inward sensation of our minds and understandings, with that of our outward senses." Common notions would have to be squared with knowledge derived from sense experience. Acts of the mind, he argued, were reducible to three types. The first was simple apprehension or the perception of single objects. The second was judging, essentially the comparison of single objects to make propositions. The third was ratiocination, the connection or dependence between propositions which permitted inference. All men agreed on the first, that is, all perceived green as green. And all those "apprehensions wherein all men do agree . . . are called natural

Notions." Thus natural notions might well be based on common sense experience. They included all opinions which "have in them a suitableness to the minds of men, as to be generally owned and acknowledged for true, by all such who apply their thoughts to the consideration of them."[48]

Instruction could foster but not eradicate natural notions based on experience. Instruction in no way undermined their naturalness because mankind was naturally social. Without society, mankind would have "wild and gross apprehensions of things as are in themselves very plain and obvious." In a lengthy but important example, Wilkins suggests that a solitary individual who had lived in some deep cavern would, if he entered the world, possess an enormous number of erroneous opinions due to lack of knowledge of the most common things. It would not initially seem credible that trees were produced by tiny seeds or birds from eggs. Such knowledge required both the use of one's faculty and mutual society and conversation. It was in this sense that the "Notion of God is natural to the soul."[49]

While Wilkins's approach is not devoid of traditional doctrines of common consent, he has moved a long way toward indicating that natural notions were not innate and were derived from shared experience. It was only a short step to an outright and explicit denial of innate ideas. Yet the participants in these pre-Lockean discussions were unclear about their own evolving solutions, leaning at some points in a Lockean direction and at others toward something like innate ideas. Even Wilkins could speak of "Natural conscience" as "God's Deputy which provided natural notions of good and evil which were independent of custom and positive law."[50] Not until Locke himself do we encounter the final onslaught on innate ideas that led many natural theologians to turn away from common consent and common notions arguments.

Theological explorations by natural theologians, particularly those with links to the scientific movement, thus contributed substantially to the explorations of epistemology which have too often been examined as if they had developed solely within the context of an independently evolving philosophy of mind. More particularly, the tension created for natural theologians when they sought to employ notions of innate ideas and common consent in theology, a tension that was already causing them difficulties in science, led to significant epistemological advances. For the tension could only be resolved by moving toward a translation of innate ideas and common consent from the realm of the purely rational or intuitive into the realm of collective sense experience.

PROOFS FROM THE EFFECTS OF NATURE

Proofs from the "Effects" of nature and from Providence were not so troublesome. Rather than relying on innate ideas, John Ray preferred to take his proofs "from the Effects and Operations" of nature, which were exposed "to every man's view" and could not be "denied or questioned by any." Such a proof could not only convince subtle and sophisticated adversaries, but was "intelligible also to the meanist Capacities."[51] If John Ray's *Wisdom of God* provided the most lengthy and elaborate proof from effects, his position was echoed by many natural theologians. They argued that God's existence could be proved by examining the admirable contrivance of natural things. As plants, animals, and the human body were lovingly admired, their admirers must see that they could only have been produced by an infinitely wise and beneficent agent. The "Being of God" could thus be "Evicted from the Creatures"[52] or from the "Frame of the World."[53] Only the most stubborn and prejudiced minds could conclude that the perfections of nature could have been the result of chance. Locke, who in so many ways summed up the position of the natural theologians, insisted that the works of nature were crucial in providing evidence for belief in a deity.[54] It would be difficult to find a seventeenth-century English scientist who did not express this idea at one time or another. The investigation of nature itself became almost an act of worship.

The study of "God's handiwork," which proved the deity's existence with a moral certainty, also contributed to a change in aesthetic sensibilities. Naturalists and natural theologians rhapsodized over the "Elegance and Beauty" of the Creation. Nature was "so symmetrical in Proportion, so exquisite in pulchritude" that one could not help appreciate its "comeliness and splendor."[55] Mountains, once considered ugly excrescences on a once-smooth globe, were now praised for their beauty. So were fleas, so admirably contrived to pursue their annoyance of man and beast. All things natural might be considered beautiful, having been produced by the goodness and Providence of God. Man-made objects suffered by comparison.[56]

Proofs based on the effects of nature merged with proofs based on God's Providence, His governance, and care of man and nature.

The emphasis was increasingly on the usual course of nature. The stress on Providence as the ordinary operations of nature left the problem of miracles. An omnipotent God could not, after all, be constrained to act in any particular way. In the "Resolution of Natural Events," however, investigators "should not fly unto the Absolute Power of God, and tell us what he can do, but what according to the usual ways of Providence, is most likely to be done."[57] Miracles too often served "for the Receptable of Lazy Ignorance: which any industrious Spirit would be asham'd of."[58] Although it was possible to trace a convergence between the "usual ways" of Providence and the laws of nature, the possibility of miracles was still vigorously asserted. Virtuosi defended the truth of biblical miracles, while at the same time excluding them from the realm of contemporary, scientific explanation of natural events. Yet the line between what was and was not a special intervention remained somewhat blurred. The Plague and Fire might be considered simultaneously as God's punishment for sin and the result of natural causes. The observed regularities of nature and divine intervention could still be subsumed, albeit with increasing difficulty, under the rubric of Divine Providence.[59]

Still another proof for God's existence centered on showing that the universe had been created rather than being eternal, and that Creation had been accomplished by a wise agent rather than by some chance collision of atoms. This argument was also used in connection with establishing the truth of Scripture. The natural theologians were thus led to discuss atomism, Aristotelian notions of eternality, and the Mosaic account of Creation. In this connection, Scripture was most often treated as a history "most likely to be a true account of the first original of things." This "proof" resulted in complex chronological calculations and elaborate speculations on what the world would have been like if mankind had existed from infinity.[60]

This proof is interesting, too, in charting changes in use of the term "hypothesis." In this particular arena, the term might be used either in a positive way to suggest some position supported by a great deal of evidence or, alternatively, to indicate an opinion without much support. Sir Matthew Hale thus defended the truth of the Mosaic or "Divine Hypothesis," while Wilkins labeled the doctrine of eternality "a mere precarious Hypothesis," that is, one without adequate evidence. Hypotheses in religion as well as science might, if well supported, be considered "morally certain" or highly probable, and, if not, be equated with "mere opinion."[61]

A final point stressed by natural theologians was the compatibility of natural and revealed religion. Natural law and Revelation were equally the law of God.[62] The "Duties of Natural Light" were identical to those provided by God's Grace, though Revelation provided a clearer statement of those principles and duties. Given the difficulty of the "unassisted reason to establish morality in all its parts upon its true foundation with a clear and convincing light," God, Locke and others argued, had sent someone "to tell [men] their duties and require their obedience."[63] Latitudinarians made little if any distinction between moral righteousness and evangelical righteousness, and natural theologians would have agreed that both scriptural precepts and the duties of natural religion demanded "a good life and repentence."[64]

This compatibility was also highlighted in reiterating that God had revealed Himself to man in two books: the Book of Revelation and the Book of Nature. Men must study both. The idea of a book of nature was not new in the seventeenth century, but its use was vastly expanded by virtuosi-theologians like John Ray, who reveled in reading "the vast library of Creation."[65] The greatly increasing use of the metaphor of the book of nature was a by-product of attempts to prove the existence of God by natural means.

The proponents of natural religion necessarily became involved in complex problems relating to moral philosophy, epistemology, natural science, and even aesthetics. Their efforts to produce a natural religion based on arguments from common consent, the effects of nature, and God's Providence, and the concomitant efforts to develop a natural morality, exposed a number of difficult epistemological issues which the natural theologians explored with varying degrees of success. Any serious discussion of major philosophical developments between Hobbes and Locke must take account of the mid- and late-seventeenth-century natural theologians. Theology and natural science were not seen as autonomous or competing epistemological realms. Rather, they were complementary endeavors, together facing one of the foremost intellectual problems of the age—the problem of accumulating and evaluating evidence to arrive at proofs less certain but no less true than those of mathematical demonstration.

THE RATIONALITY OF CHRISTIANITY

Theories of knowledge involving moral certainty were also used to prove the rationality of Christian religion as revealed in Scripture. There was, in particular, a concerted attempt to refine the nature of rational belief. The primary stimulus continued to be polemical exchange between Anglicans and Roman Catholics over the certainty of Scripture and the inadequacy of oral tradition. A second arena was the effort to repudiate the irrational "enthusiasm" of those religious groups emphasizing divine inspiration and private revelation. A third involved refutation of atheism. Again, latitudinarians, who firmly believed in the compatibility of natural and revealed religion and the rationality of both, took the lead.

Hugo Grotius's *The Truth of the Christian Religion* in many ways provided the starting point for English thinkers seeking a rational basis for scriptural truth. For Grotius, Scripture was an historical record of God's miracles and prophesies. Unlike mathematics, physics, or ethics, such matters of fact could be proved only by testimony that was free from suspicion of untruth. One must not despise testimony of even seemingly impossible events if "testified by a sufficient Witnesses living in the time when they came to pass."[66]

Grotius's views were expanded by Chillingworth and then by Restoration era latitudinarians and virtuosi. John Evelyn, for example, insisted that reason had been given by God "to judge and determine the truth of things," Scripture not excepted.[67] He noted:

Had it not been originally manifest, and evidenced bright as the meridian sun, that such things were done as they relate, the world would never have embraced them.... And since all cannot be eye-witnesses on what is passed, let it suffice that we have the suffrage of all who are gone before us, and which common reason makes to be as authentick evidence, as are our senses. For, by the same means that all records of learning are transmitted to us, as the Scriptures prove to be matter of historical faith.[68]

Stillingfleet's *Origines Sacrae* (1662) was directed against atheism, his particular target being those who insisted that belief with respect to the origin of things was explicable by philosophy alone. In the process, it became necessary to explain belief. Complex and detailed discussions of epistemological problems and the nature of proofs are scattered throughout the work, whose primary aim was to show why one should believe the Mosaic account.

For Stillingfleet, matters of fact could not be proved by mathematical demonstration, but only by moral certainty. Only those "destitute of reason" would question every matter of fact not personally observed, for one frequently had to act on no other foundation than the testimony of others. Those who acquired land by the transfer of centuries-old titles, traders who dispatched ships to distant places they had never seen, children who honored those they believed to be their parents—none of them could rely entirely on their senses or on mathematical demonstration. All relied on historical faith and moral certainty. Such beliefs were not infallible, but their truth was not to be lightly denied. In loving detail, Stillingfleet indicated why the Mosaic account should be attributed to Moses, and why it should be accepted as true. For this purpose, Moses was treated as an historian, and Scripture as an historical account.[69]

Stillingfleet also compared mathematical truth with knowledge involving "the existence of things." The latter, "because of the manner of conveyance" to the mind, could not be as clear as in purely abstracted matters involving "purely intellectual operations." The "highest evidence for the existence of things" was either "the judgement of sense, or clear and distinct precepts of the mind," and there was no "infallible certainty" in either. The precepts of the mind were caused by "Ideas" conveyed to the understanding via sense impressions which might be fallacious. Conversely, a "clear and distinct perception" of something not immediately available to the senses could not support absolute belief in the existence of that thing. There obviously could be no clear perception of a thing after it ceased to exist. One may have a real and distinct perception of imaginary as well as real things, a Phoenix as well as a partridge. In the realm of perception, certainty equal to mathematical demonstration was clearly impossible. Stillingfleet, like Descartes, felt it necessary to assume that God would not allow men's minds to be deceived in those things where they have a "clear and distinct perception," and from these perceptions one could infer things advantageous to our certainty in matters of faith. Knowledge, then, presupposed not only the existence of God, but that He would not deceive mankind in matters He Himself revealed. There was thus, for Stillingfleet, less danger of deception with respect to revelation than in matters of sense.[70]

Stillingfleet made a great point of his rejection of scholastics who had sharply distinguished "between the foundation of faith and knowledge," insisting that both implied the veracity of God and had the same foundation of certainty. The only difference between them was that faith dealt with divine testimony and knowledge did not. He argues that Revelation has "the same ground of certainty, which we have as to any natural causes." One can believe in the Trinity and the Incarnation without fully comprehending them, in the same way that one can believe that the sun shines without having proved the "undoubted truth of the Ptolemaic or Copernican hypothesis."[71]

Stillingfleet also criticized natural philosophers who prematurely claimed to have demonstrated general maxims from "an universal undoubted history of nature." That history remained "too dark and obscure to pretend to the full knowledge of." No "jejune unproved hypothesis" should dictate "matters of faith." Only when philosophical principles were "collected from a most certain and universal inspection into the nature of all beings," and "the manner of process be showed how they were collected," would he "make Reason . . . bring the Scriptures as the Prisoner to its Bar."[72]

In dealing with Scripture, mathematical proofs and philosophical hypotheses were inappropriate. Where truth depended on testimony, the issue was the credibility of that testimony. A discussion of the means of judging testimony is therefore introduced, and comparisons made between human and divine testimony. Thus, Stillingfleet's attempts to establish a rational basis for the "moral certainty" of scriptural history were grounded on a complex set of arguments involving the nature of human knowledge and its relation to philosophical and scientific argument.[73]

Sir Charles Wolseley's *Unreasonableness of Atheism Made Manifest* also emphasized Scripture as capable of moral rather than either "ocular or mathematical demonstration." The wish to see a past event was as foolish as the demand for a mathematical demonstration of it. The reality of things past must be accepted "by the credible testimony of others" and by any "remaining Effects." Limitation of knowledge to what each individual actually observed would have disastrous consequences, eliminating all civil and natural history. Wolseley therefore concluded that Scripture was true and that the miracles reported there ought to be believed.[74]

Sir Matthew Hale's ponderous *Primitive Origination of Mankind* (1677) strove to repudiate atheism and the doctrine of the eternality of the world and man by showing that mankind had had a beginning in time and that the Mosaic hypothesis of its origins was the most credible. Since his proofs were to be derived from the "Light of Nature and Natural Reason," he began with a discussion of the varities of knowledge, the appropriate modes of proof for each, and the varieties of certainty available. "Opinion" occurred "when . . . assent is . . . gained by evidence of probability" and merely inclined the investigator to one persuasion over another. It thus retained a "mixture of incertainty or doubting." "Science or Knowledge" consisted of demonstration, and "Faith or Belief." Faith or belief had two aspects: belief in the senses and belief in the testimony of others "that we have no reasonable cause to suspect." This category included the data of the natural sciences as well as history and was made up of "moral evidence" which could never result in "demonstrative or infallible" knowledge. Hale thus linked the empirical, natural sciences with historical knowledge. Although the senses provided the best evidence of matters of fact, reasonable acquiesence in the relations of others, that is, the sense knowledge of others, was appropriate for matters of fact "transacted before our time and out of the immediate reach" of sense. A significant ingredient in eliciting assent was "the veracity" of the reporter and the number of eyewitnesses making the report. Historical knowledge, and for Hale the origin of man was a question of historical fact, could be proved with moral certainty "so highly credible" it would "elicit the assent of reasonable men." Hale then turned to elaborate proofs of the Mosaic account of the origin of man, concluding that the biblical account was highly probable, if not demonstrable.[75]

Mathematician and theologian Isaac Barrow explored similar epistemologically related religious issues ranging from the proper approach to problems of religious knowledge to the nature of faith and belief and their relationship to other varieties of knowledge. Barrow first insisted that consideration of such matters required precisely the same kind of "sober, composed, wakeful inquisitive after truth" approach required of all intellectual investigation.[76] He stressed the need for "great humility" and a sense of imperfection. Faith is defined as a kind of knowledge or "possession of Truth," distinguishable from both sensory knowledge and ratiocination. Although it dealt with things beyond the reach of reason, it was nevertheless a kind of knowledge "comparable to that whereby the Theorems of any science are known." Indeed, it benefited by not being grounded on the "slippery deductions of reasons." Instead, faith was conveyed "by powerful evidence." It was not produced by "precipitate assent," but required rational assent resulting from "diligence and industry."[77]

In one of his sermons, Barrow employed a far broader term, "belief," which he defined as the product of a mind

fully convinced and persuaded of the truth of the propositions . . . not excluding any objects there contained . . . (either being apparent to sense or demonstration by reason, or credible by any sort of testimony) nor abstracting from any kind of reason persuasive of their truth.[78]

Barrow has thus placed testimony and sense data in the same category and suggested that religious belief was not very different from belief in facts or even inferences from reason. Barrow used this notion of belief to show that Christ had not required his followers

to rely upon his bare testimony concerning himself, but to consider rationally the quality of his works; and upon that to ground their faith; which kind of persuasion seems grounded rather upon than principles of reason, than any authority.[79]

He thus argued the first and main "Article of the Creed, that there is a God," could not be grounded solely in authority. It was equally necessary to employ the senses and reason.[80]

Christian belief, then, was to be based on a combination of sense data, reason, and credible testimony. All possible evidence and all kinds of data and knowledge could be united to produce belief. In the process of bolstering scriptural belief, Barrow was obliterating the differences between scientific and religious conclusions. A variety of means could be employed, in what particular combination he is not willing or able to say, to produce religious belief. Presumably, the same combination might be used to produce scientific belief.

A somewhat more complex approach was presented by Robert Boyle. After distinguishing between reason and experience, he proceeded to defend Christianity on the basis of experiential knowledge of a special type. There were three varieties of experiential knowledge. The first two were personal or individual experience and historical experience conveyed by testimony. The third, theological experience, consisted of what is known by Divine Revelation. Thus, we know by personal experience that there are stars in Heaven, by historical experience, that a new star was seen by Tycho Brahe in 1572, and by theological experience, that the stars were made on the fourth day of Creation.[81]

Boyle recognized that he employed the term "experience" in a new way. Experience is

the knowledge we have of any matter of fact, which without owning it to Ratiocination, either we acquire by the Immediate Testimony of our own Senses and other Faculties, or accrews to us by the Communicated Testimony of others.[82]

Theological experiences, then, are the "Revelations that God makes concerning what he has Done, or purposes to do, are but Testimonies of things, most of them matters of Fact."[83] On the basis of competent testimony, one could believe things which seemed strange or irrational.[84] Earlier, Boyle had made a similar argument about scientific matters, insisting on the reasonableness of accepting the phenomenon of magnetism despite the fact that one did not understand it. He also reminded his readers that natural philosophers assented to matters of fact when the proofs in these matters were only available by relation and testimony.[85] The better qualified the "Witness is, in the capacity of a Witness, the Stronger Assent his Testimony deserves."[86] If experimental philosophers increased the knowledge of natural things by means of observations made by ignorant men who might nonetheless be conversant with the works of nature, one should be far more willing to receive the doctrines of revealed religion, given the honesty of religious teachers and their opportunity "to know the Truth of the Things they" declare.[87]

The belief in miracles was supported similarly. While we can have no knowledge of past miracles through our own senses or immediate observation, we must believe in them because of the vicarious experience contained in "duly transmitted Testimony" of those who were "Eyewitnesses . . . of the things they relate."[88]

And since we scruple not to believe such Prodigies, as Celestial Comets, Vanishing and Reappearing Stars . . . and like amazing Anomalies of Nature, upon the credit of Human Histories; I see not that Vicarious Experience should not be more trusted, which has divers peculiar current Circumstances to Confirm it, and particularly the Death that most of the first Promulgators chearfully Suffer'd to Attest the Truth of it.[89]

Clearly, the "vicarious experiences" of suitable witnesses was sufficient evidence for natural phenomena, human history, and revelation.

John Locke's *Reasonableness of Christianity* was in many respects the culmination of the effort to use concepts of belief grounded on moral certainty to support the Christian religion. Locke attempted to show that Christianity rested primarily on Revelation and that reason could certify and interpret that Revelation. He noted the slight results obtained in hundreds of years of effort to develop a scientific ethics as compelling as mathematics. Such an ethics would be ineffective in any case, since few possessed the leisure and intelligence required for comprehending demonstrative knowledge and the elaborate proofs which normally accompanied it. Most men "cannot know, and therefore they must believe." And the Gospel contained a "perfect body of ethics," far better and clearer than any provided by natural reason.[90]

Such belief was equally suited to intelligent and vulgar persons. Many truths were difficult if not impossible to discover oneself. We take them from others, assenting to them because they are consistent with our reason.[91] Indeed, Locke was forced to rely on Scripture somewhat more heavily than his immediate predecessors, who were more confident about a natural system of ethics based on innate ideas or common consent. When Locke eliminated innate ideas, he undercut a major prop of natural ethics, and thus was driven back toward scriptural support for ethical truths.

Locke's major statement of epistemological principles is the *Essay Concerning Human Understanding* of 1690. Here again Locke insists that what God has revealed is true, but "whether it be a divine revelation or no, reason must judge."[92] The century's most complete discussion of the nature of human knowledge, itself derived from a 1670-1671 discussion of morality and religion, reminds us how much the epistemological formulations of the seventeenth century owed to the search for a reasonable basis for religious belief.[93]

PROTESTANT-ROMAN CATHOLIC POLEMIC

Continued polemics between Protestants and Roman Catholics remained an important area for the fruitful application of epistemological arguments to religion. This "rule of faith" controversy reiterated and developed the approaches of Falkland and Chillingworth. Here, again, we are concerned with the defense of rational scripturalism against Roman Catholic assertions of the infallibility of oral tradition. The Restoration controversy focused even more sharply on the question of infallibility as Roman Catholic apologists attempted to repudiate Protestant arguments based on mere moral certainty. In the process of defending moral certainty, Anglican theologians from Stillingfleet and Tillotson in the early 1660s to a host of their successors at the end of the century were forced to examine the concept in greater and greater detail. Intra-Christian religious controversies were thus a major component of the epistemological development of the late seventeenth century. The examples of Stillingfleet and Tillotson will suggest something of the discussion, although it would be easy to multiply authors and texts.

Stillingfleet's *A Rational Account of the Grounds of the Protestant Religion* (1665) set the tone for Restoration efforts to prove that

101

Protestants did have "certain grounds" for their faith, and that Roman Catholic claims to infallibility were unsupportable. His discussion, as well as his rivals', centered on belief: whether or not it might have a rational basis, how it might be distinguished from other kinds of knowledge, and the level of certainty it might achieve. Central to Stillingfleet's argument was the assertion that faith consisted of rational assent based on evidence.

Stillingfleet insisted that only moral, not infallible, certainty was available in religious matters. Moral certainty provided the basis not only for current religious beliefs but also for the beliefs of the original Christians who witnessed miraculous events. In asserting infallibility, Roman Catholics were asserting the impossible, and thus were striking at religion itself. There was no need to assert infallibility in order to banish religious doubt, for there was no more reason to doubt the moral certainty on which religion was based than the mathematical and physical certainty which provided the basis for other kinds of belief.[94]

Stillingfleet's attempt to refute the papists did not end in 1665. His 1688 *A Discourse on the Nature and Grounds of the Certainty of Faith* suggests the process by which seventeenth-century intellectuals refined their notions of what kinds of data under what conditions yielded what kinds of knowledge and certainty. By 1688, Stillingfleet had become even more critical of scholastic modes of argumentation. He also extended the realm of things incapable of infallible certainty, insisting now that infallibility was available in neither moral nor physical things. He went out of his way to insist that those involved in physical and natural investigations were wrong to state their conclusions as demonstrative when they, too, were capable only of a moral certainty.[95] As we have suggested, this epistemological approach was crucial in realigning the relationship between the natural sciences, history, and religion. If, in the end, Stillingfleet could not accept Locke's rejection of innate ideas, his contribution and that of other anti-Roman Catholic polemicists attempting to find a rational basis for Protestantism should not be underrated when attempting to understand the shaping of Lockean epistemology.[96]

We can see these lines of development in the works of John Tillotson, who entered the polemical arena with his much-read *Rule of Faith* (1666). By 1666, Tillotson was already making a reputation as a latitudinarian divine, sharing the pulpit of London's St. Lawrence Jewry with his father-in-law, John Wilkins.[97] Tillotson's work dealt with the nature of belief and the issues of infallibility, assurance, and probability, and did so even more thoroughly than Stillingfleet's. Building on Falkland, Chillingworth, and Stillingfleet, he, too, attempted to refute the opposition's contention that religion required an "infallible assurance . . . wrought by Demonstration." Like many others, he quoted Aristotle's notion that things of a civil and moral nature were incapable of demonstration. He categorized the varieties of knowledge, focusing particularly on the varieties of faith and the appropriate methods of handling matters of fact. He noted, as Barrow had, that in common usage, faith implied "persuasion or assent in the mind, to anything, wrought . . . by any kind of argument." Unlike Barrow, however, he preferred to use faith, as divines traditionally did, as a term of art indicating assent produced by testimony or authority. His subject was divine faith based on the testimony of God, and his particular enquiry was the ways and means by which the knowledge of God is conveyed with certainty to men separated from the crucial events by "many ages."[98]

Although Tillotson devoted a great deal of attention to refuting the possibility of an infallible oral tradition, the other side of his argument was the reasonableness of belief in Scripture. Tillotson argued that the general testimony of man ought to be believed in plain matters of sense, while the generality of experts was to be preferred in matters of special skill and knowledge. The plain text of Scripture was among those things of which all might be certain. Scripture, like history, involved matters of fact, and thus necessarily fell short of demonstration. It could nevertheless be believed on the same basis that one believed in the existence of America. He analyzed the reasons why it was reasonable but not certain to believe in the existence of America, and that all Frenchmen would not die tonight, and that the sun would rise again tomorrow. Having shown that we have no satisfactory reason to doubt these propositions, he concluded that, on the same basis, Scripture was believable. Because moral certainty was all that could be demanded of Scripture, which dealt after all with matters of fact, we could fully believe in its truthfulness.[99]

Thus natural philosophers and theologians increasingly discussed their own particular problems in terms of common concepts of belief, moral certainty, and matters of fact, and the common proposition that it was reasonable to believe in any matter of fact provided there was no contrary evidence which led one to doubt. Scripture was increasingly treated as an historical document containing the facts of the Resurrection and miracles. In the process, more and more areas of inquiry were placed under the heading of matters of fact which might be known with moral certainty. A larger and larger portion of human knowledge entered the realm of moral certainty rather than that of infallible certainty or mathematical and logical demonstration. Thus the effort to save religion from skepticism and atheism on the one hand, and Catholic infallibility on the other, led the rational theologians to elaborate a religious epistemology that reinforced and in part shaped the more general epistemology of Locke, Boyle, and the Royal Society. The search for truth in religion not only resulted in a new school of rationalizing theologians and a rational theology which played an increasingly important role in late-seventeenth-century and eighteenth-century religious thought, but helped shape the overall intellectual culture as well.

LATITUDINARIANS

The proponents of natural theology and rational Christianity were not a scattering of isolated individuals, but a recognizable group of laymen and clerics called latitudinarians. This group of largely Anglican intellectuals emerged about 1650 and contributed importantly to intellectual life. Our description will focus primarily on those aspects of latitudinarian thought that bear on seventeenth-century theories of knowledge. Indeed, the latitudinarians' approach to epistemology is one of the hallmarks that distinguish their views on religious doctrines and ecclesiastical policy from those of more traditional churchmen. The chief characteristics of this group, many of whom were involved in or sympathetic to natural science, were their emphasis on morality and ethics as opposed to theology and the distinction they made between the fundamentals and nonfundamentals of religion. They identified the nonfundamentals of religion with "opinion," and this identification led them not only to discussions of the nature of opinion but to considerations of how to construct a single church in a society where opinion was diverse.

From their earliest public emergence, the latitudinarians were identified with a concern for morality and ethics. Even during the Interregnum, John Wilkins and Seth Ward were accused of being "meer moral men, without the power of Godliness."[100] Emphasis on ethical behavior, accompanied by a disinclination to concern themselves with doctrinal issues, was one of their chief characteristics. Their ethically oriented sermons on charity and moderation were often characterized by a kind of calculating utilitarianism that many historians of religion have found unattractive.

The individual was to calculate the advantages and disadvantages of various courses of action with an eye toward maximizing the sum total of his happiness in this world and the next. This approach owed a good deal to a long tradition of casuistry. During the course of centuries, churchmen had worked out a system to guide individuals in making decisions with moral implications, decisions which had to be made even though all the relevant facts or consequences might not be known. A tradition, sometimes called probabilism, developed to weigh probabilities and possible consequences involving cases of conscience. While clerics admitted that this weighing of possible consequences and advantages might be self-delusive and could not be anchored in absolute truth, the tradition continued because of the need to assist parishioners with the moral implications of daily decision making.

Moral probabilism continued to be characteristic of casuistry in the early modern era. Anglican casuists saw conscience primarily as a rational activity, not one of emotional reaction or social convention, and their application of knowledge to actions represented an elaboration of the Thomist tradition.[101] The casuist tradition, which survived the Reformation, contributed not only to shaping English latitudinarianism but also to the style of calculating interest and advantage found in Restoration political and economic writing.

Though influenced by medieval moralists, the latitudinarians recoiled from "Jesuitry." They rejected the then-current Roman Catholic versions of probabilism, which they characterized as holding that nearly any opinion could be safely followed because any opinion held by even a single grave doctor was sufficiently probable to inform social conduct. Jeremy Taylor roundly condemned this position because it did not recognize that some opinions were more probably true than others. They contrasted their method to casuist notions of probability which relied on concepts of plausibility and authority derived from traditional rhetoric. Moral decision making, like religious belief and scientific evaluation, required a reasoned calculation of probabilities based on the best and most complete information and evidence available. Ethics and casuistry were necessarily linked to views of human knowledge because human actions could only be judged and guided by what one can know and do. It was thus not at all inappropriate for the popular *Whole Duty of Man* to begin with a discussion of "Human Capacity," the "Human Understanding," and the rightly informed conscience.[102]

The new emphasis on marshaling complete evidence in an unbiased manner before reaching a decision was, in one sense, a repudiation of rhetoric as well as of traditional casuistry to which it was related. In another sense, however, it was the revitalization or reform of those traditions, which had always been based on some notion of probability. What is new is the specification of what constitutes appropriate information, evidence, and arguments in those realms which rhetoric had always treated as closed to logical certainty, and therefore open to the techniques of persuasion. Whichever way one wishes to view the change, it was an important one, which was subtly altering English intellectual life. Decision making and judgment, moral and otherwise, had to be based on evidence rationally considered, not on opinion, mere plausibility, convention, or authority.

One strand of latitudinarian thought was represented by the Cambridge Platonists. The relationship between Platonists and other latitudinarians has puzzled scholars.[103] Although their kinship to natural religion, moderation, natural theology, and the promotion of natural science has often been noted, there has also been detected a subtle difference which has generally made the Platonists more appealing than the other latitudinarians. The rationalism of the Platonists has been viewed as more truly religious than the more calculating, practical, worldly rationalism of the Wilkins-Tillotson set, and the Platonist "Candle of the Lord" more attractive than the careful and full use of one's reasoning faculties.

Although both groups were deeply committed to rational theology, the Platonists tended to prefer innate ideas while the Wilkins-Tillotson group concentrated more on bringing common notions into closer harmony with experientially derived knowledge. John Smith, a leading Platonist, argued, for example, that everyone possessed an innate knowledge of God and of virtue, and that these principles of religion and morality were clear, distinct, and easily understood. More's *Enchiridion Ethicum* (1666), too, offered an easily comprehensible system of morality based on self-evident moral principles which, being rather like mathematical axioms, needed no real proof.[104] Being immediately recognizable, they required little defense in terms of either evidence or assessment of the advantages to be gained from accepting them. If common consent consisted of collective learning, then ethical principles had to be accompanied by incentives and evidence.

There were other differences as well. All latitudinarians were worried about atheism, but the Cambridge men tended to place their first line of defense in proving the existence of a spiritual substance in nature, or the possibility of spirit acting on matter. These interests led not only to the development of the concept of "plastic nature," influential in biological thought, but also to proving the existence of witches and to the investigation of occult phenomena. The two wings of latitudinarianism were thus attracted to different physical theories. Even the first description of the "Latitude Men" noted that some favored the "Platonic Philosophy," and others the "Mechanick" Philosophy and the "atomical Hypothesis."[105] While most latitudinarians favored a clear and simple prose style, Platonists often produced an obscure and allegorical style.

Their lives were spent rather differently, the Platonists preferring the retired scholarly life to the hurly burly of an active city pulpit, or efforts to gain the high ecclesiastical posts which would enable them to pursue actively their moderate policies. It was Wilkins, William Lloyd, Sprat, Stillingfleet, Tillotson, and Gilbert Burnet, not the Platonists, who became the deans, bishops, and archbishops. Their reputations were tarnished in the process, particularly by high churchmen who felt that comprehension would destroy the historic role of the established Church. The reputations of the Platonists, by and large aloof from ecclesiastical politics, remained unscathed. The distinctions between the Platonists and non-Platonist wing of the latitudinarians, however, must not be drawn too sharply, and one might puzzle a long time before deciding whether to include John Ray, Benjamin Whichcote, or Joseph Glanvill in one or the other category. At best, they represent tendencies within latitudinarianism, with More representing one model and Tillotson or Boyle the other.

A major characteristic of all latitudinarians was their emphasis on the distinction between the fundamentals and the nonfundamentals of religion, and their enlargement of the scope of nonessentials. The fundamentals of religion were few: the principles of natural religion and the essentials of Christianity. The fundamentals seemed to consist primarily of "Practice," and were identified with leading "a good life and repentence." Rarely willing to cite the fundamental doctrines revealed in Scripture, the latitudinarians indicated that the purpose of Scripture was to reform men's lives and make them good. They refused to provide a list of fundamentals not only because they thought such lists would themselves generate religious dispute but also because moral behavior and the worship of God were the heart of religion. It was clear that sin and immorality were far more reprehensible than doctrinal error.[106]

It was important not to confuse nonfundamentals with the essence of religion. Nonessentials, which included not only ceremonies, vestments, and forms of prayer but most theological doctrines, were easy to identify since substantial disagreement about a practice or proposition indicated that it was unlikely to be a fundamental.[107] The institutional shells wherein men worshipped and their theological opinions were nonfundamentals. While most Anglicans agreed on the distinction between essentials and nonessentials, or *adiaphora*, the latitudinarians expanded the latter category to such an extent that little except the principles of natural religion and the basic principles of morality exhibited by natural and revealed religion remained in the essential category.

Nonessentials were identified with opinion, that category of knowledge characterized by a very low level of certainty. Religious opinions, like opinions in any other field of study, might or might not be true, and were considered as propositions of "less certainty and consequence."[108] Echoing and sometimes citing Bacon, the latitudinarians emphasized the role of custom, education, and upbringing in shaping and perverting the judgment of individuals. The role of "Interest, Pride, Passion and Prejudice" was noted with considerable regularity, as was the need to recognize the "obscurity of things."[109] The problems stemming from passion, "which doth cloud and darken the understanding," was particularly bothersome to those who had experienced the civil war and Interregnum.[110] Passion led to unnecessary contention and resulted in bad judgment, while pride clouded the understanding and resulted in dogmatism.

The fact that men's opinions resulted from differences in custom and education meant that diversity of opinion was inevitable.[111] A number of conclusions followed. The very fact that opinions differed indicated that the matter in question was not clear and therefore unnecessary to salvation. Good men would naturally differ. Such differences, even if erroneous, were not damnable. Wilkins, noting that it was "next to impossible for men to agree in the same apprehension of things," was, like Erasmus, quite willing to let theological doctrines be settled on the Day of Judgment.[112] The clash of opinion, therefore, must not be permitted to destroy the public peace. To achieve greater truth and maintain public peace it was necessary to recognize the fallibility of man's judgment, and understand that excessive confidence in the "Truth and Certainty of their opinions" was misplaced.[113]

Joseph Glanvill conducted the most extensive campaign against excessive zeal and enthusiasm. Repeatedly, he warned his fellow men to "Beware of Zeal about Opinions," those propositions of "less certainty and consequence." "Every vain Opinionator is as much assured as if he were infallible . . . and the contrary Doctrine Heretical and Abominable." This stance had resulted in unnecessary "Disputes, Hatreds, Separations, Wars." Glanvill's message was clear: a mistaken theory of religious knowledge led to religious war.[114]

The latitudinarians tended to express the pacifying role of their epistemology by urging a particular tone and style for religious argument. Such argument should be conducted without "magisterially imposing" on one another, "disputatious wrangling," bitterness, fierceness, and vehemence, and finally, without the assignment of "odious names" to those of differing opinions.[115] Zeal, the "Bitter juice of corrupt affections," which produced "rigid Censurers," must be avoided.[116]

The Dissenters and their Puritan forerunners were the groups most often castigated,[117] but fault was also placed at the door of theologians generally because they attempted to define what was unknowable. Predestination and free will were doctrines about which one could have opinions, but little more. A simple faith had been warped by those who had not only insisted on their respective opinions with inappropriate zeal but had turned simplicities of faith into an elaborate, ill-founded metaphysical system, and then imposed their authority on others. An honest recognition that they were dealing with opinion would do much to mitigate the dangers of dogmatism and zeal among all students of religion.

This unwillingness to elevate opinion to the status of authority helps explain the decline in the reputation of the Church fathers among the latitudinarians.[118] Increasingly aware of the disagreements among the fathers, the latitudinarians insisted that respect did not imply reverence. Using a comparison more frequently employed in natural philosophy, one latitudinarian indicated that while his contemporaries might be pygmies compared to giants, if they stood on pygmies' shoulders they might see farther.[119]

The reciprocal of these repeated attacks on dogmatism was a prescription for proper religious discourse. Latitudinarian writing is liberally sprinkled with calls for "indifferent, impartial inquiry" and individual, open-minded judgment, as opposed to collective authority. "Liberty of judgment" was to rest on a modest and cautious search for truth informed by an awareness of human fallibility.[120]

In philosophical terms, then, the latitudinarians attempted to take a position somewhere between skepticism and dogmatism. They rejected the skeptical position which denied the possibility of any knowledge. They also rejected a zealous dogmatism which was overly confident in opinions that lacked adequate certainty and which, given the opportunity, would impose its opinions on others. It was far more important to preach moderation and charity for the views of others than to quarrel over any doctrine or ceremony.[121]

The humble and impartial search for truth, not the correctness of the position reached, was the true mark of piety.

We are not to think the worse of others for their differences . . . for though they should be erroneous and mistaken in their judgment in such things, but if their conversations be more just and righteous than ours, if more humble and peaceable, they are thereupon to be accounted better than we are, both more acceptable of God, and approved by men.[122]

Sin was more reprehensible than error; one of the worst sins was the lack of charity for those who differed in opinion.

POLICY IMPLICATIONS

To their critics, the impartiality and indifference of the latitudinarians suggested a "luke warm temper," a "detestable neutrality," and/or the absence of true religious feeling. This criticism, flowing from Dissenters and high churchmen alike, was combined with distaste for the practical policies of the latitudinarians, policies that stemmed directly from their epistemology. For the latitudinarians urged that only those few Christian doctrines which attained to the level of moral certainty should be enforced by the Church, and that matters of nonfundamental opinion should be left to the independent search for truth. In this way, the public authority could promote both religion and public peace. Accordingly, latitudinarians steered a center course through the religious conflicts of the day. They coupled an acceptance of divine Providence with their indifference to nonfundamentals in accepting both Puritan Interregnum and Anglican Restoration, and then the Revolution of 1688. With the partial exception of Locke,[123] they favored comprehension rather than toleration. They proposed to make those modifications in ritual and governance necessary to achieve the broadest possible comprehension.

The Anglican doctrines of the *via media*, "things indifferent," and the secular origins of ecclesiastical institutions might focus either on the need for obedience and conformity to things admittedly "indifferent," or on the prudence of altering these forms before imposing conformity. Although their readiness to alter the establishment as a means of accommodating various dissenting groups placed them in conflict with the high churchmen, the latitudinarians, or low churchmen as they were later called, were squarely within the Anglican tradition of a national Church imposing a uniform worship. The uniformity they sought, however, was an external uniformity, not a uniformity of belief.[124]

Wilkins, Tillotson, Hale, Stillingfleet, Thomas Tenison, and other latitudinarians were repeatedly active in the political arena, attempting to achieve a broader comprehension through parliamentary modification of the Act of Uniformity.[125] Their ecumenical thrust, however, should not be exaggerated, for it never extended to Roman Catholicism. Their enemies frequently accused them of Socinianism, but never of excessive friendliness to Papists. The latitudinarians remained convinced and committed Protestants.

RELIGION AND SCIENCE

The religious debates of the seventeenth century produced both a theory of probabilistic knowledge and a technique of inquiry based on that theory. This theory and technique were the hallmarks of the proponents of natural religion and, more generally, of the latitudinarians. Religious epistemology did not, however, develop in theological isolation. Both the persons propounding the new theory and the ideas themselves were simultaneously active in both religious and scientific inquiry. The remainder of this chapter examines some connections between religious and scientific theories of knowledge in seventeenth-century England.

It is, of course, impossible to detail here the religious views of every seventeenth-century English scientist. It is possible, however, to illustrate our hypothesis by focusing on one figure, John Wilkins, whose central position in the scientific movement of the period is indisputable. If there was any single individual who tied the scientific and latitudinarian movement together, it was certainly Wilkins. Not only did he establish a scientific center at Wadham College, Oxford, during the stormy years of the Interregnum and promote a particularly moderate religious climate in the College itself, but in the early years of the Restoration, he was one of the most important contributors to the creation of the Royal Society, while at the same time gathering together a circle of young latitudinarian clerics. In both periods, Wilkins served as a rallying point not only for those who wished to avoid religious conflict but for those who sought to establish a climate of opinion which would end the conflict itself and lead to calmer, more pragmatic levels of discourse and action.[126]

Wilkins was not an isolated phenomenon. The Wadham circle contained an extremely high proportion of religious moderates, as did the leadership of the Royal Society. Sir William Petty, for example, rejected all dogmatism and expressed disgust for sectarian squabbles. Ralph Bathurst, a devoted Anglican, was also known for his dislike of religious controversy. Jonathan Goddard, the celebrated biologist who was a member of the Oxford circle, was noted for his willingness to defend scholars of any and all religious parties, having "none of that narrowness of mind which was the common failing of the great men of these times." Robert Boyle intensely disapproved of the religious quarreling he saw around him. "It is strange," he wrote, "that men should rather be quarrelling for a few trifling opinions wherein they dissent than to embrace one another for those many saving truths, wherein they agree." Boyle vigorously opposed "all severities and persecutions on account of religion," refusing to "shut himself up within a party, nor neither did he shut any party out from him."[127]

A similar pattern appeared among the scientifically inclined at Cambridge. The latitudinarian and scientific interests of Cambridge Platonists such as More and Ralph Cudsworth are well known. When Wilkins moved on to Cambridge, he "joined with those who studied to propagate better thoughts, to take men from being in parties, or from narrow notions, from superstitious conceits and fierceness about opinions."[128] John Ray and his student, Francis Willughby, were also latitudinarians, as was Isaac Barrow. Isaac Newton, Barrow's successor in the Lucasian Chair, was also a latitudinarian. Although there are notable exceptions,[129] the more closely we look at scientists involved in the Oxford group, and later the Royal Society, the more we realize that the most striking thing about their religious views and the progress of their careers was their ability to make peace with whatever government was in power, their toleration of disparate views, and their repudiation of all forms of dogmatic religion, that is, their latitudinarianism.

Many latitudinarians who were not themselves active scientists were sympathetic to the scientific movement. William Lloyd, Edward Stillingfleet, Simon Patrick, Samuel Parker, Joseph Glanvill, John Tillotson, and Gilbert Burnet did not themselves engage in scientific activities, but were enthusiastic about the new philosophy.[130] Joseph Glanvill and Thomas Sprat were propagandists for both science and latitudinarianism. In John Locke and his patron, Lord Ashley, the combination of liberal religion and scientific interest again occurs. It is no accident, then, that contemporary admirers and detractors alike noticed the association between latitudinarianism and science. Simon Patrick, for example, noted that the latitude men were "followers for the most part of the New Philosophy."[131] There was every reason that contemporaries should note the connection, since the proponents of both tended to emphasize the point themselves. The emphasis on natural theology, and particularly the proofs of God's existence from an examination of his Creation, was common to both. The study of His effects was obviously the task of the devout virtuoso, while the study of nature would itself lead to a belief in the Creator. Natural theology and science were thus thought to be mutually reinforcing.

Both also demanded the rejection of the principle of authority. Employing his own rational and observational faculties, the individual, himself, must consider and evaluate the point at issue. There could no longer be a finding from authority in either religious or philosophical matters. The opinions of theologians and natural investigators might be accepted, but only after they had been fully investigated.

Thomas Sprat's official apologia for the Royal Society made the alliance between liberal religion and scientific inquiry very clear, insisting that the quality of the Christian and the scientific experimenter were the same. He argued it was "requisite" that the virtuosi "be well practis'd in all modest, humble, friendly Vertues; should be willing to be taught, and to give way to the Judgement of others."[132] Good science could never be produced by "high earnest, insulting Wits," who could "neither bear partnership or opposition."[133] Wilkins, Glanvill, and Boyle all noted the parallel between the moderate Christian and the scientific experimenter, particularly emphasizing consciousness on one's own and others' fallibility as the mark of the true Christian and the true scientist.[134]

Joseph Glanvill went further, insisting that scientific inquiry itself provided a remedy for religious dissension. It "dispose[d] men's Spirits to more calmness and Modesty, Charity and Prudence in the Differences of Religion, and even silence[d] disputes there."[135] For wherever scientific investigation prevailed, "the Contentious Divinity loeseth ground; and 'twill be hard to find anyone of those Philosophers, that is a zealous Votary of a Sect."[136] Sprat noted that the real philosophy bred "a race of . . . men invincibly armed" against the enchantments of religious enthusiasm. The meetings of the virtuosi provided the unusual sight of "men of disagreeing parties, and ways of life, [who] have forgotten to hate." Their pursuit of natural philosophy would produce religious calm, for "Spiritual Frensies, can never stand long, before a clear and a deep skill in Nature."[137]

It is not difficult to see why scientific activities attracted so many during this period of religious and political upheaval. Natural science provided a respite, a noncontroversial realm of discussion, where men might have "the satisfaction of breathing a freer air, and of conversing in quiet one with another, without being engaged in the passions and madness of that dismal Age."[138]

For such a candid, and unpassionate company, . . . and for such a gloomy season, what could have been a fitter Subject to pitch upon than *Natural Philosophy*? To have been always tossing about some *Theological question*, would have been, to have made that their private diversion, the excess of which they themselves dislik'd in the publick: . . . It was *Nature* alone, which could pleasantly entertain them, in that estate. The contemplation of that, draws our minds off from past or present misfortunes . . . that never separates us into mortal Factions; that gives us room to differ, without animosity; and permits us to raise contrary imaginations upon it, without any danger of a *Civil War*.[139]

The alliance between latitudinarianism and science, however, went far deeper than a common core of practitioners and a mutual distaste for dogmatism. Fundamentally, the two movements shared a common theory of knowledge, and members of both became the principal proponents of a rationalized religion and natural theology based upon that theory. In their respective areas, both scientists and theologians sought a *via media* between skepticism and dogmatism. As we have seen, the scientific side of this search resulted in an emphasis on hypothesis and a science without overt metaphysics. In spiritual matters, it led to an emphasis on broad fundamentals and the eschewing of any detailed, orthodox theology claiming infallibility that we have traced earlier in this chapter.

This theory of certainty permitted the latitudinarian scientists to direct attention away from traditional theological disputes, for most of these disputes were over matters that fell into the category of opinion. The inevitable limitations on human certainty that were clearly operative and significant in science were equally decisive in religion.

Moreover, just as some scientific truths could be established to a high degree of certainty and thus become the foundation for further scientific investigation, so certain fundamental propositions of religion could be similarly established and similarly used to guide the conduct of religious life. There was a core of religious and scientific truth upon which rational agreement could be attained. Beyond that, the limits of certainty should establish the limits of dispute, particularly violent dispute.

It being utterly impossible . . . that we should always agree in the same apprehension of things. If upon every difference men should think themselves obliged to prosecute matters to the utmost height and rigour, such eager persons may easily from hence be induced to have recourse to Arms rather than such precious things as truth and justice shall suffer; and being once thus engaged, it will be impossible . . . to end their differences by any accommodation, and they must fight it out to the last till one side be wholly subdued and destroyed. And thus would men grow wild and savage, the benefits of Society would be lost, and mankind destroyed out of the world.[140]

It was thus a theory of knowledge which incorporated the factor of human fallibility that led many members of the Royal Society to emphasize natural religion as a core of established truth on which all men could agree. This core would be sufficient to guide men's spiritual lives without attempts to settle insoluble questions that could only lead to more heat than light.

This scientific commitment to a nondogmatic religion naturally went hand in hand with the scientists' constant need to re-emphasize the necessity of free inquiry and experiment, unconstrained by rules accepted a priori on the basis of authority. John Wilkins insisted those in "search of Truth" must "preserve a Philosophical Liberty," which must be used to make impartial inquiries. The "indifferent seeker after truth" must approach his task "with an equal Mind, not swayed by Prejudice, but indifferently resolved to assent unto that Truth which upon deliberation shall seem most probable."[141] Robert Hooke seconded Wilkins with the warning that it was poor scientific procedure to "dogmatically define" or "fix axioms." The better course was to "question and canvass all opinions adopting . . . none, till by mature debate and clear arguments, chiefly such as are deduced from legitimate experiments, the truth of such experiments be demonstrated invincibly."[142] If there were "any doubt or obscurity" on one or another point, it was necessary to "suspend our Assents," and although continuing to "dispute pro or con" on the matter, not to settle one's "Opinion on either side."[143]

As we have seen, the scientists were not only reluctant to accept traditional authorities but hesitant to create new ones. Overconfident assertions constrained investigation by presenting hypotheses as unquestionable truths. Two of the basic qualities of the scientific attitude were humility before an ever-increasing body of facts and willingness to give way to the judgments of others. Their humility was coupled with the intense feeling that freedom to differ and investigate was the most important tool of the scientist.

Scientific discussion as well as religious discussion required restraint. Wilkins advised that in all matters where "Victory cannot be had, Men must be content with Peace."[144] The virtues of the scientist are summed up by Joseph Glanvill. He has:

a sense of his own fallibility . . . and never concludes but upon resolution to alter his mind upon contrary evidence. Thus he conceives warily and he speaks with . . . caution . . . with great deference to opposite persuasion, candour to dissenters, and calmness in contradictions . . . he gives his reasons without passion . . . discourses without wrangling, and differs without dividing. . . . He suspends his judgment when he does not clearly understand.[145]

The Royal Society insisted that this approach rule their meetings. Sprat described the Society's "singular sobriety of debating, slowness of consenting, and moderation of dissenting," and compared the "yielding compliant" temperament of the scientists to that of "Bold, and haughty Asserters."[146]

Thus, it is not surprising that so many scientists espoused the new latitudinarian currents of the Restoration. For the cooperative and tentative attitudes of the scientists were easily translated into the sphere of religious discourse, and they reduced the temperature of religious debate. Perhaps even more significant, however, were the mutually reinforcing elements of latitude, moderation, and modest, tentative rationality that the spokesmen of the Royal Society advocated in both the religious and scientific spheres. Not only was science a haven from religious dogmatism and conflict, but the methods of science could contribute to improvement in the religious climate. The virtuosi hoped that eventually science and a moderate, latitudinarian, natural religion might serve as the two pillars supporting an intellectual life in which the calm, friendly and practical pursuit of truth and goodness could replace abstract debate and ideologically motivated civil strife.

All of this is not to say that the development of scientific ideas sketched in Chapter I caused the religious developments noted in this chapter or vice versa. Rather, it is to argue that there was a group of seventeenth-century Englishmen who pursued religion and science as parallel occupations. They conceived of them as parallel precisely because they saw both as being not in the realm of logical demonstration, but somewhere between the realm of opinion and that of moral certainty, and thus largely subject to probabilistic knowledge derived from the critical evaluation of sense data and testimony.

CONCLUSION

This chapter has not attempted to cover all the religious issues which, in one way or another, relate to seventeenth-century theories of knowledge. One might argue that it would have been desirable to investigate in greater detail the contribution of the hermetic tradition, neo-Platonism, and the mid-century sects for whom the latitudinarians expressed such distaste. Our aim here, however, has been to demonstrate that religious investigations, particularly those pursued by the latitudinarians, played a significant role in the development of seventeenth-century theories of knowledge. Those theories, in turn, resulted in a fruitful exchange and overlap between religion and the development of the natural sciences.

Efforts to demonstrate the compatibility of faith and reason, or of religion and philosophy, and the concepts of faith, belief, and moral certainty are not new to the sixteenth and seventeenth centuries. We have traced the further development of theological positions stemming from Aquinas and extending to Hooker, Grotius, Chillingworth, and Tillotson. What is significant for our purposes is that this further development was fully compatible with, and often identical to, developments in seventeenth-century philosophy of science. Early modern English attempts to provide rational but not mathematically demonstrable proofs for natural and revealed religion, and to meet the challenges of Roman Catholic arguments for infallibility, contributed to epistemological theory in general and thus provided a basis for various aspects of scientific and historical theory. By the end of the century, the latitudinarians had contributed enormously to a theory of knowledge capable of drawing together many aspects of theology, the natural sciences, and history. In each, the equation of knowledge with mathematical or logical demonstration, and the distinction between knowledge and opinion, had been replaced by the same probabilistically graded categories of relative certainty. In each, findings ranged from mere opinion or speculation on the one hand, to a moral certainty which no reasonable man might doubt on the other. Had the concepts of moral certainty and highly probabilistic knowledge been limited to the religious sphere, their influence would no doubt have been considerable; but it was their simultaneous development and use by overlapping groups of investigators engaged in a number of different intellectual pursuits that elevated religiously related epistemological issues into the mainstream of intellectual life.

IV

History

IN THE SEVENTEENTH century, English historical thought first reached its modern state of methodological ambivalence, poised between the competing claims of literature and science. Some of the historiographical writings of the period invoke the kinship between history and literature, and many contemporary historians have emphasized the connections between early modern historical thought and Renaissance humanism and rhetoric.[1] Nevertheless, in this period some historians began to see themselves as men of science, confronted with the same epistemological problems as other scientists.[2] One of the primary functions of this chapter will be to place seventeenth-century historical thought in the context of then-current theories of knowledge and to suggest that changes in conceptions of evidence and proof brought historical thought into closer contact with the natural sciences. The same concern for evidence linked historical knowledge to religious belief. Although an examination of the important relationship between historical and legal thought will be postponed to the next chapter, the reader will immediately note the intrusion of legal language and concepts when theologians and historians deal with the veracity of witnesses and reporters.

The attempt to reconstruct the natural sciences on an empirical basis had major implications for history, which, since the early Renaissance, had become closely related to rhetoric. As the natural sciences became more empirical, more grounded in facts gathered by imperfect observation, it became possible for history, which also dealt in uncertain observation of matters of fact, to develop serious intellectual contacts with the natural sciences. The growth in intellectual power of the natural sciences was accompanied by changes in the reputation and function of rhetoric, which was increasingly linked to poetry and conceived as an instrument of moral instruction and aesthetic pleasure. Poetry and rhetoric appeared less truth-oriented, and history, once closely connected with rhetoric, now shed some of these associations and entered into a new alliance with an empirically grounded natural science.

That history and natural history share their name was something more than a linguistic accident. For the seventeenth century, a "history" was a true account of the facts—any facts—physical, biological, social, and/or "historical." We will consider the overlapping subject matters of history and natural history with particular emphasis on the inclusion of what we today would call historical, anthropological, and sociological data in the numerous natural histories produced during the period. We will examine common methodological problems faced by historians and natural scientists, especially the need to evaluate the degree of reliability of data sources. We will also briefly comment on the overlapping membership in the historical and scientific communities, and certain shared ideological positions which further indicate that contemporaries saw nothing incompatible about pursuing historical and scientific topics simultaneously, as intimately related parts of a larger intellectual endeavor.

THE CONTINENTAL BACKGROUND

To assess English historiography, it will be necessary to place it in the context of Renaissance historiography more generally. We must, of course, begin with Italy where humanistic and historical studies developed. It is generally agreed that early Italian humanism was associated with disinterest in the formal theology, philosophy, natural science, and logic of the scholastic tradition. Humanists concerned themselves with grammar, rhetoric, poetry, moral philosophy, and history. In all of these endeavors, persuasive power and eloquence were more valued than factual accuracy. The alliance between rhetoric and history in the Renaissance was a close one, so close that it is often difficult to distinguish history from panegyric.[3]

Although history was supposed to be truthful, there was little interest in the nature of historical truth or historical method. In the sixteenth century, however, following the models of Polybius and Tacitus rather than Cicero, the reigning favorite of the preceding era, attention shifted from the moral lessons of history to its political lessons. The realistic, utilitarian, and politically oriented history developed in Florence by Machiavelli and Guicciardini soon

120

shifted to Venice as Bruto, Paruta, Davila, Sarpi, and others moderated the didactic moralism of Ciceronians.[4] The intellectual interests of humanist historians also broadened. Philosophy, mathematics, and natural science were less likely to be rejected. A number of historians, including the much-admired Sarpi, were interested in the natural science of the day.[5] Italian, and particularly Venetian humanists and historians, also became more sensitive about the nature of historical sources. Italian historians began to stress the necessity of assessing the character, associates, and "personal worth" of sources and of comparing various accounts, and Sarpi insisted that his history was based on documents, reports, and letters.[6]

We must also take note of the antiquarian movement and the new genre which combined history and geographical description. Flavio Biondo's pioneering *Roma instaurata*, firmly based on archaeological remains of the Roman past, was designed to provide historically accurate information. His *Italia illustrata*, a geographical and historical survey of Italy, combined the methods of the humanist scholar with those of the naturalist, perhaps for the first time since antiquity. He not only applied the best critical and philological techniques to the ancient sources but insisted on firsthand observation and travel. He rejected the oratorical style for a more detached, accurate narrative based on the sources. This type of scholarship, which would eventually combine geography, history, and all the descriptive natural sciences, became popular first in Germany and then in England, where it merged imperceptibly with natural history. The form adopted by its practitioners was usually the systematic survey rather than a chronological, narrative account.[7]

As history moved away from the rhetorical tradition, now increasingly associated with imaginative literature and fiction, and emphasized impartial accuracy,[8] it was forced to relate its claims of truth to those of logic and "science," and thus to confront disciplines it had earlier rejected and epistemological issues it had previously ignored. Some tentative beginnings in this direction were made by such men as Patrizzi, who combined interests in natural philosophy and mathematics with an interest in history. Patrizzi, a correspondent of Galileo, concluded that history, though it aimed at truth, could at best achieve only a rough approximation of certain knowledge because it ultimately depended on sources whose reliability could not be fully known. Despite the lack of certain knowledge of the past, critical evaluation of the reliability of the sources would enable historians to narrate the probable course of events.[9] This type of analysis was continued by a number of Italian historiographers, including Acontio whose writings on historical methodology were soon translated into English together with Patrizzi's.[10] These historiographical developments, however, soon came to a halt in Italy. It has recently been suggested that seventeenth-century Italian historical thought underwent a "crisis of content" which resulted in coupling the rhetorical platitudes of ancient rhetoricians with historical writing devoid of politics. A "baroque" historical tradition emerged, characterized by a complex and unclear style and no pretense to practical utility. There was also a split between history as literature and history as "research." Although detail was prized, accuracy was not, and research often meant that absurdities were coupled with irrelevancy.[11]

North of Italy, philological techniques were applied to the sources of Christianity by Erasmus and his disciples, and historical scholarship was used by Protestant and Roman Catholic controversialists and theologians. It is important to focus on the somewhat less well-known German topographical-historical school in which humanist scholars, following Biondo and Aeneas Silvius and the ancient models of Ptolemy and Strabo, began to investigate and describe their country. The practitioners of chorography, as the genre was called, combined descriptive geography and narrative history, built on the critical study of sources, firsthand observation, and the increasingly scientific knowledge of geographers, mapmakers, and naturalists. It profits little to label the practitioners of this genre humanists or scientists. They were obviously simultaneously something of each.[12]

In similar fashion, the Spanish described the New World. Government sponsorship created the post of Cosmographer and Chronicler of the Indies, whose responsibilities involved preparation of histories and geographies. Questionnaires, similar to those developed later by the Royal Society, were designed to provide information concerning politics, geography, botany, customs, mineral and economic resources, and history. The result, again, was a combination of natural history, geography, and ethnography.[13]

The most influential and methodologically most sophisticated work to emerge from Spain was José de Acosta's *Historia natural y moral de la Indias* (1590),[14] which provided still another model for combining physical description—from the heavens down to plant and animal life—with "the deeds and customes" of men. The latter, Acosta labeled "Morall History." Under this rubric he recorded not only the current religion, customs, government, and law of the Indians but also their history. Acosta, like Bacon, insisted on the superiority of modern over ancient knowledge, assumed that knowledge was progressive and cumulative, and insisted on the necessity of firsthand observation and experience. Yet, as an historian, he was acutely conscious of the difficulties in reconstructing history. Like Patrizzi, he was sensitive to problems of method and the kinds of certainty one could expect to achieve from various kinds of investigation. In natural and physical matters, experience was "the most perfect rule." One should not expect "infallible and mathematical" rules in such matters, for they were simply not available. Concepts of relative certainty or degrees of certainty, which were employed by Acosta in Spain and Melchor Cano, a Dominican theologian, were further developed by English scholars—religious, scientific, and historical.[15]

In France, developments took a somewhat different turn. Here the critical techniques and philological methods developed by Lorenzo Valla and others were applied to Roman law and history, and then to French law and history, by a group of historically oriented jurists.[16] French historians were less involved in combining natural and civil history than their German and Spanish counterparts, although Jean Bodin's much-admired work recalls French efforts to comprehend all kinds of knowledge.[17] French historians were interested in problems of historical method. They took to heart the Polybian attack on hearsay evidence and sought firsthand accounts. Some even noted that eyewitnesses themselves might be biased. Etienne Pasquier, for example, who first applied the critical techniques of the philologists and jurists to the history of France, not only insisted on staying close to the sources, the "démonstrations oculaires," but recommended including texts wherever possible so that readers could touch them personally "with their fingers." Conflicting accounts thus might be compared and evaluated according to the "worth" of the reporter and his proximity to the event. It would, he thought, be possible to reconstruct the past with certainty beyond dispute. By labeling his efforts "researches" rather than "history," Pasquier limited himself to topics where sources existed.[18]

If few were as sensitive and critical as Pasquier, the trend in French scholarship was, nevertheless, increasingly toward a concern for historical accuracy. By the 1580s, the fabulous and the legendary, including the popular legend of the Trojan founding of France, were being rejected. Consensus was forming that, without research in the sources, the historian could never get at the truth, let alone at the causes and explanations which were the aim of "perfect history." As the new history became dependent on erudition in the sources, scholars' efforts turned to the collection of documents and the creation of libraries and archives, which in turn led the "erudites" to join in what has been described as an unchartered society of antiquaries practicing a kind of cooperative scholarship.[19]

By the 1560s, French historical thought was faced by the threat of skepticism. Christian anti-intellectualism, culminating in Agrippa's attack on all arts and sciences, was a continuing problem. But the attack on knowledge became sharper and more widespread as the sources of ancient skepticism became known. Now, not only were the rational products of men's minds ridiculed, but the validity of historical knowledge and knowledge based on sense experience was also repudiated. For the true skeptic, no knowledge was possible. Thus, French theologians, philosophers, historians, and scientists, indeed all intellectuals, were forced to come to grips with the problem of knowledge and belief itself.[20]

For Cartesians, statements based on sense observation or the reports of others could, at best, reach only probable or conjectural status and were therefore downgraded. The mathematical sciences, which alone were capable of certainty, were to be cultivated, while historical knowledge, and even the physical sciences to the extent that they were based on sense information, could be dismissed as being built on an uncertain foundation. In many respects, the Cartesian conception of science continued medieval and Renaissance rejection of observation and report as a basis for truth. The popularity of Cartesianism appears to have had an inhibiting effect on necessarily probabilistic historical scholarship.[21] Even in France, however, a number of academies and literary circles explored a combination of scientific and historical topics. Rationalism predominated but did not still the combination of empirical and humanistic interest.[22]

ENGLISH HISTORICAL THOUGHT

The English seem to have been more willing than the French to accept and live with less than certain knowledge. English intellectuals were far less deeply affected by skepticism and, perhaps for that reason, were less prone to accept a Cartesian solution that devalued all but the certain knowledge to be derived from logic and mathematics.[23] Yet English intellectual life exhibited many of the same features we have seen elsewhere. Long before the 1580s, the decade frequently suggested as the take-off period of historical creativity, the English had absorbed the values and scholarly concerns of Continental humanism: its hostility to scholastic logic and dialectical studies, and its literary, philological, rhetorical, and educational interests. Polydore Virgil's *Anglica historia* (1534) provides something of a landmark in English historical thought by introducing the values and methods of Renaissance historiography. Familiarity with critical methods, a growing sensitivity to sources, and patriotic enthusiasm led the English as well as the French to a concern for the preservation and collection of records and documents. By the late sixteenth or early seventeenth centuries, collections and libraries had made serious historical research possible. Because of their rather late entry to Renaissance historiography, English historians were exposed to both the Ciceronian rhetorical and the Tacitean-Polybian views of history, the latter becoming the dominant but not exclusive view. Humanism and patriotism, both secular and religious, united to make historical studies extremely popular in England.

The achievements of Tudor and Stuart historians have been described by others and we need not retrace their steps.[24] But it is necessary to discuss certain features of those developments. The first of these is historical classification. There were, of course, a number of ways to classify history, but that of Francis Bacon is particularly significant. For Bacon and for his many followers, there were two major varieties of history—natural and civil. Both dealt with individual instances and with particular events and experiences which, in time, would become the sources of general principles of natural philosophy or axioms of civil knowledge.[25]

Although Thomas Hobbes held a very different view of how philosophical principles were to be derived, he, too, identified all knowledge of fact with history.

The register of Knowledge of Fact is called History. Whereof there be two sorts: one called Naturall History, which [is] the History of such Facts, or Effects of Nature . . . Such as the Histories of Metalls, Plants, Animals, Regions, and the Like. The other is Civil History, which [is] the History of the Voluntary Actions of Men in Commonwealths.[26]

The coupling of natural history and civil history was to be found not only among philosophers but in such conventional works as Richard Braithwaite's treatment of the varieties of history.[27] Civil history, for most Englishmen, consisted of the conventional political and governmental topics.[28] Natural history was extraordinarily broad,

125

including all the "Phenomena of the Universe." Natural history, for Bacon and many of his countrymen, thus came to include the history of the heavens, comets, meteorology, cosmography, geography, botany, zoology, physiology, and anatomy.[29]

Though civil history dealt with the deeds and works of man, and natural history with the works of nature, Bacon did not view the categories as mutually exclusive or totally distinct. The history of arts and trades, though included among the varieties of natural history, was defined by Bacon as the history of nature as altered by the activities of man. Cosmography, for Bacon, was

mixed of many things; of Natural History, in respect of the regions themselves, their sites and products; of History Civil, in respect of the habitations, governments, and manners of the people; and of Mathematics, in respect of the climates and configurations of the heavens, beneath which the regions of the world lie.[30]

In order to show the methodological links between history and science, it will be necessary to examine natural history, civil history, and mixed forms somewhat more closely. Like Bacon, we shall begin natural history with astronomy, to all appearances a field of study as far from history as one can imagine, given its mathematical orientation and its traditional home among the physical sciences. Yet, Robert Hooke as well as Bacon used the term "history" in connection with astronomical observation, employing it to cover any kind of accurately reported data devoid of theoretical speculation. Indeed much of the parallelism between history and natural science in the seventeenth century was based on the notion that history—any kind of history—consisted of an accurate report of past and present facts and events. Thus, the description of celestial phenomena, comets for example, was history. So were accurately recorded observations of the earth's atmosphere, weather, and climate.[31]

Cosmography was natural history on the grandest scale, for it included both heavens and earth. Hydrography (we would perhaps call it oceanography) referred to the seas, and geography to the study of the earth. The study of particular geographic regions was often labeled chorography or topography. Terminology was not consistent. Whatever the terms employed, however, these studies were frequently combined with what we are accustomed to call history. Peter Heylyn, seemingly unaware of the Continental chorographic tradition, thought of his combination of history and geography as a "new method." His *Microcosmus* of 1621 soon ex-

126

panded into the often reprinted *Cosmographie*. It covered the world from the time of creation, combining not only geography and history, but politics, theology, chorography, and heraldry. Heylyn argued that especially history and geography had to be united for a proper understanding of past ages and present nations. The two were like Sidney's lovers: "Her being was in him alone / And she not being, he was none."[32]

Heylyn's views were echoed in Moses Pitt's huge and far more modern Royal-Society-sponsored *Atlas*, designed to provide a comprehensive description of the entire world. The descriptions of physical surroundings and cities were only a segment of his ambitious plan:

> In every Nation also account shall be given of their original Language, Manners, Religion, Employment, &c. that if any art or science useful to society be there eminent, it may be transferred into our own Country. Much more considerable are their Governments, Civil and Military, their Magistrates, Laws, Assemblies, Courts, Rewards and Punishments, and such like. Neither must we omit the manner of educating their youth in arts liberal and mechanick. . . . Lastly, it will be expected, that we give an account of the History or actions and successes of each Nation, or their Princes, remarkable actions, &c.[33]

Heylyn and Pitt easily mixed the subject matters of nature and man.

Geology was a less mixed form. Yet, when seventeenth-century geologists went beyond description to offer explanations of the physical changes they observed, they encountered documentary evidence. Explanations had to be fitted into the scriptural account of the earth's past—the Creation and the Flood—and the earth's future—its dissolution and final conflagration. Geologists had to confront the written text in much the same way as the historian whose topic touched Scripture. Virtually all geologists agreed with Thomas Burnet's statement that the Mosaic account of the Deluge was "a true piece of Natural History," and with John Ray's comment that Moses had provided "the History and Description of the Creation."[34]

Geology was thus among the sciences most closely connected with history. Cecil Schneer has demonstrated that geology and archaeology were advanced at the same time by an overlapping group of naturalists and antiquarians clustered around the Royal Society. Investigators such as Robert Hooke noted similarities between fragments of the natural and the man-made past, suggesting that shells and other natural forms were "the Medals, Urnes, or Monuments of Nature."[35]

If geological studies began to flourish only in the second half of the seventeenth century, enthusiasm for chorography and topography had begun much earlier. These studies were a mixture of natural and civil history. The study and investigation of England began in earnest in the 1540s when John Leland began work on his never published "Britannia." His successors reached in a number of directions—topographical description, natural history in the conventional sense, map making, and the study of the language, institutions, and physical remains of the English past. His inspiration resulted in John Speed's *Theatre of the Empire of Great Britaine*, whose importance lay in its maps, in Laurence Nowell's old-English studies, and in William Lambarde's Anglo-Saxon legal studies. It also led to William Harrison's "Historicall Description of the Islande of Britayne," included with Ralph Holinshed's *Chronicles* (1577), which contained a physical description mixed with accounts of political and legal institutions and comments on ancient languages. Holinshed's chronicles of England, Ireland, and Scotland were, in fact, each preceded with a Biondo-like description. Richard Brathwaite's volume on the proper writing of history recommended that all histories include physical description and a description of the trade, customs, and manners of the inhabitants.[36]

These developments culminated in William Camden's justly famous *Britannia*, an historical chorography of ancient Britain, which immediately became the model for later efforts. Camden began with geography of England, moving on to more "historical" topics: the nature of England's early inhabitants and the historical development of the Roman through the Norman periods. Camden's range was enormous—we would say it included history, geography, topography, natural history, antiquarianism, and anthropology.[37]

Camden's example also resulted in the historico-geographical treatment of the English counties, first by those, like himself, associated with the Society of Antiquaries, and then among antiquaries and naturalists connected with the Royal Society. William Lambarde's *Perambulation of Kent* and Richard Carew's *Survey of Cornwall* are examples of the first. Their chorographies described soils and minerals as well as the social, economic, and legal environment, both past and present. If Lambarde was more involved with history and antiquities, Carew heralds the interest in natural phenomena and contemporary description which became so popular in the post-Baconian decades. And if William Dugdale's *War-*

wickshire and Robert Thornton's *Nottinghamshire* concentrated on political, legal, and ecclesiastical antiquities, topics heavily dependent on documentary and archaeological evidence, other post-Restoration works, like those of Robert Plot and John Aubrey, gave greater attention to natural phenomena and less to history and institutions. The breadth of Camden's *Britannia* and of Bacon's civil and natural history categories effectively held together the varied factual aspects of county history.[38]

A similar breadth is to be found in John Stow's *Survey of London* (1598), which follows the structure and method of *Britannia* and initiated a spate of smaller regional studies. Stow critically examined every kind of relevent data and evidence, past and present, physical and documentary.[39] Like Stow and Camden, Richard Hakluyt, author of *The Principall Navigations, Voiages and Discoveries of the English Nation* (1589), not only made use of contemporary observations and reports, but researched "old records, patents, [and] privileges."[40] The voyage tradition, like regional history, also became associated with the Royal Society, which undertook an entrepreneurial role in connection with reports and histories of voyages, foreign lands, and English colonies.[41] In 1671, for example, it requested John Winthrop to compose

a good History of New England, from the beginning of ye English arrival there, to this very time, containing ye Geography, Natural Productions, and Civill Administration thereof, together with the Notable Progresse of ye Plantation, and the remarkable occurences in the same.[42]

The Society was thus seriously committed to a mixture of natural and civil studies. Indeed, its "General Heads for the Natural History of a Countrey, Great or small," largely the work of Robert Boyle, which included items on the physical environment, plant and animal life, customs, antiquities, natural and manufactured products, traditions, and learning, represented an effort to standardize the genre.[43]

English studies of other countries, treated in much the same way as English counties and towns, also allow us to trace the growing role of the scientific community. Gerard Boate's study of Ireland, published by Samuel Hartlib, combined natural history with the "Fashions, Lawes, and Customes" of the Irish. Sir William Petty's *Political Anatomy of Ireland* (1691) was in the same mold, though its emphasis was on historical development and current social, political, and economic conditions. Laurence Echard's *Exact Description of Ireland* (1691) included the "Chorographical and Modern" with the "Historical and Ancient," without any sense that it might be an inappropriate combination. When emphasis was on physical and biological description, we are on the familiar territory of natural history; when these were mixed roughly equally with political, economic, and historical information, we have chorography. When the center of attention was such political, economic, and historical data, we might want to speak of history and of a new socio-economic political genre which resulted in titles like "The present state of X" or "The ancient and present state of Y." Taken one step further, the process led to John Graunt's *Natural and Political Observations* (1661) in which mathematical calculations were applied to both "political" and "natural" phenomena.[44]

All the forms mentioned slid back and forth between natural history, chorography, history, and simple description without any sense that these subject matters should not be mixed together. John Ray felt no more uneasiness in combining a narration of his voyage and travels with some "Observations Topographical, Moral and Natural"[45] than an Annales-school historian does in combining demographic, climatological, and geographic topics with agricultural and social history.

A great deal of historical writing, of course, remained unadulterated by natural history and cosmography, and concerned itself with the traditional historical topics—politics, war, and diplomacy. We thus must discuss "civil history" if we are to assess the place of historical investigation in the context of seventeenth-century intellectual endeavor. The most successful and most admired variety of civil history was "politic history," inspired by Machiavelli and Guicciardini, and more remotely by Polybius, which aimed ultimately at deriving practical political maxims. Its practitioners, the most outstanding of whom were Francis Bacon, Sir John Hayward, Samuel Daniel, and William Camden, wished to describe men and events as they were rather than as they should be, and thus moved away from the earlier moralizing, rhetorical, political history, exemplified by Sir Thomas More's *History of Richard III*, which lauded good men and brave actions and condemned their opposites.[46]

"Politic history," sometimes identified by contemporaries as "perfect history," was also characterized by explanations and causal analysis which might provide guidance for future policy makers and political actors. From Camden to Clarendon and beyond, admirers of "perfect history" insisted that the mere compilation of facts without causal explanations was a waste of time.[47] Such explanations became increasingly more secular. While few, if any, historians would deny God's providential role, the second causes they sought were less likely to refer to the consequences of violating moral injunctions. Their approach corresponds roughly to the tendency of naturalists to refer to the "ordinary" ways of Providence. This allowed natural and, in the case of the civil historian, human explanations without denying God's ultimate oversight. The speed of this development, however, must not be exaggerated, for God's intervention might be invoked to explain not only the defeat of the Spanish Armada but the outcome of mid-century civil war battles and the Revolution of 1688. Nevertheless, victory and defeat were increasingly, if not consistently, explained in secular terms.

"Politic" or "perfect history" was at its height between 1580 and 1630, and both the quality and quantity of its productions seem to have declined well before 1640. Despite the decline, perhaps caused by the development of antiquarian history and the difficulty of producing perfect history, the ideal, with its emphasis on the "true Relation of the Actions of Public Persons and the Great Business and Affairs of Kingdomes" and causal analysis, remained the central goal of the civil historian.

Although historical terminology was rather confused and became even more so as the century wore on, we must at least identify the dominant varieties, if for no other reason than the fact that the confusion and difficulties of these categories reveal important features of seventeenth-century historical thought. Sir Francis Bacon's well-known attempt to classify the varieties of history was typical, and thus will be useful in describing the major strands of historical writing and conceptualization. We have already noted his division into natural, civil, and mixed history, and have now dealt sufficiently with the first and third. Perfect history, clearly the most esteemed variety of civil history, contained three subcategories—a period of time, a "person worthy of mention," or an "action or exploit of the nobler sort."[48] Most of Bacon's contemporaries would have agreed that only important events and personages were worthy of the label perfect or politic history. The first, a period of time, needs little explanation. It typically recounted the reign of a monarch and was typified by Camden's *Annals of the Reign of Elizabeth.*

Although Bacon and his contemporaries considered "Lives" or biography one of the varieties of perfect history, it was, and remained, an undeveloped genre. As Bacon recognized, "Lives," in fact, were "sadly neglected," and he suggested that there were "many worthy personages," not all of them royal, who deserved "better than dispursed report or dry and barren eulogy."[49] Lives should not be treated moralistically nor rhetorically. They should describe, not prescribe behavior.

Not all historians, however, were ready to exclude the "ought" from history. Even as some derived empirical generalizations from the examination of historical experience, others continued to point out examples of good and evil according to pre-established moral principles.[50] The humanist view that history is philosophy teaching by example assumed, however, that the principles of moral philosophy were already known. When the principles of moral philosophy themselves were uncertain or in dispute, as they were by mid-century, we should expect to see less history as moral illustration. Indeed, this genre does decline. Nevertheless, although Bacon himself initiated some efforts to make biography the basis for an empirically derived, naturalistic ethics and psychology, the effort to derive empirically and historically based rules of human behavior did not develop very far.

Biography did undergo some changes. Initially the genre was associated with the brief, literary, character sketch aimed at describing different types of personalities. With Clarendon, such sketches became more individualized and realistic, depending more on direct observation of particular individuals. Another development, which may have owed as much to the collection of saints' lives as to Baconian admonitions, was the collective biography. Yet, Thomas Fuller's *Worthies of England*, Lloyd's *Memorials*, Aubrey's *Brief Lives*, and Anthony Wood's *Athenae Oxoniensis* remind us that prosopography, or group biography, was practiced by those of antiquarian bent and would never have been considered "perfect history."

The third subcategory of perfect history involved particular events of limited duration, such as the Peloponnesian War or the Council of Trent. This type of history was thought to have important advantages since the historian could obtain more complete information than he could for a more lengthy period. Bacon and his successors nevertheless noted that there were in fact few extant examples of this type.[51] Clarendon's *History of the Rebellion and Civil Wars in England* was among the few English works admitted to this category.

While extolling it as a goal and a type, Bacon, his contemporaries, and successors bewailed the lack of perfect history, particularly the lack of an English history. Perfect history was more an ideal than an extant variety of historical writing. "True and perfect Civil History" was thought to be remarkably difficult to achieve. In order to write it, it was necessary:

to carry the mind in writing back into the past, bring it into sympathy with antiquity; diligently to examine, freely and faithfully to report, and by the light of words to place it as it were before the eyes.[52]

Not only was it enormously difficult to ascertain the truth of past transactions, but it required "great labour and judgement." It might also be dangerous to tell the truth of more recent events, and not a few historians encountered difficulties when dealing with topics having current or potential political relevance.

The civil history actually produced was usually considered fault-ridden:

some (and these are the greater part) write only barren and commonplace narratives, a very reproach to history; others hastily and disorderly string together a few particular relations and trifling memoirs.[53]

Some were too detailed and others too brief. Still others showed the influence of passion or party. Civil history, as written, was anything but perfect history, and fewer attempted it as they became conscious of its difficulty.

The term "perfect history" was troublesome. It was used to denote both the three varieties of history and a standard for the historian. Frequently, the term "historian" was equated with "perfect historian." This usage suggests that others were engaged in imperfect work, and that those engaged in historical enterprises not covered by "Times," "Lives," and "Actions" must be something other than historians.

Categories of imperfect history existed which were considered lesser than, and sometimes preparatory to, perfect history. Less-than-perfect history was composed of "Memorials," the "unfinished" or "rough draughts of history" according to Bacon. "Memorials" or "Preparatory History" included "Commentaries," the narration of events devoid of causal explanations, and "Registers," which were collections of laws, speeches, etc., with little or no narrative thread.[54] We may wish to think of this material as akin to data or sources, though considerable labor and intellectual effort on the part of the compiler and commentators might be involved.

The notion was common that contemporary reports, though not "history" themselves, would contribute to history, much in the sense that the practitioner of natural history felt he was contributing to natural philosophy. The mid-century newspaper reporter who insisted on the importance of leaving "true Memorials of our present affaires to all succeeding generations, that posteritie may see the truth of their forefathers actions," thus echoed Camden's and Bacon's comments that contemporary reporting, if done well, would contribute to producing a true history.[55]

The category "antiquities" proved more conceptually troublesome. Antiquities, for Bacon, were the "remnants of histories," comparable to the "spars of a shipwreck, decayed and almost lost," which might be recovered somewhat "from the deluge of time" by "acute and industrious persons." The deficiency of antiquities lay not in the intelligence or diligence of the practitioners but in the nature of the enterprise itself.[56] Antiquarian research, however well done, could not yield perfect history. It was presumably a different kind of historical enterprise produced by a different set of researchers.

If the concept of perfect history and its less perfect subsidiaries remained current throughout the century, it was not universally held. Some historians, perhaps out of modesty, would call their work "narrations" or "memorials." Others rejected the notion that true history had to be written on a grand scale or had to concern itself with serious topics of great consequence. John Selden rejected the notion that history consisted solely of accounts of various states and ages where the action was connected by "continued discourses or threads of time." For him, it also included that which dealt with "some narrow particulars, and sometimes under other names."[57] John Evelyn insisted all history was good "if it were true and matter of fact, though the subject of it were never so trivial."[58] Nevertheless, Daniel Defoe found it necessary to justify "giving the Name of a History" to his *A General History of the Pyrates*, given the fact that it dealt with "nothing but the Actions of a Parcel of Robbers," suggesting that there was some question of whether his readers would consider piracy worthy of the name "history."[59]

Different notions of history might even exist simultaneously in the same individual. James Howell, writing on the reign of Louis XIII, contrasted "perfect history" with "downright confus'd Narrations" which bundled together facts without digestion or analysis.[60] Yet, when he turned to an antiquarian investigation of London, modeled on Stowe, he stressed the similarity between antiquarian and historian. Indeed, the only difference was the historian's somewhat greater freedom in putting materials together elegantly.[61] As more historically minded intellectuals engaged in antiquarian research, they became less willing to give the palm to the historian.

134

Yet in theory, a distinction remained between the historian and the antiquarian or memorialist. The seventeenth century was an enormously important period in the development of historical scholarship and understanding, but few would or could claim to be "historians." Indeed, much of the best historical work was labeled something other than history. History was simultaneously the term used for any truthful record of facts or events, natural, human, or mixed, and for the specially elevated branch of civil history which few hoped to achieve. Those producing memorials, narratives, or reports on antiquarian research might have historical interests and contributed to history, but did not merit the title "historian." Indeed, hardly any mid- or late-seventeenth-century Englishmen were awarded that august title.

This segregation of imperfect and perfect history created a number of problems. At times, the two were viewed as distinct tasks to be undertaken by different individuals. The terms were rarely, if ever, employed to suggest something like phases of a single process. Indeed, many felt the true historian need not become deeply involved in research, but might work from the collections of others. The much admired histories of Bacon and Lord Herbert were thus only very partially built upon original research. The division, if maintained, meant that perfect history was likely to be both more superficial and more readable than the more historically sound but often cumbersome antiquarian studies. Seventeenth-century historians were not sure whether readable, political history could be combined with painstaking, documentary research.

It was antiquarian scholarship that produced most of the important historical achievement of the seventeenth century, particularly after the decline of perfect history in the 1620s, and we must examine these historical studies more closely if we are to assess the place of history in seventeenth-century intellectual endeavor. The practitioner might view himself as the appropriate interpreter of the remains of the past or as simply a compiler of materials to be used by future "historians." If some individuals limited themselves to recording, locating, and describing archeological remains or documents, others considered themselves to be historians engaged in interpretation and analysis. Their emphasis on "facts" and "things" was in keeping with the growing demand for accurate evidence and convincing proof. Antiquarian research tended to limit itself to topics where visible remains and documentary evidence were available.

Some antiquarian effort was devoted to legal and political institutions. The study of ancient parliaments, Anglo-Saxon political institutions, the Norman conquest, and the development of feudalism—matters of intense political as well as scholarly concern—are clearly "historical" from the vantage point of modern scholarship. Contemporaries, from the time of the founding of the Elizabethan Society of Antiquaries, often labeled those who dealt with nonnarrative political and legal topics "antiquarians." The lack of a sustained narrative structure and of the central role of individual actors seems to have been a critical element. Thus, the best historical work on institutions and customs was undertaken by intellectuals who might not even consider themselves historians.[62]

Many antiquarians, particularly those involved in chorography and county history, had close connections with the scientific movement.[63] Stonehenge, England's most impressive "antiquity," was investigated by men as different as William Camden, England's most admired antiquary; Inigo Jones, the classically inspired architect; John Aubrey, the natural historian and antiquary; and Walter Charleton, the atomist virtuoso and man of letters.[64] It was not unusual for a man like Camden to collect fossils or for Martin Lister, known primarily as a man of science, to devote himself to the study of Roman urns as well as spiders and shells.[65] Indeed, the distinction between what was a stone, an animal fossil, or a human artifact was not always clear to those who studied and collected them.

While there was a close connection between antiquarian and scientific research, many of the best antiquarians were accomplished classicists and linguists. Indeed, the attraction of Roman Britain, one of the earliest fields of antiquarian study, was that it was the sole portion of Roman history which had not been pre-empted by the Romans themselves.[66] Those who accomplished most in this area possessed a mixture of linguistic and observational skills. The antiquarian had to be at home with a combination of documentary materials, coins, inscriptions, statuary, roads, and fortifications. Like the modern archeologists, firsthand observation was combined with more sedentary linguistic pursuits. The contrast seems to have been less between humanist and scientist than between generalist and scholarly specialist.

It was the more painstaking antiquarian scholarship, with its closer links to natural history, the scientific movement, and philological specialization, which, more often than "history," produced a sensitivity to the pastness of the past, to problems of development, and to the uniqueness of various institutions and periods. "Perfect history," whose links with Renaissance historical thought are obvious, may in the end have contributed more to general social science than to history itself. For it was practitioners of perfect history who were particularly interested in causal explanation and political generalization.

Seventeenth-century conceptions of the nature of history were thus rather confused. On the one hand, we have seen that the links between history and natural history were extremely close and helped produce some of the outstanding historical works of the period. At the same time, we have also seen that when theorists and practitioners considered civil history alone, it appeared as if history, at least perfect history, had far closer ties to literature and political and moral philosophy. How the varieties of imperfect history related to perfect history remains even more ambiguous than how natural history, scientific observation, or natural phenomenon related to natural philosophy. In both science and history, the "building blocks" were to be related to eventual goals, but precisely how remained an open issue. Many investigators were willing to limit themselves to the probable truths of physical observation and antiquarian analysis, leaving others to worry about the future use of their work.

Bacon and Camden provide instructive examples of the interconnections. Bacon not only insisted on the close connections between natural and civil history but also emphasized "perfect history" as both different from and superior to "antiquities." Camden was the author of both the *Britannia*, chorographic history and antiquarian scholarship at its best, and the *Annals of the Reign of Elizabeth*, often considered by contemporaries to be the most outstanding specimen of perfect history. History gained a great deal from the precise and careful observation of the new science, and was able to absorb scientific technique without abandoning its connections with literature or its goal of political generalization.

It is significant, however, that after the initial successes of Bacon, Lord Herbert, and Camden, few attempted perfect history. For the remaining portion of the century, it was evidently thought to be more interesting, more valuable, or more truthful to pursue the less prestigious, "matter of fact" underpinnings. In the process, a good many antiquarians became convinced that their own work was as important as perfect history and equally historical, and some seem to have begun to reject perfect history as a goal. A good deal of research and scholarly effort was thus devoted to collecting, ordering, dating, collating, and then finally analyzing difficult-to-handle historical sources. Simply compiling lists of the holders of a given office over a period involved an enormous amount of time, energy, and erudition. Many researchers contented themselves with such immensely valuable "Registers," or with "narratives," "memorials," ar.d "collections" or "histories" which dealt with fairly manageable topics, and which they sometimes regarded as the building blocks of true history and sometimes as ends in themselves.

It seems reasonable to compare the decline in efforts to produce perfect history to the decline in efforts to produce natural philosophy. In both history and science, there is a movement away from premature generalization and theory. The development of antiquarianism and mixed forms of history roughly parallels the upswing in natural history and experimentation. In both natural science and history, there is increasing concentration on discrete topics which might be based on facts and visually inspectable evidence and testimony. Perfect history and natural philosophy might remain the distant goals, but man's knowledge could best be increased by sticking more closely to verifiable matters of fact.

As historical scholarship became more thorough, sensitive, accurate, learned, and technical, however, it became increasingly difficult for the layman to read and enjoy. As the seventeenth century neared its end, there was a reaction, and renewed demands for a readable, narrative history, perfect history, were again voiced. This demand was often coupled with a distaste for the achievements of the scholars whose search for truth had led them to musty records and artifacts. Perfect history was to be literary history shorn of pedantry, and many early eighteenth-century intellectuals assumed that perfect history and scholarship were distinguishable and independent intellectual efforts.[67]

Having noted some of the difficulties embedded in seventeenth-century historical classification, we will consider various aspects of historical methodology and the research attitudes involved in describing and recounting the natural and social worlds—past and present—again drawing attention to similarities between history and science.

The first, and perhaps most basic, common assumption of historical inquiry was that the stuff of history, both natural and civil, was "matter of fact." Though fundamental, this assumption was rarely discussed from either a practical or philosophical point of view.

Another common though less universal assumption was that, once discovered, the facts of history as well as the facts of nature would yield "true" generalizations and axioms. Several basic positions could be found among scientists and historians. The first, perhaps most vocally represented by Bacon and his followers, was that findings of fact, both civil and natural, would become the basis of a civil philosophy and a natural philosophy whose principles would be established on the basis of demonstrative certainty. This approach would make civil history the basis of political science, sociology, and psychology.[68] A second school of thought took the position that generalizations drawn from civil and natural history would yield probable rather than certain conclusions. Explanations and causal statements might be comprehensively phrased in terms of general principles of probable truth or confined to the data or evidence offered. Scientists holding the probabilistic position were more likely to seek general rules than their historian counterparts, who more often confined themselves to particular explanations. There was also a third group for whom the collection and presentation of data, or matters of fact, constituted an intellectual task completely separate from explanation and causal analysis. Some members of this third group were hostile to generalization, others simply thought it premature. Naturalists belonging to this group could, at least in theory, distinguish natural history from natural philosophy. History lacked a clear, dual terminology. If on some occasions, the terms "memorial," "narration," "antiquities," "annals," or "documents" suggested something less than perfect history or explanatory history, increasingly, the single term "history" came to cover both, thus submerging the distinction between data and analysis.

None of these schools drew a fundamental distinction between natural and historical knowledge.[69] For our purposes, however, the second approach is the most interesting. It was primarily among those who viewed most human knowledge as being in the realm of less than absolute certainty that we find the development of a theory of knowledge which placed the description and explanation of historical events and natural events on the same plane. For this school of thought, the basic distinction was between science, that is, certain or demonstrative knowledge on the one hand, and probable knowledge sometimes capable of moral certainty on the other. Although the distinction has obvious Aristotelian origins, it was, as we have seen, developed very considerably as the problems of knowledge became more acute in the sixteenth and seventeenth centuries.

Despite the efforts of Bacon, Descartes, and others to establish knowledge on a certain foundation, there were opposing voices, for example, that of the Spaniard Acosta, who felt that, in "naturall and physicall things" as well as in the historical, "we must not seeke out infallible and mathematicall rules, but that which is ordinarie and tried by experience."[70] As we have seen, sixteenth-century Italian, French, and English historians often suggested that they were working in the realm of the probable and insisted that history, unlike mathematics or logic, could never reach the status of certain knowledge. Generally, however, the term "probable" was losing its rhetorical sense of the merely plausible and taking on the connotation of statements made on the basis of good evidence. The development, if clear, was not complete in historical circles, and "probable" continued to be used in both senses.

By the mid-seventeenth century, there were modes of thought stressing probability which, if developed, might be used to form a coherent view of knowledge that would place natural, religious, and historical knowledge into a single framework of probable knowledge. We have indicated in earlier chapters the exploration of this approach by Boyle, Hooke, Charleton, and Locke in the scientific realm, and in religion by Chillingworth, Wilkins, Tillotson, and the latitudinarians, some of whom, like Stillingfleet and Gilbert Burnet, were prominent historians as well as respected theologians. This approach distinguished mathematics and logic from religious, historical, and natural knowledge based on matters of fact. Conclusions drawn from investigation of historical and physical phenomena might be highly probable, reaching moral certainty, or they might be less probable, being little more than opinion. What was critical to the elevation of historical and natural findings from mere opinion to moral certainty was the quantity and quality of the evidence and the credibility and impartiality of the investigator or observer. For Locke, who summarized these developments, history and the physical sciences operated in the same probabilistic realm and were to be evaluated by the same rules or standards. Historians, however, being somewhat more reliant on secondhand testimony at greater distance in time from the event, would typically reach conclusions of less certainty than the naturalists.

The term "experience," though frequently employed in connection with both natural and civil history, was not often examined. Indeed at times "experience" was used synonymously with "history." The term "matter of fact" was also widely employed and like "experience" was applied to the data of both history and natural history. Matters of fact based on firsthand experience and reliable reports of observations and experiences were held to be basic to both historical and scientific knowledge. As historians and scientists came to recognize that evidence could not be taken at face value, both developed similar criteria for evaluating and weighing it.

Historians constantly emphasized the desirability of eye- and "ear witnesses." Firsthand observation was just as important for them as for the naturalists, and was considered the highest type of evidence. Statements to that effect were repeated so frequently as to represent an historical given. Only gradually was it recognized that eyewitnesses' accounts themselves might be marred by error or bias, and that these, too, would have to be assessed for credibility. Emphasis on firsthand observation, suspicion of hearsay, and stress on the need for credible witnesses thus reinforced the preference for those who wrote the history of their own times and the belief that those engaged in political affairs were best qualified to write political history. Both ancient and more recent historians, such as Machiavelli, Guicciardini, Davila, and Sarpi, who wrote contemporary history, were much admired.

A gradual change seems to have occurred, however, in the second half of the century. While retaining this belief that "conversation and familiarity" with the "insides of courts and the most active and eminent persons in the government" was essential, Clarendon indicated that records and state papers were also important.[71] Gilbert Burnet, a considerably more document-oriented historian, expressed identical sentiments.[72] Documentary materials increasingly supplemented firsthand information. Nevertheless, the Classical and Renaissance preference for firsthand reporting, reinforced by the preference for firsthand observation among naturalists and lawyers, continued despite the enormous gains in knowledge of the distant past and in the constantly increasing use of documentary evidence.

Many who did not themselves write contemporary history felt it imperative to preserve firsthand materials. John Rushworth, who produced one of the great document collections "for After Ages to ground a true history," insisted that speeches, letters, and relations of battles be collected while still "fresh in memory," in order to separate truth from falsehood and things real from things fictitious or imaginary. If documents were not accurately and promptly preserved, falsehood and error would inevitably creep in and produce false and inaccurate history.[73]

Initially, few historians appreciated the difficulties of writing contemporary history. Few suggested that, despite the fact that the most politically active people were likely to be the most knowledgeable and to possess the readiest access to evidence, they were also likely to be interested parties. Bacon, however, felt that the historian who wrote "after party heat had cooled down" was more likely to achieve "a more perfect history."[74] After an enormous amount of obviously partisan history had been written, an early eighteenth-century historian suggested that contemporaries were "least able to judge of the History of their own Times," and that no prudent writer should call the history of his own times "History."[75] A tension existed between impartiality gained by time and the presumed accuracy of firsthand observation. As eyewitness testimony came to be recognized as less than conclusive, greater reliance was placed on legal, governmental, and other documents, which increasingly were considered akin to firsthand evidence.

When conflicting testimony or documents presented themselves, the historian chose between two approaches. The first was simply to present the conflicting data, giving the reader the option of deciding what was most likely to be true; the second was to take upon himself the task of making judgments and drawing conclusions. Whichever approach was chosen, historians recognized that it was essential to weigh conflicting evidence and to consider the quality and quantity of the evidence. Something confirmed by several witnesses or in several documents was to be given greater weight, although one unbiased source might in some instances be sufficient.[76]

Historians now cited sources more frequently and even included relevant documents in the text, thus making evidence available to the reader. This practice might be considered roughly analogous to the criterion of replication in scientific experiment. Indeed, Gilbert Burnet, one of the first to include such lengthy documents did so on the recommendation of Sir Robert Moray, a leading scientist.[77]

Naturalists faced similar problems in similar ways. Firsthand observation and experience were valued most highly, but naturalists recognized that they, as much as the historians, were dependent on the reports of others. No one, for example, could hope to describe all the insects, birds, or plants of the world if he were to rely on his own observations. Thus, over and over again, Evelyn, Willughby, Ray, Edward Tyson, Plot, and others writing natural history insisted that they were relying on firsthand observation and credible reports, Evelyn noting that he would include only what he had seen himself or had "received unquestionable testimony for."[78]

Following the same approach to sources as the historians, the natural historians compared conflicting reports of distant and exotic habitats in order to improve the level of confidence in their findings. Both the civil historian dealing with political events of the past and the natural historian dealing with distant natural phenomena that he could not personally observe, were forced not only to rely on the testimony of others but to evaluate it for accuracy and trustworthiness.

The culmination of this approach is to be found in John Locke's *Essay Concerning Human Understanding*, which emphasized the integrity, skill, and purpose of the reporter, the number of witnesses, internal consistency, and the presence or absence of opposing testimony as crucial factors in evaluating testimony. With Locke, if not earlier, this approach became the common property of the English learned community. Although natural historians had certain advantages, since observations and experiments might be repeated, civil historians could present their data to their readers by citing or including documentary evidence. Burnet, for example, criticized a fellow historian for failing to indicate the location of the documents in question so that other historians might check them.[79]

Late seventeenth-century historical writing was often larded with citations and lengthy quotations that made it difficult to follow the narrative. Even the most obviously partisan history was likely to be full of citations to the sources. Robert Brady insisted the reader would thus not have to depend entirely on the "Integrity and Faith of the Author, for the truth of things Related . . . but matter of Fact laid down and warranted, by such as lived in the very times when the Thing was done or nearest to them, or by sufficient Record."[80] In addition, illustrations and engravings were included for the reader by both naturalists and antiquarians as a kind of evidence, being considered a means, albeit secondhand, of observing and recording the truth of "things."[81]

We must take a few moments to examine seventeenth-century attitudes toward documents because modern historians do not, as their seventeenth-century predecessors did, consider documents as virtually synonymous with the data of natural history. Collection and use of historical documents began late in the sixteenth century, following the Continental model. By 1625, many of the sources for the period 1066 to 1485 had been recovered, deposited, and made fairly accessible.[82] Calendaring and care of records was well underway and the libraries of Robert Cotton and others were immensely valuable and widely used by lawyers, antiquarians, and

143

historians. Printed collections of documents, such as those of John Rushworth, became surprisingly popular, and there was continued if sporadic pressure exerted to establish a public archive.

Thus, despite the preference for eyewitness accounts, historians increasingly began to feel it necessary to go through the "Many dark Lobbies and dusty places, before" reaching the "Great Hall of Light." It was necessary to "repair to old Archives and peruse many mouldering and moth eaten Records" in order to see "truth" through "our Ancestors eyes."[83] It was becoming a truism, at least for some historians, that history required painstaking research,[84] and that the clarity of firsthand observation might be almost recaptured by use of historical sources.

Not all historians took this view. Sir Philip Sidney, praising poetry over history, might be forgiven for his negative comments on "mouse eaten records," but Bacon, too, insisted that document grubbing was "somewhat beneath the dignity" of the true historian.[85] The seventeenth century engaged in an enormous amount of documentary research, but remained ambivalent about its ultimate value. Indeed, as the new document-based scholarship gained momentum, impatience was expressed with manuscript-based research. The ridicule of antiquarian scholarship, most striking in Sir William Temple, Lord Bolingbroke, and Voltaire, ran roughly parallel to the ridicule of the scientific virtuoso who foolishly engaged in microscopic investigation of fleas, lice, and other "unworthy" creatures. Early eighteenth-century ridicule of antiquarian research, however frequent, came from within the historical community, while that of the virtuosi came from nonscientists. The documentary and antiquarian approach to history, so important in the long run, was thus not adopted with complete enthusiasm.

In part, this countercurrent can be attributed to the concept of perfect history, with its goal of insuring that the general reader have access to historical scholarship in a readable, narrative format. The very success of philological and technically complex documentary history meant that the period of nonprofessionalized readership was passing in certain areas of learning. If scientists produced some popularizations, they did not often record their basic findings or present their hypotheses in a form particularly accessible and palatable to the general public. In the seventeenth century, history as a discipline became torn, as it still is, between the requirements of scholarship which often result in highly technical, monographic treatments of rather small topics or events based on documentary analysis, and the need for readable narrative. It was not until almost the end of the eighteenth century that Edward Gibbon demonstrated that it was possible to produce a thoroughly scholarly yet elegantly written history. The development of historical scholarship in the seventeenth century thus created a dilemma which, since there have been so few Gibbons, continues to haunt the historical profession.

Few seventeenth-century historians faced up to the task of historical analysis. Antiquarians dealing with nonwritten materials probably came closest to what a modern historian would consider "historical understanding" because they were forced to consider the meaning and significance of their nontestimonial finds. Perhaps because so many historians were lawyers, documents were often viewed as testimonies, whether or not they were the report of an individual. The task became one of authentication rather than analysis. Although a few historians recognized that the documents might contain false information or misrepresentation, most were more critical of live or recent "witnesses" than of documents. While recognizing that a contemporary report might willingly or unwillingly be biased, they often looked at the mere existence of documentary evidence as providing a truthful foundation for history. There are many references to "credible authors" and "credible testimony." If denial of the credibility of "monkish sources" was commonplace, most other documents were assumed to be adequate. Camden suggested that eyewitnesses to events keep diaries, since these would contribute toward the "History of those Times" by replacing the historians' "inferences from matters of fact."[86] The drive for "authentick" documents may have somewhat slowed down critical evaluation of nondocumentary source materials. A similar problem was related to the historian's use of the concept "experience." At times it was employed almost synonymously with "history," and at others with firsthand observation, which might or might not be incapsulated in a document. The nature of that "experience," once authenticated, was typically left unexamined.

Thus historians tended to treat each document as a unit to be tested for overall authenticity rather than as a collection of data, some parts of which might contribute to historical understanding. Despite the great achievements of historical scholarship based on documentary sources, the seventeenth-century search for historical truth and accuracy meant that "historical meaning" and interpretation played a subsidiary role.

Historians, natural and civil, constantly expressed their devotion to truth above all else. While the model of the historian as truthful

145

and "faithful recorder" was not new, the constant emphasis on truth seeking was, and Polybius, the ancient historian who most often enunciated this view, was preferred to other ancient historians. Any element of older historical writing which detracted from that ultimate goal became suspect.

This disposition led to efforts to dispel fabulous and legendary accounts of the founding of Britain. The "Romantic Fables" of Arthur and Brutus soon disappeared from history and, along with the giants and fairies which had made pre-Norman history in particular "look like Scenes of Fairy Land,"[87] were relegated to romance and fiction. "Authentick documents and antiquities" would now put English antiquity on a "firm and solid Foundation."[88] By mid-century, Milton was one of the few to express ambivalent feelings on the subject. Recognizing that myth and fable were excluded by "judicious Antiquaries," he felt that they contained, if not truth itself, at least the "footsteps of something true."[89] Milton therefore retained the Brute legend in his history of England, if only for the use of poets and rhetoricians, expressing the hope, however, that they would use it judiciously.[90] Naturalists, too, were anxious to eliminate the spurious. They removed fabulous and mythical beasts, as the historians removed legendary heroes. This task was not an easy one, however, because naturalists received descriptions of animal life from non-European sources that seemed as implausible as those being rejected as mythical.[91]

The problem of the "invented speech," however, which owed so much to the early intimate connection between history and rhetoric, was unique to civil history. Professional rhetoricians, who were among the first laymen to develop a taste for history, had assigned "appropriate" speeches of their own making to historical personages. These speeches, also justified by classical example, had proved particularly useful to historians wishing to draw particular moral and political lessons. Under the rhetorical canon, such invented speeches were permissible if they were plausible, that is, appropriate to the historical figure in question. Despite the fact that invented speech was still employed in the early seventeenth century by Bacon, Hayward, Lord Herbert, and "politic" historians more generally, approval of what was clearly fictitious waned rapidly. Increasingly, it was felt that the historian must not "fayne any Oration nor any other thing."[92] If speeches were to be included, they must be authentic ones.[93] Although historical writing had developed in alliance with rhetoric, that alliance was becoming strained. Verisimilitude remained a standard for poet and orator, but not for the antiquarian or historian whose goal was verity. The seventeenth century had little sympathy for flights of historical imagination.

If the search for historical truth required the elimination of fable and invented speech, it seemed even more obvious that prejudice and bias were inimical to the historian's task. Concern for impartiality was not entirely new, having been expressed by some ancient historians, but the concern had never before been so central or dominant. Indeed, it is difficult to find an historical work that failed to point out the dangers of prejudice and bias and the need for impartiality in the search for historical truth. The qualifications for the "faithful historian" were "fidelity, disinterest," and a "sincere Affection for Truth."[94]

Partiality and partisanship did not, of course, disappear. History was too closely tied to political, ecclesiastical, and theological controversy to live up to the standards which its practitioners so frequently and resoundingly proclaimed. Nevertheless, the dispassionate investigator had become the ideal for scientist and historian alike.

Some historians attempted to deal with the problem of bias. Rushworth, for example, thought that it was possible "to be of a Party, and yet not Partial." His not uncommon solution was to stick to "a bare Narration of matter of Fact" without interposing his "own Opinion" or "interpretation."[95] Selden's view was similar. History was limited to fact and phenomenon. Any expression of his own opinions and views would thus be inappropriate and violate impartiality. Historians were not to give a "verdict" on what they related.[96] If opinion implied partiality, it had no place in history.

Yet, such "bare narrations of matters of fact" included Andrew Marvell's obviously partisan *Account of the Growth of Popery and Arbitrary Government*,[97] and Gilbert Burnet's extremely biased *A History of My Own Times*. Only a few historians were truly sensitive to the danger of using "apparitions of Records, to justify the cause for which they wrote."[98] It was always easier to recognize partiality in the work of others, and Gilbert Burnet, who provides an excellent example both of the goal of impartiality and the inability to achieve it, noted that a great many recent histories were more like "Panegryick or Satire" than the impartial relation of truth.[99] The "Indifferency" which was the "Glory of Historians" was rarely achieved, however much lauded,[100] and statements of objectivity often screened polemical argument.

Nevertheless, the model held up for the historian was the impartial judge, not the partisan advocate. "Indifferency," the "Glory of Historians," was also the prime requisite of a judge, and partisanship in either was inappropriate and reprehensible.[101] History must be separated from advocacy, appeal to the passions, and the persuasiveness associated with rhetoric. Historical judgment must thus be free from both passion and advocacy. Yet, Thomas Sprat was one of the few historians who realized how difficult it was to "Write a plain History without falling sometimes unawares in its praise." He admitted that Part III of his own *History of the Royal Society* was a "Defense" or "Apology," not a true history.[102]

It was particularly difficult to avoid partisanship when dealing with religion and politics. Historians were most successful in avoiding obvious bias when they dealt with topics without obvious contemporary significance. For this reason, too, naturalists seem to have found it easier to approximate their goal.

But the continuity of the traditional rhetorical approach to history also played a role. Ciceronian rhetorical history had never been rejected as decisively or as explicitly as the scientists rejected Aristotelian physics or scholastic disputation. Its reputation was impaired, but not destroyed. Furthermore, there were elements in the Ciceronian position which, if they did not make truth telling absolutely central, at least indicated that nothing false might be included, and expressed distaste for flattery and hatred. This tradition, too, instructed historians to comment on the justice and injustice of causes.

If his investigative stance linked the historian increasingly with the scientist, the problems of writing narrative reinforced his link with the man of letters. Many of the technical and artistic problems of writing narrative were shared by the reporters of matters of fact and the new novelists.

There was, then, in the seventeenth century a tension between two views of history, one which related it to literature, morality, and rhetoric, and another which related it to science, the truthful and accurate recording of facts, and suspicion of rhetorical skills. The modern tension between the claims of art and science thus owes much to the seventeenth century which, perhaps for the first time, leaned in the direction of science, technical accuracy, and truth telling. Since that time, individual historians as well as historical epochs have inclined in one direction or the other. History, then as now, stood somewhere between science and rhetoric. The claims of accuracy and the goal of truth telling exist alongside those of readability, persuasiveness, significance, and literary grace.

The seventeenth-century emphasis on truth telling and the accurate narration of events implied that truth telling was possible. Such a view could not maintain itself in an intellectual environment in which skepticism ran deeply. If, in France, the skeptics' proclamation of the inevitability of bias led some to despair of any historical knowledge, the partially skeptical views of Bacon and others in England provided a more constructive sensitivity to the issue. Bacon's famous "Idols," echoed in the work of so many later writers, pointed out bias and distortion resulting from education, custom, and prejudice, as well as from the general fallibility of reason and the senses. The historical investigator, like the naturalist, must walk a difficult path between skepticism and dogmatism, frequently reminding himself and his readers of the necessity of impartiality in the investigator, the readers, and all those involved in collecting materials and making judgments on the matter at hand. Over and over, appeals were made to the "impartial judgment of unprejudiced Readers."[103]

If, on the one hand, interest and passion meant that historians seldom achieved the "impartial representation of the Truth" they sought, it was also recognized that they must try, and that some historical facts could be established with moral, if not mathematical, certainty. A mild but incomplete skepticism thus proved as beneficial to historical as to scientific effort. These benefits were explicitly recognized by John Selden, who noted that, while the skeptics would never admit "they had found a Truth" and were thus excessively scrupulous, they had found "the best way to search for any."[104] David Douglas has shown that the Restoration era was marked by the highest pitch of skepticism consistent with effort, and has linked this attitude with the enormous achievement of historical scholarship of that era.[105]

Historians were aware that explanations of the facts they verified might require speculation or theorizing that went beyond the facts themselves, which in some sense might be the creation of the mind or the imagination. The search for explanations and causes thus brought with it the dangers of a return to the imaginary, the fictional, and the unproved. Yet some practitioners in both the natural and historical sciences felt required to employ what they called "conjecture," "hypothesis," and "theory."

If the intellectual problem was a shared one, the two groups of intellectuals did not respond to the problem in quite the same ways. Historians were more likely to use the term "conjecture" than "hypothesis" or "theory," and used it for explanations offered when little or relatively little data or evidence were available. When applied under these circumstances, "conjecture" was sometimes associated with the fictional or imaginary, and might even be condemned on these grounds. But conjecture might also be used, as it was by John Selden, in the process of applying philological principles to documents, or as an estimation of general plausibility or probability.[106] Selden thus noted, "In conjectures I durst not be too bold . . . but when they seem to offer themselves, they deserve the choice of judgment."[107] Conjecture was thus not simply wild fancy. But exactly what it was is not so easy to say.

While it is fair to argue, as Frank Fussner has, that by the end of the century historical scholars had learned not to frame hypotheses on the basis of unverified facts, seventeenth-century historians were reluctant to discuss the nature of conjecture and hypothesis. Perfect history may have required explanation and causal analysis, but few historians devoted much attention to the intellectual processes or epistemological issues involved in making such explanations. Sir Walter Raleigh was something of an exception. He was concerned with the problem of causes, and recognized that all historians who examined things in terms of second causes were dealing in the realm of conjecture. He suggested that the line between valid inference and conjecture was a thin one, and that some conjecture or theorizing was inevitable. Camden also defended the use of conjecture, noting that it was needed in all the sciences. Spelman adopted the term "Theoreme" in connection with the interpretation of feudalism, employing it in much the same way as natural philosophers used the term "hypothesis."[108] Nevertheless, few historians made explicit their use of "theory" or "hypothesis" in offering historical explanations. For some historians, impartial relation of matter of fact was inconsistent with theory and even interpretation. Many simply asserted that the faithful historian was to report nothing but matter of fact and make no comments or interpretations of his own.[109] Others would present the relevent documents, asking the reader to assume the responsibility for drawing conclusions. If opinions were to be formed, many thought this function should be performed by the reader, not the historian. The reluctance to interpret and theorize was thus related to the goal of impartiality and a desire not to go beyond the facts. In this respect the historical community, like the scientific community, was divided as to whether theorizing or commenting on the facts was desirable.

The willingness of some historians to admit "plausible" or "probable" conjectures when the data were largely or completely absent suggests the continued use of the rhetorical concept of plausibility. Walter Charleton, one of the main promoters of the atomic hypothesis, offered his views on Stonehenge as a conjecture precisely because there were no credible facts to assist on the questions of dating and origins. He felt he had "reasonable grounds for a conjecture" which had the "Livery and colours of Truth," but did not claim he was offering the truth. At one point, he explicitly identified such speculation with "Opinion." He thus felt uncomfortable about rejecting the rival theories of Camden and Inigo Jones, insisting on their similar devotion to truth. He defended his own speculations saying, "it is no dishonor even to the best Marksman, not to hit the white, when he is forced to shoot in the dark."[110] In Charleton, then, plausible historical explanations retain their rhetorical origins and remain in the realm of unverifiable opinion. As the century wore on, the more document-bound historians felt somewhat uncomfortable with this practice but did not entirely abandon it. White Kennett was willing to offer some conjectures where the documents were lacking, but promised to keep them "short and modest."[111]

It is difficult to find historians who use the term "hypothesis," as did the scientific community, as a theory whose validity and usefulness is measured by the quality and quantity of evidence. The reluctance may have resulted from its early association with mathematical suppositions in astronomy. When Thomas Gale, an historian with scientific interests, used the term, he made it clear that hypothesis was not the same thing as conjecture. He offered:

fuller evidence and convictive Arguments, touching the veritie of this Hypothesis. . . . From so great a Concurrence and Combinations of Evidences . . . we take it for granted, the main conclusion will appear more than conjectural, to any judicious reader.[112]

His conclusions, then, were not mere conjectures, and he felt no embarrassment in referring to the "moral certainty" and "strong probability" of his hypothesis.[113]

Although naturalists began the seventeenth century with a Baconian distrust of conjecture, hypothesis, and theory, the attitude of many, as we have seen, had changed by mid-century. Mid-century scientists engaged in considerable theory building, although at the close of the century, Newton's pronouncements led some to renewed suspicion of moving beyond the limits of the data. The historical community, faced with somewhat similar methodological and epistemological problems, made far less self-conscious use of theory and hypothesis than did many of their scientific contemporaries. Many historians insisted on the necessity of historical explanation, especially for perfect history. Some felt that their explanations and conclusions must be based on careful analysis of factual data. Few were prepared to confront the intellectual processes involved in theory building or historical explanation.

The epistemological basis of historical and scientific thought was thus a partially shared one, although the historians were perhaps less self-conscious about it than the scientists. The overlap was most characteristic of the mid- and late-seventeenth century, when historical and scientific facts or data were seen as matters of fact, when scientific as well as historical theory emphasized probable rather than certain knowledge, and when history and physics were governed by similar methodological assumptions. This shared approach allowed both groups to discuss their hypotheses, conjectures, conclusions, and inferences in terms of greater or lesser probability, conclusions in both disciplines ranging from mere possibility to moral certainty. This link between the two communities, however, began to disintegrate during the eighteenth century. Then at least a portion of the scientific community, following Newton, again asserted that they were operating in the sphere of certain rather than probable knowledge, and a portion of the historical community returned to a more rhetorical and literary history, with its lack of interest in factual accuracy and antiquarian research.

In addition to overlapping subject matter and similarity of certain methodological assumptions, a number of other common elements linked historical and scientific communities. First, there is the overlapping membership of the two communities. It would be difficult to decide whether John Dee, Sir Henry Savile, Harriot, Lord Brooke, Bacon, and Raleigh, in the early period, and Aubrey, Plot, Ray, Charleton, and Thomas Gale, in the latter, belong among the historians or the naturalists.[114] When referring to sixteenth-century intellectuals, we often employ the term "humanist," which includes a wide range of interests. In dealing with the seventeenth century, we revert to more specialized terms: "poet," "philologist," "antiquary," "historian," "scientist," "virtuoso," and so forth. These terms obscure the fact that such knowledge was neither specialized nor professionalized, and that intellectuals still moved with relative ease from one kind of intellectual enterprise to another.[115] The scientific community might be unsympathetic to fabulous "history," but not to history.[116]

There are some suggestive, institutional similarities between the

Royal Society and the short-lived Society of Antiquaries (1586-1607). Both emphasized loyalty to the search for truth and insisted that no final or authoritative statements or decisions might be made by the group.[117] Members viewed themselves as investigators, not authorities. Historians as much as scientists emphasized the need for free inquiry, mutual criticism, and painstaking and laborious investigation. The two societies announced a common belief in progress and a consequent willingness to revise their views as more or better evidence was offered. Humility, whether real or feigned, became part of the ideology of all kinds of seventeenth-century intellectuals. Both organizations, no doubt to avoid any possible difficulties with secular and ecclesiastical authorities, officially excluded discussions of religious topics and matters of state, and both thought of the search for knowledge as an ongoing, cooperative enterprise.[118]

Although the stress on cooperative, intellectual enterprise is most often associated with science and the Royal Society, collective effort, albeit on a more modest scale, also characterized a good many historical enterprises. Camden's *Britannia* provides something of a model in this respect. Not only did Camden owe a great deal to the information collected by Leland and others, but he felt his own efforts merely "broke the Ice." He never considered the *Britannia* a finished work. His vision of an ongoing, cooperative enterprise continued to provide inspiration and direction after his death as subsequent editions were contemplated. In 1658, Sir Thomas Browne, a man of scientific and antiquarian interests, suggested the timeliness of a new edition. In 1673, a new edition based on the collections of "hundreds of experienced persons" was issued. The same year, "queries" for yet another revision were reviewed by John Aubrey, Christopher Wren, Gregory King, Sir John Hoskins, and Robert Hooke. Yet another cooperative revision was organized by Bishop Edmund Gibson. The fact that his scholarly team, too, included a significant number of contributors connected with the Royal Society again suggests the overlap between scientific and historical research.[119]

Other collective efforts were contemplated. Realizing the unlikelihood that any single historian would possess the requisite skills to produce the still-unwritten history of England, William Nicolson proposed a "club" of historians which would include specialists in ancient and modern langauges, specialists in the British and post-Conquest periods, and experts in geography and law. Though he concurred in the desirability of Nicolson's project, White Kennett

153

suggested a less ambitious substitute, a collection of separate histories which would cover the history of England. Kennett, a friend of Gibson, the coordinator of the 1695 *Britannia*, also hoped for a cooperative publication of English historical documents.[120]

Secular explanations became increasingly characteristic of both groups: we hear less of God's direct intervention in natural and historical processes and more of second causes. While both groups assumed the operation of God's Providence in the world, in practice they dealt with secular explanations and second causes.

A number of areas, then, point to a closer relationship between history and natural history in particular, and history and science more generally, than is conventionally thought to have existed. The relationship between history and natural science appears closest in the decades from about 1630 to 1700. In emphasizing natural history, we do not wish to suggest that natural history should be equated with natural science, nor that the enormous creativity of mathematicians and physicists should be ignored. Indeed, Thomas Kuhn's distinctions between the classical mathematical physical sciences and the Baconian sciences may be helpful here, for those aspects of scientific development which seem to be particularly closely related to historical thought fall primarily in the inductive category.[121]

First, there was the development of the genres which combined historical and natural materials and whose aim was to make accurate statements on matters of fact, both past and present. Second, there were developments in epistemology and methodology revolving around the concepts of certainty, probability, evidence, matters of fact, and impartial investigation which were shared by practitioners of the natural and historical sciences. Last, there were overlapping attitudes or institutional and intellectual styles largely deriving from the new probabilistic approach they shared, particularly humility, modesty, and cooperative effort.

HISTORY AND RELIGION

If the bulk of this chapter has been devoted to viewing historical thought in the wider context of natural history and natural philosophy, we would be remiss if we did not at least touch on the relationship between historical and religious thought. In doing so, we will briefly note the impact of new developments on ecclesiastical history and chronology, note the overlapping concepts of historical faith and religious belief alluded to in the last chapter, and point to some of the problems resulting from treating Scripture as an historical document.

Ecclesiastical history was gradually being absorbed into civil history, though theological controversy and denominational rivalries insured that it would continue to be a lively field of study. Historical controversies between Protestants and Roman Catholics, which had resulted in the *Magdeburg Centuries*, in Baronius's huge historical output, and in Sarpi's admired *History of the Council of Trent*, continued to inspire religio-historical scholarship. Anglican scholars from Jewel to Stillingfleet combined historical investigation and analysis with anti-Roman polemic. The attempt of many Anglican scholars to recover a primitive Protestant church staffed by bishops yet independent from Rome resulted both in an enormous amount of historical research[122] and in a growing sensitivity to the process of institutional development and change. The Anglican doctrine of "things indifferent," which condoned ecclesiastical variation resulting from differing times, places, and customs, produced an historical-mindedness not often shared by Puritan contemporaries, who were more wedded to pre-established biblical models of church government and worship.[123]

Bacon's suggestion that ecclesiastical history, once within the province of theology, be at least partially subsumed under civil history, was generally adopted.[124] Indeed, the connection between ecclesiastical change and English Reformation politics contributed to this awareness of the relationship of religion and politics. Camden's treatment of the reign of Elizabeth made clear the linkages between political and church history.

Values expressed by ecclesiastical historians now became the standard ones—truth and impartiality. A recent study has suggested that a new standard of impartiality had been established with Thomas Fuller's *Church History of Britain* (1655).[125] As in secular history, impartiality was more difficult to practice than preach. White Kennett and Gilbert Burnet, who were among the most scholarly research- and "truth"-oriented church historians, were far from impartial when it came to Roman Catholicism. Indeed, Burnet's *History of the Reformation* was even voted a public thanks by the House of Commons for its service to the Protestant cause.[126]

Ecclesiastical history was affected by, and contributed to, the importance of documentary evidence. Fuller not only begged documents and copies of documents but trudged the countryside in search of sources like any antiquary or naturalist, and Burnet advertised in the *London Gazette* for relevant manuscripts.[127] The desire to eliminate myth and fable was also felt. Stillingfleet's *Origines Britannicae* was designed to rescue church history from "Fabulous Antiquities."[128] Not surprisingly, several of the great ecclesiastical historians were associated with the Royal Society and admirers of the new science.[129]

So ecclesiastical history followed the course of secular history. Historical and religious faith became parallel phenomena. Belief in Scripture was to be subjected to the tests of historical belief. While explicit concern with this parallelism is most frequently found in the context of Protestant-Catholic polemic, it is also found in various rational defenses of Scripture against private revelation. By the end of the seventeenth century, the comparison between historical belief and scriptural belief had become almost a commonplace in some intellectual circles. While not exclusive to Anglican latitudinarians, the comparison seems to have been stressed most by those comfortable with a probabilistic basis for religious belief.

One of the lengthiest treatments is contained in Seth Ward's *A Philosophical Essay Toward an Eviction . . . of God.* A mathematician and astronomer as well as Anglican theologian, Ward attempted to deny enthusiasts' claims of private revelation and to defend the primacy and truth of scriptural revelation. He began with the by now familiar insistence that "demonstration" was inappropriate in such matters, and that assent to historical statements was very different from assent to mathematical propositions. A full chapter on the nature of "historical faith" was included in order to show that the same considerations govern belief in scriptural history as any other history.[130] Where improbable events were related, it was particularly important to evaluate critically the relators and the manner of their relation. First, one must determine whether the event in question was knowable and then assess whether "the parties had sufficient means" to obtain such knowledge, whether the relators were "eye or ear" witnesses, and whether the occurrences "were publically acted and known." The integrity of the reporter and the probability that he might have an interest in deception must also be considered.[131]

These principles, Ward argued, applied to all reports and all historical statements. It was on this basis that one believed that such cities as Rome or Paris existed without personally having observed them. The accounts of events by Caesar, Sallust, indeed all historians, were to be believed because the relators had the opportunity to observe the events they recorded and no one had contradicted their accounts. To be sure, historians might engage in fabrications, but there was little reason, given the lack of conflicting accounts, to doubt the events they reported. If it was madness to doubt secular history, it was surely even more unreasonable, Ward argued, to reject the "History of Holy Scripture." In what became the standard approach among Anglican ecclesiastics, Ward attempted to show that no impartial person could reasonably doubt the truthfulness of biblically reported events and matters of fact.[132]

The same line of argument based on the absence of "reasonable doubt" rather than absolute certainty was used by Stillingfleet to establish the greater certainty of scriptural history as compared to heathen histories. Moses, he argued, had knowledge of what he wrote, was an eyewitness, and his account was unbroken and uncontroverted. Moses, an impartial and truthful historian with no interest in deceiving, was thus to be believed.[133] Tillotson, another Anglican latitudinarian, adopted a similar approach in his refutation of the Roman Catholic claims that oral tradition was capable of greater certainty than Scripture. After making the initial argument that infallible demonstration was impossible in things of this nature, he insisted that Scripture was of far greater certainty than oral tradition. Like Ward, he stressed the similarity between belief in Scripture and belief in any historical statement or, indeed, any statement involving a report of matters of fact not personally observed.[134]

Miracles and other difficult to believe events were thus to be accepted as true on the basis of accurate reporting by faithful and unbiased reporters. The fact that one could not comprehend how an event occurred was not sufficient basis for rejecting such a central Christian "fact" as Christ's Resurrection. Even if one could not mathematically demonstrate many of these facts, one could, nonetheless, be "morally certain" that the events had occurred.

The comparison between historical belief and belief in scriptural history was not entirely novel in the seventeenth century, and can be traced through medieval and then Protestant and early Anglican theology. Its repetition, centrality, and elaboration, however, particularly by rationalizing Anglican divines, made it a characteristic feature of mid- and late-seventeenth-century thought. All accounts of matters of fact—scriptural, physical, or human—had to be evaluated according to what were then considered to be the strictest critical standards. By the early eighteenth century, this view had become a commonplace, and Joseph Addison reiterated the argument without comment. Pagan historians were guided by the common rules of historical faith, that is, they examined the nature of the evidence which was to be met with in common fame, tradition, and the writings of persons who related them, together with the number, concurrence, veracity and private characters of those persons; and being convinced, upon all accounts that they had the same reason to believe the history of our Savior as that of any other person to which they themselves were not actually eyewitness, they were bound by all the rules of historical faith, and of right reason, to give credit to this history.[135]

This approach, too, helped to reinforce the preference for contemporary history.

The emphasis on the truth of Scripture did not imply a narrow literalism. Most of the writers just mentioned would have agreed with Locke that one must attempt to understand the biblical text as one would any other historical text, that one must consider the plain meaning of the words and phrases as they were used in "that time and country wherein they lived," and that it was necessary to treat the text "without learned, artificial and forced senses," and avoid constructing "systems of divinity" from the text.[136] Indeed, Locke represents a culmination of this line of argument.

Insistence on the rationality of belief in the accuracy of Scripture, however, sometimes led to difficulties, particularly when natural scientists found scriptural statements which seemed to be at odds with the experience, findings, or speculation of contemporary scientific investigators or historians using nonbiblical historical evidence. As early as the 1620s and 1630s, Galileo and John Wilkins, his disseminator in England, were insisting that Scripture was not a source of natural truths and that God's penmen accommodated their language to ordinary use. For Galileo, Wilkins, Glanvill, and others, who wrote in support of Copernicanism, Scripture was intended to provide moral and religious truth, not philosophical speculation and theory.[137]

When it came to accounts of Creation and the Deluge, however, Scripture was defended as an accurate history of matters of fact. Sir Matthew Hale's *Primitive Origination of Mankind* (1677), one of many anti-atheistic works, insisted on the accuracy of the scriptural account of man's origin. In the process, he made the standard comparisons between secular and scriptural history. His investigations, some of them quite original, which dealt with chronology, population growth, linguistic change, the growth of technology, and the advancement of knowledge, were an outgrowth of his effort to show that mankind had indeed had a beginning in time, and that the scriptural account of that beginning was correct.[138]

The accuracy of the Mosaic account of Creation and the Deluge was explored at the turn of the century when a spate of publications, engendered by Thomas Burnet's *Sacred Theory of the Earth* (1681), considered various theories of the earth's formation and development. Virtually all of them insisted on the truthfulness of the Mosaic account and attempted to show the consistency of their respective hypotheses with the "facts" of Scripture and the "facts" of natural history. The difference of attitude between Wilkins and the biblically oriented "geologists" can perhaps be explained by the fact that Scripture dealt only incidentally with astronomy and very centrally with the Creation and Flood.[139]

Chronology, of concern to ecclesiastical historians, secular historians dealing with the ancient world, theologians, and geologists, made considerable strides by combining astronomical calculations with documentary sources, some scriptural, some secular. It was necessary to draw from both the Book of Scripture and the Book of Nature, which revealed the eclipses and other critical astronomical phenomena.[140] Thus Joseph Scaliger's combination of astronomical and Near Eastern sources, which derived primarily from philological scholarship, was not fundamentally different from the chronological studies of Newton and Whiston.[141]

Historians, theologians, and geologists dealing with the origins of man, the Creation, refutations of the eternality of the world, or the dating of fossils, all confronted the scriptural chronology. In most instances, Scripture was treated as an historical document, albeit a true one, and few would have disputed the statement that, for the period between the Creation and the Deluge, "We are informed by no other History besides Scripture."[142] Biblically oriented studies might result in elaborate calculations of the date of Creation and the minimum size of Noah's ark, as well as investigations of demographic growth and the development and dispersion of languages, learning, and the mechanical arts. If efforts to support the truthfulness of scriptural statements were linked to seventeenth-century theories of knowledge of matter of fact, biblically oriented studies also seem to have stimulated studies in the social, linguistic, and natural sciences.

CONCLUSION

This chapter has stressed the relationship between historical thought and both religion and science, particularly the latter. If the relationship between history and the natural sciences is as close

159

as we have suggested, it will be necessary to modify the traditional view that the humanities and the natural sciences belonged to different, and perhaps mutually exclusive, traditions. There is thus a need for a general re-evaluation of humanistic and scientific culture and scholarship in seventeenth-century England, a re-evaluation which would modify the views of a generation of literary scholars who have proposed a fundamental antagonism between science on the one hand and literature, religion, and the humanistic disciplines, such as history, on the other. Even if the notion of two conflicting traditions or cultures is to be maintained, history as a discipline belonged fully to neither.

The question, however, is not whether history as an intellectual discipline "really" belongs to the humanist literary tradition, or whether its connection with the scientific movement made it a science. What is important is that, from the seventeenth century to the present, history has partaken of and contributed to both traditions. In the seventeenth century, the period when history first clearly established links with both traditions, its practitioners more often emphasized its kinship with empirical science and repudiated certain aspects of the humanist rhetorical tradition. In the eighteenth century, the pendulum shifted back somewhat toward a more literary conception of history. In the nineteenth century, it moved again toward a rapprochement with the natural sciences and positivism. Since the seventeenth century, however, it has never shifted all the way in either direction. If some historians stress precision and accuracy of facts, and others aspire to the generalizations of the social sciences, still others emphasize the literary aspects of historical writing and the creativity of historical reconstruction.

Addison, an admirer of both science and literature, exemplifies the tension. On the one hand, he disassociated history from poetry and fiction, clearly identifying it with those "who are obliged to follow Nature more closely," that is, "Historians, natural philosophers, Travellers, Geographers, and . . . all who describe visible Objects of a real Existence;" on the other, he recognized that the historian required a special talent in presenting that reality. He admitted that the ability to describe a picture in a lively manner, so that the reader "becomes a kind of Spectator," required an ability to gratify the imagination, and this talent "shews more the Art than the Veracity of the Historian."[143] History somehow, for Addison, was to combine factual accuracy and literary artistry—"Art" and "Veracity." Just how this combination might be achieved remains a dilemma for the practicing historian, but it is a goal that suggests that the dual claims of literature and science continue to be an important legacy of the seventeenth century.

This approach to seventeenth-century historiographical development may be helpful in dealing with Frank Fussner's claim of an historical revolution in England running parallel to and linked with the scientific revolution. Others have suggested that a revolution occurred, but have seen it as essentially philological and have associated it with humanist textual analysis. Still others have denied that there was a revolution, viewing early modern historiography as a continuation of Renaissance humanism. Whether or not there was a revolution, there certainly was a continuation of the humanist tradition combined with a rejection of some of its rhetorical features, and that rejection, in turn, was made possible by the reorientation of the natural sciences toward probabilistic knowledge.[144]

Without that reorientation, which gave a new place to observation of facts and phenomena and associated them with truth and moral certainty, it is difficult to see how any elements of the humanist tradition could have come into contact with scientific studies. We must remind ourselves not only that the humanist tradition of the seventeenth century was somewhat different from that of the fourteenth and fifteenth centuries but that the scientific assumptions and methodology of the seventeenth century were different from those of the fifteenth or even the sixteenth centuries.

Reluctance to see the dual claims of humanism and empirical science may owe something to the fact that much of the best work on early modern historiography has centered on the origins of historicism. Praise and blame have thus been awarded to individuals or communities of historians who appear to move in the desired direction. While this scholarship has enormously enriched our knowledge of early modern historical craft and consciousness, its sensitivity to the period's growing relativism and recognition of the historical uniqueness of events leads us to ignore those aspects of seventeenth-century historical thought which moved in different directions.

In recent years, historians of science have recognized that seventeenth-century science cannot be understood simply by investigating those lines of thought which seem to lead directly to present science, and that to ignore or give demerits to hermeticism and magical interests of early modern "scientists" inhibits historical understanding of scientific development. Whether or not historians of historical thought feel that history is, or ought to be, a part of the humanities, seventeenth-century historians did form an alliance with the early modern scientific movement. The seventeenth-century emphasis on the centrality and provableness of historical facts is as significant as any nascent historicism.

The seventeenth-century re-examination of the problem of knowledge affected history as it did other varieties of intellectual endeavor. Although historical thought exhibited much continuity with early traditions of historical writing, the character of English historical thought was, at the same time, indelibly affected by changing theories of knowledge and research strategies. Indeed, its uneasy but continuing relation with both Renaissance humanism and the scientific tradition has been a characteristic feature of historical thinking since the seventeenth century.

V

Law

Law, no less than other disciplines, was affected by the changing conceptions of evidence that are the subject of this book. This chapter will describe the interrelations between lawyers and other intellectuals concerned with fact-finding, particularly historians and scientists. It will seek to show that certain ideas about proof, which were then becoming part of the general intellectual climate, shaped the development of the English law of evidence.

LAW AND HISTORY

In the Greco-Roman world, history and law were linked to the rhetorical tradition and normally contrasted with logic, which was thought to yield demonstrative knowledge or science. Rhetoric could yield only probable knowledge, judged by a standard of plausibility or cogency rather than truth. The orator, rather than the logician or philosopher, provided the initial European model for both lawyer and historian. The association of law and history with rhetoric was maintained in an attenuated fashion during the medieval period and was reaffirmed with the revival of classical studies in fourteenth- and fifteenth-century Italy. Indeed, it was the lawyers and notaries, whose professional work linked them with the Roman past, who took the lead in reviving and developing humanist studies.[1] Many of the most outstanding historians of the Italian Renaissance were connected with the legal profession. The names of Valla, Guicciardini, Biondo, and Sarpi are sufficient to remind us of the close connections between history and law in the Italian Renaissance.[2]

The application to legal materials of the philological, linguistic, and historical techniques developed by the humanists created a new school of jurisprudence. Under the leadership of Andreo Alciato, it insisted that critical methods might be applied to Roman legal texts as well as to literary ones. Although this school did not produce a purified Roman law for contemporary use, it did produce a more detailed and accurate knowledge of Roman legal and constitutional history. In a parallel development, French legal historians gradually abandoned the notion that a purified, classical Roman law was desirable for France. Their historical interests, however, did not remain fixated on Rome, and they came to view the contributions of the medieval centuries in a more positive light. As the chapter on history has already indicated, in the rhetorical tradition of which these legal historians were a party, emphasis on literary values and plausibility imperceptibly gave way to a search for truth, defined as some degree of moral certainty. Thus Continental legal scholarship tended to move from the literary analysis of classical texts toward an assessment of the accuracy of somewhat more recent historical data.[3]

Beginning in the sixteenth century, first in Italy and then in France, a group of legally oriented historians, deriving from Alciato, attempted the careful examination of evidence. Both as historians and lawyers, French scholars searched for reliable witnesses and sought to date documents and assess the good faith, knowledge, and credibility of those who initially had prepared them.

Legally oriented history, first in France and later in England, came to focus on the "ancient constitution." In order to determine what the early nature of the constitution had been and how it had been altered, historical-legal records were collected and critically examined. By the mid-sixteenth century, it became difficult to disentangle the techniques, methods, and values of historically minded lawyers from those of legally oriented historians.[4]

In England, this substantial interbreeding of history and law is best exemplified in the late sixteenth century by the Elizabethan Society of Antiquaries. The Society, which was dominated by lawyers and students from the Inns of Court, engaged in a wide range of historical studies. A substantial number of the discussion and research topics involved investigation of the laws, customs, and institutions of England. Professional familiarity with documentary evidence and techniques of historical proof became important for their historical studies, just as it had for French lawyers.[5]

Most of the active historical scholars and antiquaries of the late sixteenth century were connected with the Society of Antiquaries. William Lambarde, a lawyer and author of a popular handbook for justices of the peace, best exemplifies the Society's combination of legal and historical interests. Lambarde's historical studies focused not only on the history of English law and courts but extended to topographical studies. His *Perambulation of Kent*, the first county history, introduced the new topographical history to England.[6]

Sir Francis Bacon, a far more important lawyer than Lambarde, was equally at home in both legal and historical studies. In addition to his learned professional writings and activities, the Lord Chancellor wrote the most thoughtful of the period's discussions concerning the nature of civil and natural history, as well as one of the outstanding political histories of the era. Richard Braithwaite, associated with Gray's Inn, was the author of a number of historiographic works. Edmund Bolton, who also wrote on the theory of history, had legal training. John Hayward, a civil lawyer, was the author of a major historical work dealing wtih the reign of Henry IV. Sir Henry Spelman, one of the many lawyers connected with the activities of the Society of Antiquaries, is credited with being the first English historian to understand the essential nature of English feudalism.[7]

John Selden, one of the most learned men and respected lawyers of the era, was deeply involved in historical investigation, his *Historie of Tithes* being enmeshed in both legal and historical controversy. He explicitly took his terminology of historical proof from the courts. Historical facts, he insisted, like those accepted by courts, had to be established with a very high degree of certainty, if arguments built upon them were to have any validity.[8]

While Sir Edward Coke is best remembered as a lawyer's lawyer and not as an historian, we should not dismiss his historical interests. Much recent scholarship has attacked the lack of historicism among common lawyers like Coke who manipulated their findings about the past to serve their present interests. Such attacks, however, do not sufficiently distinguish between historical interest and activity, on the one hand, and modern historical consciousness, on the other. If the seventeenth-century English historians and lawyers lacked a modern historical sense, the Whig history they created was history nonetheless. Their research was still historical research, even if motivated by political and constitutional concerns. We must not dismiss the connection between law and history simply because we now have different notions of what professional historians ought to be doing. Together, common lawyers and historians made great strides in archival collection. Cotton's great library, which became the center for English historical research, was widely and regularly consulted by lawyers and historians alike.

In England, as elsewhere, constitutional problems provided a great stimulus to historical research. Coke and those of his persuasion chose to magnify the common law, Magna Carta, and the like to their advantage. Others searched the records to find precedents which favored the Crown. Both sides thus investigated the past, collecting and analyzing historical-legal documents. As long as political positions and theories were justified by conformity to some real or mythical "ancient constitution," historical research and constitutional argument would necessarily be linked. The relationship between law and history was thus particularly close during the pre-civil war era and remained strong during the Interregnum. Radical efforts to reform the law, for example, were again discussed in terms of the return to pristine Anglo-Saxon law.

Restoration historical thought and scholarship continued to be linked to the law. Judges Francis North and Matthew Hale during the Restoration era, and Geoffrey Gilbert in the early eighteenth century, suggest the continued relationship. North, Lord Guildford, one of the leading Restoration judges, was extremely involved in historical studies, joining with a number of judges and lawyers to collect public records and to promote their scholarly study.[9] North's historical judgments were often colored by political and constitutional preferences. He hoped to produce his own history of Parliament to counter that of Paul Foley, "a facetious lawyer."[10]

Sir Matthew Hale provides a more important example of lawyer-as-historian. Like many lawyers, his historical interests focused on English legal institutions. His *History of the Common Law* of England and his *History of the Pleas of the Crown* are monuments to both historical and legal scholarship. Hale's unpublished collections of Gloucestershire Antiquities suggest the wide-ranging character of his historical interests. Nevertheless, his historical research continued to be shaped by constitutional issues and political bias. The cult of England's "ancient constitution" remained the focus of many historical studies. Only Hobbes was willing to jettison the traditional alliance between history and law by establishing the latter on an abstract rational basis. Hale's response to Hobbes underlined the historical continuity of English law and helped to cement further the traditional relationship between law and history. Hale even implied that the lawyer's knowledge was historical knowledge.[11]

Although the historical learning of Sir Geoffrey Gilbert, whose legal scholarship dominated the early eighteenth century, could not rival that of his predecessor Hale, he, too, cast many of his legal works in historical format. His numerous posthumously published writings were, in fact, part of an effort to compass a "general History of the Courts of Justice."[12]

While we do not wish to suggest that seventeenth-century English historians and lawyers were engaged in absolutely identical tasks, they often dealt with the same materials—the documents of the past. Both groups were anxious to expand the store of ancient manuscripts, particularly those which bore on legal, ecclesiastical, and political institutions and privileges. A basic task of both lawyers and historians was the authentication of documents. In our earlier examination of historical technique, we saw the extent to which historians consciously adopted a lawyer-like role and legalistic figures of speech in seeing their work as that of determining the credibility and reliability of witnesses and documents. Conversely, the common lawyer, resting his analysis of legal institutions on the evidence of the ancient documents, necessarily affected the mantle of the historian. It is little wonder, then, that the lawyer-historian is a commonplace figure of English intellectual life.

LAW AND SCIENCE

While the link between law and history has long been apparent in English intellectual history, the links between law and the scientific revolution of the seventeenth century have not been so obvious. Yet they are certainly there. In this connection, we must first recognize that what we call the scientific revolution was not confined to a narrow group of professional scientists. Not only was there no such professional category, but those with scientific interests and accomplishments came from many different professional and non-professional groups. The philosophical and scientific ideas associated with Copernicus, Bacon, Descartes, Galileo, Boyle, Gassendi, Hooke, Ray, Locke, and Newton became the common property of the entire literate community of England, and certainly of the community of gentlemen to which the barristers and judges belonged. The change was not only in beliefs about the nature of the physical world but, more fundamentally, in beliefs about what methods were best for finding the truth, how certain men could be about the truths they found, and how they might best communicate those truths to one another. New modes of thought came to shape men's views of what was and was not common sense, of what was and was not well argued, and of what was and was not assumed to be true.

We need not, however, content ourselves with linking science to lawyers by way of the general category of gentleman. Several of the major legal scholars and leaders of the bar of that day were immersed in the new science, and these men not only viewed the two activities as compatible but frequently drew on the same central core of ideas for both their legal and scientific pursuits.

Perhaps most important, two major intellectual developments of the seventeenth century occurred almost simultaneously in law and science. The first was the drive for systematic arrangement and presentation of existing knowledge into scientifically organized categories. This concern for systematization is not only a characteristic of seventeenth-century English science but is also reflected in the first comprehensive and systematic treatises on English law—Sir Matthew Hale's *Analysis of Law* and *History and Analysis of the Common Law*.[13] Hale's work is part of the distinctly seventeenth-century concern for organized and simplified presentation in which he participated as both lawyer and scientist. A similar point could be made about casebooks and court reports, which are usually treated as purely independent developments. They began to flourish only after Bacon, again both a scientist and a lawyer, emphasized the need for the careful and accurate collection and correlation of data from which generalizations might be drawn.

The second major movement of the century shared by law and science was the concern with degrees of certainty or, in more modern terminology, probability. There was a new emphasis on the grading of evidence on scales of reliability and probable truth. In science, statements about the real world became probabilistic hypotheses. In law, an examination of the credibility of witnesses and a concern for truth beyond a reasonable doubt became the standard. Here, again, there are striking overlaps between the vocabularies and methods found in law and science, as well as in the actual persons employing these notions.

Law, then, like religion, philosophy, and literature, was touched by scientific and philosophic changes. We have already noted the pivotal role of Sir Francis Bacon, a central figure in the revolution and also one of the leading lawyers and jurists of his day; the connection between his leadership in science and his contributions to the legal profession and jurisprudential writing is not frequently noted.[14] Bacon was, of course, a lawyer by training and profession. He rose in turn to the posts of Solicitor General, Attorney General, and finally, Lord Chancellor.

Bacon's contributions to legal thought were closely connected with his scientific views. His approach toward both law and nature was inductive, for he argued that one should keep close to the particulars of each. The source of legal generalizations should be statutes and court cases rather than deductive reasoning.[15] Moreover, generalizations should not be of the highest order, such as statements describing the nature of justice, but those of the middle order, for these, he thought, were more productive in both natural science and the law. This inductive approach to legal maxims was novel, and Bacon, himself, thought it a new and distinctive path. He advocated the approach because he believed it would yield practical results in law as well as science; utilitarian considerations were never far from his mind. Through systematic analysis, Bacon hoped to make law into a useful "rational science." He expressed the common view that law should be in conformity with nature and reason, and to him, nature had a scientific as well as a traditional and moral connotation. For Bacon, then, the similarities between law and natural science were not coincidental. He insisted that the proper method of gaining knowledge was the same for all areas of inquiry, and that law was simply one branch of knowledge.[16]

Law and the new philosophical currents were also linked on the Continent. Grotius, a practicing lawyer who attempted to transform international law into a juristic science, was learned not only in the law but also in theology, philosophy, and astronomy. Samuel Pufendorf, another lawyer-philosopher, reflected on the similarity of findings of fact in a number of different disciplines, including "the Proceeding in humane Courts of Judicature."[17] And Leibniz emphasized his legal training as a source of his doctrine. It has been suggested that his approach to mathematical logic and degrees of truth and probability derive from a jurisprudential model.[18] Continental learned societies, such as the Académie Française, the Cabinet of the brothers Dupuy in France, and the Academia dei Lincei in Italy, dealt with legal and historical as well as scientific and philosophic topics.[19]

Philosophers such as Bacon, Grotius, Pufendorf, and Leibniz were not the only prominent legal figures to become associated with the scientific movement. Although Edward Coke and John Selden were more fully immersed in historical studies, they were not immune to the scientific developments of the day. Coke's library contained many books by prominent Elizabethan scientists, and Selden was an enthusiastic supporter of the new astronomy and of Samuel Hartlib's and John Drury's effort to instill Comenian ideas of scientific and educational reform in England.[20] There were many opportunities for lawyers and would-be lawyers to discover the new science. Not only was a very considerable proportion of the books published in the seventeenth century devoted to scientific subjects, but the Inns of Court were conveniently located near the Royal College of Physicians, the Society of Apothecaries, and Gresham College—the center of London scientific activity. At Gresham College, scientific lectures could be heard during the law terms. A fairly substantial portion of the upper classes who were associated with the Inns of Court were exposed to the fashionable pursuits of the day. These included not only attendance at sermons and theatrical performances but the study of anatomy, astronomy, geography, history, mathematics, theology, and foreign languages.[21] Thus, those who would actually enter the legal profession, as well as those who simply used the Inns as a fashionable club, were likely to be familiar with the substantial scientific activities and contemporary literature. The point is not that all of them engaged in scientific pursuits, but that a certain amount of familiarity with science was expected of a young man who wanted to cut a fashionable figure in society. By the late seventeenth century, lawyers were being advised that it was "a vast advantage" to include mathematics and natural philosophy as part of their education.[22]

The legal profession's participation in the scientific movement is also shown by the involvement of lawyers and judges in the founding of the Royal Society. Thomas Sprat praised the legal profession and noted that "many Judges and Counsellors of all Ages" were "ornaments of the Sciences, as well as of the Bar, and Courts of Justice."[23] John Aubrey even noted that "the first beginning of the Royal Society . . . was in the Chamber of William Ball [a jurist] in the Middle Temple."[24] Sir John Hoskyns, a well-known lawyer and a Master in Chancery, was one of the original members and was considered "a most learned virtuoso as well as a lawyer." He "became so far an adept" at "philosophy and experiments" that the Society "at last advanced" him "to be their President."[25] Sir Cyril Wyche, another prominent lawyer and one of the original members of the Society, also held the post. Henry Powle was still another legal figure in the ranks of the original members. Sir Robert Atkyns, one of the most learned lawyers and judges of his time, joined the group in 1664. Several Lord Chancellors—among them Edward, Earl of Manchester; Edward Hyde, Earl of Clarendon; Anthony Ashley Cooper, Earl of Shaftsbury; and John, Lord Somers—were members. Shaftsbury, the patron of John Locke, took a substantial part in the Society's affairs. Lord Somers, an eminent lawyer and politician who became Lord Chancellor, was active in literary and scientific circles and served for a time as president of the Royal

Society. He eventually gave up his post so that Newton might succeed him. Sir Geoffrey Gilbert also combined an outstanding legal career with scientific interests. Gilbert was not only Chief Baron of the Exchequer and the author of numerous legal treatises but was almost as famous for his mathematical accomplishments as his legal studies.[26]

While membership in the Royal Society did not necessarily mean serious participation in the scientific movement, it does suggest at least a passing knowledge of what the Society was trying to accomplish and probably some acquaintance with scientific publication. Some of the judicial members of the Society undoubtedly took little more than a *pro forma* interest in scientific matters. On the other hand, there were a number of major legal figures, such as Sir Matthew Hale and Francis North, whose scientific accomplishments were considerable but who did not become members.[27]

North, onetime Solicitor General, Attorney General, and eventually Lord Keeper, is an excellent example of the lawyer and judge as virtuoso. North was "a most knowing and ingenious person, and very skillful in Music, painting, the new philosophy, and Political studies."[28]

His lordship was an early virtuoso; for after his first loose from the university, where the new philosophy was then but just entering, by his perpetual inquisitiveness, and such books as he could procure, he became no ordinary connoisseur in the sciences, so far as the invention and industry, of then latter cricks, had advanced them.[29]

North cultivated the friendship of scientists, particularly the astronomer John Flamsteed, and even became involved in a scientific dispute with his judicial colleague, Sir Matthew Hale. The results of North's own work in hydrostatics were published in the *Philosophical Transactions* and gained the approval of Robert Boyle and John Ray.[30]

Sir Matthew Hale, the greatest lawyer of his day and the model seventeenth-century judge, was, like North, engrossed in the scientific discoveries of the period. Although not a member of the Royal Society, Hale was a close friend of its chief founder, John Wilkins, and numbered many of its members as intimates. Hale, who had become interested in mathematical and scientific studies at Lincoln's Inn, was not only "conversant in Philosophical Learning and in all the curious Experiments, and rare Discoveries of this Age" but collected scientific books and instruments and performed experiments to "recreate himself" when he tired of his legal studies.

Hale also developed considerable interest and skill in anatomy and medicine.[31]

Hale also contributed to the growing body of scientific and semi-scientific literature.[32] If his somewhat old-fashioned ideas failed to make a serious scientific contribution, they did exhibit a sensitivity to problems of scientific philosophy and method. Hale distinguished two approaches to finding scientific truth. The first begins with observations of the senses, proceeds to experimentation, and ends by constructing theorems to explain the experimental results. The second was deductive. Its foundation lay in speculation and its followers manipulated natural phenomena in accordance with their hypotheses. Hale, himself, favored the inductive approach because he felt that practitioners of the deductive method tended to distort the data to fit their hypotheses.[33]

The linkage between law and science in Hale is far more extensive and important than his scientific theory alone would suggest. His considerable contributions to English jurisprudence are marked by an approach in accord with the best canons of theorizing and data collection then current in the scientific community. The basis of his legal scholarship is an inductive method that emphasized the collection of data and the construction and reform of legal principles based on cautious and tentative theorizing from past experience. Thus, in Hale, we find a combination of systematic presentation and the urge to reform and modernize on the one hand, and, on the other, the rejection of radical changes in law based on abstract rational systems, such as Hobbes's. While legal scholars have been accustomed to think of this combination as peculiar to the tradition of the common law, Hale's position is not only a part of that tradition but typical of the approach followed in the most advanced intellectual circles of his day—circles in which he, himself, played a conspicuous part.

Hale is best remembered for his attempts to systematize the law. Legal scholarship, however, has not usually recognized that his interest in such systematization was in harmony with, and perhaps even an outgrowth of, the virtuosi's effort to classify natural knowledge. Though Hale's legal classifications were the most sophisticated that the seventeenth century produced, they were not unique. John Wilkins also attempted, perhaps with Hale's assistance, to organize and classify "judicial relations" in the course of his effort to organize all knowledge into a systematic and philosophically sound system. The systematizing work of Hale, so frequently viewed as part of the progress of an essentially autonomous legal discipline, was thus related to the scientific culture of his day; a concern for classification and systematic communication was a general feature of seventeenth-century intellectual life.

There can be no doubt, then, that many leading lawyers in England were familiar with, and participated in, major intellectual movements of the sixteenth and seventeenth centuries. In the area of evidence and proof, these intellectual movements clearly influenced the development of the law itself. Judges and lawyers, no less than philosophers, scientists, historians, and theologians, had a major commitment to finding methods and procedures which best elucidated and established truth. In order to understand the basis of this commitment, we must briefly trace the evolution of European methods of legal proof.

Although most of Europe in the early medieval period shared a common framework of legal assumptions and procedures, a major divergence occurred in the later medieval period. By the early modern period, England and the Continent possessed quite different legal systems and institutions. Among the several forces contributing to this divergence was a crisis in the technology of legal proof. Trial by ordeal and trial by battle, which dominated legal proceedings all over early medieval Europe, did not involve an attempt to try causes by rational means. Proof of a litigant's assertion was left to God, who would decide which party was telling the truth. Dissatisfaction with the outcomes of ordeal and battle developed, as victory rarely seemed to coincide with justice and right. Such trials also increasingly came to be considered irrational, particularly by churchmen trained and skilled in intellectual matters. Official condemnation of the ordeal in 1215 by the Lateran Council forced secular jurisdictions to find more rational modes of evaluating evidence brought into court. The canonist procedure, which had already established itself in the ecclesiastical courts, was increasingly adopted by many secular jurisdictions on the Continent as a rational and available alternative. The substitution of one procedure for another was not simply the result of ecclesiastical command. It occurred because society, or at least that portion of it which controlled political and legal institutions, no longer found trial by ordeal intellectually and morally satisfying. Alternatives were thus sought which would conform more closely to ideas of what was rational, fair, and practical.

France, and indeed most of the European continent, adopted and then further developed and refined what is traditionally called the "Roman-canonist approach" or "rational modes of proof." Although there is considerable scholarly dispute as to precisely when and how the transformation took place, and over the respective contributions of the Roman law of Justinian's age, canon lawyers, and medieval civilians in the process, it is clear that the new procedure came to dominate Continental jurisprudence.[34]

Basically, the Roman-canon inquisition process was a system of inquiry, operated by professional judges, designed to obtain "full proof" defined by clearly established evidentiary standards. As a result, Continental procedure was based on rigidly specified rules as to the quality and quantity of proof. There were rules giving prescribed weight to testimony based on the number, status, age, and sex of the witnesses. The testimony of high status and propertied persons was ranked higher than that of the poor and lowly. Exclusionary rules were developed to disqualify the testimony of the litigants, relatives, and interested third parties. An exactly specified number of witnesses was required to prove a fact.[35] In criminal trials, full proof consisted of confession confirmed by the testimony of two good witnesses. Once full proof had been achieved, conviction was automatic. A great deal of faith was thus placed in the formal fulfillment of evidentiary rules and relatively little room allowed for judicial evaluation of the substance of the evidence.

The system of proofs involved a kind of numerical calculation, the judge being a kind of accountant who totaled up the fractions. Every evidentiary element was assigned a set value which, when added together, either constituted or did not constitute a full proof. One "unexceptional" witness, for example, constituted a "half proof"; a doubtful one, less than an half. One doubtful and one unexceptional witness, therefore, added up to something more than a half-proof but not a full proof. Other types of evidence, such as "common fame" or private, as opposed to public, documents, also were considered half-proofs. Civil procedure, even more than criminal, emphasized proof fractions and thus became a kind of numerical jurisprudence.[36] In criminal causes, one witness—no matter how good or how reliable—could never result in conviction. Without a confession, two witnesses were absolutely essential. In this way, the law encouraged and, indeed, often required, the torture of the accused in order to produce a confession, which was considered of particularly high evidentiary value.

Complex evidentiary rules determined whether there was sufficient evidence to justify judicial torture. They defined a system of "indications," "signs," and "presumptions" of various weights. In each case, the judge would establish whether the amount of this circumstantial evidence constituted "sufficient presumption" to proceed to torture. No matter how compelling these presumptions, however, they were not sufficient to convict. Indeed, they went only to the threshold question of torture and could not be considered at all in determining the guilt or innocence of the accused.

This system of "rational" or "legal" proofs left little room, at least in theory, for judicial evaluation or discretion. When the appropriate indices, signs, presumptions, or proofs were present, the judge had no choice but to torture or convict. The complexity of the evidentiary rules resulted in an enormous expansion of the judiciary and the virtual elimination of laymen from the legal process. Method of proof thus might have an enormous impact on the development of a legal system and the size and character of the legal profession.[37]

It has been suggested that the rigorous application of the mechanical process which characterized Continental courts was being undermined in the sixteenth and seventeenth centuries and replaced, at least in criminal cases, by free judicial evaluation of evidence, which is considered characteristic of English trials. John Langbein argues that sixteenth- and seventeenth-century French judges often circumvented the whole system of legal proofs in criminal cases by imposing arbitrary punishments, such as galley service, solely on the basis of circumstantial evidence, that is, on the indices and presumptions which technically were not considered proof at all. The judiciary, he argues, thus escaped both the proofs and torture, and based their judgment on "preuves considérables," freely evaluated by judges on the basis of subjective persuasiveness. Thus he argues that the law of proof was being severed from its traditional dependence on confession, evidence, and torture and came to approximate the kind of persuasive evidence standard that English juries were thought to apply.[38] France, he suggests, really possessed two systems of proof in the area of serious crime.[39] Although Langbein has clearly demonstrated that arbitrary punishments, such as galley service, were often imposed by judges who circumvented torture, it is not clear that a new theory of evidence actually came into being. It is just as likely that the notion of "presumptions" simply remained and that, where the presumptions reached a high level of sufficiency, they triggered a sentence to the galleys rather than a judicial order to torture.[40]

In England, the rejection of ordeals and other "irrational" proofs led to the development of trial by jury. Initially, trial by jury required little in the way of rules of evidence. Jurors, men of the neighborhood, were assumed to know the facts of the case and to incorporate their knowledge in the verdict. In civil cases, the facts tended to be quite restricted, involving only a single legal issue. Juries thus did not have to concern themselves with all the facts of the case, but only a small portion of them. The only critical factor thought to be essential in obtaining a fair trial was insuring that the jury was not biased in such a way as to purposely falsify its verdict. Criteria, probably derived from canonist practice, were therefore employed to exclude potentially biased relatives and other interested parties, and property qualifications were established to promote the jury's independence.

Initially, the adoption of the jury was itself a surrogate for the development of rules of evidence. Knowing most of the facts and confined by the pleadings to narrow issues, a jury could arrive at findings of fact guided by common sense and common knowledge. Thus the canonist evidentiary system, whose complexity required professional judges applying technical skills, was the very obverse of a jury system that relied on the everyday experience of laymen who could not be expected to master such complexity.

In the late fifteenth and early sixteenth centuries, several developments subtly altered English trials and created the need for some kind of law of evidence. By the sixteenth century, juries were no longer so likely to be familiar with the facts of a case. As society became more complex and as mobility increased, juries increasingly came to rely on the testimony of witnesses for information. A major turning point seemed to have occurred in 1563, when legislation created a legal process for compelling the attendance of witnesses and made perjury a crime.[41] Without giving up their right to consider their own personal knowledge in reaching a verdict, juries increasingly relied on witnesses and documents which they now had somehow to evaluate for truthfulness and accuracy. Grand jurors seem to have been placed in a similar position. They, too, were increasingly in the position of third parties who had to employ their rational and analytical faculties to reach conclusions about facts and events they had not personally witnessed or known.

From at least the mid-sixteenth century, too, justices of the peace began to play a substantial role in investigating crime, examining suspects, and determining whether there was a case to be sent to the grand jury which would, in turn, decide if the case warranted trial. These tasks, made part of the justices' duties by the Marian bail statutes, seem to have required some evaluation of the evidence given against the accused by a variety of informants.[42]

176

By the mid-sixteenth century, grand jurors, trial jurors, and the justices of the peace were necessarily faced with the problem of how to deal with the variety of evidence and testimony presented to them. The response to the new legal environment was slow and halting, perhaps partially obscured by the fact that, legally, juries could still give verdicts based on their own knowledge.

Nevertheless, the law of evidence that slowly evolved throughout the seventeenth century was clearly discernible by the beginning of the eighteenth century. When it did finally emerge, it had been shaped not only by political and legal tradition and ideology but by the enormously active and fruitful intellectual environment of the seventeenth century which affected lawyers and nonlawyers alike.

Although the English did not in general look with great favor on the Continental approach to evidence, the early stages of the effort to cope with the new evidentiary environment are occasionally marked by Continental influence, though, to be sure, the English never considered adopting the elaborate and mechanical system of "legal proof." Some elements seem to have been employed in the pretrial procedure, and were therefore unlikely to show up in later textbooks on evidence. The Continental doctrine of presumptions seems to have provided handy guidelines for justices of the peace, now routinely engaged in examination of criminal suspects. Both Lambarde's and Michael Dalton's much reprinted handbooks for the justices enumerated appropriate "suspicions" or "presumptions," which look very much like Roman-canonist "indices" of character, age, wealth, status, companions, life style, and "ill fame."[43] These presumptions which, if present in sufficient quantity, would be followed by torture on the Continent, in England became guidelines to the justices in the pretrial functions. Richard Kilbourne's 1680 handbook, for example, discusses "probable Presumptions" as "good Causes of suspicion, and sufficient for a Justice to commit the Persons suspected."[44]

Several leading English thinkers, including Coke and Hale—jurists who could not have been more protective of English procedure—occasionally borrowed Continental language. In contrasting trial by witness and trial by jury, Coke used the terminology traditionally associated with the former. Judgment was the verdict of twelve men:

and upon such evidence is given to the jury, they give their verdict. . . . And many times juries, together with other matter, are much induced by presumptions; whereof there be three sorts, viz. violent, probable and light or temerary, *Violenta praesumptio* is manie times *plena probatio*; as if one be runne throw the bodie with a sword in a house, whereof he instantly dieth, and a man is seen to come out of that house with a bloody sword, and no other man was at that time in the house. *Praesumptio probabilis* moveth little but *praesumptio levis seu temeraria* moveth not at all.[45]

Coke's language is rarely cited by later writers dealing with jury verdicts. Instead, it appears in handbooks for justices of the peace as a basis for "sufficient case of Suspicion."[46] Coke himself was at times uncomfortable with the concept of presumptions. Commenting on a case in which a man was wrongfully executed upon presumptions, he indicated he had reported the "case for a double caveat, first, the judge, that they in case of life judge not too hastily upon bare presumptions."[47]

Englishmen were, of course, familiar with Roman-canonist evidentiary concepts and terminology since they, or some variant, were employed in the ecclesiastical and admiralty courts which were largely staffed by civil lawyers trained in Roman law procedure and doctrines of proof. Chancery and Star Chamber procedure also owed something to Continental models.[48] Yet, the English did not adopt these models in the common law courts not only because trial by jury had initially provided a reasonable alternative but also because of political and constitutional ideology. From at least the time of Fortescue, English political and legal writers not only praised trial by jury but were markedly hostile to the use of torture, the absence of juries, and private rather than public trials which characterized Continental practice. These, together with distaste for the *ex officio* oath increasingly associated with Continental procedure and autocratic government, made adoption of the Roman-canonist system unlikely. Given the adulation of the jury,[49] political ideology, and the absence of any desire or ability on the part of the Crown to provide a large professional legal bureaucracy, it is not surprising that the English, while occasionally employing the language of the civil law, moved in a very different direction. Only in witchcraft trials do we see significant use of Continental concepts.

When legal thinkers, laymen, and philosophers began to deal with legal evidence, they quite naturally thought that it was to be subsumed under their general theory of evidence and knowledge and thus did not attempt to deal with it separately. John Wallis, a mathematician and one of the founding members of the Royal Society, easily linked law and history with other inquiries dealing with matters of fact:

Likewise among historians and among judges in legal cases themselves (where an inquiry is directed towards a matter of fact), a strong presumption and a great probability as to the happening (in the absence of infallible proof) suffice for settling a very great many questions; and, in doubtful matters, the major probability should prevail over the minor.[50]

This statement suggests how the concept of probability was increasingly associated with the weight of evidence and not merely with plausibility.

Robert Boyle, in describing the differing degrees of certainty and probability to be ascribed to mathematical, physical, and moral demonstration, noted that men's actions were in the realm of probability and used "the practice of our courts" as a vivid example:

For though the testimony of a single witness shall not suffice to prove the accused party guilty of murder; yet the testimony of two witnesses though but of equal credit, that is; a second testimony added to the first though of itself never a whit more credible than the former, shall ordinarily suffice to prove a man guilty; because it is thought reasonable to suppose, that though each testimony single be but probable, yet a concurrence of such probabilities (which ought in reason to be attributed to the truth of what they jointly tend to prove) may well amount to a moral certainty, i.e., such a certainty as may warrant the judge to proceed to the sentence of death against the indicted party.[51]

Boyle also indicated that this approach could be applied to witnesses:

You may consider . . . that whereas it is as justly generally granted, that the better qualified a witness is in the capacity of a witness, the stronger assent his testimony deserves . . . for the two grand requisites, of a witness [are] the knowledge he has of the things he delivers, and his faithfulness in truly delivering what he knows.[52]

Locke, too, in the course of his discussion of various kinds of evidence and the levels of certainty they produce, dealt with the evaluation of testimony and, like Boyle, easily saw the applicability of this approach to the law. For example, both he and Boyle noted that an attested copy of a record is good evidence that an event occurred, but that an unattested copy is not as good. The testimony of a witness is good evidence that an event has occurred, but "a report of his report is not and will not be admitted in a court of law. The further from the source, the weaker the evidence becomes."[53] Thus, sophisticated laymen felt that the rules for determining the truth in legal matters were the same as those in other areas of investigation.

Judges and lawyers also found that current philosophical theory suited their needs. Lord Nottingham, for example, while Lord Keeper, used the language of certainty quite naturally when he defended the King's Declaration of Indulgence in 1673: "A Mathematical security we cannot have: a moral one we have from the King."[54] John Selden also suggested the mutual borrowing of theory between fields. When discussing the truths of history and methods of historical proof, he turned to the terminology of relative certainty and reasonable doubt.[55]

More significant, however, in demonstrating the application of the theory of certainty to legal thinking is Sir Matthew Hale's *The Primitive Origination of Mankind*. Here, Hale categorized knowledge in much the same way as his friends Tillotson and Wilkins. He was most concerned with the evidence for matters of fact. Although the evidence of the senses was the "best evidence" in these matters, it was obviously inapplicable to "things transacted before our time, and out of the immediate reach of our Sense." Here, only "moral and not demonstrative or infallible" evidence was available. Yet a "variety of circumstances renders the credibility of such things more or less, according to the various ingredients and contributions of credibility that are concentered in such an evidence."[56] To elicit assent, it was necessary to weigh:

the veracity of him that reports and relates it. And hence it is, that that which is reported by many Eyewitnesses hath greater motives of credibility than that which is reported by few; that which is reported by credible and authentic witnesses, than that which is reported by light and inconsiderable witnesses; that which is reported by a person disinterested, than that which is reported by persons whose interest it is to have the thing true, or believed to be true . . . and finally, that which is reported by credible persons of their own view, than that which they receive by hear-say from those that report upon their own view.[57]

Such evidence might be "of high credibility, and such as no reasonable man can without any just reason deny."[58] While, in this instance, Hale utilized these concepts principally in the context of history and general knowledge, he readily transferred them to law. "That evidence," for example, "at Law which taken singly or apart makes but an imperfect proof, *semiplena probatio*, yet in conjunction with others grows to a full proof, like *Silurus* his twigs, that were easily broken apart, but in conjunction or union were not to be broken."[59] Hale's comments also suggest that the legal doctrine of proof beyond reasonable doubt owed a great deal to religious efforts to prove religious principles beyond reasonable doubt.

Similar concerns existed on the Continent. Leibniz attempted to establish degrees of probability for legal findings and, more generally, to develop a logic for contingent events. He, too, rejected Jesuit-style probabilism[60] for a theory of probability which linked degrees of probability with degrees of certitude, his aim being to develop a logic of probability "derived from the nature of things, in proportion to what we know about them."[61] Such propositions might not be established with certainty, but it might be possible to measure the extent to which data warranted inference.[62] Although probability theory is, for modern thinkers, linked to concepts of mathematical probability, at least one modern philosopher has suggested the similarity between nonmathematical concepts of probability and the Anglo-American approach to legal proof.[63]

The first English treatise devoted entirely to the problems of legal evidence, that of Sir Geoffrey Gilbert, followed the same approach as the rational theologians, the scientists, and Hale. Gilbert's *Law of Evidence*, which, viewed exclusively in the context of legal scholarship, has often been treated as revolutionary, in fact represents an advance only in explicitly employing the seventeenth-century doctrine of certainty as the central basis for a systematic treatment of legal evidence.[64] Moreover, its purpose was not to reform, but to describe the state of the law at the time the treatise was written, and it was not actually published until nearly three decades after Gilbert's death. Thus the work, which might casually be taken as introducing the doctrine of certainty into law in the middle of the eighteenth century, actually suggests the earlier widespread judicial adoption of that doctrine.

The work begins with a discussion of the "rules of probability" by which evidence offered to the jury "ought to be weighed and considered." Citing the observations of that "very learned man," John Locke, who, as we have seen, outlined a probabilistic theory of knowledge, Gilbert notes that:

there are several degrees from perfect Certainty and Demonstration quite down to improbability and Unlikeness, even to the Confines of Impossibility; and there are several Acts of the Mind proportioned to these Degrees of Evidence, which may be called Degrees of Assent, from full Assurance and Confidence, quite down to Conjecture, Doubt, Distrust and Disbelief.

Now what is to be done in all Trials of Right, is to range all Matters in the Scale of Probability, so as to lay most Weight where the Cause ought to preponderate, and thereby to make the most exact Discernment that can be, in Relation to the Right.

Now to come to the true Knowledge of the Nature of Probability, it is necessary to look a little higher, and see what Certainty is, and whence it arises.[65]

He proceeds to discuss certainty in terms of sense perceptions and necessary inferences from fixed data.[66] Since most litigation depends on transient data "retrieved by Memory and Recollection . . . the Rights of Men must be determined by Probability."[67] Probability is then considered in terms of degrees of credibility of witnesses and the point at which their statements of facts could be accepted without "any more reason to be doubted than if we ourselves had heard and seen it."[68] This line of thought was subsequently adopted by Blackstone and incorporated into nineteenth- and twentieth-century texts on evidence, where, of course, it is still to be found.[69]

Hale's and Gilbert's treatment of questions of evidence and matters of fact is in accord with the most advanced thinking of the period. Both were aware that contemporary developments in epistemology and scientific method were having an impact on law and saw their own work as a vehicle of that impact. Given the pervasiveness of these ideas in the intellectual community of the time, a community in which the lawyers participated, they could not have immunized themselves from developments in the theory of relative certainty that occurred in the scientific, philosophical, historical, and religious fields during the seventeenth century.

The failure of legal historians to acknowledge the seventeenth-century contribution can be explained in several ways.[70] There is a major gap in legal historical scholarship between the medieval period and the mid-eighteenth century, and a resulting tendency to assume that medieval conceptions continued to rule until they were suddenly replaced at the point where legal historians pick up again. In the realm of evidence, part of the difficulty no doubt arises from excessive concentration on rules of procedure and admissibility of evidence rather than principles of proof—the ratiocinative process of continuous persuasion that Wigmore recognized as of far more importance than rules of admissibility.[71] Concern with this latter process has been very limited, and Wigmore felt himself to be the first scholar since Bentham to call attention to the principles of proof as distinct from admissibility. It is this area that "bring[s] into play those reasoning processes which are already the possession of intelligent and educated persons."[72] Yet, it is also

precisely the area of persuasion and belief that changed so substantially in the course of the seventeenth century. Because such
matters of evaluation lie largely in the habitual patterns of thought
of judges and juries rather than in the formality of procedure, they
leave few skeletal remains in the form of changes in rules of admissibility. Yet, there can be no doubt that the major shift in intellectual climate created by the introduction of notions of probability and relative certainty in historical, theological, and scientific
discourse played an important role in shaping English legal practice
long before Gilbert recorded them, and certainly long before the
publication of his work in the middle of the eighteenth century.

Still another reason that these seventeenth-century developments
have been obscured is the notion that a sophisticated and consistent
treatment of the law of evidence could not develop until the jury
had ceased to be witnesses as well as judges of matters of fact.[73]
Yet Sir Matthew Hale, whose highly developed views on probability
and certainty of evidence we have already examined, announced
these ideas at a time when he was still permitting jurymen to know
and present information somewhat in the manner of witnesses. He
sought to harmonize his two positions by arguing that additional
information contributed by jurymen could be used to improve the
court's assessment of the credibility of ordinary witnesses.[74] The
transition was thus quite slow. Although, technically, juries could
know things on their own, in practice, they rarely possessed knowledge which bore on the case. In 1650, a judge ruled that jurymen
who wished to present evidence must be heard on oath in court
like any other witness.[75] Two years later, the judge in Bushell's Case
(1670) ruled that jurors could still act on their own knowledge.[76]
And this continued well into the eighteenth century. Thus, the new
ideas on evidence had come in long before the old jury practices
went out.

It has also been suggested that the medieval practice of treating
all evidence given under oath as of equal weight continued into
the eighteenth century.[77] Some residues of the older notions undoubtedly did survive, but seventeenth-century judges and juries
clearly made judgments about credibility. Locke's six criteria for
evaluating testimony—"the number of witnesses, their integrity,
their skill at presenting the evidence, their purpose, the internal
consistency of the evidence and its agreement with the circumstances, and lastly the presence or absence of contrary testimony"—
and John Wilkins's statement, "and as for the evidence for Testimony which depends upon the credit and authority of the Wit-

nesses, these may be so qualified as to their ability and fidelity,"[78] are echoed in greater or lesser degree in the legal literature and in several important cases of the period. In *The History of the Common Law*, Hale made several comments that suggest how well-established was the notion of credible, as opposed to merely lawfully sworn, witnesses during the Restoration period. He noted that the testimony of legal witnesses can be attacked "either as to competency of the evidence, or the competency or credit of the witnesses."[79] If the jury has:

just cause to disbelieve what a witness swears, they are NOT bound to give their verdict according to the evidence, or testimony of THAT witness. And they may sometimes give credit to ONE witness, though opposed by more than one. And indeed it is one of the excellencies of this trial [the jury trial], above the trial by witnesses, that although the jury ought to give a great regard to witnesses and their testimony, yet THEY ARE NOT ALWAYS BOUND BY IT; but may either upon reasonable circumstances, inducing a blemish upon their credibility, though otherwise in themselves in strictness of law they are to be heard, pronounce a verdict CONTRARY to such testimonies; the truth whereof they have JUST cause to suspect, and may, and DO OFTEN, pronounce their verdict upon one single testimony, which the Civil Laws admits not of.[80]

The jury "are to weigh the Credibility of Witnesses and the Efficacy of their Testimonies."[81] Hale's *The History of the Pleas of the Crown* similarly notes the distinction between legal and credible witnesses, indicating that the jury is to judge the "probability or improbability, credibility or incredibility of the witness and his testimony."[82] It is in the context of this approach to evidence that Hale noted the superiority of the jury trial over civil law procedure. The former was "the best Method of searching and sifting out the Truth."[83] The ability to question witnesses in open court was also very important because it permitted judge and jury to observe contradictory testimony and increased "Opportunities" for "the true and clear Discovery of the Truth."[84] Juries were thus enabled to "weigh the Credibility of Witnesses, and the Force and Efficacy of their Testimonies," uninhibited or "precisely bound to the Rules of the Civil Law," which required "two Witnesses to prove every Fact . . . nor to reject one Witness because he is single, or always to believe Two Witnesses if the Probability of the Fact does upon Circumstances reasonably encounter them."[85] Trial by jury, Hale insisted, was far superior to its civil law and equity rivals not only with respect to "cheapness," "dispatch," and "certainty," but especially as a means "to investigate the Truth."[86]

The distinction between credible and lawful witnesses became increasingly common, particularly in the latter part of the seventeenth century. Although Coke did not discuss the matter at any length, he notes that a partial and interested witness may be sworn, but jurors "who are tryers of the fact" will consider "his credit upon the exceptions taken against him."[87] A legal writer in 1663 noted that jurors might doubt "the clearness and veracity of positive statements," and a 1681 tract clearly distinguished between legal and credible witnesses.[88] Standards for doubt often turned on the credibility and impartiality of witnesses.

Judge Hale, summing up evidence for a jury, noted that a witness was "a person, I think, of no great Credit."[89] In a 1681 case of assault and battery, the defense counsel indicated that "we shall prove (by substantial and credible men) that not one blow was given."[90] In 1679, Lord Chief Justice North also distinguished between lawful and credible witnesses,[91] and, in a 1696 conspiracy trial, the judge instructed the jury to consider the "Fairness and Crediblity" of the evidence that was given.[92]

In cases where certain defense witnesses were not permitted to testify on oath, the notion of credibility also appeared. The Solicitor General, summing up the evidence in the case of Lord Mohun before the House of Lords, noted that the peers were to believe the defendant's witnesses, though not under oath, "so far, as your Lordships shall Judge was said Credible, about Consideration of all that you have heard."[93] Several of the numerous Popish Plot trials turned on the question of the credibility of the witnesses. When the defendant Langhorn, himself a lawyer, indicated that his "whole Defense must run to disable the witnesses," and that he could "have no defense unless it be by lessening their Credit,"[94] Lord Chief Justice North advised him: "Do lessen it if you can." In the process of his defense, Langhorn further noted that "If I can Disprove a Witness in any one material thing that he says then it will take off from his Credit in every thing he says." In summing up, North instructed the jury that it must judge the credit of the witnesses on both sides—those who had testified under oath, as well as those who had not been so permitted.[95] Just a year earlier (1678), Judge Scroggs, too, had instructed the jury "to be governed . . . according to the credibility of the person and the matter."[96] In the famous treason trial of Algernon Sidney (1683), the Lord Chief Justice told the defendant: "If you can give any Testimony to disparage the witness" or "that they are not Persons to be believed, do it."[97]

Juries had serious obligations in the truth-finding process. They were to go over the evidence carefully, making notes if necessary.[98] They were to judge whether "any Matter is sworn, Deed read, or offered, whether it shall be believed or not, or whether it be true or false in point of fact."[99] In the process, they were to consider whether there might be any possibility of "Subornation, foul practice, or Tampering" with witnesses, and whether they "have any Malice or sinister Design."[100] They must have "special regard to the Circumstances or Incoherences of their Tales, and evidence." By "apt questions," they were to "sift out the Truth." They were even to consider whether the judges had summed up the evidence "trully, fully, and impartially." In the end, it was they who must "be fully satisfied in their Consciences."[101] A fully satisfied conscience obviously involved a good deal of careful, reasoned thought.

The transition to evaluation of testimony for credibility, if definite, was not always smooth, and older notions continued to jostle the new. Some time after the 1679 conviction of the Earl of Stafford, it became clear that "Very few, if any, of the peers that condemned him would own that they believed the witnesses who swore the treason against him."[102] When Judge North, who was appalled at such statements, "expostulated with some of them" as to how they could have "declare[d] him guilty," they replied they were "not free" and had been "bound to judge according to the proof of the facts." Since the witnesses had "sworn the facts," they felt they had no choice but to accept them.[103] The indignant Judge therefore informed them:

that this was contrary to the very institution of trials; for it is the proper business of peers and juries to try not the grammatical construction of words . . . but the credibility of persons and things; which require collation of circumstances and a right judgment thereupon; and God forbid that the worst Villains should have it in their power, by positive swearing, to take away a man's life or estate . . . if you believe the witnesses find, else not.[104]

Attitudes toward oaths seem to have been involved in this instance. Increasingly, however, testimony under oath was no longer assumed to be truthful. Oaths, in general, were not taken as seriously as they had been in earlier centuries. No doubt the growing concern over perjury was linked to declining belief in the awesomeness of the oath. Yet, in all these matters, change came slowly. Only after 1691 could defense witnesses in treason trials be sworn. This privilege was extended to all felonies in 1707. Before the eighteenth century, defense witnesses in criminal cases "spoke upon their Credits," not upon their oath.[105] But long before 1707, the testimony of witnesses for defense and prosecution was being evaluated for credibility in substantially the same way.

In a related development, the employment of multiple witnesses testifying as to the same event lost its oath-helper quality and became, instead, a means of improving the scientific certainty of judicial fact finding. Hale suggests:

> If to any one quantum of fact there be many but probable evidences, which taken singly have not perchance any full evidence, yet when many of those evidences concur and concenter in the evidence of the same thing, their very multiplicity and consent makes the evidence the stronger; as the concurrent testimonies of many Witnesses make an evidence more concludent.[106]

Isaac Barrow and Robert Boyle, writing in another context, indicated that the preference for a larger rather than a smaller number of witnesses was based on considerations of probability.[107] Thus, although the rhetoric of oaths and the multiplication of witnesses may not have been substantially altered between the thirteenth and seventeenth centuries, their meaning and significance in the evidentiary system were imperceptibly changing.

The newer views are particularly evident in several late seventeenth-century court decisions in which judges sought to distinguish levels of proof needed for various kinds of cases. The recorder in a 1681 case insisted that in assassination cases, "exact and positive proof" was unattainable, so that the court "must not expect it should be so clear as in a Matter of Right between Man and Man."[108] In the trial of Carr for publication of a libelous book, this position was even more clearly elaborated. The presiding judge argued that "you very well know, that Evidences of Fact, are to be expected according to the Nature of the thing."[109] Forgery could not be proved in the same way as the sealing of a document because witnesses were not ordinarily present: "in things of that nature, we are fain to retreat to such probable and conjectural Evidence as the matter will bear."[110] In cases involving murder, juries should not expect "a direct Proof of the Act of the actual Killing; but yet, you [have] such Evidence by Presumption as seems reasonable to conscience."[111] The judge therefore advised the jury:

> You must take Evidence in this case, as you do all the Year long; that is, in other Cases, where you know there is an absolute certainty, that the thing is so: for human frailty must be allowed; that is, you may be mistaken.

For, you do not Swear, nor, are you bound to Swear here, that he was the Publisher of this Book: but, if you find him guilty, you only Swear, you believe it so.[112]

The jury was, therefore, instructed to reach their verdict "according to reason and the probable Evidence of Things."[113]

Similar issues arose in the context of grand jury proceedings. Here, too, the problem must have been generated by instances in which grand juries were required to reach decisions based on the testimony of witnesses. We begin to see discussion of what kind of evidence should result in an indictment. While indictment usually seems to have involved a lower standard than that required for conviction, there was no clarity as to what that standard was. In 1681, for example, C. J. Pemberton advised the grand jurors reviewing the evidence against Shaftsbury that the petty jury, not they, would evaluate the credit of the witnesses. Several grand jurors, however, disagreed, arguing that if they were not permitted to consider the credibility of the witnesses, they would be unable to satisfy themselves about reaching an indictment.[114]

The pamphlet, *The English Man's Right* (1680), which first appeared in the context of the Popish Plot excitement, again raises these issues. The author, Sir John Hawles, a leading barrister who eventually became Solicitor General to King William III, rejected the notion that grand jurors were to be mere passive recipients of the allegations brought by accusers. Instead, like other investigators, they must be men of "understanding and integrity, indifferent and impartial."[115] Their task was to "search out the truth" from the information brought to them and to reject indictments "not sufficiently proven." "Diligent inquiry" was essential if they were to adequately investigate "as to the time, place, and all other Circumstances of the Fact alledged." They must, for example, thoroughly inquire into the character, reputation, and probity of all witnesses in order to evaluate their credibility. Indeed, they must take advantage of all means available "to make a more exact and effective Enquiry and to present the whole truth," and must not be overly deferent either to judges or prosecutors.[116]

Hawles combatted various "vulgar errors." Among them was the notion that the oaths of grand and petty jurors implied the application of different standards of proof. He suggested that the former had the advantage in the truth determination process because grand juries could summon persons and papers themselves and could examine witnesses for conflicting testimony. As for the proofs, the principal and most certain is the Juror's personal knowledge, by their own Eyes and Ears. . . . Or so many pregnant concurring Circumstances, as to fully convince them of the guilt of the accused. When these are wanting the Depositions of Witnesses and their Authority are the best guides in finding Indictments.[117]

Another error to be disposed of was the idea that grand juries were to inquire less strictly than trial juries and might indict on a "Superficial Inquiry, and bare Probabilities." If such a view were adopted, there would be no difference between arraignment and presentment.[118]

It is interesting for our purposes that the author felt it necessary to preface his remarks with a discussion of the term "probable," a term obviously undergoing considerable modification in meaning and usage during these years. Insofar as it was given its traditional association with rhetoric and opinion, that is, as it related to "propositions" having only "an appearance, not certainty of truth," it was to be completely rejected in the courts. The "probable" might be appropriate to the rhetorician who "works on the passions," but should be forbidden "where the object is truth."[119] The "best judicatures of the world" thus

utterly reject the use of Rhetorick, looking upon the Art of persuading by uncertain probabilities, as little differing from that of deceiving, and directly contrary to their ends, who by knowledge of Truth desire to be led into the doing of Justice.[120]

Guided by the rhetorician's use of the term, juries would soon be led to consider "the more or less probable, or what degree of probability is required to persuade them to find a Bill: This being impossible to fix, the whole Proceedings would be brought to depend upon the Fancies of Men." If, on the other hand, "probable" was employed according to common usage, it was equally offensive, for it "signifies no more than likely, or rather likely than unlikely." While wagers might be "good grounds for betting in a Tennis court, or at a Horse Race," they had no place in a court of law. Thus, the notion that all that grand juries required for Indictment is "a Verisimilar or probable charge" is roundly rejected.[121]

Yet, Hawles is clearly influenced by the new thought about probability, although he does not identify that word with the concept that there may be degrees of certainty. For instance, he says that legal decisions are incapable of "infallible Mathematical demonstration." Juries make their decisions on the basis of a satisfied conscience. They "often find that which in their Conscience, doth fully persuade them, that the accused person is guilty. . . . They don't swear the Bill is True, but that they in their Consciences believe that it is so."[122] Justice, in fact, "must be built upon these moral assurances."

Hawles seems to be just at the tipping point between the older, rhetorically based notions of probability and the newer ones that are the subject of this book. Condemning the "merely probable" and "slight proofs" on the one hand, and the quest for absolute certainty on the other, he is reduced to expressing the newer, middle ground in terms of "conscience" and "moral assurances," where some of his contemporaries were speaking of degrees of certainty, probabilities, as well as satisfied conscience and belief beyond reasonable doubt.[123]

Statutes, particularly those concerned with treason, also exhibit the growing concern with problems of credibility and standards of proof. While sixteenth-century statutes confined themselves to demanding the testimony of "lawful witnesses,"[124] the revised treason statute of 1661 required "two lawful and credible witnesses."[125] In effect, the later statute instructed the jury to evaluate the testimony it received. The statute of 1696 was even more rigorous in its demands of proof and in the opportunities it afforded the accused for his defense; it has been characterized as embodying "almost the difference between medieval and modern."[126] In 1697, the Blasphemy Act provided that conviction be based on the testimony of two or more credible witnesses.[127]

Closely related to this more sophisticated approach to evidence was the increasing concern for the impartiality of judges to be found after the Restoration. Judicial practice might still have been far from ideal, but the judicial model shifted more and more from the prosecuting servant of the Crown toward the detached seeker of truth. By the end of the century, impartiality was expected of judges as much as of scientists. One measure of the change is the contrast between the acceptance of the highhanded judicial behavior of Coke and the indignation inspired by the behavior of Jeffreys and Scroggs.[128] It should thus not be totally unexpected that Sir Matthew Hale, one of the most scientifically inclined judges of the period, was so widely acclaimed as an ideal judge. It was Hale's impartiality that made him famous in his own day.[129] Hale's rules for his own conduct on the bench included laying aside his "passions and not giving way to them however provoked," eliminating "prepossessing with any judgment, till the whole business and both parties be heard," and "reserving himself unprejudiced till the whole be heard."[130] He evidently concealed his views so carefully that other judges sitting with him could not determine his position.[131]

Judge Holt, the most respected judge of the next generation, was most often praised for his impartiality and concern for evidence. Indeed, the movement to insure the irremovability of judges owed much to the growing sentiment that security of judicial tenure and judicial impartiality were closely related.[132]

We do not wish to suggest that the idea of judicial impartiality was a creation of the seventeenth century but only to indicate that those most affected by the new views concerning the search for truth were most sensitive to the ideal of impartiality. Isaac Barrow provides a good example of what was expected of judges:

A Judge should never pronounce final Sentence, but . . . upon good grounds, after certain proof, and upon full conviction. Not any slight conjecture, or thin surmise; any idle report, or weak pretence is sufficient to ground a Condemnation upon: the Case should be irrefragably clear and sure before we determine on the worse side. . . . Every Accusation should be deemed null, until both as to matter of fact, and in point of right, it be firmly proved true; it sufficeth not to presume it may be so; to say, It seemeth thus, doth not sound like the voice of a judge. . . .

Moreover, a Judge is obliged to conform all his determinations to the settled rules of Judgment, so as never to condemn any man for acting that which is enjoyned, or approved, or permitted by them; he must not pronounce according to his private fancy, or particular affection, but according to the standing Laws . . . he that proceedeth otherwise, is an arbitrary and a slippery Judge . . . a Judge should be a person of good knowledge and ability; well versed and skilful in the Laws concerning matters under debate; endowed with good measure of reason, enabling him as to sift and canvas matters of Fact, so to compare them accurately with the rules of right. . . .

Lastly: It is the property of a good Judge to proceed with great moderation, equity, candour and mildness.[133]

Restoration judges do not seem to have been entirely clear as to whether they ought to comment on the evidence presented in their court. Hale's *Pleas of the Crown* was explicit in stating that judges, in addition to directing the jury in matters of law, had the duty "in matters of fact, to give them great light and assistance, by his weighing the evidence before them, and Observing where the Knot of the Business lies; and by Showing them his opinion even in matters of fact."[134] As a judge, however, Hale apparently sometimes did and sometimes did not perform this task.[135]

Writing in 1680, Hawles noted that judges "do often recapitulate

191

and sum up the Heads of the evidence," but claimed that juries were not required to accept the judge's views. The judge, he thought, should present the evidence in a "hypothetical, not coercive" way. "If you find thus or thus . . . then. . . ."[136] After making the conventional point that judges might not know everything that the jury does, he insists that judge and jury could honestly differ "in the opinion or Result from the evidence," as, of course, could different judges.[137] In this instance, one suspects that this late emphasis on the independent knowledge of the jury, which no longer reflected actual experience, was introduced to bolster the independence of juries against judicial dictation, particularly in politically relevent cases.[138]

Roger North, a leading Restoration jurist, was uncertain about appropriate judicial behavior in such matters. Commenting on the Popish Plot trials which were widely criticized in later years, he noted favorably that the judges, Scroggs excepted, had been essentially "passive." They had not interposed "their opinion of the evidence" which he recognized "is often done by judges for the assistance of the jurymen in common trials; and many in later times have thought that the same ought to have been done here."[139] He attempted to excuse the judges on the grounds of the political nature of the trials in question and the general upheaval of the times, which had made the judges rather "let a vessel drive which they could not stop."[140] Yet, he remained somewhat unsure whether a judge should be essentially passive or whether he should more actively assist the jury in the truth-winnowing process.

These discussions of judge and jury are highly revealing in their assumption that evidence is to be evaluated rather than witnesses counted or proofs, in the Continental sense, introduced. The ideal of impartiality and impartial fact determination did not automatically provide precise rules for judges, any more than the ideals of scientific and historical impartiality prescribed precise rules for scientists undertaking experiments or historians attempting to reach conclusions from documentary evidence. All of these discussions, however, were touched by, and responded to, the demand for careful and impartial fact finding and for conclusions carefully derived from those facts. All cautioned against overambitious claims of certainty based on inadequate or "merely" probable evidence.

Although the scarcity of sixteenth- and seventeenth-century legal records makes it difficult to generalize with confidence about the development of the law of evidence, it is obvious that evidentiary matters had to be dealt with, and that decisions based on matters of fact had to be made. As it was increasingly realized that obtaining the truth about matters of fact was not a simple matter either in theory or practice, rules and practices were developed to deal with witnesses, jurors, testimony, and judicial behavior, all of which were aimed at refining the process of reaching truth. Philosophical theories, particularly those developed by Wilkins, Boyle, Locke, and others roughly in the same tradition, played a substantial role in this process. Concepts borrowed from this tradition were applied in the legal sphere, first somewhat haltingly by Hale and North, and later more confidently by Gilbert and his successors. By the eighteenth century, the English legal community possessed a law of evidence that not only provided practical rules adapted to a jury system which routinely employed the testimony of witnesses but was felt to rest on a sound philosophical basis. The philosophical underpinnings of Locke and the treatises of Gilbert thus firmly established a tradition which has been modified since only in particulars. Later authorities on legal evidence, from Sir James Stephen and Wigmore to current writers, routinely attempt to base their treatises on what they consider the best theory of knowledge of the day. Contemporary law journals concern themselves not only with the practical problems relating to the law of evidence, but also attempt to deal with these problems in terms of modern empirical philosophy, and even notions of mathematical probability. The "fit" between philosophy on the one hand, and legal procedure and the law of evidence on the other, is rarely perfect, the latter being greatly influenced by the force of tradition and the difficulties of practical application. Yet, at least since the late seventeenth century, it has been felt that these should be at least roughly compatible, and that determinations of fact in the courtroom should not be too far divorced from what are considered to be the soundest means of evaluating factual evidence in the scientific disciplines.

Statements of historical causation are notoriously difficult to formulate or, at least, to prove. We do not wish to argue that the developments in science, or history, or theology caused developments in law. But parallel developments in so many areas of thought make it equally foolish to assert the autonomy of law. It is enough to say that in seventeenth-century England, certain aspects of legal thought developed as an integral part of the intellectual life of the times, and that religion, science, and philosophy were such a central part of that life that their influence was felt by all who thought and wrote.

VI

Witchcraft

THE FACT that witchcraft was a crime as well as a phenomenon and thus had to be proved to a learned judge and an unlearned jury, as well as being subjected to the scholarly inquiries of scientists and theologians, provides an unusual opportunity to observe theories of evidence at work. For the courts, witchcraft was a matter of fact and, like all questions of fact, turned on the nature and sources of the testimony, including in some instances the confession of the accused. During the course of the seventeenth century there was a marked decline in English prosecutions and convictions. That decline seems to have been somewhat retarded, however, by differing standards of evidence held by the diverse classes of participants in the judicial process. Those classes included justices of the peace, judges, grand jurors, and trial juries and exhibited wide variations in their depth of exposure to that new body of ideas about the probable that is the subject of this book.

We now know a good deal about the social role and substantive content of witch belief and the rise and fall of legal prosecution of witches, both in England and on the Continent, in the early modern era.[1] The discussion which follows will touch on recent scholarly research only insofar as it relates to theories of knowledge and changing standards of evidence and proof.

Seventeenth-century witch belief cut across lines typically labeled scientific, philosophical, religious, and legal. Witchcraft simultaneously involved one's views of God and the Devil, explanations of the operation of the physical world and how one might comprehend its operations, the nature of matter or substance, the relationship between matter and spirit, how one reached reliable information of any past event, and the appropriate means of proving that a capital crime had occurred. The machinery of·justice was thus called upon to evaluate testimony about various events and

194

occurrences, and to attempt to determine who, if anyone, had employed diabolic or supernatural means to harm another individual.

Although prosecutions for witchcraft had occurred with some frequency during the medieval period, a greatly increased rate of prosecution characterized the early modern period. Both learned discussion of and prosecution for the crime, which, on the Continent, tended to be associated with heresy, grew rapidly all over Europe during the fifteenth and sixteenth centuries, regardless of differences in religion, geography, nationality, or legal tradition.

In England, the practice of witchcraft and conjuring with spirits became a statutory crime in 1542. This legislation, which emphasized *maleficium*, or harm done, rather than heresy, was replaced in 1563 with a harsher statute which made it a capital crime to invoke evil spirits, even without maleficent activity. This statute was replaced in 1604 with one meting out still harsher penalties. It required the death penalty, even if the victim did not die, and added a compact with the Devil as a necessary component of the crime. Although popular English witch belief centered on *maleficium*, that is, in harm to the bewitched, legal proof of the crime now increasingly came to focus on the diabolic compact.[2] Curiously, the harsher act of 1604 may itself have contained some seeds of decline. It has been suggested that the statute's emphasis on the compact helped push aside the formerly adequate presumptions, and replaced them with stricter standards of proof. In any event, it now became necessary to prove the compact itself. Evidence thus came increasingly to center on use of a familiar, the existence of a devil's mark on the witch, and the confession of the accused. Critical or skeptical investigators, however, might find familiars to be ordinary pets, the witch mark a natural growth, and confession a delusion. The necessity of proving the diabolic compact may thus, itself, have contributed to the increasing English acquittal rate, especially since without torture confessions were not often forthcoming.[3]

During the period in which legislation was enacted and enforced, belief in witchcraft was very widespread among literate and illiterate alike. Without the support of the parliamentary class, which had made the legislation possible, and the willing participation of justices of the peace, grand juries, and judges, there would have been neither statute nor enforcement. The beliefs of these particular groups were therefore crucial. For when they ceased to believe in witchcraft or, more significantly, that it could not be proved with sufficient conclusiveness, enforcement would end and the statute become inoperative. Although the statute was not repealed until 1746, rapid decline in enforcement can be charted from the mid-decades of the seventeenth century.

A number of factors thus must be considered. The first involves the operation of the English legal system, the second, changes in standards of evidence as applied to witch belief. English prosecutions involved a number of different processes, each involving a different set of people who might hold different beliefs and make decisions according to different critical standards. The first stage typically involved the justice of the peace, who heard the accusation, examined the accused, and collected the relevant testimony. His views and his methods of collecting evidence were thus important. A second decision was made by the grand jury as to whether there was sufficient evidence to present or indict. The grand jurors' views on the nature of evidence and proof and how to handle testimony would have considerable bearing on whether they recorded an *Ignoramus* or *Billa vera*. Only in the latter case would evidence be presented to a trial jury, who would then determine whether there was sufficient evidence to prove that a crime had taken place and that the accused was guilty of that crime. The presiding judge, too, might play a substantial role in shaping this decision. If a guilty verdict appeared to involve a great injustice, he might use his influence to obtain a reprieve. Thus, the opinions of the educated classes, from which the judges, the justices of the peace, and the grand jurors were drawn, would have an enormous impact on both the prosecution and conviction rate. On the other hand, if the case actually came to trial, the views of the less educated trial juries also played an important role. Some attention to the juries' views on fact finding and fact evaluating procedures is also essential to charting the decline in witch trials.

It is probably no accident that both the high point of witch belief and its decline occurred during a period when traditional standards of knowledge were undergoing rapid transformation. Witch belief and prosecution were at their height at a time when the natural world, indeed the entire universe, was viewed as being full of magical and mystical powers, when the physical and spiritual were difficult to distinguish, and when the line between scientist and magician was difficult to draw. We should thus not be surprised to find that those who held this world view should also accept the notion that individuals were capable of employing supernatural powers for both good and evil purposes. The fifteenth and sixteenth centuries were also those in which hermetic and neo-Platonic

196

doctrines, with their notions of spiritual substance, were at their most popular. If the decline of witchcraft does not precisely coincide with the adoption of the new science and the mechanical philosophy, the decline of neo-Platonism and the development of belief in an orderly world, created and kept in motion by an everpowerful Creator, left little room for the activities of witches and other beings capable of wielding supernatural powers, either on their own or in cooperation with good or malevolent spirits. The orderly mechanical world of the scientists of the mid- and late-seventeenth century left even less room for the supernatural.

The decline, however, also coincides with the heightened concern for methods of establishing truth and sifting evidence which was so characteristic of the seventeenth century. Even witch trials exhibited a clear concern for conclusive proof. The search for witch marks and the like, often by respected physicians, was a search for needed empirical evidence. Keeping an accused awake for unreasonable lengths of time to obtain a confession and keeping a sharp watch for familiars were steps undertaken precisely because they were thought to provide appropriate evidence. When such proofs as confessions or the sighting of familiars were taken at face value, convictions were likely to occur, especially given the community pressures which produced English witch accusations with considerable regularity. But as Englishmen became more concerned with and had available to them more critical standards which they could apply, witch trials evaporated rather quickly.

This hypothesis cannot be documented systematically since few trials were adequately reported and the literary evidence is sporadic. Nevertheless, the surviving materials reveal something about the way theories of knowledge and approaches to evidence affected both witch belief and witch trials. These critical attitudes and procedures, as we shall see, occurred both among those who favored and those who opposed increased prosecution.

The terminology employed by English commentators was a curious amalgam of common and civil law language. This can be explained either as the result of direct Continental borrowing or, what is more likely, the fact that witchcraft cases were initially handled by both ecclesiastical and lay courts.[4] The ecclesiastical courts, as well as Chancery and Admiralty jurisdictions, employed civil law-like procedures and standards of evidence. The terminology, however, may also be related to the nature of the crime. Witchcraft, secret and difficult to prove, was thought to be so unique a crime that the normal rules of evidence might be modified.[5] The civil law terminology of "sufficient and full proof" and "light and weighty presumptions" is far more common in discussions of witchcraft than in those of any other type of crime. As we noted in the last chapter, a system of presumptions governed the initial decision to torture under the civil law, while a system of partial and full proofs, with full proof consisting of a confession confirmed by two witnesses, governed the decision to convict or acquit. By analogy, the English could and did readily link presumptions to their presentment and indictment processes, and proofs to their trial processes in witchcraft cases. In the course of the seventeenth century, English writers gradually shifted from a mix of ideas and arguments that tended to give first place to the rather formal and mechanical Continental system of presumptions and proofs, to one that gave far greater prominence to the grading of evidence in terms of the credibility of the witnesses and the probability of the events to which they testified.

The first, and the most devastating, attack on the English law and belief was Reginald Scot's *Discoverie of Witchcraft* (1584). Without going quite so far as to deny that there were witches, Scot exposed one type of trickery and fraud after another and denounced Continental legal procedures which, in cases of witchcraft, permitted excommunicants, infants, and "infamous" and perjured persons to testify, and allowed "presumption and conjectures" to be taken as "sufficient proofes."[6] If men would only "credit" their "owne experience and sense unabused, the rules of philosophie, or the word of God," they would realize that witches possessed only the same powers of other human beings.[7] The implications for the law were obvious:

And because there is nothing possible in lawe, that in nature is impossible; therefore the judge dooth not attend or regard what the accused man saith; or yet would doo: but what is prooved to have beene committed, and naturallie falleth in mans power and will to doo. For the law saith, to will a thing unpossible, is a signe of a mad man, or of a foole, upon whom no sentence or judgement taketh hold. Furthermore what jurie will condemne, or what Judge will give sentence or judgement against one for killing a man a Berwicke; when they themselves, and manie other sawe that man at London, that verie daie, wherein the murder was committed; yea though the partie confesse himself guiltie therein, and twentie witnesses depose the same. But in the case also I saie the judge is not to weigh their testimonie, which is weakened by lawe, and the judges authoritie is to supplie the imperfection of the case, and to maintaine the right and equitie of the same.[8]

Scot, however, had adopted a position that few would support at the end of the sixteenth century, for he attempted to show that most claims of witchcraft exceeded the natural order and, therefore, that most reports of witchcraft were based on illusion. Even confession, normally the best form of evidence, was dismissed by Scot as "idle, false, inconstant, and of no weight."[9] If confessions were examined by "divinitie, philosophie, physicke, lawe or conscience," they would be found false and "insufficient."[10]

A few years later, George Gifford, a clergyman, also emphasized the search for natural explanations and cautiousness with respect to evidence. One of his major points was that different standards of proof were required in indictment and conviction. The former required only "liklihood," the latter "proof." Thus, "suspicion and common fame" were not appropriate evidence for conviction. "Sufficient witnesses" and confession, not idle gossip, were necessary for the level of proof that would support conviction. If adequate proof were unavailable, the suspect must simply be acquitted.[11] If Gifford was, like many of his contemporaries, unclear as to the grounds upon which a jury should doubt the testimony of a sworn witness, he had no doubts that spectral and hearsay evidence should not be given serious consideration.[12] His work suggests how attention to more careful handling of evidence and testimony alone might contribute to the diminishing force of the English witchcraft statute.

The changing attitudes of King James I also suggest a good deal about the process by which belief in witchcraft might be undermined. James began as a firm believer, and, in fact, wrote his *Daemonologie* in 1597 as an attack on Reginald Scot. Once he had become King of England, James, now the author of one of the leading works on the subject of witchcraft, took a personal interest in the prosecution of English witches. Yet it was this very experience which led him to caution and, perhaps, even doubt. Contact with contradiction and outright admissions of fraud resulted in a loss of his earlier confidence. On one occasion, he stopped a trial. Soon James was advising his judges to be especially careful in dealing with witnesses and evidence in witchcraft cases, and he sharply criticized Justice Winch and Sergeant Crewe for condemning nine witches on the basis of inadequate evidence.[13] The King's doubts and the disgrace of his judges insured there would be no royal pressure to prosecute and condemn witches. Rationalist treatises of the Scot variety seemed to have had less influence than the personal experiences of kings, judges, and grand juries on the very rapid drop in the prosecution and conviction rate.[14]

Francis Bacon, philosopher and confidant of King James, took a similar though more detached position. Bacon's *Advancement of Learning* (1605) proposed a "history of marvels" from which the "superstitious narrations of sorceries, witchcrafts, dreams, divinations and the like, where there is an assurance and clear evidence of the fact" were not to be "altogether excluded."[15] Though Bacon admitted "the practice of such things is to be condemned," it was necessary to investigate them

not only for discerning of the offenses, but for the further disclosing of nature. Neither ought a man to make scruple of entering into these things for inquisition of truth, as your majesty hath showed in your own example.[16]

Bacon also agreed with James's position that witchcraft was "the height of idolatry."[17]

By 1620, however, the "Preparative toward Natural and Experimental History," part of Bacon's *New Organon*, suggests considerably less enthusiasm for the "superstitious history of marvels." Now, these were not only to be sharply distinguished from the history of natural prodigies but were not to be undertaken at all until "the investigation of nature has been carried deeper."[18] Bacon "would not have the infancy of philosophy, to which natural history is as a nursing mother, accustomed to old wives" fables. Later, there might be time "for a light review of things of this kind."[19]

Even the experiments of natural magic should be sifted diligently and severely before they are received, especially those which are commonly derived from vulgar sympathies and antipathies, with great sloth and facility both of believing and inventing.[20]

One of the most interesting analyses is physician John Cotta's *The Triall of Witchcraft* (1616). This work, dedicated to Sir Edward Coke and the judiciary and explicitly advocating reform of witchcraft laws, clearly illustrates how theories of knowledge and evidence were brought to bear both on the issue of belief in witches and the crime of witchcraft. Cotta explores two basic themes: the existence of witches, and proper and improper methods of identifying them. Many of the then current modes of discovery, e.g., swimming, beating, and other miraculous methods, were found faulty. Proper investigation, which Cotta explicitly related to the nature of human knowledge, was essential. Beginning with appropriate references to Aristotle, he distinguished certain from probable knowledge, noting in those things where "certainty of knowledge by manifest proofe" fails, "there remaineth no other refuge, but prudent and artificial conjecture, narrowly looking and searching through probabilities, into the nearest possibility of truth and certaintie."[21] Though probabilities were not to be equated with certainties, they often "advance into the knowledge of certainty, that is, often equall unto certainty, and doth perswade and settle discreete resolution and disposition in all affairs."[22] There was thus no reason to flee from probability. In addition, since all knowledge, including that of his own profession, medicine, was derived from sense, reason, and "artificial conjecture," there was no reason why witchcraft could not be discussed in these terms.

After establishing this epistemological and methodological framework, Cotta proceeded to discuss the activities of the Devil, performed both with and without human assistance. In dealing with the latter, he insists that he will not "recite infinite Histories and Reports which may seem to depend upon the obscure or doubted credit of superstition, or partiall Authors." He will utilize only those where "common consent" and valid reports were available, since there could be "no deceit in so many ears and witnesses."[23] Common consent and numerical weight were thus important means of distinguishing the true from the possibly false. When he turned to the Devil's activity, accomplished by covenant with man, Cotta became even more critical, suggesting a variety of means to distinguish witches from imposters and the truly bewitched from those suffering from naturally caused diseases. It is here that he pleads for a special investigative role for physicians guided by sense and reason.

Cotta also had advice for those involved in the legal aspects of investigation and detection:

concerning the first, since it clearly consisteth in that which is manifest unto the outward sense, if the witnesses of the manifest magicall and supernaturall act, be substantiall, sufficient, able to judge, free from exception of malice, partialitie, distraction, folly, and if by conference and counsell with learned men, religiously and industriously exercised in judging those affairs, there bee justly deemed no deception of sense, mistaking of reason or imagination, I see no true cause, why it should deserve an Ignoramous, or not be reputed a True bill, worthy to be inquired, as a case fit and mature for the same due triall.[24]

Though there were special difficulties arising from testimony related to sorcery and witchcraft, such testimony was as acceptable as that relating to any other act or crime. Witches thus might be discovered by "probable reason" and "presumption."[25]

And from things evident to sense, and manifest to reason, there issueth a certainty of undoubted knowledge; for so in things that carry only probabilitie, diligence doth beget and produce verity and truth of opinion. Hence it commeth to passe, that he who truely knoweth, and knowingly can distinguish and discerne the validitie, nature, difference and right use of probabilities, doth most seldome in his opinions mistake or erre.[26]

Yet Cotta also acknowledged that what seemed probable might be false and pulled back a bit in the context of prosecutions.

I do not affirme circumstances and presumption, simply in themselves sufficient to prove or condemne a Witch: what reasonable man will or can doubt or deny, where first a manifest work of Sorcery is with true judgement discerned, and knowne perpetrate: that the former circumstances and presumptions pointing unto a particular, doe give a sufficient warrant, reason and matter of calling that particular into question.[27]

Despite the problems, there was no reason "why due proofe and tryal should not always diligently be made therein."[28]

The conclusions the reader was to draw from Cotta's analysis are not clear. Investigation, indeed very careful investigation, might yield sufficiently conclusive, if not absolutely certain, results. But the concepts of conclusiveness, presumption, and circumstantiality are not analyzed with any clarity. About all Cotta can do is to inform his readers at very considerable length of all the natural explanations available, and how to detect certain types of frauds and errors. Cotta's problem was very similar to that of historians and natural historians of the same era. What means, if any, were there to distinguish true from false testimony? The notions of common consent and numerical weight had considerable currency, as we have seen, yet such evidence remained inconclusive for those who realized that large numbers of people might have mistaken beliefs, and the common consent of one era might not be that of the next. Cotta's adoption of the Continental legal terminology of presumptions and proofs does not extricate him from these problems. The significance of Cotta's work, however, is that he attempted, albeit unsuccessfully, to base convictions on the best standards of evidence available.

Evidentiary concerns were also to be found among those like Thomas Cooper, who favored rigorous prosecution. Cooper's *Mys-*

tery of Witchcraft (1617) warned magistrates not to enquire "upon every corrupt passion, or sleight occasion," but only upon "weighty presumptions" and "probable conjectures."[29] Conviction must not be based on "bare presumption," but on the higher standard of "sufficient proof" that required confession and the "testimonie of two sufficient witnesses to either the Satanic pact or some known witch practice."[30] Like Cotta, Cooper borrows Continental legal terminology to express the need for more rigorous standards of evidence in witchcraft prosecutions. It appears that Englishmen, anxious to be more precise about evidence, borrowed civil law terminology with relatively little comment or hesitation. Perhaps they had no alternative since the principles of evidence in common law had not yet been articulated.

Richard Bernard's *Guide to Grand Jurymen in Cases of Witchcraft* (1627), which was dedicated to both the common and the civil lawyers, is particularly suggestive of how changing standards of evidence might hasten the decline of witchcraft prosecutions. While Bernard did not deny the existence of witches,[31] and even offered methods of detecting them, he was concerned with protecting innocent victims from false accusations and conviction. Thus, unless the "Witchcraft be very cleere," it was better,

till the truth appear, to write an Ignoramus, then upon oath set Billa vera, and so thrust an intricate case upon a Jury of simple men, who proceed too often upon relations of meer presumptions, and sometimes very weak ones too, to take away men's lives.[32]

Bernard more than once suggested that the responsibility lay with the more educated and discriminating grand-jurymen and magistrates, and noted that the fear and superstition frequently found among the common people often resulted in unjust conviction.[33] Since much depended on the early stages of the case, it was extremely important that those who initially examined the suspect be men "in authority," able to properly handle "weak conjectures, which are commonly alledged by the weaker sort, arising out of their own imaginations, or idle speeches of some others."[34] Grand juries, in order "not to be deceived," therefore must not be too credulous "in receiving reports as true and over confidently averring them to be."[35] They must diligently inquire into "the wisdom and discretion of the witness, whether they can discern well between reall and counterfeit acts . . . what sufficient triall has been made of the supposed bewitched, as also by whom, and how long."[36] They must also determine whether trickery or fraud might have occurred, and whether the cause of the afflicted's illness might be natural. The assistance of a trained physician was highly desirable, but if none was available, medical books and other learned men should be consulted. Grand juries were not only to examine the various parties separately but to attempt to distinguish between the testimony of friends and relations of the afflicted and that of "indifferent relators." They were to give more weight to "credible persons" than to "old silly persons," children, the superstitious, or "suspected adversaries."[37] A careful analysis of testimony was not to be taken at face value. Strong presumptions, indeed, were required for indictment. Even

if the suspicion upon great probability, and very strong presumptions, yet unless these doe leade to prove, that the suspected hath made a League and Compact with the Devill . . . they [the suspects] should be released.[38]

Here the Continental language of presumption blended with notions of credibility and probability. Obviously, for Bernard, the task of the grand jury went beyond the simple collection of those bits of unevaluated evidence that would trigger presumptions. The grand jurors were urged to evaluate evidence fully in order to determine whether something like what in modern law would be called a *prima facie* case existed. That is, while not asked to hear and evaluate all the evidence so as to arrive at a final determination of guilt or innocence, they were asked to determine whether the evidence was sufficiently credible and weighty to justify moving on to a full-scale trial.

A good deal thus depended on the justice of the peace who prepared the preliminary evidence for the grand jury. It was he who typically received the accusation, examined the accused, and decided whether the presumptions were sufficient to proceed to the grand jury. Consequently, Michael Dalton's popular handbook for justices of the peace included Bernard's list of presumptions of witchcraft but not his instructions for evaluating evidence, which would be the task of grand jurors and jurors. In all felonies, and witchcraft was of course a felony, the examining justice of the peace had to consider the accused's character, mode of life, and previous encounters with the law. "Common fame," that an individual had done the criminal deed, was sufficient for an arrest.[39] The justice of the peace obviously had some discretion, but it was his job to insure that cases were prepared for the grand jury. Confession, Dalton advised the magistrates, especially in cases of witchcraft, "exceeds all other evidence."[40] Another popular, but considerably later handbook by Giles Dunscumbe, however, noted that the "truth of Witches Confessions themselves hath been often doubted; it seems therefore that [there] ought to be good circumstances concurring."[41]

We may surmise that Bernard, Dalton, and Dunscumbe, whose works were frequently reissued, played some role in the sharp drop in prosecution and conviction. Certainly, Bernard's rules for detecting errors, if followed, would have had that result. In many respects, Bernard's approach was typical. He retained the general belief in witches, yet by providing for searching analyses of particular cases, eliminated many and eventually nearly all actual convictions.[42]

We can obtain further insight as to how prosecution and conviction fell off from Edward Fairfax, a man of some standing who, in 1621, complained about the methods employed in the case of his daughter "who had been bewitched" into serious illness. When the accused were initially questioned by the justice of the peace, Fairfax found they had "counsellors . . . supporters of the best," who "moved doubts, [and] inferred a supposal of counterfeiting . . . in the children."[43] The justices, he thought, tended to be "incredulous of things of this kind." Even some divines and physicians, he felt, attributed too much to natural causes. At some stage, the authorities provided Fairfax with medical books in order to convince him that his daughter's illness was the result of natural causes. When the case went to the grand jury, six of whose members were themselves justices of the peace and gentlemen of "wisdom and discretion," it was advised by the judge to be "very careful."[44] During the trial which followed, experiments were performed on the afflicted children, who were at that time evidently in a trance. In the end, the judge informed the trial jury that the evidence "reached not to the point of the statute," and the accused were released, much to Fairfax's displeasure.

By the 1640s, many already felt that only those witches whose activities resulted in death should be executed.[45] Sir Robert Filmer evidently thought it was now time to instruct potential jurors on the matter of appropriate evidence and standards of proof. Filmer's primary aim was to refute the still popular work of Puritan theologian William Perkins, which had provided some eighteen signs or proofs of witchcraft. The main thrust of Filmer's argument was that Perkins himself had recognized that most of his signs might be wrong or misleading.[46] Filmer took great pains to distinguish presumptions and signs, which under some circumstances might appropriately be utilized in a pretrial examination, from "proofs sufficient for conviction."[47] Although Perkins had suggested that torture might be appropriate to gain a conviction in instances of "strong and great presumptions," Filmer reminded his readers that torture was not permitted in England.[48] Foreign standards were irrelevant. "[H]ere they are tyed to a stricter . . . Rule in giving their Sentence."[49] After casting doubt on all Perkins's signs and proofs, Filmer concluded by telling jurymen they must be diligent and careful "not to condemn any suspected upon bare presumptions, without sound and sufficient proofs."[50]

By 1640, then, those involved in all stages of the legal process were being counseled on the proper evaluation of testimony and evidence, with higher and higher standards of proof requested as each case moved from preliminary examination, through indictment, and on to trial. While one cannot prove that it was the greater concern for evidence that was responsible for the decline in witchcraft prosecutions and convictions, it seems reasonable to suggest that it played some role in that process.

The downturn was not quite unbroken. A brief but deadly upsurge stimulated by professional witch hunter Matthew Hopkins alone resulted in several hundred trials and about two hundred convictions, actually a considerable portion of the total number of English executions during the century. Significantly, the outbreak occurred during the breakdown of judicial institutions, the assizes having been temporarily suspended as a result of civil war.[51] Eventually Hopkins's irregular methods, which included a kind of torture, were questioned by some judges and laymen.[52] Despite Hopkins's irregular methods, acquittals still ran at forty-two percent.[53] And nine of those convicted were pardoned by the House of Lords in 1646. The Hopkins interlude, however, did not prevent the overall downturn of prosecution and conviction.[54]

The judiciary, on the whole, appears to have used its influence to prevent conviction, and helped to make the witchcraft statute inoperative many decades before final repeal. Keith Thomas has suggested that this process began at least as early as 1633. He notes a 1658 case in which the judge attempted to prevent a conviction on the basis of inadequate evidence. By 1676, judges gave "small or no encouragement to such accusations."[55]

The most famous exception was Sir Matthew Hale, perhaps the most learned and most respected jurist of the mid-seventeenth century. He and his close friend and neighbor, the famous dissenting divine Richard Baxter, a staunch defender of witch beliefs, were anxious to defend the existence of spirits as a means of preventing religious disbelief and "atheism."[56] The famous 1664 trial at Bury St. Edmunds seemed to have followed standard courtroom procedure. Dr. Thomas Browne, a well-known physician of literary eminence who also believed in witchcraft as a bulwark against atheism, provided expert testimony. Browne indicated both that delusion was possible and that the children in question truly had been bewitched. During the trial, Hale proposed an experiment which involved the blindfolded, afflicted children being touched by someone other than the accused to see if the reaction was the same. The experimenters, mostly gentlemen, concluded that fraud was involved. Sergeant John Keyling, soon to be Chief Justice of King's Bench, was present at the trial and thought the evidence inadequate. Hale's charge to the jury, however, made it clear that he believed witches did exist, citing the evidence of Scripture and the fact that all nations had laws against them.[57] He refused to comment or even to repeat the evidence, alleging that he might misinterpret it, although his normal practice was to sum up evidence for the jury.[58] He instructed the jury that there were two questions only: whether the children were bewitched, and whether the accused were responsible. The jury found the defendants guilty, and they were executed.

No judge was more knowledgeable about criminal law and procedure or more sophisticated about the credit to be accorded testimony both in legal and nonlegal matters than Sir Matthew Hale.[59] In his scholarly work, Hale, the leading authority on the criminal law for several generations, had insisted that judges were not only to direct the jury in matters of law but to assist it in weighing the evidence.[60] Yet in the 1664 case, Hale refused the latter role. But Hale also felt that the two most difficult crimes with respect to evidence were rape and witchcraft,

wherein many times persons really are guilty. Yet such an evidence as is satisfactory to prove it, can hardly be found, and the other side persons really innocent may be entangled under such presumptions that many times carry great probabilities of Guilt.[61]

Hale, however, offered no comment as to how one might resolve this dilemma.[62] Presumably in these cases, as in all others, the jury was to listen to the testimony of the witnesses, weigh their credibility, and then decide.[63]

Hale's refusal to sum up the evidence and his statements about witchcraft were considered extraordinary at the time, and were the subject of both favorable and unfavorable comment for many years.[64] It seems fair to conclude that this was an instance in which Hale's zeal against atheism overcame his commitment to the new methodology, with his refusal to sum up signaling his own awareness of the cognitive dissonance which he had created for himself.

By 1664, the case clearly was atypical. There were relatively few indictments and even fewer convictions by this time, executions ceasing entirely in 1682. By then, the educated classes, which comprised the judiciary, the lawyers, the justices of the peace, and grand jurors, had resolved Hale's dissonance by allowing his more critical approach to evidence to dominate their earlier witch beliefs. They became increasingly reluctant to credit the wild accusations of ignorant countrymen. The increased skepticism of the legal profession as a whole is suggested by Richard Baxter's comment that disbelief centered "at Court and ye Innes of Court."[65] Despite the support given by Dr. Browne in the 1664 case, physicians as a group were among the skeptical, as they provided more natural explanations for strange behavior and afflictions and gave "little Ear to Stories of Witches."[66]

There can be no doubt, however, that the judiciary played a key role and that Sir John Holt, Chief Justice of King's Bench between 1689 and 1710, a man of very different stamp than Hale, was its leader. Holt, like Hale, had a reputation for being especially careful about evidence and for being particularly unprejudiced. He, "[b]y his questions and manner of hemming [summing] up the evidence seemed to . . . believe nothing of witchery at all." Holt, more clearly and more openly than any other judge, brought his enormous influence and position to bear against witchcraft convictions, his directions to the jury resulting in eleven successive acquittals.[67] Not all judges, however, were as successful as Holt. Justice Powell, who presided over one of the last cases (1712), affronted the jury by making skeptical remarks, among others, that there was no law against flying. The angry jury therefore convicted the accused, though Powell was able in the end to delay execution and obtain a royal pardon.[68] This case caused considerable public discussion.[69] One pamphlet defending Powell critically examined the testimony. The author insisted that the facts alleged had not been proved, hinted at fraud, and concluded that natural explanations were to be preferred to the supernatural:

But I do not see how it will help Mr. Bragge [another pamphleteer] if, as he pretends, he has given us all the proofs for his Witchcraft, that the

Nature of the thing will admit of. It would indeed then be very reasonable in any Man to expect that he should give more: but then it would be barely for that Reason. For wherever the Thing in Question does not admit of Evidence to weigh with a reasonable Man there the Nature of the Thing is such that (be it never so true) it cannot be the object of a wise man's Faith. For our belief in anything does not depend on the intrinsick Certainty and Reality of the Thing itself, but upon the Evidence it carries with it. And therefore since it is certain a thing may be true, and yet not capable of proved to be so, it will be little to purpose to say, that we have all the Evidence that the thing will bear, if all be not enough.[70]

Another writer also gave his attention to the problem of evidence, insisting that the mere existence of records of past convictions and legislation did not amount to demonstration. Not only were judges fallible and so might wrongfully condemn witches, but the existence of records did not constitute satisfactory proof. There were, after all, "records" of such "Creatures as Antipodes," and they were no longer believed to exist.[71]

Not long afterward, Francis Hutchinson dedicated his widely known *Historical Essay Concerning Witchcraft* (1718) to the Chief Justice of Common Pleas and Chief Baron of the Exchequer. The essay was a collection of evidence and argument put together with the purpose of preventing further witch accusations and prosecutions.

As the 1712 case tried by Powell indicates, English criminal trials were never entirely in the hands of judges. Acquittals were up to the jury, and juries could be both tenacious in their views and hostile to skeptical Westminster judges. This is borne out by the observations of Roger North, who accompanied Judges Francis North and Sir Thomas Raymond at the Assizes. In one case, the "rabble" was full of "noise and fury" against the accused. "The stories of their acts were in everyone's mouth," not only in the countryside, but in Exeter where they were tried. "A less zeal in a city or kingdom hath been the overture of defection and revolution."[72] There would have been real danger of public disorder if acquittal had taken place, and Raymond's "passivity" and inability "to oppose a popular rage" had insured conviction. The evidence consisted primarily of the accused's confession, "the rest of the stuff was mere matters of fancy, as pigs dying and the like."[73] Judge Raymond, North thought, had not examined the confessions critically, and had made "no nice distinctions, as to how it was possible for an old woman in a sort of melancholy madness . . . to contract an opinion of themselves that was false." Nor had the judge informed the jury that confessions ought to be ignored "without a plain evidence that it was sensible and rational, no more than a lunatic." Instead, Judge Raymond had simply left the evidence to the jury, which convicted.[74] Judge Francis North, presiding over the civil suits on that occasion, complained to the Secretary of State about the current state of the law, noting "we cannot reprieve now without appearing to deny the real being of witchcraft . . . which is against the law."[75] As long as the statute remained on the books, and as long as cases reached juries, judges could not ignore or dismiss them. Their only alternative was to show that the evidence presented did not prove the accusation. As judges, they could not try directly to convince the jury that the event in question could not have occurred by the means alleged. Instead, they could only do their best to discredit witnesses and to suggest ways in which malice and fraud might have been perpetrated.

How this might be accomplished is shown in another case involving Judge North. North and the "better audience" thought the matter before them was "a strange imposture," despite the witnesses' "very positive swearing." The "danger" came from the jury "who were ordinary men, who, if they find an opinion against the belief of witches, are very apt to sacrifice a life to prove the contrary." North therefore proceeded slowly, examining "with great temper and moderation," being careful "not to disclose his own opinion." Only at the end did he question the examining justice of the peace, who had by then himself reached the conclusion that fraud had been involved and explained to the jury how he thought it had been perpetrated. North felt that the common people retained witch beliefs "with an inveterate obstinancy, and so much the fiercer as their superiors endeavor to rectify them." If judges openly declared against witchcraft, or ridiculed popular belief, juries were likely to "cry, this judge hath no religion, for he doth not believe in witches; and so, to show they have some, hang the poor wretches." The judge, therefore, had "to convince . . . by detecting . . . the fraud," rather "than by denying . . . such power."[76]

As late as 1712, many countrymen still felt the "least Doubt" was "a Badge of Infidelity, and not to be superstitious passes for a dull Neutrality in Religion, if not a direct Atheism."[77] Since accusations were initiated by villagers, sporadic cases were likely to occur, even though more sophisticated town dwellers, intellectuals, and the professional classes were ceasing to believe. The existence of jury trials in which jurors were judges of the fact resulted in sporadic convictions for witchcraft long after the educated classes had thrown their weight against prosecution, and country trials with "country probations" lingered even after the trials became illegal in 1736, popular belief occasionally resulting in the illegal "swimming" or "lynching" of witches.[78]

In England, judges had no role in initiating prosecution. The crucial role in bringing a case to trial was played by the examining magistrates and the grand jurors who would formally indict. As we have seen, there were efforts to insure that grand jurors would evaluate witchcraft testimony with great care. In 1692, a grand jury was told that witchcraft was, to be sure, a great crime, but "it is so hard a matter to have a full proof of it, that no jury can be too cautious and tender in a prosecution of this nature."[79] If the grand jury refused to indict, there would of course be no trial. A very late and dramatic instance of the critical role of the grand jury occurred in 1717 when a woman and her two children were accused. Despite the testimony of twenty-five witnesses to the fact that the three had made their victims vomit large stones and that a child had been bewitched to death, the indictment was thrown out.[80] The critical skills of examining justices of the peace and grand jurors, and their willingness to evaluate testimony critically thus played an important role in the decline of prosecutions. By the 1680s, the justices of the peace had almost ceased to press charges against witches.[81] The reissue of Bernard's *Guide to Grand Jurymen* in 1680 and 1686 no doubt aided justices of the peace and grand juries.

Yet one must not too readily assume that all juries were credulous or ready to believe whatever they were told. Acquittals were far from rare in England, even during the height of witch trials.[82] After 1640, juries convicted in fewer and fewer of those cases that reached them. In a case of 1682, for example, despite the fact that some nineteen or twenty witnesses testified against the accused, the jury "to the great amazement of some who thought the evidence sufficient to have found her guilty," acquitted the accused. Others present, who considered the "great difficulty in proving a Witch," however, "thought the Jury could do not less than acquit."[83]

For a few decades in the late sixteenth and early seventeenth centuries, both popular and elite cultures supported witch beliefs. Only during this period, when witch persecution had the active support of the upper classes, the government, and the legal profession, were trials numerous. When the beliefs and standards of evidence of those who controlled the legal system changed, prosecution dropped sharply and virtually ceased. This situation is obvious in England where we have seen the development of a growing divergence between popular and learned culture. Superstition and belief continued, but was no longer systematically enforced by the legal machinery.

In an earlier chapter, we saw that the potential dangers of materialism and atheism that inhered in the new mechanical philosophy had led the scientific community to a defense of the basic principles of religion based on a new approach to knowledge and certainty. On the whole, this group adopted a version of the mechanical philosophy which emphasized God as Creator of the natural world. The study of His works became a means of appreciating His existence, power, and continued action in the natural world. If this group found that they could combine mechanism and atomism with natural theology and Christianity, there were others who concluded that religion could be defended only by a repudiation of atomism, materialism, and mechanism, and by a revival or reworking of neo-Platonic doctrine that allowed for immaterial or spiritual substances which might act on material ones. In the process, Henry More, Ralph Cudsworth, Joseph Glanvill, and others associated with the Cambridge Platonists defended the existence of witches, thus prolonging, at least in some quarters, the philosophical respectability of witch beliefs. For the Cambridge group, belief in witchcraft was linked to belief in the world of the spirit, and ultimately to a defense of religion against the encroachments of materialism. In making and developing these connections, they attempted to employ a philosophically sound theory of knowledge and belief.

Henry More, writing against Hobbes, Descartes, and, later, Spinoza, expounded the idea of an immaterial agent which guided and shaped material phenomena.[84] Witchcraft and psychic phenomenon were crucial to his argument because they provided the evidence, the empirical proof, for the existence of spirit. A belief in "bad Spirits will necessarily open a Door to the Belief that there are good Ones: and lastly that there is a God," and case histories would provide "fresh examples of Apparitions and Witchcrafts."[85] A similar view was expressed by Ralph Cudsworth, who was sure that the "exploders" of witch belief "can scarcely escape the suspicion of having some Hankring towards Atheism."[86] More and Cudsworth, therefore, willingly cooperated in Joseph Glanvill's effort to find the necessary evidence, More even taking responsibility for the expansion of the posthumous editions of Glanvill's *Sadu-*

cismus Triumphatus: Or, A Full and Plain Evidence Concerning Witches and Apparitions.

Joseph Glanvill is interesting for our purposes not only because he collected the proofs desired by More but because it was he who most explicitly attempted to link these proofs to the theoretical conceptions about the nature of empirical knowledge being developed by Boyle, Wilkins, and others. Glanvill's efforts may also stem from Bacon's demand for a variety of history which would include witchcraft as well as other marvels. Platonist concerns might thus be linked to Baconian natural history. By 1666, the date of his first publication on witchcraft and spirits, Glanvill was no stranger either to neo-Platonism, having written a defense of the Platonic doctrine of the pre-existence of souls, or to the work of the Royal Society.[87] Over the years, Glanvill reported and embellished his arguments, evidence, and proofs for the existence of witches. His basic position was that knowledge based on matters of fact could demonstrate the same levels of certainty, or rather probability, in the matter of witches and psychic phenomena, as could any well-documented account of natural phenomena or historical events. His argument consists primarily of establishing the level of evidence necessary to prove matters of fact and demonstrating the variety of inferences which might properly be drawn from them.

Thus, whether "there have been and are unlawful confederacies with evil spirits . . . by virtue of which their hellish accomplices perform things above their natural powers," was simply a "Matter of Fact" capable only of the "evidence of authority and sense." Not only did the history both of rude and civilized ages testify to the existence of witches, but "[w]e have the attestations of thousands of eye and ear witnesses, and those not only of the easily deceivable vulgar only, but of wise and grave discerning, of whom no interest could oblige them to agree together in a common Lye." As in natural, civil, or sacred history, it was the quality and quantity of the relators that was significant. Like many historians, Glanvill cited the "standing public Records of these well-attested Relations," and the cases tried by "wise and reverent Judges upon clear and convictive evidence."[88]

To the by now common suggestion that witch beliefs were merely the result of melancholy and imagination, Glanvill replied that imagination might indeed deceive, but he would not accept the notion that "all the Circumstances of Fact, which we find in well-attested and confirmed Relations" were the result of the "deceivable imagination." After all, if one were to reject everything not personally observed, all historical knowledge would be relegated to the category of "Dreams and Fond Imaginations." Such a position would "quite destroy the Credit of all humane testimony."[89] In these matters, Glanvill emphasized the observations of the common man. In "things of Fact the people are as much to be believ'd as the most subtile philosopher and Speculators; sincere Sense is the Judge."[90] He admitted that all accounts could not be accepted at face value, for cheats and impostors did exist. The frequency of deceit warranted "greater care and caution," but imposture in any given instance did not mean a "universal Negative" might be concluded.[91] That some witnesses might not be trustworthy was recognized as a problem, but not as an insurmountable one. The senses did not always deceive, and "all Mankind are not Lyars, Cheats and Knaves."[92] A single "relation of an Affirmative sufficiently confirmed and attested is worth a thousand Tales of Forgery."[93] Although it might seem unlikely that the Devil was at the beck and call "of a poor Hag," it was even more improbable that "all the world should be deceived in matters of Fact and Circumstances of the Clearest Evidence and Conviction."[94]

Glanvill attacked his opponents on methodological grounds. They either ignored the evidence or based their position "simply on an apprehension that such a belief is absurd, and such things impossible."[95] But it was unreasonable to deny a "matter of Fact well proved" simply "because we cannot conceive how they can be performed." The natural scientist, after all, did not deny facts simply because he had no explanation for them. If one could not understand how the fetus was formed or how plants grew, it was hardly surprising that one did not comprehend the "Constitution and Powers" of witches.[96]

It was thus not he, but his critics who were credulous, for they rejected evidence in favor of their own unsupported belief. Furthermore, they reasoned from a false basis. Facts can only be proved by "immediate Sense or the Testimony of Others." To try to "demonstrate" fact by abstract reasoning and speculation "was as foolish as trying to prove Julius Caesar founded Rome by means of Algebra or Metaphysics."[97]

Serious investigation was clearly necessary, given that "the Land of Spirit" was "a kinde of America" which "stands on the Map of humane Science like unknown Tracts."[98] "Histories" must therefore be collected and experiments performed.[99] From 1668 on, Glanvill began collecting "evidence" for his "Cautious and Faithful History." First he added the story of the Demon of Tedworth, a contemporary witch disturbance that he himself had investigated, to his published work. Successive editions enlarged the "empirical proofs." The posthumous editions of 1681 and 1688, to which Henry More contributed, added more reports, most of which dealt with psychic phenomena rather than the *maleficium* and diabolical compact so essential for prosecution.[100] Glanvill was particularly anxious to find contemporary evidence, recognizing that "things . . . long past are either not believed or forgot; whereas those being fresh, and near, and attested withall . . . for credibility, may" be expected to have "more success upon the Obstancy of unbelievers."[101] The Royal Society demanded the same kind of reliable reports of earthquakes and other nonrepeatable natural events.

Indeed, Glanvill initially hoped that the Royal Society would "direct some of its . . . luciferous enquiries towards the World of Spirits."[102] This expression of hope, dropped in later editions,[103] perhaps suggests that the organized scientific community was not receptive to Glanvill's enterprise, despite its Baconian pedigree. Thomas Sprat's *History of the Royal Society*, for example, emphasized that "It is matter, a visible and sensible matter, which is the object of the Society's labors."[104] Sprat referred contemptuously to "the terrors and misapprehensions which commonly confound weaker minds, and make men's hearts to fail and boggle at Trifles."[105] Sprat associated fairies and apparitions with other cobwebs of the past. From the "time in which the Real Philosophy has appeared," such beliefs had declined:

Every man is unshaken at those Talkes, at which his Ancestors trembled. The course of things goes quietly along, in its own true channel of Natural Causes and Effects. . . . Which though they have not yet completed the discovery of the True world yet they have already vanquish'd those wild inhabitants of the false worlds, that use'd to astonish the minds of men.[106]

When Glanvill's first essay appeared, Samuel Pepys, a man with wide interests in science, found it "not very convincing."[107] Yet shortly after the publication of Glanvill's 1668 effort, several of Henry Oldenburg's correspondents suggested that the Royal Society investigate the subject of witchcraft.[108] The Royal Society itself did not take up the subject of witchcraft and did not associate itself with Glanvill's cause. The views of Robert Boyle are instructive, for they exhibit both his customary caution with respect to evidence and a religiously motivated urge to believe in the possibility of spiritual influence in the natural world. Unlike Glanvill and More, Boyle was not a Platonist, but one of the leading proponents of the mechanical philosophy. In defending the mechanical philosophy, he was highly critical of the dark and intricate doctrines of the Platonists and chemists with their "Archeus, Astral Beings, and other odd notions." Effects often attributed to "an effect of witchcraft" were to be explained instead by appropriate "optical and mathematical laws."[109] Boyle was equally skeptical of diseases reported to be the result of "incantations," and thought "Sober Physicians" should attempt to "reduce those extravagent symptoms to . . . known and stated disease."[110] Most relations of witchcraft were false and "occasioned" by the "Credulity or Imposture of Men."[111]

Yet Boyle did not deny the possibility of witchcraft and psychic phenomena. In a letter attached to Peter du Moulin's *The Devil of Mascon*, he wrote not only of "the powerful inclinations, which my course of life and studies hath given me to diffidence and backwardness of assent, and the many fictions and superstitions . . . which are wont to blemish the relations where spirits and witches are concerned," but also of his belief that the narrative in question was true.[112]

Boyle's correspondence with Glanvill again reveals both his tentative belief and his critical approach to evidence.[113] Glanvill, who had recently been attacked in John Webster's *The Displaying of Supposed Witchcraft* (1677), which had been licensed by the vice president of the Royal Society, approached Boyle, among others, in the hope of obtaining "some modern well-attested relations to fact, to prove the existence of witches and apparitions."[114] A later letter to Boyle reported that he now had "a collection very considerable, for plainness and strength of evidence . . . to shame all atheists, sceptics, Sadduccees and witch-advocates. . . ."[115] Boyle's replies focused on the issue of adequate verification:

the main circumstances of the relation may be impartially delivered, and sufficiently verified, either upon your own knowledge, or by the judicial records, or other competent vouchers; for we live in an age, and a place, wherein all stories of Witchcrafts . . . are by many, even of the wise, suspected; and by too many, that would pass for wits, derided and exploded.[116]

Boyle thought nineteen out of twenty witch stories circulated were untrue. As for the twentieth, he would have considered it false himself if "I had not had particular and considerable advantages to persuade me, upon good grounds, that, though most of these stories be untrue . . . they are not all so."[117] Boyle, however, warned that well-meaning men with "improbable and ill verified stories of witches and sorceries . . . erred in presuming, that the multitude of such relations would compensate their want of credibility." Instead, false and dubious accounts made the "judicious suspect that the rest were of the same kind."[118] It was therefore absolutely essential that Glanvill's:

narrations resume the credit of this kind of stories in the opinions of the unbiased men, by having its circumstances warranted with testimonies and authorities, which, the nature of thing consider'd, may suffice to satisfy those that are diffident, out of cautiousness, not prejudice. . . . I doubt not, but one circumstantial narrative, fully verified, such as I hope you may prove, will be preferred by the curious and judicious, to a hundred improbable, and slightly attested ones.[119]

Boyle eventually contributed an Irish story to "accommodate" Glanvill's "design." In forwarding it, Boyle reiterated that Glanvill must be

very careful to deliver none but well attested narratives; the want of which cautiousness has justly discredited many relations of witches and forgers, and make most of the rest suspected; since in such stories, the number of the whole can no way compensate the want of truth, or of proof in some of the particulars.[120]

The quality, not the quantity of evidence was paramount.

Boyle's comments on Glanvill are echoed in John Ray's reservations on John Aubrey's collection of occult phenomena. Though Aubrey himself admitted that only one in a hundred reports was likely to be true, and preferred natural to supernatural explanations, he accepted several accounts that inspired Ray to comment that Aubrey was "a little too inclinable to credit strange relations. I have found men that are not skillful in the History of Nature very credulous, and apt to impose on themselves and others."[121]

Others were even less sympathetic than Boyle or Ray. John Wagstaffe argued that there was no such thing as a witch and attempted to demonstrate that proofs based on matter of fact were completely unsatisfactory. Matters of fact necessarily involved the senses. While Wagstaffe was prepared to believe in spirits composed of incorporeal matter "too fine to be perceived by the senses," such belief could not be based on "matter of fact." He did not deny "matters of fact witnessed by oaths" in matters of sense, e.g., the existence of Julius Caesar, the River Thames, or the existence of America, but he rejected such claims when they did not and *could not* involve the senses. Witchcraft activity was thus by definition excluded from matters of fact. In addition, witnesses in such matters were so often

217

deluded that it was more rational to believe that they were liars and perjurers than that an old woman had turned herself into a cat.[122]

One of the most influential antiwitchcraft tracts was *The Displaying of Supposed Witchcraft* (1677) by physician John Webster who explicitly associated his repudiation of Casaubon, More, and Glanvill with the goals of the Royal Society.[123] This volume sought to undermine Glanvill's data and methods. Webster begins by noting that belief in the powers of demons and witches had been "pretty well quashed and silenced" by Reginald Scot and Thomas Ady, as well as by the proceedings of learned judges and other "judicious magistrates." It was necessary to examine the issue again because Glanvill had "newly furbished" the "old Weapons" and arguments.[124]

Although Webster dealt extensively with Scripture and other aspects of the controversy, we will mention only his position relating to questions of evidence and proof. Like many seventeenth-century defenders of natural science, Webster insists that the advancement of truth frequently required the rejection of "common and deep-rooted Opinion." Therefore, he associated his position with scientific innovators like Harvey, Descartes, Boyle, and Galileo, noting all inventions and opinions were "in their beginnings opposed and censured . . . [and] all acquired Knowledge, and all Arts and Sciences were once new."[125]

Webster also denied that "the generality of an opinion, or the numerousness of the persons that hold and maintain it" was a satisfactory proof. Indeed, "not one of an hundred" was "qualified to search for and understand truth."[126] If numbers alone were a sufficient basis for belief, then the pagans who far outnumbered the Christians would be correct, as would the Aristotelians, whose views had dominated men's minds for generations. It was therefore neither safe nor rational "to receive or adhere to an opinion because of its Antiquity; nor to reject one because of its Novelty."[127] Opinions, old or new, should not be accepted unless "we be fully satisfied, from indubitable grounds."[128] Strange and wonderful effects in Art or Nature, "require much diligence truly to discover and find out their causes; and we ought not rashly to attribute those effects to the Devil, whose causes are latent or unknown unto us."[129]

Previous writers on the subject were dismissed as having treated witchcraft either in a "confused and unmethodical way," or for having expressed their views in such a "far fetcht . . . metaphorical, and improperly applied" language "that no rational . . . man can tell us what to make of them."[130] Still another cause of witch belief "was an evil education." Custom and education about apparitions, fairies, ghosts, and the like were instilled early, and were difficult to eradicate. "A melancholick complexion and constitution" also might be involved. Custom, education, temperament—several of the Baconian "idols"—were thus important elements in continued belief.

Although Webster took great pains to refute the notion that the denial of the existence of spirits and witches would result in denying the existence of God,[131] he was even more concerned to show that Glanvill's proofs were inadequate. Many of the authors Glanvill cited had not been eye or ear witnesses, and had "taken it up by hearsay, common fame, or the relation of others."[132] And if what they related was:

not of their own certain knowledge . . . then it is of little, or no credit at all; for the others that relate it might be guilty of active or passive deception and delusion, or might have heard it from another . . . of all which there is no certainty, but leaveth sufficient grounds for dubitation, as is sufficient to caution a prudent person altogether to suspend his assent, until better proof can be brought.[133]

If the fact in question was witnessed by a single person, even an eye or ear witness, it was still "not sufficient" because that individual's sense organs might be defective. If matters of fact were witnessed by many

ear and eyewitnesses, yet may their testimony bear no weight . . . because they may be corrupt in point of interest, and so have their judgements misguided and biassed by the corruption of the desires and affections, or relate things out of spleen, envy, and malice.[134]

Webster went still further and insisted:

But if the Authors that report matters of fact in reference to these . . . particulars, were ear and eyewitnesses, and not single, but a greater number, and were not swayed by any corrupt or self interest whatsoever; yet all this is not sufficence to give evidence in these matters, except they be rightly qualified.[135]

Witnesses must be "perfect in the organs of their senses." Fearful and melancholic individuals were excluded as likely to take a black sheep for a demon and the noise of wild swans for spirits.[136] They must "be clear and free from those imbibed notions of Spirits, Hobgoblins and Witches . . . instamped . . . through ignorant and superstitious education." Lastly, they should "be free in the judgements as *in aequibrio*."[137] It followed that virtually all known reports would be disposed of as inadequate, and those which appeared:

to carry with them a great splendor and weight of truth and reason . . . if . . . looked into, and narrowly weighted in the balance of sound reason, and unbiassed judgment . . . will be found too light, and will soon vanish into Rhetorical fumes and frothy vapours.[138]

The stance of the scientific investigator and the methods of the virtuosi would thus dispose of witch belief as it had disposed of other chimeras. What is perhaps most interesting for our purposes is that the advocates and opponents of witch beliefs, the Glanvills and the Websters, attempted to capture both the prestige and the methodology of the empirical scientists.

It is difficult, given the scarcity of evidence, to generalize, but we believe that the greater part of the scientific community, at least those who were supporters of the mechanical and atomic "hypothesis," preferred to fight atheism on somewhat different grounds than More and Glanvill. One could "prove" the existence of God by the study of His creation, rather than by means of a neo-Platonic theory of nature or demonstration of the existence of witches and other effects of spirit on matter. The response of some members of the scientific community was to find flaws with all the witchcraft evidence and testimony presented. The response of others was to find at least one or two reports that were adequately supported by the evidence. But, at least theoretically, the same exacting standards of evidence and investigation were to be applied to this evidence as to any other disputed matter.

Nevertheless, the inclination to search for such evidence declined rapidly. As the physical universe was increasingly associated with order, harmony, and regularity, without the capricious intervention of God, it became more difficult to suggest that lesser spirits, good or evil, were likely to intervene in natural processes.[139] If the development of natural philosophy, and particularly the mechanical philosophy, was not solely responsible for the decline in belief, there were those, among them Richard Bentley, who thought it played a significant role:

What then has lessen'd in England your stories of sorceries? Not the growing sect [of free thinkers], but the growth of Philosophy and Medicine. No thanks to atheists, but to the Royal Society and the College Physicians: to the Boyles and Newtons, the Sydenhams and Ratcliffs.[140]

Francis Hutchinson, too, associated the disappearance of witch belief with the rise of learning and knowledge, and specifically with natural science and the Royal Society.[141]

At the same time, few were willing flatly to deny the possibility of witchcraft. John Locke seems to have been somewhat puzzled about how to handle the problem, for he wished to maintain a belief in spirit as well as matter. If one introduced the young to natural philosophy, one ran the danger of instilling the notion that all was matter and that there were no immaterial beings. The opposite danger, however, was that the young might receive "early impressions of goblins, spectres and apparitions," which would leave their minds subject to undesirable fears and superstitions. He thought perhaps the dilemma might be resolved by introducing the subject in a simplified version of Scripture. Thus armed with Revelation, one could study nature without fear of materialism. He emphasized his point by noting that gravity was a phenomenon of nature which could not be explained solely by the "natural operation of matter, or any other law of motion."[142] Another midway position was offered by Thomas Tenison, who defended the possibility of incorporeal substance against Hobbes's denial. While admitting fraud and delusion and the fact that many accounts were "hatched in chimney corners" or in the "disturbed imagination of fearful people," he nevertheless felt that all accounts need not be considered fables. The rejection of romance, after all, had left the truth of history.[143]

Joseph Addison perhaps best represented the view of early eighteenth-century English intellectuals: "I believe in general that there is, and have been such a thing as Witchcraft; but at the same time, can give no Credit to any particular Instance of it."[144] Religious men may not have wished to deny completely the possibility of spiritual activity in the world, but the standards of verification which had developed in the course of the seventeenth century now made specific cases impossible to verify to the satisfaction of critical intellectuals, scientists, and judges, and even to a large part of the general English population. If, by the Newtonian era, there were few who vigorously defended the existence of witches and demanded their prosecution,[145] we must recall that Newton's exposition of gravitation seemed to some to reintroduce the issue of occult forces and powers in nature.

The decline in England was paralleled on the Continent, despite the existence of a different legal system and a somewhat different structure of witch belief.[146] In France as in England witchcraft was increasingly transferred from ecclesiastical to secular tribunals. In France all stages of the criminal process were controlled by the legal profession, and lawyers produced manuals to assist fellow professionals in the detection and punishment of witches. It has been suggested that Bodin's widely read *La Démonomanie des sorciers* (1580) was designed to replace the outdated *Malleus Maleficarum*, which had provided guidance for the Inquisition. Like its predecessor, Bodin's work combined a philosophical disquisition with a practical, procedurally oriented handbook for those involved in detecting and punishing witches.[147]

One of the chief characteristics of these French, lawyer-produced volumes was a relaxation and modification of normal evidentiary rules. Bodin indicated that in cases of suspected witchcraft the testimony of only one reliable witness was sufficient to justify torture. The accused might be put to torture if there was any corroborating evidence, a practice forbidden in normal criminal cases. He stressed the reliability of presumption and conjecture, noting that in cases of witchcraft "common rumour" was "almost infallible," and that "When a woman is reported to be a witch, there is most grave presumption that she is one."[148]

Henri Boguet's often reprinted handbook, *An Examen of Witches*, illustrates the standard approach in France. Two themes predominate in his work. The first was that a great increase in the incidence of witchcraft required increased judicial activity. The second was that judges were not bound by the "usual legalities and ordinary procedures."[149] The procedures he outlined deviated from the norms of civil law and judicial investigation largely by giving more weight to "common rumour." Common rumour together with certain other indices and presumptions were sufficient to initiate the torture that would elicit the confession so essential to Continental criminal procedure. Confession required corroboration by witnesses. In witchcraft trials, however, accomplices, children, "infamous and notorious" characters and even "personal enemies," all of whose testimony would normally have been excluded,[150] were to be heard. Boguet felt it entirely appropriate to condemn on the "strength of those indubitable indicators and conjectures" that traditionally allowed for torture but were not normally sufficient for conviction. Given these evidentiary rules, accusations were likely to lead to conviction either through reliance on lower standards of evidence alone or by the use of these lower standards to justify extorting confessions under torture.

The initiative to end prosecution in France seems to have come from the intellectually sophisticated Parisian judicial class, which, despite strong popular belief and a series of powerful outbreaks, forced a new, more skeptical mentality on lesser jurisdictions. It has been suggested by Robert Mandrou that the increasingly critical mentality of the Parisian parlementaires resulted from intellectual contact with theologians, physicians, and savants, and particularly with the philosophic and scientific circles of Mersenne and Théophraste Renaudot. These overlapping groups of legal, scientific, and theological intellectuals, all with professional interests in the distinction between supernatural and natural, and in the evaluating of evidence, now urged all investigators—judicial, scientific, and philosophic—to greater caution, both in the investigative process and in reaching conclusions.[151]

These currents probably owed a good deal to Michel de Montaigne, who despite factual evidence, "proofs and free confessions," refused to believe in the deeds of witches. His 1588 essay on witchcraft emphasized the cautiousness required in assenting to evidence of this nature. It was more likely that two men lied than that one travelled on the wind. One should believe the best rather than the largest number of witnesses. "Luminous, clear-cut evidence" was essential. If Bodin was inclined to accept virtually anything he heard or read on the subject of witchcraft, Montaigne felt it was "putting a very high price on one's conjectures to roast a man alive for them."[152] Bodin's writings show how powerful, legally trained minds could provide support for witchcraft prosecutions. Montaigne's suggest how those of a similar professional background, but one tinged with skepticism, could move in the opposite direction. The Parisian-based intellectuals increasingly expressed disdain for popular credulity and urged greater caution in crediting witnesses.[153] Cyrano de Bergerac, for example, combined open contempt for the witch beliefs of ignorant peasants with concern for the critical evaluation of witnesses and testimony, claiming he would accept no opinion simply because "many people hold it, or because it is the thought of some great Philosopher." He would "admit no Witches until someone proves it to me." Most cases Cyrano had heard about simply did not meet his standard of evidence.[154]

By 1640, the Parisian judiciary, whose jurisdiction covered almost half of France, had instituted a new policy. If the parlementaires did not go so far as to suggest that witchcraft was impossible, they became increasingly unwilling to accept the proofs of Bodin or Boguet. Robert Mandrou concludes that their critical examination of evidence constituted a virtually "new Jurisprudence."[155] But just as important as the revised standards was the ability to enforce them on lesser jurisdictions. Automatic review by the Parlement of Paris was becoming the norm for all cases involving torture or capital punishment. The judges were thus in a position to educate and control provincial magistrates, and insure more rigorous and scrupulous analysis of evidence.[156]

Alfred Soman rejects Mandrou's thesis, suggesting that it was rigorous implementation of traditional Roman law standards of proof in lesser jurisdictions which yielded these results.[157] There is every reason to suppose that the developments in the capital described by Mandrou, and those in the provinces described by Soman were occurring simultaneously and interactively. The Parlement of Paris may have chosen to dress its skepticism about witchcraft in the language of the new philosophy. Provincial magistrates, more wedded to tradition, might achieve the same results by rejecting the laxness of Bodin and Boguet, and working the traditional formal system of proofs to its fullest rigor. It would occur only very rarely that a witchcraft prosecution that succeeded under a rigorous application of the old proofs would nonetheless fail to meet the standards of proof of the new philosophy. Gradually the standards affected most royal bureaucrats and provincial parlements, though inferior judges were occasionally recalcitrant. Had provincial authorities not been controlled by the sovereign courts, they would undoubtedly have continued to employ Boguet's standards much longer. In France, as in England, traditional beliefs remained strong in rural areas long after the educated elite, which composed the governing classes, refused to enforce them.

A new epidemic in the 1670s finally resulted in royal intervention and the imposition of the stricter standards of evidence employed by the Parlement of Paris.[158] The Edict of 1682 ended the era of witchcraft prosecution in France, for the edict implied that magic was merely an illusion pretended by imposters.

Similar patterns of decline occurred elsewhere on the Continent. Both E. W. Monter's study of the Swiss-French borderlands and H. C. Erik Midelfort's examination of Southwestern Germany suggest a similar chronology. Midelfort notes that the decline occurred before philosophical currents of the Enlightenment could have had any very great effect on general beliefs about witchcraft. He suggests witch hunters stopped hunting and executing witches not because people no longer believed in them, but because judges no longer knew how to find them. It was thus a crisis of confidence in traditional judicial procedures and fact finding which brought the panics to a halt.[159]

Increasing cautiousness, if not skepticism, was clearly developing in Europe. The *Cautio Criminalis* by the Jesuit Friedrich Spee, which went through sixteen editions in the century after its publication in 1631, provided a scathing indictment of German criminal procedure. Spee's critique of the improper use of the proof system was thought to have influenced several German princes to end witchcraft prosecutions in their domain. In 1635, the Roman Inquisition itself concluded it "has found scarcely one trial conducted legally."[160] Its 1657 ordinances dealing with witchcraft accusations attempted to provide a far more careful set of rules for handling accusations and testimony. A more rigorous application of evidentiary standards and procedures was thus extremely important in the decline of prosecution and conviction of continental witches.[161]

The role of the scientific movement in this decline has been discussed by a number of historians. Most now agree that the decline began before the scientific and philosophical movements often associated with it were widely disseminated. Nevertheless, from at least the beginning of the seventeenth century, we can trace the erosion of a world view that peopled the natural environment with spirits and occult forces. It was no accident that the most intellectually sophisticated supporters of the spirit world, More and Glanvill, were deeply influenced by neo-Platonic thought, which had been at its height in the sixteenth century. A mechanical world simply left little room for the world of spirits. The religious scientists and scientific theologians who dominated the late seventeenth-century intellectual community in England found an orderly, mechanistic, but providentially guided universe, religiously and intellectually satisfying.[162] More important than the general popular belief in witches and spirits was the attitude of those educated individuals who were required to deal with evidence in witch accusations and trials. All over Europe, in the course of dealing with large numbers of accusations, these people came to realize that it was very difficult to prove to their own satisfaction the actual witch activities of the particular persons accused, no matter what their beliefs about witchcraft in general. Thus, the evidentiary standards and procedures of the age had a substantial impact on the rate of success in witchcraft prosecutions, even before the more general aspects of philosophy and science undermined the beliefs that fueled the initiation of such prosecutions. Greater care in handling accusations led to a rapid increase in acquittals, as judges and juries found they had inadequate tools to discover witches. In France, critical standards were imposed on lesser tribunals. In England where, due to the absence of torture as a means of obtaining confession, mass executions had never been a serious problem, judges, justices of the peace, grand juries, and eventually juries applied more rigorous standards of evidence and proof. While we do not wish to suggest that theories of evidence and proof alone were responsible for the rapid decline of witch trials and witch belief, we should not underestimate their role.

In the whole complex of factors leading the rise and decline of witchcraft prosecutions in the sixteenth and seventeenth centuries, the concern for evidentiary standards served as the leading edge of a new world view that would eventually have the profoundest impact on all of Western culture. Precisely because witchcraft raised problems of fact finding within a practical area and within the interlocking contexts of historical authority, religious belief, and legal technology, it was a forcing ground for working out the implications of the new approach to evidence. The intellectual elite of judges, theologians, and scientists who did the working out bore a direct responsibility for shaping public policy in an area that literally involved life and death. As a result, the witchcraft controversy provides an early and sharply focused episode in the development of a central belief in the modern world—the belief that, in the empirical realm, the issue is not absolute truth or falsehood, but the degree of certainty or probability that can be attributed to a factual proposition.

VII

Language, Communication, and Literature

SEVENTEENTH-CENTURY intellectuals were acutely aware of problems of language and communication. Neither the traditional models of logic and rhetoric nor the modification of these models in the hands of Rudolph Agricola, Peter Ramus, and other humanist reformers suited their needs. Particularly those individuals concerned with utilizing fact and experience rejected both syllogistic science based on Aristotelian logic and the Ciceronian derived rhetoric which was in some respects its companion art. A critique of traditional logic and rhetoric thus went hand in hand with the new methodology. What was required was a new mode of communication for the new knowledge and particularly for statements of fact, one that presented information with a minimum of distortion or bias.

The search for new forms of language to replace traditional logic and rhetoric pervades seventeenth-century intellectual life. Following our earlier practice of separating for analytical purposes what were in reality overlapping disciplines, we will examine how the reaction to traditional logic and rhetoric affected science and natural philosophy, history, law, and religion. Then we will note that the mutual concerns for language in all of these disciplines combined to produce a substantial shift in prose style. We will then briefly examine linguistic developments which grew out of the pervasive concern for unbiased communication. Among the principal concerns of the new linguistics were the development of universal languages that would enable scholars to communicate accurately across linguistic barriers, the exploration of the relation between language and thought, and the development of systematic grammars and dictionaries.

From linguistics we will move to literature. For efforts to devise a theory of knowledge, and consequently of language, that would allow a more complete synthesis of theoretical and empirical findings led to a revised attitude toward the literary arts, and particularly toward poetry. Where a principal item on the intellectual agenda is to render factual statements more precise and to distinguish carefully statements supported by evidence from mere speculation, there is bound to be an impact on literature. This impact must be all the greater when a principal literary form—poetry—is closely linked to rhetoric, and rhetoric in turn is seen as a barrier to precise factual statement. The development of a literature of exploration, travel, and description is an obvious response to the new concerns. So is the introduction of the newspaper designed to present reports of events uncolored by rhetoric or bias. Less obvious but more important responses were the development of a new fact-oriented form of fiction—the novel—and a major shift of poetic style away from the "contaminations" of traditional rhetoric. Thus, our survey of literature must be a broad one, because the new theories of knowledge both created new forms and deeply affected the old forms of literary expression.

Before beginning this march from philosophy through science and history to linguistics and literature, we must say something of the traditions of logic and rhetoric against which thinkers in all of these areas were in revolt.

Sixteenth-century thought was characterized by an Aristotelian derived logic that had evolved over several centuries and a fundamentally Ciceronian rhetoric that had been revived and given new prominence by Renaissance humanists. Learned communication was dominated by logic and its associated art—dialectic—while rhetoric was expected to shape various forms of popular discourse, that is, preaching and most forms of oratory. If learned argument and communication, the realm of logic and dialectic, were to be devoid of emotional appeals and literary effect, popular discourse was expected to draw sustenance from just such appeals and effects. In theory at least, philosopher and orator were to devote themselves not only to different subject matters and audiences but also to different standards of excellence and different methods of presenting their material.

Neither logic nor rhetoric, however, remained static in the sixteenth and seventeenth centuries.[1] Nor did the relationship between them. While poetry was not considered identical to rhetoric, the two had become closely linked as rhetoric became increasingly associated with amplification and ornamentation. Rhetorical texts focused on the means of enlarging and expanding similitudes, and many had simply become compendiums of rhetorical tropes and figures. One popular text, for example, suggested that the function of rhetoric was to enable one "Copiously to dilate any matter or sentence."[2] Amplification and ornamentation were skills taught by rhetoric and employed by poets as well as writers aspiring to eloquence. These practices were so deeply ingrained that they were not employed as mere illustration, but had become part of Renaissance proof and argumentation.[3] "Good utterance," according to neo-Ciceronian theorist George Puttenham, "riseth altogether in figurative speaches."[4] At its height, the linkage could produce the profuse and vivid imagery and elaborate language of Spencer as well as the complexities of the metaphysical poets and prose writers. It could also produce verbosity, excess, and ambiguity.

We have seen that seventeenth-century philosophers, scientists, and historians were attempting to reconstruct knowledge by grounding it on fact and experience. This realm of the "probable" rather than the logically certain was traditionally the realm of rhetoric. By the seventeenth century, however, rhetoric appeared to be too emotional, too personally biased, too ready to accept common opinion, and too amplified, verbose, and poetic for their purposes. Practitioners of the new fact-oriented learning became restive with the standard models of writing and thinking.

Rhetoric certainly offered techniques for dealing with facts and was accustomed to handling the world of common experience, but its goal was not truth nor "science." Its goal was persuasiveness based on probability. Probability, however, was taken to mean plausibility. Rhetoric's emphasis on popular persuasion also made it unsuitable if not dangerous to truth-seekers. Not only might rhetoric involve conscious deception but, perhaps even more important, its aim was persuasion, not the transfer of knowledge. The rhetorician varied his arguments with different audiences and was not required to produce contrary evidence. He buttressed his position with the force of his personality and the authority of others and was expected to play on the passions and deeply felt prejudices of his audience. The new scholarly community of historians, naturalists, and empirically oriented philosophers, on the other hand, did not wish to rely on authority or the long standing prejudices of the common people. Indeed, the rejection of the principle of authority was one of the hallmarks of the new community. Nor did it seek mere plausibility. When seventeenth-century scholars spoke of probability, they increasingly shifted away from the rhetorical notion of plausibility and verisimilitude. Instead, they referred to the degree to which conclusions and judgments were based on evidence rather than the rhetorical skill of the writer. They sought a mode of communication that could transfer information, findings of fact, theories, and arguments with a minimum of appeal to emotion, bias, and authority. Traditional rhetoric did not provide an adequate model of communication for the newer style of intellectual. Thus, Gilbert insisted that his *De Magnete* would be presented without "the grace of rhetoric" or "verbal ornateness," and would include only "such terms as are needed to make what is said intelligible."[5]

Yet neither Gilbert nor his many successors felt it desirable to return to the Aristotelian directives for philosophical discourse, though Aristotle had insisted on the need for a straightforward, undecorated, plain style. Scholastic logic and dialectic, and the modes of scholarly argumentation and disputation associated with them, were increasingly under attack in the sixteenth century, first by humanists and then by naturalists. Aristotle was so identified with the defects of scholastic philosophy and logic that it became difficult to return to explicitly Aristotelian canons of scientific discourse.

The early humanists, newly embued with the goals of eloquence, ridiculed logic and dialectic for their verbal barbarism and lack of moral utility. Subsequently, natural philosophers and empirical investigators rejected the claims of logic and dialectic. The syllogism and its variants were increasingly considered an unsatisfactory means of producing knowledge, and the terminology employed by its proponents was increasingly viewed as largely meaningless. As natural science and other branches of knowledge became more empirical, terminology and modes of communication based on logic and dialectic no longer proved adequate.

Other developments of the sixteenth century blurred the distinctions between rhetoric, on the one hand, and logic and dialectic, on the other. In the interests of an improved pedagogy, a number of humanists, most importantly Agricola, Philipp Melanchthon, and Ramus, developed a reformed dialectic to organize and present the subject matters of all disciplines. At about the same time, humanists began to reject a fundamental Aristotelian distinction. For Aristotle, if one began from premises that were certain and proceeded by arguments that were logically correct, one arrived at a demonstration of truth. This was the realm of logic. If one began from plausible but uncertain premises and proceeded by logical

230

argument, one had entered the realm of dialectic. Many humanists believed that this was a distinction without a difference because both involved the same operations. Accordingly, dialectic became the appropriate means of handling all kinds of argument, and all kinds of subject matters. Such humanist teachers whose influence was widely felt in England were not concerned with the creation of new knowledge but with the appropriate presentation of an existing body of knowledge. In their hands, dialectic would take over much of what had previously belonged to rhetoric, as well as what had belonged to logic. Rudolph Agricola, whose 1515 textbook became well known in England, was one of the first to introduce the new mode of teaching which combined dialectic and rhetoric into a single art of discourse. Thus, the arts of "copia," that is, techniques for amplifying, embellishing, and illustrating, which had traditionally belonged to rhetoric, were now included in the new dialectic. Philipp Melanchthon's "dialectic," too, encompassed most of the traditional aspects of logic, dialectic, and rhetoric; and John Seton's elementary text, designed to provide rules for all kinds of writing, not just formal disputation, was composed of a mixture of logic, dialectic, and rhetoric.[6]

Although the enormously influential work of Peter Ramus observed the traditional distinction between logic and rhetoric, it created a single art of discourse, "dialectic," that handled arguments leading to "science" as well as those that dealt with probability and opinion, traditionally the realm of rhetoric. His system was designed to serve preachers, logicians, mathematicians, lawyers, poets, indeed all writers. Ramus, no more than Agricola or Melanchthon, espoused the new philosophy, for he retained the assumption that argumentation and dispute were the appropriate means of eliminating error and establishing truth. Ramist reorganization also contracted the scope of rhetoric. Rhetoric was limited to delivery and to style, by which Ramus meant the ornamentation and enrichment of speech largely by means of tropes and figures. Ramism thus merged all types of thought and discourse but separated these from the language in which they were clothed. Rhetoric now involved garnishing thought which had been arrived at by other means. Ramism, which spread to England in the 1570s, and was particularly favored by Puritan divines, had a wide though never overwhelming influence in England.[7]

The new blends of logic, dialectic, and rhetoric created special problems for those whose interest focused on the search for truth. Rhetorical devices, such as amplification and the use of figures and tropes, now might creep into writing about "truth" and "science," thus creating ambiguity and obscurity where precision and clarity were desired. The conflation of rhetoric, logic, and dialectic meant that there was no longer a variety of distinct models of communication and style from which one suitable for scientific discourse might be chosen.

In England, no school of thought became dominant. Neo-Aristotelians and neo-Ciceronians confronted Ramists and others who sought to create dialectics of their own. As a result, linguistic issues remained unresolved both for those who did not have an interest in the newer epistemological developments of the seventeenth century and those who did. Unresolved issues were whether learned and popular discourse should or could share a common theory of communication; whether logic, either Aristotelian or Ramist, was a viable system of communication; and what role any of the old or new systems of discourse might play in communicating new knowledge. There were also questions involving the relationship between language and thought, between words and things, and as to whether embellishment and figures were essential or decorative. All of these issues were further complicated by the difficulty of relating any of the available modes of discourse or any combination of them to inductive or partially inductive methods. Those who sought knowledge in experience, matter of fact, and experiment had no agreed mode by which to communicate their findings.

A linguistic crisis thus arose when philosophers, and especially natural philosophers, invaded the everyday world and made experience and matter of fact central to their concerns. The problem arose with the realization of the difficulties of employing an imprecise and nontechnical language associated with common experience. This unsatisfactory situation had a number of results. The first was an effort to produce a more precise language for the data and processes of interest to naturalists and philosophers, leaving everyday speech and literary language much the same. The other was to modify all language in the direction of greater clarity and precision. The new emphasis on matter of fact and experience thus would leave its impact not only on those disciplines which had always dealt with facts but on language and literature as well.

NATURAL SCIENCE AND PHILOSOPHY

Philosophers and natural scientists were deeply troubled by these problems of language. From at least the time of Gilbert, we see a growing concern for finding a suitable means of communication. The first major effort was made by Francis Bacon, who hoped to establish an essentially new logic, a New Organon, and an appropriate mode of communication to deliver its findings.

Indeed, it would be difficult to discuss the growing hostility to scholasticism and scholastic terminology or the development of the plain style so characteristic of the late seventeenth century without reference to Bacon. Bacon's role in the process is complex and ambiguous, and it has attracted the attention of many scholars.[8] The famous Baconian Idols, however, suggest something of his position.

Bacon numbered the misuse of words among the Idols afflicting mankind. "The idols imposed by words" were of two types, being "either the names of things which do not exist" or "the names of things which exist but yet confused and ill defined and hastily and irregularly derived from realities." The first variety, which included concepts like "Fortune, the Prime Mover, Planetary Orbits . . . and like fictions," had its origin in "false and idle theories" and might be largely eliminated by the adoption of the Baconian methodology. The second, more deeply rooted, having its origin in "faulty and unskilful abstraction," might be improved but not fully eradicated.[9] The "juggelries and charms of words" would always remain to "seduce and forcibly disturb the judgement."[10]

The disposition to study words rather than things, Bacon felt, owed a good deal to the humanist revival of classical literature and learning. Although the revival of ancient learning had increased the store of knowledge, excessive admiration for ancient eloquence had led his contemporaries to be more concerned with:

choiceness of the phrase, and the round and clean composition of the sentence, and the sweet falling of the clauses, and the varying and illustration of their works with tropes and figures, than after the weight of matter, worth of subject, soundness of argument, life of invention or depth of judgment.[11]

The Renaissance revival and development of the rhetorical and literary arts thus aggravated the problems posed by the Baconian Idols.

Bacon's reform aspirations were anything but modest. He proposed to create both a new inductive logic and a reformed mode of communication. The new philosophy based on Bacon's inductive method was to be grounded on a collection of natural histories which would in time yield the certain principles of natural philosophy. A simple direct prose was required in this initial phase of collecting natural histories.

> And for all that concerns ornaments of speech, similitudes, treasury of eloquence, and such like emptinesses, let it be utterly dismissed. Also let all those things which are admitted be themselves set down briefly and concisely, so that they may be nothing less than words. For no man who is collecting and storing up materials . . . thinks of arranging them elegantly, as in a shop, and displaying them so as to please the eye; all his care is that they be sound and good, and that they be arranged as to take up as little room as possible. . . . And this is exactly what should be done here.[12]

These influential comments, however, referred only to the preliminary stage. Later stages required other modes of presentation.

These issues led Bacon to a discussion of the various audiences that might be involved. Unlike the scholastics, Bacon's new philosophy might have a popular as well as a learned audience, and perhaps for this reason, his discussion of philosophical communication tended to take on a somewhat rhetorical cast. Currently there was a "contract of error between the deliverer and the receiver" of knowledge which derived from the fact that the former wished to "deliver it in such a form as may be best believed, and not as may be best examined."[13] Scholars thus tended to be "magisterial and peremptory" rather than "ingenius and faithful."[14] Although Bacon wished knowledge to be communicated by "the same method wherein it was invented," his goal was immensely difficult to realize because no one, as he himself recognized, could actually determine the processes by which he obtained knowledge.[15] In the end, Bacon concluded that the aphorism came closest to his goal. The aphorism was not merely the pithy statement, commonplace, or maxim traditionally favored by rhetoricians, but a "sure foundation." It enabled philosophers to convey "knowledge broken," a form which invited further inquiry. It could present the "pith and heart of sciences," and required no illustration. The aphorist avoided any need to show order and connection. Initially, aphorisms, a kind of condensed knowledge, would be fragmented, but they would eventually be used as "bricks" to build and communicate a true inductive science.[16]

The Baconian aphorism, however, did not commend itself to later philosophers and scientists in the way his prescriptions for the preliminary stage of compiling histories did. In this respect, as in so many others, Bacon was more propagandist than practitioner of the new philosophy, and he himself employed analogy and im-

234

agery for the purposes of argument as much as did his contemporaries.[17]

Despite his critique of rhetorical excess, his concern for the distortion of words, and his efforts to provide new models for scientific and philosophic communication, Bacon found traditional "rhetoric, or the art of eloquence" to be "a science excellent and excellently well laboured," whose "duty and office" was to apply "reason to imagination for the better moving of the will."[18] Rhetoric thus had its place in the moral or active life where decisions partook of good and evil. This rhetoric included the traditional political and forensic discourse and speeches of praise or blame. Nevertheless, Bacon attacked Nicholas Car and Roger Ascham for deifying Cicero and Demosthenes, suggesting that "the whole inclinations of those times was rather towards copie than weight."[19] The rival Senecan style, so popular in the early seventeenth century, he found overly concise and cryptic, even considering it as one of the "distemper[s] of learning."[20] If Bacon admired rhetoric in principle, employed many of its techniques in his own work, and felt it served an important function in morals and politics, at the same time he felt impelled to stress its current ambiguity and distortion.

The linguistic views of Thomas Hobbes were in many respects even more traditional than Bacon's. For instance, Hobbes retained the division between science and rhetoric. Nevertheless, he exhibited the growing hostility to scholastic logic and rhetorical excess that marked many of his contemporaries. Indeed, his work points the way toward the possibility of reviving Aristotelian norms of a nonrhetorical philosophical style. Despite his hostility to Aristotelian logic, physics, and metaphysics, Hobbes, more than most seventeenth-century English philosophers, stressed definition and deduction. Nor did he, like most of his seventeenth-century scientific contemporaries, ignore Aristotelian standards of scientific prose and Aristotelian rhetorical analysis. He even produced an epitome or condensed version of Aristotle's *Rhetoric*. Hobbes, like Bacon, emphasized the acute need to improve the communication of knowledge. His investigation into the nature of human knowledge also led him to explore the relationship between knowledge and language.[21]

Words for Hobbes were simply the names for the ideas or conceptions of things, and the purpose of speech was to transfer mental into verbal discourse.[22] "True and false," he insisted, were "attributes of speech, not of things."[23] Like Bacon, he felt that the growth of knowledge had been impeded by abuses of language. If ge-

235

ometry, the model science for Hobbes, was the only science that had begun "at settling the significations of the words," precise definition could and should be extended to all areas of knowledge.[24] Many words were "insignificant" sounds without any meaning. In "all rigorous search for truth," ambiguity and especially metaphor must "be utterly excluded."[25] All "obscure, confused, and ambiguous Expression" and metaphorical speeches that stir up the passions must be cast aside.[26]

Perhaps even more influential were Thomas Sprat's famous pronouncements made on behalf of the Royal Society. The Society's position, which in large part involved a rejection of the use of rhetorical and metaphoric language in the natural sciences, may well have stemmed from the fact that for several generations Englishmen had been taught via the new "dialectics" to combine rhetorical and scientific subjects and language. This unified art of discourse contributed to the problems faced by the Society. The Royal Society now "indeavor'd to separate the knowledge of Nature, from the colours of Rhetoric, the devices of Fancy, or the delightful deceit of Fables."[27] Any old-fashioned, Aristotelian, scholastic philosopher would have agreed, as indeed did Alexander Ross, defender of Aristotle and scholasticism. The Society's members did not really return to Aristotle, however, nor did they uncritically follow in Bacon's footsteps. Although they adopted Bacon's advice about the language to be used in the collection of natural histories, and indeed extended it to all scientific communication, they did not follow his efforts to develop the maxim and aphorism as an appropriate method of scientific communication.

The Society was very seriously concerned with the "manner of their discourse," feeling that unless it was extremely vigilant, "the whole spirit and vigour of their Design" would soon be "eaten out, by the luxury and redundance of speech," the "ill effects" of which had "already overwhelm'd most other Arts and Professions."[28]

Who can behold, without indignation, how many mists and uncertaintyies, these specious Tropes and Figures have brought on our Knowledge? How many rewards, which are due to more profitable and difficult Arts, have been . . . snatch'd away by the vanity of fine speaking. . . . I dare say; that of all the Studies of men, nothing may be sooner obtained than this vicious abundance of Phrase, this trick of Metaphor, this volubility of Tongue, which makes so great a noise in the World.[29]

The "evil," so deeply ingrained by the educational system, made it "hard to know whom to blame, or where to begin to reform."[30] The evil threatened international peace, religion, and philosophy.

The Royal Society, however, had done something

toward correcting of its excesses in Natural Philosophy; to which it is, of all others, a most profest enemy.

They have therefore been most rigorous in putting in execution, the only Remedy, that can be found . . . and that has been, a constant Resolution, to reject all the amplifications, digressions, and swellings of style: to return back to the primitive purity, and shortness, when men deliver'd so many things, almost in an equal number of words. They have exacted from all their members, a close, naked, natural way of speaking; positive expressions; clear senses; a native easiness: bringing all things as near the Mathematical plainness, as they can: and preferring the language of Artizans, Countrymen, and Merchants, before that of Wits, or Scholars.[31]

The Society's statutes required "In all Reports to be brought into the Society, the Matter of Fact shall be barely stated, without any Prefaces, Apologies, or Rhetorical Flourishes."[32] "The Language employed," Sprat insisted on behalf of the Society, must "bring Knowledge back again to our very Senses from whence it was first derived to our understandings."[33]

Similar views are found in a substantial number of those interested in the new philosophy. We should not be surprised that John Wilkins's views were very close to those of Sprat, since Sprat was his protégé and Wilkins guided much of what was contained in the History. His own Essay Toward a Real Character and a Philosophical Language also emphasized "the ambiguity of words" resulting from "Metaphor and Phraseology." Although such devices seemed "to contribute to elegance and ornament of Speech; yet, like other affected ornaments, prejudice the native simplicity of it, and contribute to the disguising of it with false appearances."[34] Wilkins also noted the difficulties caused by linguistic change. Modes of expression were "very changeable, every generation producing new ones; witness the present Age, especially the late times, wherein this grand imposture of Phrases hath almost eat out solid knowledge in all professions."[35] His own reform scheme, which we shall discuss shortly, would reduce the number of words, "prevent much circumlocution, contributate to perspicuity and distinctness, and very much promote the elegance and significancy of speech."[36]

Samuel Parker, like Wilkins and Sprat a defender of both experimental science and latitudinarian religion, insisted with Sprat that metaphor be excluded from natural philosophy:

Now to Discourse of the Natures of Things in Metaphors and Allegories is nothing else but to sport and trifle with empty words, because these Schems do not express the Natures of Things but only their Similitudes

237

and Resemblances. . . . All these Theories in Philosophy which are expressed only in metaphorical Terms, are not real Truths, but meer Products of the Imagination. . . . Thus their wanton & luxurious fancies climbing up into the Bed of Reason, do not only defile it . . . but instead of real conceptions and notices of Things, impregnate the mind with nothing but Ayerie . . . Phantasmes.[37]

True statements and useful theory must avoid dealing in mere resemblances and must accurately represent the phenomenon itself.

Although he did not begin as an advocate of the plain style, Joseph Glanvill became one. Glanvill directed his attention to the obscurities and empty verbalism of scholastic philosophy rather than to excessive metaphor and ornamentation.[38] Removing "unnecessary Terms of Art" and stating things in "clear and plain words" would themselves end many contentions, thus promoting "both . . . truth and peace."[39] The traditional framework of scholastic science was argument, disputation, and debate. Glanvill and others speaking in behalf of the new philosophy repudiated its contentious mode of argumentation as well as its excessively verbal character. The Royal Society claimed it was not interested in "winning" adherence to any particular position. All were humbly to present their findings.

Although not all members of the Royal Society consistently conformed to the new standard of scientific communication, a remarkable number of them promoted it. Ambiguity had to be removed or at least mitigated by excising metaphor, similitude, and the tropes and figures of rhetoric from natural philosophy. According to Sir William Petty, contemporary writing consisted "only of words, opinions, and theories," instead of "descriptions" of things. To remedy this he began "A Dictionary of Sensible Words" to state "what sensible Matter, Thing, Notion or Action every word therein doth mean and signify,"[40] to "curtail verbal superfluity and insignificancy, in short . . . sweep away all the fogginess of words."[41] The Royal Society, he felt, helped eliminate such fogginess by making "Mysterious Things plain," and eliminating "insignificant and puzzling words."[42]

Robert Hooke, too, insisted on the use of plain, unrhetorical style particularly in reporting scientific data.

The next thing to be taken care of is the manner of Registering . . . so that as nothing be wanting in the History, so nothing also be superfluous in the words. In the Choice of which, there ought to be great Care and

Circumspection, that they be such as are shortest and express the Matter with the least Ambiguity, and the greatest Plainness and Significancy, avoiding all kinds of Rhetorical Flourishes, or Oratorical Garnishes, and all sorts Periphrases or Circumlocutions.[43]

Robert Boyle hoped for the introduction of "more significant and less ambiguous terms and expressions" in natural philosophy,[44] and Baconian Joshua Childrey adopted the plain style, insisting he would "not disfigure the face of Truth by daubing it over with the paint of Language." Childrey was particularly sensitive to the difficulty of translating "exactly what we have seen or heard" into words. Ambiguity might be introduced despite conscious efforts to avoid it.[45]

That the Royal Society and other virtuosi concerned with the development of natural knowledge almost unanimously joined in attacking poetic language, metaphor, similitude, and rhetorical flourishes in scientific writing is hardly surprising in the light of their common concern for the accurate reporting of facts and the existence of a similar tradition in Aristotelian logic. What is most interesting is that they felt it necessary to repeat and restate this position with such vehemence. They re-emphasized this position for several reasons. First, logical and rhetorical techniques and language had essentially become merged in a single mode of discourse, so that the tactic of assigning one language to science and another to literature or daily affairs was no longer available. Second, that single mode of discourse had become so closely linked to poetry, and thus to amplification of thought and language, that those opposed to amplification in their own discourse felt constantly embattled. Third, Bacon's curious combinations of plain style, aphorism, and traditional rhetoric did not promise good results for scientific communication. Fourth, Aristotelian philosophy and science were in increasing disrepute. Their terminology was considered vague and confusing and was often thought to refer to nothing at all, or to be the creation of the imagination. Their basis was ratiocination not observation and their mode of presentation was contentious and argumentative. The new scientists thus were reluctant to identify their search for a more adequate form of communication with the Aristotelian tradition. Instead, they sought a new standard of plain, unadorned language for science and tended to identify it with mathematics, ordinary speech, or sometimes even Scripture.

The extent to which epistemological and philosophical exploration were linked to the critique of existing modes of communication can be seen in Locke's *An Essay Concerning Human Understanding* (1690), which was as concerned with language and the communication of knowledge as with the character of knowledge itself. Locke was convinced that the "extent and certainty of our knowledge" was closely linked to words. Indeed "unless their force and manner of signification were first well observed, there could be very little said clearly and pertinently concerning knowledge." For Locke, the problems engendered by language were twofold, one caused by the natural imperfections of words, the other by the willful abuse of language. The purpose of language was to transfer one man's thoughts or ideas to another, to accomplish that "with as much ease and quickness as possible" and "thereby to convey the knowledge of things." Language was "abused or deficient" if it failed in any of these.[46]

Communication for Locke was of two varieties: civil, which included common conversation and the ordinary affairs of life, and philosophical, "to convey the precise notions of things, and to express in general propositions, certain and undoubted truths." Although the former required "less exactness," the goal of both was understanding, something impossible to achieve if words did "not excite in the hearer the same idea which it stands for in the mind of the speaker."[47] Although Locke's distinction between civil and philosophical discourse is reminiscent of the traditional dichotomy between rhetoric and logic, he does not suggest, as tradition had, that they be governed by different standards or rules. For Locke it is the philosophical use of words, with its emphasis on precision and truth, which established the proper standard for *all* communication.

For Locke, the basic linguistic problem resulted from the problematic relationship between words and things and more importantly between words and ideas. This is the problem of the "signification" of words. The signification of many words was arbitrary or vague because the word signified a complex combination of ideas, or because the idea signified was not itself precisely related to a natural phenomenon or because the word denoted a moral rather than a physical phenomenon.[48] In all these instances there existed no standard in nature by which to "rectify" and adjust their significations.[49] Even where a word signified a natural substance so that it was possible to "follow Nature . . . and regulate the signification of their names by the things themselves," problems might arise.[50] It was often impossible to determine the real essences of things, and thus the appropriate words for them. Having pointed to the natural imperfections of language, Locke denounced "willful faults and neglects"—the use of words that did not clearly signify any particular idea or phenomenon, inconsistent usage, ambiguity, and the belief that having coined a phrase or term one had proved the existence of a phenomenon. These faults were liberally attributed to "Schoolmen and Metaphysicians," Aristotelians, Peripatetics, and Platonists.[51]

Despite these natural and humanly created imperfections, language remained the "great bond" that held society together and was the means "whereby the improvements of knowledge" were conveyed. Those who "pretended seriously to search after or maintain truth" must therefore "study how they might deliver themselves without obscurity, doubtfulness, or equivocation."[52] First, it was necessary to "take care to use no words without a signification, no names without an idea for which he makes it stand."[53] The second was to insure that words annexed to simple ideas "be clear and distinct"; and those annexed to complex ideas "be determinate." This was particularly crucial for moral terms which had "no settled objects in nature, from whence their ideas are taken."[54] The difficulty of defining such complex notions as justice did not excuse the failure to follow his rule. Indeed failure to do so would insure continued obscurity, confusion, and unnecessary "wrangling."[55] Third, the names of substances had to be made "conformable to things as they exist," and the definition of things to "the truth of things." That truth was to be determined by inquiry into "the nature and properties of the Things themselves."[56] A natural history to present the "properties" of things was thus essential not only to the progress of knowledge but to the improvement of language.[57]

Greater precision was not only "absolutely necessary" in philosophical inquiry but highly desirable in common speech. Echoing Sprat, Locke suggested that philosophers might learn something from ordinary people, "merchants and lovers, cooks and sailors," who frequently expressed themselves with greater clarity than philosophers. One must therefore "take care to apply . . . words as near as may be to such ideas as common use has annexed them to." Words must not be permitted to become the private possession of learned men, but instead serve as "the common measure of commerce and communication."[58]

"In all discourses wherein one man pretends to instruct or convince another, he should use the same words constantly in the same sense." If this alone were done:

many of the books extant might be spared; many of the controversies in dispute would be at end, several of those great volumes, swollen with ambiguous words, now used in one sense, and by and by in another, would shrink into a very narrow compass; and many of the philosophers' (to mention no others) as well as poets' work, might be contained in a nut-shell.[59]

Locke attacks the traditional arts of rhetoric in both the philosophical and civil sphere. If one wished to

speak of things as they are, we must allow that all the art of rhetoric, besides order and clearness; all the artificial and figurative application of words eloquence hath invented, are for nothing else but to insinuate wrong ideas, move the passions, and thereby mislead the judgment; as so indeed are perfect cheats; and therefore, however laudable or allowable oratory may render them in harangues and popular addresses, they are certainly, in all discourses, that pretend to inform or instruct, wholly to be avoided.[60]

Where truth, knowledge, and morality were concerned, rhetoric—the "arts of fallacy"—had no place, for it was an "instrument of error and deceit."[61]

The seventeenth-century desire to improve scientific and philosophical communication seems to have taken two general directions. One approach retained, or perhaps it would be more accurate to say returned to, the essentially dualistic scheme of the ancients. This first approach, exemplified by Bacon, Hobbes, and Sprat, at least in some of his moods, involved the elimination of inappropriate rhetorical devices and poetic language from natural science and philosophy, leaving rhetorical expression, properly pruned, to the civil sphere, to moral discourse, ordinary conversation, poetry, and the realm of the imagination. The philosophy to be pursued in unadorned language was no longer scholastic philosophy but some version of the new philosophy, with its strong mathematical and empirical orientation. The scholastic disputation based on traditional logic and dialectic no longer formed the substance, the method, or the mode of presentation of science. A reformed scientific language and a reformed rhetoric might thus exist side by side.

The alternative approach, sometimes suggested by Sprat and stated most explicitly and comprehensively by Locke, involved a rejection of the logic-rhetoric or philosophy-rhetoric dualism and the adoption of a new single art of discourse informed by the requirements of science and philosophy. According to this view, the arts of rhetoric and eloquence were pernicious, producing error and deceit, and so must be removed from all communication. This approach implied a single linguistic standard, informed by the demands of truth and clarity, to be used in all forms of communication.

The dualistic approach allowed science and the new philosophy to coexist comfortably with poetry, eloquence, and literature. Such an approach made possible the simultaneous commitment to science and the neo-classic standard of literary taste that characterized many late seventeenth- and early eighteenth-century thinkers. The other approach tended to disparage poetry and rhetoric as undermining the truth-conveying functions of language. Both, however, developed in the context of the philosophical and methodological discussions of seventeenth-century truth-seekers.

Efforts to reform the modes of communicating knowledge also resulted in efforts to understand the nature of language and of communication. The most characteristic efforts were directed at creating a universal character by which to communicate across linguistic barriers and at developing a universal language that would precisely designate all things and ideas. Related activity involved dictionary-making and an interest in codes including sign languages for the deaf and dumb. Most of these activities were pursued by overlapping groups of individuals stimulated first by Francis Bacon and then by John Wilkins.[62]

As scholars increasingly employed the vernaculars rather than Latin to expand domestic audiences, the European audience was in danger of being lost. Francis Bacon and others were attracted by the example of Chinese characters, which were understood and employed by those who did not themselves speak Chinese. It was thought that an analogous, albeit much simpler, system of characters might be devised for use across linguistic barriers. The increasingly widespread adoption of common symbols for numerals, algebraic functions and musical notation also stimulated the search for a common system of verbal notation, as did the growing number of shorthand systems being devised in England for the purpose of recording sermons.

The notion of arbitrary signs to designate words or concepts underlay the early efforts of John Wilkins and Cave Beck.[63] Wilkins's earliest linguistic effort explored the possibility not only of a universal character but communication by various types of codes. A universal set of symbols representing concepts and objects of the physical world would reduce the effort expended on learning languages. Time "now required on the Learning of Words, might then be employed in the Study of Things."[64] Wilkins's early work, the beginning of a lifetime effort at creating a universal language, thus echoed the view of many educational reformers that too much time and energy were being spent on linguistic study that might be better devoted to practical, utilitarian, or scientific ends. Promoters also envisioned religious benefits. The character would help repair the damage of the Fall and reverse the effects of the Tower of Babel, which had introduced the multiplicity of tongues. Religious controversy might be reduced since many theological disputes stemmed from differences over theological terms.

A number of approaches were attempted, the most common being to reduce the number of radicals to the fewest possible and then translate these into numbers. Cave Beck's effort resulted in a kind of numerical dictionary in which letters were added to the necessary words (numbers) to provide for tense, case, gender and number. William Petty, Robert Boyle, and Samuel Hartlib were among the early enthusiasts of a universal character.[65]

Even before these efforts were well under way, Descartes and Mersenne had begun to discuss the possibility of a "philosophical language." Their rather undeveloped speculations soon influenced English linguists, who moved away from simply translating existing languages into a universal character and toward creating a language that would describe and reflect reality itself. The new approach was far more difficult, requiring the classification and ordering of all knowledge and the enumeration of all things and concepts. Such efforts obviously could not be separated from questions about the nature of reality and man's ability to perceive it and communicate it to others.

A significant number of scholars in and around Oxford in the early 1650s were involved in both efforts as well as in other linguistic projects. The cryptographer and mathematician John Wallis worked on his *Grammatica Lingua Anglicanae* (1653), which dealt with the articulation of sounds and the relation between sounds and meanings.[66] Wallis and William Holder, later members of the Royal Society, developed rival systems of teaching the deaf and dumb to speak that grew out of efforts to relate language to sign and gesture.

The major shift occurred as George Dalgarno and John Wilkins began to develop both a universal character and a philosophical language. Dalgarno's originated as a shorthand that eventually became a character based on a philosophical classification. Wilkins, who worked on Dalgarno's tables,[67] became involved in a more complex scheme, based on the suggestions of Seth Ward, then Savilian Professor of Astronomy at Oxford.

But it did presently occure to me, that by the helpe of Logicke and Mathematics this might soon receive a mighty advantage, for all Discourse being resolved in sentences, those into words, words signifying either simple notions or being resolvable into simple notions it is manifest, that if all the simple notions be found out, and have Symboles assigned to them those will be extremealy few in respect of the other, (which are indeed Characters of words . . .) the reason of their composition easily known, and the compounded ones at once will be comprehended, and yet will represent to the very eye all the elements of the composition.[68]

Walter Charleton soon reported "considerable progress toward the invention of Symbols or Signs, for every Thing and Notion."[69] These efforts culminated in Wilkins's *Essay Toward a Real Character and Philosophical Language*, licensed by the Royal Society. The *Essay*, the fruit of a cooperative effort directed by Wilkins, included discussions of the origin, change, and diffusion of existing and past languages and alphabets. A rational language and character to express all things and ideas was to be created as all things and ideas were systematically classified and organized. By this means the names of things might be made to correspond to the things themselves. The classification included abstract metaphysical concepts, objects of the nature world—e.g., animals, plants, and insects—and the basic concepts of the military, ecclesiastical, and political worlds. Creations of the imagination such as fairies were omitted, as having no existence in nature.

Wilkins's attitude that "Things are better than words, as real knowledge is beyond the elegancy of speech" was shared by most of the philosophical and scientific community, though he perhaps carried the position to its logical extreme. Wilkins hoped his language and character would not only improve scientific and philosophical communication but "prove the shortest and plainest way for the attainment of real Knowledge, that hath been yet offered to the World." It might also benefit international commerce, lead to the dissemination of religious knowledge, and "contribute to the clearing of some of our Modern differences in Religion by unmasking wild errors, that shelter themselves under the guise of affected phrases."[70]

As several of his contemporaries pointed out, one problem with Wilkins's scheme was that the language could be no better than the classifications. To the extent that these were flawed, outmoded, or irrelevent, so the language itself would be. If the project easily lent itself to ridicule, however, it nevertheless continued to attract serious attention.[71] Robert Hooke, for example, thought:

it being a Character and Language so truly Philosophical, and so perfectly and thoroughly Methodical, that seemeth to be nothing wanting to make it have the utmost perfection, and highest Ideas of any Character and Language imaginable, as well for Philosophical as for common and constant use.[72]

Among its advantages was that it was "perfectly free from all manner of ambiguity, and yet the most copius, expressive and significative of any thing or Notion imaginable."[73]

In one way or another a substantial portion of those of the intellectual community with mathematical, empirical, and philosophical interests hoped to bring either words and things or words and concepts into closer relationship. If individuals differed on the question of whether a universal philosophical language or even a universal character was feasible, they agreed that language must be used with greater clarity and precision.

Most of our discussion thus far has focused on the relationship between natural philosophy and linguistic attitudes. As we have seen, a plain unadorned prose and an increasing use of symbols came to characterize philosophical and scientific writing. As the comments of Sprat, Wilkins, and Locke have already suggested, the same currents were felt beyond the world of philosophy or science in the realms of history, law, religion, and morals. While the impact on these areas was often diluted and somewhat more difficult to trace, we will now briefly examine the extent to which the standards of appropriate communication in these areas seem to have been altered by changes in scientific and philosophic epistemology and methodology.

HISTORY

The problem of appropriate language and style was more complex for historians than for philosophers. Both medieval and seventeenth-century scientists and philosophers had sought clarity and precision, the former by the employment of the scholastic method and terminology, the latter by its rejection. Although there were a few efforts at scientific popularization, the scientific community did not often feel required to make major concessions to the general reader. History, as we have seen, forged new links with the natural sciences as the empirical and factual became more central, and to some extent historians adopted the linguistic position of the scientific community. But historians did not fully abandon either their long-term association with rhetoric and literature or their concern for the general reader.

Like the naturalists and philosophers, historians increasingly emphasized the need for a plain, unadorned style and became extremely hostile to the elaborate language and linguistic tricks, which they associated with rhetorical embellishment and poetic fancy. By the sixteenth and seventeenth centuries, simplicity and clarity were viewed as the principal virtues of historical prose. One must "plainly" set forth the Truth, "which shew always best with its own proper colors, without the elaborate dresse and vernish of Rhetorick."[74] There was no need for the "jingling of words and phrases in ostentation of writing."[75] An "unaffected and familiar Style," not "Wit and Eloquence," were proper for the historian who aimed at truth.[76] The association of plain language and truth, in this case the truth of history, had become a commonplace for historians of the seventeenth century.[77]

As we have seen earlier, fables, invented speeches, and other obvious fictions were gradually excised from history. The decline of historical poetry and the history drama also suggests the effort to disassociate the veracity of the historian from the imaginative in literature.[78] The poetic language and the copiousness prized by Renaissance writers were to be reduced or excised in the name of truth. If there were any beauty to be associated with historical prose, its aesthetic standards were clarity, simplicity, and naturalness. These values, however, were not only those enunciated by the natural scientists but also those of neo-classicism. Whether or not one chooses to locate the new models of historical prose in science, in neo-classicism, or elsewhere, it is clear that historians as much as philosophers were rejecting the intricate, embellished, and to their mind, confusing, and therefore deceptive, Renaissance style for a simple prose more appropriate for presenting the truth.

Most historians attempted to free themselves from linguistic embellishment and the "flowers of eloquence." Camden insisted he would use plain language and would not provide the reader with the "Nosegay of Flowers" which one met with "in the Garden of Eloquence."[79] Most historians would have agreed both with Sprat that "purity and shortness" are "chief beauties of Historical Writings" and with the Frenchman Rapin that the historian was to narrate matters of fact and make them "sensible, palpable, evident."[80] Although it was not clear exactly how this might be achieved, few would have disagreed with the statement that history, both natural and humane, must avoid "Rhetorical Hyperbole, or the least flourish of Eloquence."[81]

Some historians went beyond repudiating the elaborate prose they associated with rhetorical excess and attacked the principal rhetorical forms as antithetical to history. History was thus to be distinguished from the pleading of causes, from defense or apology, and from panegyric and invective.[82] Although the separation of history from rhetoric was often accompanied by a hostility toward the latter, this was not always the case. Rushworth, who was adamantly opposed to the use of rhetoric in historical writing because history aimed at truth and rhetoric did not, nevertheless admired the rhetorical skills of the great parliamentary orators.[83] Though historical thought owed a great deal to the rhetorically oriented humanist culture, seventeenth-century historians had come to feel that historiography and rhetoric were concerned with antithetical goals.

We can also trace the growing separation of history from poetry, which had become so closely connected with rhetoric. History was to present the truth of fact while poetry, unlimited by fact, might fictionally present universal truths. Although the distinction might be used to elevate the status of poetry above history, e.g., by Sir Philip Sidney, it was often employed during the seventeenth century to extoll the truthfulness of history over the fictions of poetry.[84] By mid-century both Hobbes and Charleton sharply distinguished poetry from history. Poetry could no longer be permitted to "infect" historical prose.[85] By mid-century, too, the efforts of Michael Drayton and Samuel Daniel to present historical narrative in poetic form would have appeared not only old-fashioned but also inappropriate. The late seventeenth-century equivalent of Drayton's *Poly-Olbian*, a poetic county-by-county description of England, was the matter-of-fact natural history of Robert Plot which emphasized the need for a "plain, unartificial stile, studiously avoiding all ornaments of Language."[86]

While epistemological change, science, and the search for truth clearly influenced historical writing, we must at the same time note the influence of certain ancient historians and the fact that the origins of modern historiography were to a very considerable extent an outgrowth of the rhetorical environment of Renaissance humanism. Lucian and Polybius were often cited to the effect that historians must write in a clear, natural style, and the latter was

248

mentioned to support views on the inappropriateness of rhetorical ornament and "Artful Eloquence" in historical writing.[87] These views had been reiterated by the Tacitean-Polybian school of historians, who likewise emphasized fidelity to truth presented in a clear, unadorned style. While it is possible to discuss the development of historical prose in terms of a return to particular classical models without any reference to the development of science, it seems foolish to take such a narrow position given the overlap in subject matter, method, and personnel of seventeenth-century historians and natural historians. It would be equally foolish, however, to ignore the existence of similar ancient and late Renaissance prescriptions. It is perhaps the coalescence of these two traditions that helps to explain the identical prescriptions offered by virtuosi and historians for the proper mode of expression. Seventeenth-century historians chose precisely that historical tradition most compatible with the stylistic preferences of the contemporary scientific and latitudinarian community.

Seventeenth-century historiography also produced certain technical problems for historians that have continued until our own day. The new document-oriented history with its unfamiliar technical vocabularies, erudite footnotes, marginal citations, lengthy quotations, and scholarly digressions often resulted in less and less readable productions in which the narrative thread, if present at all, was sacrificed to other goals. History, whether or not one chooses to link it with the new science, was in danger of losing both the general reader and its status as literature. John Milton thus decided to exclude "controversies and quotations" from his *History of England* because they would "delay or interrupt the smooth course of History."[88] By the end of the century, the problem had become so acute that a number of critics, beginning with Sir William Temple, were ready to jettison antiquarian scholarship in order to win back the general reader to the easily flowing literary narrative of "perfect history."

As we have seen, many seventeenth-century historians, especially those who were linked to the new empirical sciences, emphasized historical truth and scholarly exactitude over literary values. Their very success in creating new, if less readable, genres of history helped produce the reaction of the early eighteenth century, which favored sweeping political narrative presented with literary grace. Only Gibbon seems to have been able to combine successfully historical erudition and an admirable literary style.[89] Whether inspired by neo-classic norms or romantic yearnings, the literary mode dominated until a revived emphasis on scientific history brought the problems of style and audience again to the forefront. Twentieth-century historians have most often opted for the small, scholarly audience leaving less knowledgeable popularizers and historical novelists to provide historical fare for the general reader. Few have been willing, and still fewer able, to achieve the desired combination of scholarly and literary values. Since the seventeenth century, and largely because of its advances, the tension between scholarly and literary values, between truth and pleasure, has shaped the writing of history.

LAW

Somewhat parallel developments can be traced in attitudes toward the language of the law, although it is less clear how much influence linguistic reformers had in this area. Under the influence of Cicero and Quintillian, Roman law had forged an alliance with rhetoric that seems to have continued into the medieval and early modern period. Such an alliance does not seem to have been characteristic of the English common lawyers at least at the conscious level. Some sixteenth-century humanists hoped to improve the barbarous language of the law by bringing legal proceedings into closer conformity with the new emphasis on trying to achieve eloquence in English. The most powerful plea of this type was contained in civilian-trained humanist Sir Thomas Elyot's *The Book Named the Governor*, which was designed to improve English political culture and education by reviving the ancient rhetorical classics and using them to reform the language and form of the English common law.[90]

Another effort to bring the law into closer relationship with the sixteenth-century standard of Ciceronian eloquence was that of Thomas Wilson, an Italian-trained civilian, whose popular *Art of Rhetoric* (1553) was extremely influential. There is little to suggest any direct influence on the legal profession for whom proficiency in the technicalities of pleading counted for more than oratorical skill. The fact that both Elyot and Wilson were civilians rather than common lawyers perhaps suggests the greater receptivity of Roman law to the Renaissance standards of eloquence.[91] Neither did the effort of Abraham Fraunce to apply Ramist principles of logic and rhetoric to the law have much effect. Indeed, the claims by laymen to deal with the substance of the law on the basis of any ordinary reasoning procedures were explicitly repudiated by both Coke and Hale.[92]

If, on the one hand, there is little direct evidence to suggest that the efforts of Ciceronian or Ramist rhetoricians were successful in modifying the language and modes of argument characteristic of lawyers, there is equally little to suggest legal antagonism toward rhetoric. Indeed, the success of the humanists in the educational sphere meant that lawyers would have been exposed to rhetorical training during their grammar school and university years.

The seventeenth century witnessed a great deal of dissatisfaction with the legal profession, but legal language and argumentation were criticized less for an excess or absence of eloquence than for their incomprehensibility to laymen. The lawyers responded that Law French was not obscure to the initiated and that it provided a necessary, technical language.

Matthew Hale best represents the position of the late seventeenth century. Hale, who was seriously interested in the origin and function of language, had come to the conclusion that "Words" were "just Signs of Conceptions and Thoughts."[93] He demanded an uncomplicated and unadorned speaking and writing style when serious matters were at stake. He therefore "became a great Enemy to All Eloquence or Rhetoric in Pleading" feeling that these arts would confuse and corrupt jurors by "bribing their Fancies, and biassing their Affections."[94] He disapproved of French lawyers who modeled themselves on Roman orators, feeling that the function of counsel was not to persuade the court but to state the facts and the law as clearly and succinctly as possible.[95] Echoing the credo of the Royal Society, he insisted "you must not speak that as upon knowledge which you have by conjecture and opinion only." One's views should be presented in "significant, pertinent and inoffensive" expression.[96]

A similar distrust of legal eloquence and its association with the emotions and imagination appears in Sir John Hawles's *English Man's Right*. Hawles, who eventually became Solicitor General to William III, claimed that all the "best judicatures of the world" "utterly reject the use of Rhetorick."[97] For Hawles, like Locke, rhetoric consisted of the arts of deception and was thus "directly contrary" to the aim of the courts "who by knowledge of Truth desire to do Justice."[98] This distrust of elaborate language which played on the emotions and was associated with deceit was also echoed by non-lawyer Isaac Barrow, who insisted that a "simple manner of speaking to the point" in a "clear and compendious way" was as appropriate for the courtroom as in any deliberation of great importance.[99] A 1671 Assize Sermon similarly suggests that the "Flowers" of "Art and Eloquence" were used to "dress up and maintain" bad causes and that the substitution of "Noise and Passion" for "Reason and Evidence" could only serve to confuse juries.[100]

We possess insufficient evidence to say with assurance that the late seventeenth-century legal profession as a whole shared the views of Hale and Hawles. It is significant, however, that two of the most respected lawyers of the day felt that, in law as well as in science and history, elaborate language was likely to obscure and distort rather than reveal truth. Indeed, Hale's and Hawles's rejection of eloquence in the law courts should be compared with Elyot's and Wilson's admiration of those same qualities a hundred years earlier. The distance between Elyot and Hale was roughly that which lay between Spencer and Sidney, on the one hand, and Sprat and Dryden on the other. In law as in literature reformers sought to replace eloquence, rhetoric, and linguistic embellishment with the newer, more truth-oriented standards of clarity and precision.

RELIGION

Even before St. Augustine extensively explored the subject,[101] Christian thinkers had been concerned with the extent to which it was appropriate to integrate the tools of classical rhetoric into Christian teaching, preaching and scriptural interpretation. Although sermon construction and style were obviously of concern to all Christians, Protestants tended to give these matters greater prominence because of their special emphasis on preaching. In England, widely divergent practices emerged as preachers and theologians responded to changes in theology, rhetorical, and logical theory, and other aspects of the intellectual and literary scene. Many late sixteenth- and early seventeenth-century religious writers and preachers, especially those connected with the court, produced highly literary and even poetic sermons, full of imagery, wit, plays on words, paradox, and rhetorical display. In the hands of such masters as Lancelot Andrewes and John Donne, sermons were both learned and highly ornamented.

Such an approach was rejected by Ramist preachers, who viewed rhetoric and style rather negatively, as a decorative element to be applied after the logical structure of a sermon had been established.

Puritans, the most enthusiastic converts to Ramism, thus viewed eloquent language as mere embellishment which too easily detracted from the essential argument. Puritans attacked the sermons favored by the court as much for their literary allusion, elaborate metaphor, and classical citation as for the theological positions they espoused. Ramist-inspired sermons, whether delivered by Puritans or non-Puritans, tended to be plain. They were logically organized according to the elaborate system of dichotomies. Organizational complexity was accompanied by minute dissection of the scriptural text and a concern for theological argumentation.

The civil war and Interregnum decades added a new dimension to discussions of appropriate modes of religious communication. Many of the new religious sects rejected all logical and rhetorical traditions. For them, divine inspiration was all that was necessary for the effective communication of the Christian message. Sectarian preaching was often highly emotional, unstructured, and full of mystical language. It was thus in sharp contrast to both the elaborately constructed, unadorned sermons of Ramists and the embellished, carefully wrought style associated with the court. These same years were characterized by acrimonious debate over doctrinal and ecclesiastical issues. Out of these conflicts of style and content a new theory and practice was created which was a response to the enthusiasts, and to the dogmatism of civil war polemics. It also incorporated the newer intellectual developments in philosophy and science.

The chief theorists of Restoration religious communication were latitudinarian clergymen, many of whom were deeply involved in creating the theories of knowledge we have discussed in earlier chapters. As we have seen, this group rejected the zealousness of Puritans and non-Puritans alike, favoring a peaceful, nondisputatious approach to religion which emphasized practical morality over doctrinal precision. But they were also preachers with a strong desire to move and influence audiences to pursue a moral and virtuous life. The appeal to reason was essential, but the affections too must be moved if the desired result was to be obtained. Their philosophical and scientific interests made them suspicious of elaborate theological terms and doctrines which resulted in confusion and ambiguity. They rejected the disputatiousness and contentiousness of scholastic and Ramist logic. Their combined positions as preachers and intellectuals led them to seek a rather plain sermon style perhaps derived from Scripture. Ornateness, elaborate metaphor, and poetic language would be curtailed and organizational

253

complexity reduced, but sufficient stylistic appeal must be introduced to persuade men to live a more virtuous life. Their attack was directed against the undisciplined enthusiasm of the sects, the overly complex sermons of Puritans and other Ramists, the syllogistic approach of traditional theologians, and the highly rhetorical and poetic sermons so favored by the pre-civil war court. The catchwords of the latitudinarians were simplicity, plainness, clarity, and morality. The rhetorical arts might be employed but had to be very carefully controlled. If language were properly employed, one could eliminate confusion, misunderstanding, and unnecessary obscurity and still persuade men that a virtuous life was reasonable, scriptural, and in their interest. The problem of the religious writer was therefore slightly different than that of the naturalist or historian, for he needed a language that would simultaneously communicate truth and alter behavior.[102]

John Wilkins was perhaps the first to exhibit the combination of scientific interest, latitudinarianism, and advocacy of the new prose style. The new values are exhibited in his often reprinted companion volumes, *Ecclesiastes* and *Gift of Prayer*, the first a manual for preachers, the second a handbook for laymen.[103] The preacher, according to Wilkins, required method, that is, organization, matter, and proper expression, if he were to gain the understanding of his audience. A simple organizational pattern was proposed. Sermons

must be plain and natural, not being darkened with the affection of Scholasticall harshness, or Rhetoricall flourishes. Obscurity in the discourse is an argument of ignorance in the mind. The greatest learning is to be seen in the greatest plainnesse. The more nearly we understand any thing ourselves, the more easily we expound it to others. When the notion itself is good, the best way to set it off, is the most obvious plain expression.[104]

Wilkins favored a basically unadorned yet carefully crafted prose. He rejected both careless prose and excessive neatness and elegance.[105] He also rejected the preaching of the sects that

deliver only a kind of Caballisticall or Chymicall, Rosecrucian Theologie, darkening wisdom with words, heaping together a farrago of obscure affected expressions and Wild Allegories, containing little of substance in them but what is more plainly and intelligibly delivered by others.[106]

In later years Wilkins also hoped his universal language might

contribute to the clearing of some of our Modern Differences in Religion, by unmasking many wild errors, that shelter themselves under the disguise of affected phrases: which . . . rendered according to the genuine and natural importance of Words, will appear to be inconsistencies and contradictions. And several of those pretended, mysterious, profound notions, expressed in great swelling words . . . will appear to be, either nonsense, or very flat and jejune.[107]

Yet Wilkins did not expect sermons to have the same character as natural history. Some rhetorical expression might be employed, it being very "powerful" for expressing and exciting the affections.[108]

Wilkins's position became the standard latitudinarian one. Not only was his *Ecclesiastes* frequently reissued, but a growing circle of young friends and disciples adopted his views, among them William Lloyd, John Tillotson, Edward Stillingfleet, and Joseph Glanvill.[109]

John Tillotson became the most famous practitioner of the latitudinarian style. Gilbert Burnet suggested that Tillotson and Lloyd, later bishop of Worcester, learned a great deal from their participation in Wilkins's projects for a universal character and philosophical language and owed their ability to write "clear and correctly" to their association with that enterprise.[110] Tillotson insisted on the elimination of "sublime notions and unintelligible mysteries, with pleasant passages of wit, and artificial strains of rhetoric; and nice and unprofitable disputes, with bold interpretations of dark prophesies."[111] With Tillotson the stylistic prescriptions of the latitudinarians became the standard for a new generation. As Burnet put it, "This set of men contributed more than can be imagined to reform our way of preaching."[112]

In John Locke, also a latitudinarian, similar concerns appear. Locke was not a clergyman faced constantly with the task of leading the average man to a better and more religious life. He discussed the issues of communication in the more abstract context of moral philosophy. For Locke, the principal problem was that "moral words" were discussed in the context of "mixed modes," that is terms made up of combinations of ideas. If these combinations were broken up into their constituent parts, moral words, as well as others, might be assigned a "certain and undoubted signification." The proper analysis of concepts and definition eventually would bring "moral knowledge" to "great clearness and certainty."[113]

Preaching and moral discourse, then, could be, indeed must be, improved. It should not be surprising that those who sought clarity and precision in philosophy should aspire to those same values in religion. The same names—Wilkins, Glanvill, Tillotson, Stillingfleet, and Locke—constantly reappear, linking together the new approaches to religion, natural science, and philosophy. Latitudi-narians with scientific, epistemological, and linguistic interests were the first and most consistent advocates and practitioners of the new style in religious writing and speaking. By the end of the century, the new values had permeated far beyond the Church. Tillotson became the model not only for the young preacher but for the prose stylist more generally. Simplicity and naturalness had become the new standard of eloquence.

PROSE STYLE

All the disciplines described in the preceding sections—natural science and philosophy, history, law, and religion—were moving toward simplified forms of presentation. Natural history and nat-ural philosophy became intolerant of ambiguity and figurative lan-guage. Historians and lawyers moved in the direction of a plain, unadorned style, though perhaps not with the same unanimity and firmness of purpose. In the realm of religion and moral philosophy, too, a concerted effort was made to remove unnecessary embel-lishment and meaningless phrases without losing the ability to move audiences. All these fields were characterized by a desire to elim-inate abstruse and unverifiable terms, concepts, and doctrines and to eliminate the style of the disputation. Contentious debate and argumentation were to be replaced by a dispassionate, unbiased, basically rational presentation. A clear contrast can be drawn with the sixteenth- and early seventeenth-century emphasis on copi-ousness and amplification which was now giving way to standards of clarity and precision. Increasingly the most admired style was one that could most clearly express the thoughts of the writer and most clearly and accurately describe things, events, procedures and individuals. The elaborate prose of Sidney, Donne, or Andrewes simply could not serve the needs of the new generation.

Literary men of the mid- and late-seventeenth century simulta-neously express antagonism toward traditional rhetoric and lin-guistic practice and the search for a new eloquence based on clarity and naturalness. If at his angriest moments Sprat denounced the "luxury and redundance of speech" which was destroying knowl-edge, peace, and religion, he also admitted that the "ornaments of speaking" had once been "an admirable Instrument" to describe "Goodness, Honesty, Obedience: in larger, fairer, and more mov-ing Images." Now these arts were put to worse uses: They make the Fancy disgust the best things, if they come sound and unadorned: they are in open defiance against Reason; professing, not to hold such correspondence with it; but with its Slaves, the Passions.[114]

Sprat also desired a new style that embodied natural easiness and unaffected grace consistent with reason. Abraham Cowley thus looked on Sprat as someone who had "vindicated Eloquence and Wit."[115] Similar stylistic standards were announced by Dryden, Locke, and Addison. Dryden insisted that wit and good writing required "deep thought in common language," the best style being a mean between "ostentation and rusticity." Locke wished to cultivate "facility, clearness and elegancy in expression," and Addison, writing somewhat later, advocated a "natural way of writing . . . and beautiful simplicity." At the end of the seventeenth century, a popular work on style not only advocated "Propriety, Perspicuity, Elegance and Cadence" as the standard for that generation but held up Sprat and Tillotson as models of a superior writing style.[116]

The multifarious search for truth helped cultivate a taste for a new mode of expression which spread far beyond that rather small group of intellectuals who were so deeply committed to finding a better means of presenting empirical findings. The reformed prose style, characterized by clarity, precision and naturalness, was in close touch with the intellectual assumptions and needs of a new and more fact-oriented generation.

OLD AND NEW LITERARY FORMS

The concluding portion of this chapter will examine the ways that some of the new approaches to knowledge, particularly the emphasis on matters of fact and disapproval of the openly fictitious and imaginary, contributed to a reshaping of literary values and to the creation of new literary forms.

Poetry, like rhetoric, was reshaped by the intellectual currents of the day. Modern literary critics and historians, struck by the vehemence of the mid-seventeenth-century attack on poetic language, have noticed that the new scientific and philosophical currents helped modify Renaissance attitudes toward poetry.[117] Yet critics have gone too far in suggesting that hostility to poetic language in scientific, philosophical and "factual" communication necessarily implied hostility to poetry itself. Indeed, several propagandists for the newer philosophical and linguistic views felt that a proper understanding of the new philosophy and natural science might itself make a

257

positive contribution to a reformed poetic. The fact that Dryden's poetry and conceptions of poetic language differed substantially from those of Spencer does not mean that poetry itself was eclipsed.

Poetry came under considerable criticism during both the sixteenth and seventeenth centuries.[118] Earl Miner, who has surveyed poetic development from the Renaissance to the Restoration, has even suggested that sixteenth-century poets were more defensive than those of the mid- and late-seventeenth century.[119] Some contemporary critics quoted Plato to the effect that poetry was not only the father of lies but an inappropriate activity for those committed to the search for truth. Others thought poetry a waste of time, time better spent in the practical affairs of the world or devoted to more serious religious concerns. Thus several lines of criticism that have often been assumed to be characteristic only of the post-Baconian age were present even during the heyday of Renaissance poetry.[120] Yet, it is true that Renaissance humanists did believe that poetry was worthy of great esteem, and they justified it as an ethical discipline capable of revealing and communicating truth. In the seventeenth century, poetry continued to be associated with ethical teaching but was losing its association with truth. Increasingly we hear comments that poetry like rhetoric was designed to foster falsehood. In the new intellectual climate, poetry was labeled fiction and so could hardly represent something better and truer than mundane reality. As poets were accused of practicing the false and the fabulous, poetry's truth-conveying functions were being challenged. Poetry had to respond not only to traditional assertions of its inferior status to logic and dialectic, on the one hand, and Christianity and Scripture on the other, but also to new attacks on its ability to deal with the truth at all.

Matters related to truth were now to be expressed in prose rather than poetry and in a language that was clear and precise rather than metaphoric and elaborate. But there was no inherent reason that poets also could not adopt clarity and a more natural language. Most members of the scientific and intellectual community did not desire that poetry disappear. Even the most vociferous critics of poetic and metaphoric language in scientific and philosophical presentation were often anxious not only to retain but often to reform poetry and poetic theory.[121]

Writing at the end of the century, Locke and Newton expressed the most extreme position. When language was properly used, Locke thought, the same word would be constantly used for the same sense. He not only looked forward to the time when the "poet's

258

works" might be "contained in a nutshell,"[122] but thought it best to stifle poetic aspiration in children. Poetry was "a pleasant air, but a barren soil," and at best an idle pastime.[123] Newton felt poetry "was a kind of ingenius nonsense."[124]

Other spokesmen for the new philosophy, however, looked forward to the improvement of poetry. These efforts were often consistent with the growing neo-classicism of the era. We might expect that Hobbes, whose linguistic radicalism we noted earlier, would take a position similar to Locke's. Quite the contrary, Hobbes, himself a translator of Homer, felt that poetry fulfilled one of the primary functions of language, "to please and delight ourselves and others by playing with words, for pleasure or ornament."[125] For Hobbes, poetry consisted of two elements, judgment and fancy. The first "begets the strength and structure" and the latter, "the ornaments of a Poem."[126] Hobbes insisted, however, that the beauty of a poem did not consist "in the exorbitancy of the Fiction," for "Resemblance of truth is the utmost limit of Poeticall Liberty."[127] If not governed by verity, poetry was at least bound by verisimilitude. The "Strange fictions" of the ancient poets were no longer acceptable. The "impenetrable Armours, Inchanted Castles, Invulnerable Bodies," and the like that had been dismissed by naturalists and historians were now also to be rejected in poetry.[128]

Poetic language, too, was in need of reform. Poets, like philosophers, employed far too many words which:

though of magnific sound . . . have no sense at all; and . . . others that lose their meaning by being ill coupled . . . this palpable darkness, the ambitious obscurity of expressing more than is perfectly conceived.[129]

Obscurity and ambiguity in poetry as elsewhere should be rejected in favor of "clarity and propriety." Hobbes wanted poetry, but the poetry he desired would obviously not be that of Spenser or Donne.

Thomas Sprat was also anxious to reform English poetry. Sprat felt that literature, poetry, and "Wit" might be improved by natural philosophy, for the "best and most delightful Wit" was based on "images which are generally known, and are able to bring a strong, and sensible impression on the mind." Traditional wit, derived from ancient fable and religion was "well nigh consum'd." Indeed, it has been flawed from the start because "they were only Fictions . . . whereas Truth is never so well express'd or amplify'd as by . . . Ornaments which are True and Real in Themselves." English poets would do well to draw inspiration from Scripture and from their own history. The "Manner, Tempers, and Extravagances of men," too, would provide a foundation for wit. Indeed these, "gathered from particular observations," already provided the basis for England's excellent dramatic poetry. If logic, grammar, and mathematics were unsuitable for poetic comparison, being "removed from the senses," wit founded on the "Arts of mens hands" might be cultivated precisely because it consisted of "Images that are generally observ'd, and such visible things which are familiar." The "Works of Nature" were therefore among the "most fruitful Soils for the growth of Wit."[130] The new natural knowledge based on sense data could not only increase the available images and comparisons but would be

intelligible to all, because they proceed from things that enter into all mens Senses. They will make the most vigorous impression of mens Fancies, because they do even touch their Eyes, and are neerest to their Natures. Of these the variety will be infinite: for the particulars are so, from whence they may be deduc'd.[131]

Similar views are to be found in Abraham Cowley and John Dryden, again suggesting the compatibility of the Hobbes-Sprat position with neo-classicism. Indeed Cowley seems to have drawn much of his poetic theory from Bacon and particularly Hobbes. Cowley, who for Sprat embodied the best in contemporary poetry, was the author not only of the "Ode to the Royal Society" that prefaced Sprat's *History* but of the Baconian-inspired *Proposition for the Advancement of Experimental Philosophy* (1661).[132] Like Sprat, he was confident that scientific advance was compatible with good poetry. He, too, was opposed to elaborate imagery and complicated literary devices, feeling that true style was exhibited in the ability to express truth with appropriate clarity. Heroic poetry ought not to be "like some farfetched Fairyland" with witches, giants and other such imaginary creatures.[133] It was no more necessary for poets than for natural philosphers to serve up "the cold meats of the Ancients."[134] Instead, Cowley and Sprat offered a vision of a new poetry based on the truth of Scripture, nature, and history.

Dryden, who immediately brings to mind English neo-classicism and the influence of Boileau, too suggests how poetry was linked to seventeenth-century intellectual change. Not only did his concept of the relative role of judgment and fancy in poetry correspond closely to that of Hobbes, but he defended English poetry and drama in terms almost identical to those of Sprat.[135] And Dryden, a member of the Royal Society, also advocated a literary standard that emphasized clarity of expression. He, like Cowley, favored a narrative mode. Narrative, increasingly shorn of fantasy and myth, seemed to suit the temper of the age.

Earl Miner has drawn attention to this development in Dryden's *Annus Mirabilis* (1667), which dealt with the events of contemporary history: the Plague, the Fire and the Anglo-Dutch war. The poem was, of course, an artistic version of historical events, but the sense of reality Dryden created was so powerful that critics have subsequently attempted to verify his portrayal of events with historical evidence. For Dryden, poetry became a "lively imitation of truth."[136]

While it would be an enormous oversimplification to suggest that the new poetic theory and practice were solely related to the denigration of fiction by those with a heightened concern for matters of fact and simplified language, one cannot ignore the role these concerns played in the literary changes of the era. As the truth-conveying functions of poetry were questioned and its Renaissance practioners viewed as creators of fictions, a new poetic theory attempted to bring poetry into a new relation with reality. Once poetry was shorn of ambiguous language it could, especially if modified to take advantage of the countless new, natural, historical and scriptural images and themes available, and if kept closer to a standard of verisimilitude, regain an honored position. While it is not our place here to investigate fully the relationship between the new intellectual currents and the development of neo-classicism, it should be obvious that standards of naturalness, clarity, and propriety were the very hallmarks of neo-classicism as well as of the new science, history, and religion. It is thus noteworthy that Cowley and Dryden should have been enthusiasts of the new learning. If not all literary critics will agree that poetry and literary arts were improved by the seventeenth-century search for truth, fact, and credibility, it would be difficult to argue that the status and standards of poetry were uninfluenced by these concerns.

The shift in philosophical interest from metaphysics to epistemology which led to the reevaluation of rhetoric, logic, and poetry resulted in the reshaping, not the demise of literature. If poetry and history gradually came to terms with a new intellectual environment that emphasized truth and factual accuracy rather than imagination or fancy, there were also new literary forms that even more readily adopted the impartial presentation of matters of fact as their standard.

By the late seventeenth century, writers and intellectuals of most kinds were familiar with and put great emphasis on matters of fact and the importance of reliable testimony. They were aware of problems of bias and the role of education and custom in creating bias. They were accustomed to weighing both the quality and quantity of testimony by all kinds of reporters. Three new or newly popular literary forms of the seventeenth and early eighteenth centuries—the narrative of travel and discovery, the novel, and the newspaper—all suggest how such epistemological interests and standards might help shape literary forms and genres.

Accounts of voyages to distant and exotic lands were, as we have seen, widely read, as were the more familiar fact-oriented descriptions of England and Europe. Practitioners of this genre, which was associated with the needs of navigation and trade as much as with science and natural history, attempted to describe events, physical environments, customs, and other matters of fact with accuracy and detail. The early appetite for Richard Hakluyt's *The Principal Navigations, Voyages Traffiques and Discoveries* (1589) suggests the public interest in this kind of reporting. From Hakluyt on, travel literature self-consciously adopted a plain, clear style. This genre simultaneously appealed to scholarly, professional, and general audiences, and helped break down traditional distinctions between learned and popular audiences. Travel literature and related descriptive forms faithfully recorded matters of fact in a straightforward, unembellished style for the instruction and/or pleasure of all who might be interested.[137]

Familiarity with this genre also made possible the imaginary voyage. While some examples of this genre were devoid of any credibility, others resembled the reports of actual investigators and travelers. Indeed it is not always a simple matter to fully disentangle fact from fiction. Two striking examples of a seeming intermingling of fact and fiction are Thomas More's *Utopia*, perhaps the first pseudo-travel account, and Jonathan Swift's *Travels into the Remote Nations of the World by Captain Lemuel Gulliver*. Large portions of both works take the form of chorography or natural history, providing detailed physical and ethnographic description. At the same time, however, both writers combine great attention to verisimilitude with literary devices that make it crystal clear to the reader that their work is fiction not fact.

The works of More and Swift were part of a larger literary movement that exploited the new interest in matters of fact to create new forms of fact-oriented fiction. Fancy is no longer contrasted to and elevated above the mundane world of fact. Instead fancy and fact are united to the greater satisfaction of the reader who has come to see the realm of fact as providing joys comparable to those that early generations had found in the realm of poetry. Swift could thus simultaneously employ and mock what had become conventional statements about truthful reporting. Although Swift scholars have often pointed out that he was thoroughly familiar with the *Philosophical Transactions*,[138] it is less well-known that he was immersed in the epistemological issues and discussions relating to knowledge and certainty.[139]

Indeed, writers of the late seventeenth and early eighteenth centuries employed this mixture of fact and fantasy to create what eventually became a new form of fiction, the novel. Ian Watt has persuasively argued that the early novel, which he associates with Lockean epistemology, involved a self-conscious rejection of the romance. It employed realistic individuals in realistic settings. Swift and Defoe donned the mantle of the reliable and truthful reporter as a means of presenting their fiction. Indeed, even before the achievements of Defoe and Swift, lesser "novelists" such as Alphra Behn borrowed some of the format and subject matter of natural and moral history.[140]

Daniel Defoe, who transformed the travel narrative into the novel, provides the most striking example of these developments. He provided realistic description and created plausible persons to report his or her direct observations and experiences. *Robinson Crusoe* put itself forward as a "just history of fact" without "any appearance of fiction."[141] So intimately had fact and the new fiction become intertwined that one annoyed rival insisted Defoe had forged the story and had imposed it on his readers as if it were a true story.[142] In *Moll Flanders*, Defoe explicitly denies he is writing fiction, insisting that he has only edited what was "Written from her own Memorandum."[143] His *Journal of the Plague Year*, which purported to be an eyewitness account of the 1664 plague, an event Defoe was too young to have witnessed, is either fiction disguised as fact or history disguised as fiction. Scholars have not yet fully disentangled the invented and noninvented materials in that work. Defoe's imaginative work thus merges imperceptibly with his *A Tour Through the Whole Island of Britain*, a travel book full of precise descriptions of natural resources and economic and social life. This volume brings us full circle, for it easily fits into the category of the travel book and natural history.

Other fiction writers assumed the mantle of historian or reporter. The creation of the plausible but fictional personages of Isaac Bickerstaff, Roger de Coverly, and others who "authored" and peopled *The Tatler* and *The Spectator*, suggests how the essay-periodicals foreshadowed the characters of the novel. Works of the imagination increasingly were assimilated to a new kind of "feigned history," a history now associated with factual truth and accurate reporting. The new fiction was associated with the real and palpable, not the fantasy of romance. Fiction had to seem like fact. By the beginning of the eighteenth century, Spenser's *Fairie Queene* and Sidney's *Arcadia* could obviously no longer serve as appropriate models for either poetry or prose fiction.

The newspaper, a creation of the mid-seventeenth century, is another genre linked to the appetite for accurate, factual reporting. If often biased and partisan in practice, the newspaper made its bid for attention and legitimacy as a purveyor of truth. English newspapers, which originated during the Thirty Years War, initially were limited to providing foreign news derived from the letters and dispatches of continental observers. With the breakdown of the government's ability to control publication at the outbreak of the civil war, they came to include domestic as well as foreign news. Between 1640 and 1660, an incredible array of newspapers, most of them shortlived, provided military, political, and other news. Like their modern successors, many were identified with particular political groups and policy issues and thus presented stories from a particular viewpoint. Journalists, nevertheless, repeatedly emphasized their goals as the pursuit of truth and the accurate presentation of information. Even the names of early newspapers suggest this commitment. *The True Informer, True Relation of Certain Remarkable Passages*, the *Perfect and Impartial Intelligencer*, the *Impartiall Intelligencer*, and *An Exact and True Diurnal* were typical titles.[144]

It was difficult to obtain accurate first-hand information on events outside England, and journalists often had to rely on the reports of others or foreign printed accounts. In this respect their reporting problem differed little from the naturalist or historian who was also frequently required to rely on the reports of others. The credibility of eyewitnesses and other relayers of information was thus as crucial for newspapermen as for other investigators who hoped to report the facts accurately. Thus the *Perfect Diurnall* told its readers "You may henceforth expect from this relator to be informed onely of such things that are of credit . . . or such other news as shall be certified by Letters from the Army, and other parts, from persons of speciall trust."[145] Competitiors were frequently attacked for being inadequately committed to accuracy and truth. Attack on the veracity and honesty of the competition was

264

a means of emphasizing one's own commitment to truth. The editor of *The Faithfull Scout* thus noted, "I intend . . . to encounter falsehood with the sword of truth. I will not endeavour to flatter the world into a belief of things that are not; but truly inform them of things that are."[146]

Journalists were aware of the difficulties of providing accurate reports. They turned, as did other investigators, to the language of credibility, relative certainty, and faithful reporting. Thus, one paper distinguished between "certain Intelligence" and "Reports," and noted that unconfirmed news was something "begotten of ayre . . . like so many clouds which do hang upon the evening of truth."[147] Rumors were frequently labeled as such. Editors typically stated they would avoid "tart language" and stick to "simply a narration of affaires" describing action fully without discussion or speculating on intention.[148] Another insisted his "honest Post" would present the news "without misguided glossings, invented fictions or flattering Commentaries."[149] From the beginning, then, the newspaper promised the unvarnished truth to the extent that it was possible to obtain it.[150]

During the Cromwellian and Restoration eras when governmental authority was reconsolidated, the proliferation of news periodicals ceased. When newspapers revived in the late seventeenth and early eighteenth centuries, the press was again marked by claims of accurately reporting the truth of events. The *London Courant* noted:

what more acceptable service could be done, then to rescue Truth . . . from the Pretensions of Supposition and Fictions. . . . It shall be the business of the paper . . . to do Justice to all parties in representing things as they really shall happen.[151]

A straightforward and functional prose, which corresponded closely to the dictates of the Royal Society, characterized the new genre. Clarity, not ornamentation, was from the outset thought to be appropriate in factual reporting, and the news report proved no exception.

These brief comments on the development of literary genres are not intended as a summary of seventeenth-century literary history. The revitalization of the classical tradition, barely mentioned here, was obviously of great significance to the Augustan Age. Classical values and standards were, however, easily combined with those drawn from philosophy, science, and fact. Despite the pitfalls of oversimplification, it has seemed desirable to indicate some of the ways in which literary and linguistic attitudes and productions were related to seventeenth-century concerns for truth and to its increasingly careful and sophisticated attitudes toward accuracy in communicating fact by means of the spoken and written word. Not only were older modes and theories of linguistic and literary expression modified in the process but new ones were created.

VIII

Conclusion

THE THEME of this book has been the changing conceptions of truth or knowledge. While it is easy to see that knowledge was conceived of quite differently in 1700 than it was in 1550, so much so that we may wish to speak of an intellectual revolution or a paradigm shift, it is less easy precisely to pinpoint these changes either in time or in terms of causation. We can, nevertheless, point to the erosion of the traditional dichotomy between "science" and "probability" as the crucial development. This erosion began when natural philosophers and natural scientists came to emphasize observation and experiment and to focus more centrally on matters of fact, and when humanists began to seek a more dispassionate and less morally laden analysis and description of the natural and social environment. This development, which had its beginnings in the sixteenth century and was announced most emphatically by Francis Bacon, made possible new intellectual contacts between natural science and all other fields dealing with or purporting to deal with experience and matters of fact.

The changes announced by Bacon and Descartes, however, were not in the direction of conceiving knowledge probabilistically. Their generation was engaged not only in substituting a new scientific philosophy for that of the scholastics but of defending their new philosophies from skeptics who denied the possibility of all knowledge, scholastic or otherwise. A successful defense depended upon considerable confidence that the new methods provided a sure foundation for a certain natural philosophy. The post-Baconian generation, which has been the central focus of our study, was in a position to move on to more probabilistic ground. It did not need to adopt a stance so flatly opposed to skepticism because skepticism was losing ground. And in a less defensive posture than Bacon and Descartes themselves, the newer generation was prepared to acknowledge and to deal with the evident problems and flaws in their new philosophies.

As we have seen, the development of an empirical, probabilistic epistemology in mid-seventeenth-century England involved not only an adoption and reformulation of Baconianism but considerable borrowing, refining and redeveloping of concepts employed earlier in religion, law, history, and rhetoric. The efforts of English natural scientists were extremely important to seventeenth-century explorations of the nature of probability and certitude, but it would be unwise to suggest that the sole or even the underlying impetus was the movement we label the "scientific revolution." The chronology simply does not support the assignment of a pre-eminent role to science or indeed to any particular discipline. Certainly the scientists could not claim priority if for no other reason than because in the early part of the century they were still largely preoccupied with establishing the certainty of knowledge. Indeed in those years it is in religious writing that probabilistic notions are first developed systematically. And while the evidence is more scattered in law and history, gropings toward the new epistemology occur in those fields either before or at the same time as comparable developments in science. The mid- to late-seventeenth-century developments that culminate in the empirical philosophy of Locke thus evolved simultaneously and interactively in a number of different but overlapping fields.

The ultimate spokesman of this generation was John Locke, who voiced the shared concerns of scientists, theologians, historians, and lawyers. In the realm of religion, where the concern stemmed from efforts to find a basis for a reasonable, if not infallible belief, the result was a rationalized, latitudinarian Protestantism. History and law increasingly focused on techniques for gathering substantial evidence rather than the achievement of ultimate truth. For Englishmen, the central intellectual phenomenon of the second half of the seventeenth century was the peculiar interaction between efforts to establish a rational basis for an historically based, nondogmatic, Protestant Christianity and comparable efforts to achieve a probabilistic basis for the factual assertions of scientists, historians, and lawyers.

We have tended to speak of commonalities, common features, and overlaps rather than causal relationships. The nature of seventeenth-century intellectual life makes it extremely difficult to label the sources of an individual's thought or the influence of one variety of thought on another. Bacon, after all, was as much lawyer as historian, as much philosopher as man of letters. Locke was a physician, philosopher, political theorist, and religious polemicist. The mixture of intellectual traditions and experience is equally typical of most of the lesser figures with whom we have dealt. Although there is a tendency to view the seventeenth-century polymath as a curiosity, the frequency of this type suggests that intellectual life was not then as compartmentalized as it later became. It seems unwise to speak solely of the influence of science on religion, or vice versa. Although we may wish to trace the evolution of a field of inquiry or a discipline, such compartmentalization may prove to be little more than an heuristic device, particularly in an age in which intellectual life was bounded by so few professional or conceptual barriers.

The seventeenth century has always been troublesome to cultural historians, and those who have dealt with it have long been aware of, if not very articulate about, the inadequacy of conventional historical labels. Part of the problem stems from the time-honored humanism/science dichotomy, which works so well for the Renaissance and is based on the more ancient distinction between philosophy and rhetoric. Scholars dealing with the eighteenth century tend to use a different set of terms and are more likely to speak of literature and science than of humanism and science. Literature obviously implies a less wide sweep than humanism, since history, moral philosophy, theology, and religious polemic, and political and social analysis may be distinguished from it. As early as the seventeenth century, at least in England, there is no satisfactory umbrella term or overarching intellectual category like humanism to hold together those studies which do not deal with logic, mathematics, and the physical and biological sciences. "Humanism" no longer seems appropriate to contain all the fields it once did. "Philosophy" is no longer synonymous with "science," and natural and social investigations do not seem to be so widely separated. Although specialization may be part of the explanation for the disappearance or lessened utility of "humanism," we must recall that many intellectuals were quite comfortable participating in a number of fields. The philosophy/rhetoric, science/humanism, and literature/science pigeonholes simply do not work for the seventeenth century. In fact there is some affinity between certain aspects of Renaissance humanism and the new empiricism. Although humanists were not particularly concerned with epistemological issues, they were often suspicious of claims to absolute knowledge. Their emphasis on the need for evaluation and judgment which

269

would provide the basis for decision making and action was not the same as the empirical approach we have been describing. Nevertheless the empiricists' emphases on the lack of certitude in most kinds of knowledge, the need for constant but tentative evaluation, and emphasis on the usefulness of knowledge should suggest that sixteenth-century humanism and seventeenth-century English science did not stand poles apart.

For the most part, we have been dealing with that difficult and ill-defined "period" located between the "Renaissance" and the "Enlightenment." The former, it is generally agreed, was dominated by humanism and a decaying Aristotelianism, the latter, by reason, empiricism, and perhaps neo-classicism. Scholars concerned with the in-between period, particularly in recent years, have tended to direct their attention to particular problems, movements, or individuals rather than seeking some inclusive category or label to contain or characterize the whole.[1] While we have not found a label to encapsulate nicely the dominant intellectual motifs, some characteristics cut across specialized boundaries and assist us in understanding this complex period which lies between a reasonably recognizable Renaissance and a reasonably recognizable Enlightenment.

Seventeenth-century intellectual life should not be discussed either in terms of the decline of humanism or the origin of the Enlightenment but, instead, as a distinctive intellectual culture that grappled with a particular set of epistemological and methodological problems. The ways in which those problems were conceived were deeply affected by the scientific revolution, but are not contained by it.

If the culture we have been describing is distinctively seventeenth-century, is it also distinctively English? Wrestling with the implications of a Baconian science made English intellectuals both more empirical and more oriented toward probability than their cross-channel counterparts. If the traditional textbook contrast between Continental rationalism and English empiricism is often drawn too sharply, there does seem to have been a significant difference in English and Continental approaches to knowledge. The reorientation of philosophy provided by Descartes retained a dichotomized vision of demonstrable science and probable opinion. The modifications of Baconian empiricism developed in England resulted in a more complex, less sharply defined, and less dichotomized approach to knowledge and experience. English empiricism owes more to rhetorical opinion and probability than is usually recognized and to fields like history and law that had never aspired to logical, mathematical, or metaphysical certainty. It also owes a great deal to efforts to establish a rational basis for accepting a Protestant Christianity. Given the interest in both the Book of Nature and the Book of Scripture and the conviction that there was an obligation to study and understand both, it is not surprising that some of the same critical tools and modes of analysis were applied to both.

The relationship between the two models of natural science, one seeking logically or mathematically demonstrable, the other, empirically verifiable knowledge, remains unclear for the seventeenth century. Indeed, Thomas Kuhn has suggested that these are really two distinct scientific traditions joined only by Newton.[2] We need not ignore the presence of one of these traditions in England or deny Newton his nationality in order to assert that seventeenth-century English science is distinguished by its general inclination toward the empirical and the probable.

If we have been successful in our draftsmanship, what emerges from the individual chapters of this book is a family portrait. The nucleus of this family is a preoccupation with matters of fact combined with the perception that, in the realm of fact, there are degrees of probability or certainty rather than two sealed compartments, one for the truth of demonstration and the other for opinion. In science, there is a movement away from logical or mathematical demonstration toward observation and experimentation, the data from which are to be shaped by hypotheses and evaluated as more or less certain. In theology, latitudinarianism, natural religion, and the treatment of Scripture as historical evidence bear the family traits. Historians postponed the writing of "perfect history" while they turned their energies to the kind of fact and document gathering and verification that brought civil and natural history closer together and produced chorographies.

What we have subsequently come to see as distinctly different disciplines were closely related in seventeenth-century England. The fundamental document of the Christian religion is an historical account of what *in fact* happened at a particular but distant time and place. Many seventeenth-century English churchmen chose to approach the problem of religious truth or belief in terms of the degree of certainty with which one could know historical facts established by a written account. That account contained testimony not only about human and divine events but also about such events of the natural world, as Creation. So, the seekers after religious knowledge claimed kinship not only with the historian but also with the natural scientist. All three sought a middle way between skepticism and dogmatism, a middle way that refused to go beyond what the available data and tools of analysis would yield, but also refused to fall into despair over the limits imposed by the incompleteness of these data and tools or the fallibility of the senses. Natural religion and natural history are the offspring of this common approach. Seventeenth-century science and religion clearly share a tentative, nondogmatic, experimental style. Their common enterprise is the construction of a new schema running from "mere opinion," through probable and highly probable knowledge, and on to moral certainty and demonstrated truth.

Certainly, seventeenth-century law was part of the family, although the lawyer usually relied on far less certain testimony than that of the Apostles or the telescope. As the testimony of witnesses rather than the common knowledge of the jury became central to the legal process, the legal profession, too, necessarily sought a middle ground between an unattainable, absolute certainty and the reduction of all questions of fact to mere opinion that would have rendered the processes of justice meaningless. Lawyers and judges, too, spoke the langauge of moral certainty derived from the evidence of the senses, as they urged juries to assess the credibility of testimony in order to satisfy themselves beyond a reasonable doubt.

When everyday life, matters of fact, historical experience, and religious belief are treated as intermediate realms between absolute, logically demonstrable knowledge and mere opinion, literary men also may become members of the family. If a combination of direct observation and the careful correlation of second-hand accounts yields something better than mere opinion, journalism may flourish as something more than fiction, and fiction may seek verisimilitude as a halfway house between the true and the fabulous. Literary men joined historians, scientists, and preachers in the search for a prose style appropriate to the new conceptions of truth.

Whether we speak in terms of family of ideas, or climate of opinion, or dominant intellectual movement, what is distinctive about seventeenth-century English intellectuals is that they were prepared to face the imperfections of all human knowledge and, nevertheless, to seek that intermediate goal which they called moral certainty.

NOTES

CHAPTER I: INTRODUCTION

1. James Murphy, *Rhetoric in the Middle Ages: A History of Rhetorical Theory from St. Augustine to the Renaissance* (Berkeley, 1974); Richard McKeon, "Rhetoric in the Middle Ages," *Speculum*, 17 (1942), 1-32.

2. Jerrold E. Seigel, *Rhetoric and Philosophy in Renaissance Humanism* (Princeton, N.J., 1968), p. vii. Seigel provides an excellent discussion of the humanists' basic commitment to eloquence and traces the uneasy relationship between philosophy and rhetoric in the generations spanned by Petrarch and Valla. See also Paul Oskar Kristeller, *Renaissance Thought: The Classic, Scholastic, and Humanistic Strains* (New York, 1961); Paul Oskar Kristeller, *Renaissance Thought and its Sources* (New York, 1979); Eugene Rice, *The Renaissance Idea of Wisdom* (Cambridge, Mass., 1958); John H. Randall, *The Career of Philosophy: From the Middle Ages to the Enlightenment* (New York, 1962).

3. See Eric Cochrane, "Science and Humanism in the Italian Renaissance," *Am. Hist. Rev.*, 81 (1976), 1039-57; Eugenio Garin, *Science and Civic Life in the Italian Renaissance*, trans. P. Munz (New York, 1969).

4. Paolo Rossi, *Philosophy, Technology and the Arts in the Early Modern Era* (New York, 1970); J. H. Randall, *The Career of Philosophy*, I, 238-45; Joan Simon, *Education and Society in Tudor England* (Cambridge, 1967), pp. 115-21.

5. Bernardino Bonansea, *Thommaso Campanella* (Washington, D.C., 1969), pp. 64, 76-80.

6. See Neal Gilbert, *Renaissance Concepts of Method* (New York, 1960).

7. I have used the terms "scientist" and "virtuoso" interchangeably. Neither is really satisfactory. The former, a nineteenth-century term, suggests a degree and kind of knowledge that most seventeenth-century practitioners of the natural sciences disavowed, while the latter, "virtuoso," has come to have connotations of dilettantism. I have also used the term "naturalist," although it suggests a greater concern with flora and fauna than I wish to convey, and the term "natural philosopher." See Walter Houghton, "The English Virtuoso in the 17th Century," *J. Hist. of Ideas*, 3 (1942), 50-73, 190-219; Sidney Ross, " 'Scientist': The Story of a Word," *Annals of Science*, 18 (1962), 65-86.

8. Lawrence Stone, "The Educational Revolution in England 1560-1640," *Past and Present*, 28 (1964), 41-80.

CHAPTER II: NATURAL PHILOSOPHY AND EXPERIMENTAL SCIENCE

1. Francis Bacon, *The Works of Francis Bacon*, eds. James Spedding, R. Ellis, and D. N. Heath (London, 1875), "The New Organon," Book I, Aphorisms 47, 82. In Aphorism 126, Bacon carefully separates himself from the skeptical "denial of the

273

capacity of the mind to comprehend truth." He propounds "not denial of the capacity to understand, but provision for understanding Truly." For a discussion of the relationship between Bacon and Montaigne, see Ira O. Wade, *The Intellectual Origins of the Enlightenment* (Princeton, N.J., 1970), pp. 89-92, 105, 123. See also P. Villey, *Montaigne and Bacon* (Paris, 1913).

2. Bacon, *Works*, IV, 27-28.

3. Thomas Sprat, *The History of the Royal Society*, eds. J. Cope and H. W. Jones (St. Louis, 1958), pp. 238-39.

4. Joseph Glanvill, *Plus Ultra, or the Progress and Advancement of Knowledge* (London, 1668), p. 89. See also Anon., *A Brief Vindication of the Royal Society*, (London, 1670), pp. 3-4.

5. Sprat, *History of the Royal Society*, pp. 90-91, 214-15.

6. Glanvill, *Plus Ultra*, pp. 86-88.

7. See A. R. Hall, *The Scientific Revolution 1500-1800: The Formation of the Modern Scientific Attitude* (Boston, 1954), p. 167, see also pp. 275-305.

8. Sprat, *History of the Royal Society*, p. 83.

9. Robert Boyle, *The Works of Robert Boyle* (London, 1772), ed. Thomas Birch, V, 526.

10. Robert Boyle, *The Christian Virtuoso* (London, 1690), pp. 48, 51, 52, 55. See also Boyle, *Defense of the Doctrine Touching the Spring and Weight of Air* (London, 1662), Preface.

11. Comments dealing with testimony became commonplace. John Evelyn, for example, noted that his natural history of forest trees would include only his personal observations and what he had "received unquestioned testimony for"; *Sylva* (London, 1664), Preface. See also Francis Willughby, *The Ornithology* (London, 1678), Preface by John Ray; Edward Tyson, *Orang-Outang* (London, 1699). Thus, too, when Sprat included a report on the Peak at Teneriffe, he indicated that it had been received from "some considerable merchants and men worthy of Credit"; *History of the Royal Society*, p. 200. Robert Boyle, at one point, included not only the name but the rank of various observers so as to increase the credibility and validity of the experimental data.

12. Willughby, *Ornithology*, Preface.

13. Sprat, *History of the Royal Society*, pp. 83, 85, 95, 243, 245.

14. For a discussion of Sprat as spokesman for the Society see Barbara Shapiro, *John Wilkins 1614-72: An Intellectual Biography* (Berkeley, 1969), pp. 203-204; Margery Purver, *The Royal Society: Concept and Creation* (Cambridge, Mass., 1967), pp. 1-19; C. L. Sonnichsen, "The Life and Works of Sprat" (Ph.D. Dissertation, Harvard, 1931); P. B. Wood, "Methodology and Apologetics: Thomas Sprat's *History of the Royal Society*," *Brit., J. for the History of Science* 13 (1980), 1-26.

15. Joseph Glanvill, *A Praefactory Answer to Mr. Henry Stubbe* (London, 1671), pp. 143-44; Sprat, *History of the Royal Society*, p. 99.

16. Sprat, *History of the Royal Society*, pp. 95, 99, 100.

17. Glanvill, *Plus Ultra*, pp. 86-88.

18. Tyson, *Orang-Outang*, p. 25.

19. Sprat, *History of the Royal Society*, pp. 19-20.

20. Walter Charleton, *Physiologia Epicuro-Gassendo-Charletoniana* (London, 1654), p. 18.

21. For the impact of skepticism see Richard H. Popkin, *The History of Scepticism from Erasmus to Descartes* (New York, 1961); Charles B. Schmitt, *Cicero Scepticus: A Study of the Influence of the "Academica" in the Renaissance* (The Hague, 1972); J. S.

Spink, *French Free Thought from Gassendi to Voltaire* (New York, 1960); Margaret Osler, "Certainty, Scepticism and Scientific Optimism: The Roots of Eighteenth-Century Attitudes Towards Scientific Knowledge," in Paula Backscheider, ed., *Probability, Time and Space in Eighteenth Century Literature* (New York, 1979).

22. See John Wilkins, "The Discovery of a New World: or, A Discourse tending to Prove, That ('tis Probable) there may be another Habitable World in the Moon" (1638) in *The Mathematical and Philosophical Works* (London, 1708); Wilkins, "Discourse Concerning a New Planet: tending to Prove, That ('tis Probable) our Earth is one of the Planets" (1640), ibid.

23. Charleton, *Physiologia*, p. 18.

24. Ibid., p. 19.

25. Glanvill, *A Praefactory Answer*, pp. 143-44.

26. Robert Hooke, *Posthumous Works*, ed. R. Waller (London, 1705), p. 325.

27. Bacon, *The Advancement of Learning*, ed. G. W. Kitchen (London, 1915) pp. 90-95. See also Bacon, *Works*, IV, 345-47, 360-65. Bacon considered mathematics a branch of metaphysics; IV, 369-71.

28. Bacon, *Advancement*, pp. 94-96. See also *Works*, IV, 360-65.

29. Sprat, *History of the Royal Society*, p. 77.

30. Hooke, *Posthumous Works*, p. 329.

31. E. W. Strong, "Barrow and Newton," *J. Hist. of Phil.*, 8 (1970), 156-57.

32. Hooke, *Posthumous Works*, p. 334.

33. Sprat, *History of the Royal Society*, pp. 31, 38, 89.

34. Matthew Hale, *Contemplations Moral and Divine* (London, 1676), p. 161.

35. Sprat, *History of the Royal Society*, p. 100.

36. Ibid., pp. 101, 107.

37. Letter Oldenburg to Sluse, Feb. 1666/7. Quoted in M. B. Hall, "Science in the Early Royal Society," in *The Emergence of Science in Western Europe*, ed. M. Crosland (London, 1975), p. 63.

38. *The Problem of Certainty in England, 1630-1690* (The Hague, 1963). For a discussion of Bacon's efforts to produce demonstrative certainty of the laws of nature see pp. 1-12. See also John Losee, *An Historical Introduction to the Philosophy of Science* (2nd ed., New York, 1950), pp. 60-69.

39. Hugo Grotius, writing earlier in the century, identified four kinds of proof: mathematical, physical, advice and counsel, and matters of fact. *The Truth of the Christian Religion*, ed. Simon Patrick (London, 1680), p. 94.

40. See Van Leeuwen, *The Problem of Certainty*, pp. 15-32; Robert Orr, *Reason and Authority: The Thought of William Chillingworth* (Oxford, 1967).

41. John Tillotson, *The Wisdom of Being Religious* (London, 1664), p. 31. See also Van Leeuwen, *The Problem of Certainty*, pp. 32-48.

42. Quoted in ibid., p. 36.

43. Ibid., p. 37n.

44. Walter Charleton, *The Immortality of the Human Soul* (London, 1657), pp. 161-63, 186.

45. Sir Charles Wolseley, *The Unreasonableness of Atheism Made Manifest* (3rd ed., London, 1675), pp. 168ff.

46. Robert Boyle, *Works*, IV, 182.

47. John Wilkins, *The Principles and Duties of Natural Religion* (London, 1675), pp. 3-4, 5, 25.

48. Robert Boyle, "Hydrostatical Paradoxes," in *Works*, II, 739.

49. Christopher Wren, lecture delivered at Gresham College. Quoted in John

Summerson, *Sir Christopher Wren* (London, 1954), p. 52. Although most seventeenth-century English virtuosi felt that physical and mathematical proofs were not to be judged by the standards of the other, Wren felt that other discourses participated "more or less of truth, according as their subjects are more or less capable of mathematical demonstration"; Ibid., p. 52. For Wilkins, mathematical demonstration included mathematical propositions and all "such simple abstracted beings as in their own nature do lie so open, and are so obvious to the understanding" that no doubt is possible, even in the most prejudiced person; e.g., that the whole is greater than the parts; Wilkins, *Natural Religion*, pp. 7-8. For some, however, these were included with metaphysical certainty. For Glanvill, mathematical demonstration admitted "no ambiguity or insignificant obscurity." *The Vanity of Dogmatizing* (Oxford, 1661), p. 160.

50. Isaac Barrow, *The Works* (London, 1683-87, 4 vols.), I, 449-52.

51. Wolseley, *The Unreasonableness of Atheism*, p. 147.

52. Wilkins, *Natural Religion*, p. 5; Charleton, *Immortality*, p. 186.

53. Hale, *Contemplations*, p. 100. Hale's references to arguments rather than evidence, however, suggest a rather traditional view.

54. Robert Boyle, "The Excellence of Theology" (1675), in *Works*, IV, 432.

55. Boyle, "Hydrostatical Paradoxes" (1666), ibid., II, 739. Many things "given out" as mathematical demonstration simply were not. Naturalists were advised to forgo pretensions of mathematical certitude; ibid., 739-42.

56. See John Wallis, *Truth Tried* (London, 1642), p. 92.

57. Charleton, *Immortality*, pp. 186, 187.

58. Ibid., pp. 167-68, 188.

59. Hooke, *Posthumous Works*, pp. 329, 330-31. See David Olyroyd, "Robert Hooke's Methodology of Science as Exemplified in his Discourse of Earthquakes," *Brit. J. Hist. Science*, 6 (1972), 109-30. Hooke's emphasis on hypothesis also undermined his Baconianism.

60. Isaac Barrow, *The Usefulness of Mathematicall Learning . . . being Mathematical Lectures*, trans. J. Kirby (London, 1734), pp. 53, 54, 56.

61. Ibid., pp. 65, 68. See also pp. 70-71.

62. Ibid., p. 74. In some instances, however, a single experiment might "establish a true Hypothesis" to prove a "True Definition" and consequently to "constitute true Principles"; ibid., p. 116.

63. Richard S. Westfall, *The Construction of Modern Science: Mechanisms and Mechanics* (New York, 1971), pp. 41, 158-59.

64. Sprat, *History of the Royal Society*, pp. 107, 108.

65. See Van Leeuwen, *The Problem of Certainty*, pp. 121-42; R. S. Woolhouse, *Locke's Philosophy of Science and Knowledge* (New York, 1971); J. W. Yolton, *John Locke and the Way of Ideas* (Oxford, 1956); J. W. Yolton, *Locke and the Compass of Human Understanding* (Cambridge, 1970); *John Locke: Problems and Perspectives*, ed. J. W. Yolton (Cambridge, 1969); Margaret Osler, "John Locke and the Changing Ideal of Scientific Knowledge," *J. Hist. Ideas*, 3 (1970), 3-16.

66. For Carneades, who developed a kind of empirical probabilism, the truth of empirical statements was never necessary.

67. See Edmund Byrne, *Probability and Opinion: A Study in the Medieval Predispositions of Post Medieval Theories of Probability* (The Hague, 1968); Benjamin Nelson, " 'Probabilists,' 'Antiprobabilists' and the Quest for Certitude in the 16th and 17th Centuries," *Actes du xc Congrès Intèrnationale d'Histoire des Sciences, Proceedings*, 1 (1965), pp. 270-73; Benjamin Nelson, "The Early Modern Revolution in Science

and Philosophy; Fictionalism, Probabilism, Fideism and Catholic 'Prophetism,' "
Boston Studies in the Philosophy of Science, 3 (1964-66), 1-39.

68. Ian Hacking, *The Emergence of Probability* (New York, 1975).

69. Paolo Rossi, *Philosophy, Technology and the Arts in the Early Modern Era* (New York, 1970). The relationship between a probabilistic empirical science and the emergence of mathematical probability remains unclear. Ian Hacking has suggested that the development of mathematical notions of probability were linked to empiricism. The "signs" of medical and astrological phenomena might be read and predictions made, none of which would have claims to certitude. Predicting outcomes on the basis of signs shifted toward the numerical calculation when notions of credibility became linked to those of frequency. Despite the greater receptiveness of English thinkers to empirical philosophy and probabilistic science, relatively few English virtuosi were attracted to calculating chances. Graunt, Petty, and Arbuthnot were the exceptions. Hacking thus concentrates on Continental thinkers. He has suggested that the moral certainty was linked to probability in 1668 by Leibniz. Leibniz was the first to suggest that probability theory could serve as a branch of logic compared to the theory of deduction. Hacking suggests that Leibniz's ideas were derived from the law. He also notes that the *Port Royal Logic* of 1662 was the first work to combine numerical probability concerned with testimony of human and divine events with future contingent events. Huygens authored the first textbook which dealt with mathematical probability in 1657. Hacking, *Emergence of Probability*, pp. 46, 58, 77, 79, 139, 167-68.

Recently there has been an effort to develop a general theory of probability which would encompass both mathematical probability and inductive logic. This effort, which concerns itself with "gradations" and giving "weight" to evidence in the seventeenth-century manner, suggests that problems explored by seventeenth-century thinkers are still of philosophical relevance; Jonathan Cohen, *The Probable and the Provable* (London, 1977). Cohen is seeking an "inductive probability" distinct both from mathematical probability and from the loose probability associated with everyday life. His paradigm is drawn from Anglo-American legal concepts.

70. Nelson, " 'Probabilists,' 'Antiprobabilists,' " *Proceedings*, 1 (1965), 270-73.

71. See *Comité du tricentenaire de Gassendi 1655-1955, Actes du Congrès* (Paris, 1957), pp. 198-210, 240ff.; Robert Kargon, *Atomism in England* (Oxford, 1966). Gassendi's "History of Digne" conforms closely to the new archival and descriptive history discussed in Chapter IV. See *Comité*, pp. 140-54.

72. Quoted in Hacking, *Emergence of Probability*, p. 48.

73. Wilkins, *Discovery*, pp. 186, 167, 207.

74. John Wilkins, *Of the Principles and Duties of Natural Religion*; John Wilkins, *Sermons Preached upon Several Occasions* (London, 1682); John Wilkins, *Sermons Preached upon Several Occasions before the King* (2nd ed.; London, 1680).

75. Sprat, *History of the Royal Society*, p. 108.

76. Robert Hooke, *Micrographia* (London, 1665), p. 246.

77. See Joseph Glanvill, *Scire/ i tuum nihil est: or The Author's Defense of the Vanity of Dogmatizing* (London, 1665), pp. 1-2.

78. Ibid., pp. 73, 52.

79. Barrow, *The Usefulness of Mathematicall Learning*, p. 116.

80. Robert Boyle, "Some Considerations about the Reconcileableness of Reason and Religion" (1675), in *Works*, IV, 182.

81. Glanvill, *Seasonable Reflections . . . In Order to the Conviction, and Cure of the Scoffing, and Infidelity of a Degenerate Age* (London, 1676), p. 143. See also Jackson

I. Cope, *Joseph Glanvill: Anglican Apologist* (St. Louis, 1956), pp. 61-63, 106-107, 130-33. For Glanvill's association of probability with hypothesis see *The Author's Defense of the Vanity of Dogmatizing*, p. 93.

82. John Locke, *An Essay Concerning Human Understanding* (1690), Bk. IV, Chapt. LV, Sec. 1.

83. Ibid., Chapt. XV, Sec. 6. See also Chapt. XV, Sec. 4. See also Hoyt Trowbridge, "Scattered Atoms of Probability," *Eighteenth Century Studies*, 5 (1971), 1-38. Richard Aaron, *John Locke* (Oxford, 1955), pp. 247-48; Margaret Osler, "John Locke and the Changing Idea of Scientific Knowledge," *J. Hist. of Ideas*, 31 (1970), 3-16; Fulton Anderson, "The Influence of Contemporary Science on Locke's Method and Results," *Univ. of Toronto Studies, Philosophy*, II (Toronto, 1923); Maurice Mandelbaum, *Philosophy, Science and Sense Perception: Historical and Critical Studies* (Baltimore, 1966).

84. Locke, *Essay*, Bk. IV, Chapt. XVI, Sec. 6.

85. Ibid.

86. Ibid., Sec. 6, 7, 8.

87. Ibid., Bk. II, Chapt. I, Sec. 10; Bk. III, Sec. 39, and Chapt. XII, Sec. 9-12.

88. Sprat, *History of the Royal Society*, p. 127.

89. Aant Elzinga, "Huygens' Theory of Research and Descartes' Theory of Knowledge," *Zeitschrift für Allgemeine Wissenschaft*, 3 (1972), 17.

90. Christian Huygens, *The Celestial Worlds Discovered* (London, 1698), p. 10. Huygens' discussion of the probability of lunar inhabitants is similar to that of Wilkins.

91. Letter to Perault, quoted in A. E. Bell, *Christian Huygens* (London, 1947). Geometry is described as a science which gives such a "full comprehension and infallible certainty of Truth, as no other knowledge can pretend to"; *The Celestial Worlds Discovered*, p. 29.

92. Huygens, *Treatise on Light*, Preface quoted in Elzinga, "Huygens' Theory of Research," p. 19, see also pp. 16-22.

93. Ralph M. Blake, "Theory of Hypothesis among Renaissance Astronomers," in *Theories of Scientific Method: The Renaissance Through the Nineteenth Century*, ed. E. Madden (Seattle, 1960), pp. 23-24.

94. Copernicus privately held that his was not just a possible account of the phenomena, but the only possible and therefore true one. The suggestion that geometrical hypotheses did in fact represent reality was first offered by defenders of the Ptolemaic position; ibid., pp. 28-35.

95. Ibid., pp. 35-37.

96. Some of Kepler's views were not published until the nineteenth century. For Kepler "That astronomer well performs his office who predicts with the greatest measure of approximation the motions and situations of the stars; but he does better and is held worthy of the greater praise who in addition to this furnishes us with true opinions concerning the form of the world"; quoted in ibid., p. 43. See also Jurgen Mittelstraus, "Methodological Elements of Keplerian Astronomy," *Studies in the History and Philosophy of Science*, 3 (1972), 203-32. Mittelstraus argues that Kepler's laws of planetary motion are empirical propositions based on Tycho's calculations. Since hypotheses were dependent on empirical data, they could be falsified by empirical data; ibid., pp. 206-209. Robert Westman suggests that Kepler preferred "probable conjecture" to fictitious hypothesis and that his hypotheses were not developed inductively from nature but rather were derived from neo-Platonic sources. Kepler thus provided aesthetically appealing ratios which were in reasonably close agreement with relevant observations. Astronomers were not to conceive of anything

they pleased but to establish the probable causes of the hypotheses they recommended as the true causes of the appearances. "Kepler's Theory of Hypothesis and the Realist Dilemma," in ibid, pp. 233-64. See also Richard Westfall, *The Construction of Modern Science: Mechanism and Mechanics* (New York, 1971), pp. 3-12.

97. See Mary Hesse, "Francis Bacon's Philosophy of Science," in B. W. Vicars, ed., *Essential Articles for the Study of Francis Bacon* (London, 1972). For a view of Bacon which suggests that Bacon did allow some role for theorizing, see L. Jonathan Cohen, "Some Historical Remarks on the Baconian Conception of Probability," *J. Hist. Ideas*, 41 (1980), 219-32; Margery Purver, *The Royal Society: Concept and Creation* (Cambridge, Mass., 1976), pp. 20-62. For Descartes see Ralph Blake, "The Role of Experience in Descartes' Theory of Method," in *Theories of Scientific Method*, pp. 75-103. For a different view see L. Lauden, "The Clock Metaphor and Probabilism: The Impact of Descartes in English Methodological Thought 1650-1685," *Annals of Science*, 22 (1966), 73-104; John Morris, "Descartes and Probable Knowledge," *J. of the Hist. of Philosophy*, 8 (1970), 303-12; Gerd Buchdahl, "The Relevance of Descartes' Philosophy for Modern Philosophy of Science," *Brit. J. for the Hist. of Science*, 1 (1962-63), 227-49.

98. For the ambiguous function of experiment in Galileo's thought see Rupert Hall, *The Scientific Revolution, 1500-1800* (Boston, 1956), pp. 168-77; Westfall, *Construction of Modern Science*, pp. 21-22; John Losee, *An Historical Introduction to the Philosophy of Science* (Oxford, 1977), pp. 54-59; William R. Shea, *Galileo's Intellectual Revolution* (London, 1972).

99. Wilkins, *Discourse*, pp. 214-15. Galileo's *Dialogue Concerning the Two Great World Systems* (1632) considered the Copernican hypothesis as physical truth.

100. See Westfall, *The Construction of Modern Science, passim*; Robert Kargon, *Atomism in England*; Marie Boas, "The Establishment of the Mechanical Philosophy," *Osiris*, 10 (1952), 412-541.

101. Sprat, *History of the Royal Society*, pp. 32, 100, 101, 107. See also p. 108.

102. Bacon, *Works*, III, 156.

103. Sprat, *History of the Royal Society*, pp. 255-56. These included hypotheses dealing with astronomy, gravity, air pressure, fire, the form and spring of air, clouds, petrification, light, colors.

104. Ibid., p. 257. Causal explanations and hypotheses were admissible only if they were not made the "perpetual Objects of our Contemplation."

105. Ibid., pp. 311-18.

106. Wren to Hooke (1665) quoted in J. A. Bennett, "Hooke and Wren and the System of the World: Some Points Towards an Historical Account," *Brit. J. for the Hist. of Science*, 8 (1975), 55.

107. Joseph Glanvill, *Scepsis Scientifica* (London, 1665), Address to the Royal Society. All existing hypotheses might be built on "too narrow inspection of things." Further experiments might disclose phenomena which fit no extant model.

108. See Glanvill, *The Vanity of Dogmatizing*, p. 189. See also pp. 189-93.

109. Joseph Glanvill, "Against Confidence in Philosophy and Matters of Speculation," in *Essays on Several Important Subjects in Philosophy and Religion* (London, 1676), p. 15. Jackson I. Cope, *Joseph Glanvill: Anglican Apologist*; Richard Popkin, "Joseph Glanvill, A Precursor of David Hume," *J. Hist. of Ideas*, 14 (1953), 292-303; Van Leeuwen, *The Problem of Certainty*, pp. 71-89.

110. Glanvill, "Modern Improvements of Useful Knowledge," in *Essays*, p. 10. Even the most idealized philosophers would "not set down any System or Body of Principles as certain and established." They "gave but timorous assent to any notions

in Natural Philosophy: They held no infallible Theory here." They believed that the best foundation for natural philosophy would be a good history of nature and that remained "defective." Hypotheses, though not infallible, were permitted. They must not "be raised from abstractions" or "operations of the mind" but "collected leisurely from a careful observation of particulars"; ibid., pp. 48, 49. Fruitful hypotheses were dependent both on an ever-expanding empirical base and in a hesitancy dogmatically to establish theory and speculative doctrine; Glanvill, *Plus Ultra*, p. 89, see also p. 81. Glanvill seemed to excuse Descartes, whom he very much admired, by suggesting that he had really only intended "his Principles" as hypotheses. *Scepsis Scientifica*, p. 211. Kargon suggests that Glanvill's position at this point (1665) was consistent with Cartesian "hypothetical physics" and that in later years he moved toward a more Baconian empiricism. *Atomism in England*, p. 113.

111. Glanvill, "Against Confidence in Philosophy," *Essays*, p. 15. "Science" or "the knowledge of things in their causes which cannot be otherwise" was rarely, if ever, achieved. With hypotheses things "may be and may be otherwise"; ibid.

112. *Letters and Poems in Honour of the Incomparable Princess Margaret, Duchess of Newcastle* (London, 1676), p. 124.

113. Samuel Parker, *A Free and Impartial Censure of the Platonicke Philosophie* (Oxford, 1666), pp. 44-45, 47-48. Although Parker preferred the "mechanical hypothesis" to others he nevertheless felt "their contexture" to be "too slight and brittle to have any stress laid upon them"; ibid., p. 46.

114. Quoted in M. B. Hall, "Science in the Early Royal Society," in Crosland, *Emergence of Science*, pp. 65, 64. This article provides an excellent treatment of the role of empiricism, rationalism, and hypothesis.

115. Barrow, *The Usefullness of Mathematicall Learning*, p. 116.

116. Charleton, *Immortality*, p. 36.

117. Robert Hooke, *Micrographia* (London, 1665), Preface. For Hooke's commitment to and modification of Baconianism see D. R. Olyroyd, "Robert Hooke's Methodology of Science as Exemplified in his Discourse of Earthquakes," *Brit. J. for the Hist. of Science*, 6 (1972), 110-30. See also Margaret 'Espinasse, *Robert Hooke* (Berkeley, 1962), pp. 28-33.

118. Hooke, *Micrographia*, Preface.

119. See Olyroyd, "Hooke's Methodology of Science," *Brit. J. for the Hist. of Science*. Robert Hooke, *Lectures . . . Explaining the Power of Springing Bodies* (London, 1678), pp. 39-40.

120. Robert Hooke, *Philosophical Collections* (London, 1681), p. 25. He also noted that the "Schemes for explication of Muscular motion" used by another experimenter were the same as his. The similarity of ideas and experiments "has made me have a better opinion of this Thought than else I should ever have had; . . ."

121. Hooke, *Micrographia*, p. 6.

122. Quoted in Bennett, "Hooke and Wren," *Brit. J. for the Hist. of Science*, 8 (1975), 43. See also pp. 35-37.

123. Robert Hooke, *An Attempt to Prove the Motion of the Earth from Observations* (London, 1674), p. 4.

124. Robert Hooke, "Cometa," in *Lectiones Cutlerianae* (London, 1679), pp. 24-25.

125. Ibid., p. 53.

126. Hooke, *Micrographia*, Preface.

127. Ibid., pp. 46, 246.

128. Robert Boyle, "A Discourse of Things Above Reason" (1681), *Works*, IV,

461. See G. A. Rogers, "Boyle, Locke, and Reason," *J. Hist. of Ideas*, 27 (1966), 205-16; Maurice Mandelbaum, *Philosophy, Science and Sense Perception*, pp. 88-112.

129. *Robert Boyle on Natural Philosophy*, ed. M. B. Hall (Indiana, 1965), pp. 234, 239. Hall has suggested that Boyle initially felt that his experiments "illustrated" the corpuscularian hypothesis and later claimed they could prove it. Hall, "Science in the Early Royal Society," in Crosland, *Emergence of Science*, p. 73.

130. G.A.J. Rogers, "Boyle, Locke and Reason," *Journal Hist. Ideas*, 27 (1966), 205-16.

131. Robert Boyle, *The Christian Virtuoso* (London, 1690), pp. 4-6. "The Organs of Sense" were "but the Instruments of Reason in ye Investigation of Truth." R. S. Westfall, "Unpublished Boyle Papers Relating to Scientific Method," *Annals of Science*, 12 (1956), p. 67. Reason devised "apposite Experiments and judged their value"; ibid., p. 69.

132. Boyle, *Works*, V, 538-40; I, 302.

133. Robert Boyle, *Hydrostatical Paradoxes* (Oxford, 1666), Preface.

134. Robert Boyle, *Defense of the Doctrine Touching the Spring and Weight of the Air*, Preface.

135. Robert Boyle, "Certain Physiological Essays" in *Works*, I, 302. In some sense all generalizations in the natural sciences were hypotheses for Boyle. Most "theorems and conclusions in philosophy and divinity" were hypotheses in the sense that they were not absolutely certain, "Discourse of Things Above Reason," in *Works*, IV, 461.

Boyle, for example, treated his work on the consistency of gems as a "Conjectural hypothesis." On this occasion he first attempted to show that his hypothesis was possible and then "set down some particulars to make it very probable." The "explication" was meant to stand or fall according to the data. Robert Boyle, *An Essay about the Origin and Nature of Gems* (London, 1672), Preface, p. 123.

136. *Boyle on Natural Philosophy*, pp. 134-35; Westfall, "Unpublished Boyle Papers Relating to Scientific Method," p. 70.

137. Thomas Sydenham who wished to completely eradicate "philosophical hypotheses" from the natural history of disease contributed a great deal to medical science. Sydenham preferred a minute and clear description of the "natural phenomena of Disease." Hypotheses necessarily introduced error because phenomena were employed selectively. *The Whole Works of . . . Dr. Thomas Sydenham*, trans. J. Pechy (London, 1696), Author's Preface; Kenneth Dewhurst, *Dr. Thomas Sydenham* (Berkeley, 1966), pp. 65, 80-81, 92-93. For a more favorable view of hypotheses in seventeenth- and eighteenth-century medicine, see Joseph Levine, *Dr. Woodward's Shield: History, Science and Satire in Augustan England* (London, 1977), p. 13; William Coleman, "Mechanical Philosophy and Hypothetical Physiology," in ed. R. Palter, *The Annus Mirabilis of Sir Isaac Newton: 1666-1966* (Cambridge, Mass., 1971), pp. 322-29.

138. Charleton at times leaned toward the Continental mode and Huygens in the English direction. See Charleton, *Immortality*, pp. 36-37; Charleton, *The Natural History of the Passions* (London, 1674), Preface, p. 4. In physics Huygens thought it desirable to "start from experiment" and proceed by conceiving hypotheses. Theory would control experiment and experiment inform intelligent reasoning. He was convinced physical principles and physical hypotheses could never reach beyond probability to certainty. See Elzinga, "Huygens' Theory of Research," Pts. I, II (1971), 174-94; III (1972), 9-25; H.J.M. Bos, "Huygens," *Dictionary of Scientific Biography*, pp. 608-609; Bell, *Huygens*, p. 210. Conjectures were often desirable in natural philosophy though some were of a "higher degree" of probability than

others. Determining which conjectures lay "nearer Truth than others" was the "chief exercise of our Judgement." Huygens, *Celestial Worlds Discovered*, Preface. See also Richard Watson, *The Downfall of Cartesianism, 1673-1712* (The Hague, 1966).

139. Burnet, *Sacred Theory of the Earth* (London, 1684), I, Preface, 78, 109. Even then he admitted he might not be able "to command the Assent and Belief" of all (p. 78).

140. Ibid., 85.

141. Ibid., 149.

142. Ibid., 150.

143. William Whiston, *New Theory of the Earth* (London, 1697), p. 32. Whiston attributed the deluge to the impact of the tail of a comet.

144. L. P., "Two Essays" (1695), in ed. Sir Walter Scott, *A Collection of Scarce and Valuable Tracts*, (2nd ed., 13 vols. London, 1809-15), XII, 21.

145. *An Essay Toward a Natural History of the Earth* (London, 1695), p. 245. Woodward also criticized the conjectures of Steno and Ray for lack of "due warrant from Observation" (p. 40). See also ibid., pp. 1-3, 52, 245, and Joseph Levine, *Dr. Woodward's Shield*, pp. 33, 35, 55.

146. Thomas Robinson, *New Observations on the Natural History of This World of Matter* (London, 1696), Epistle dedicatory; John Arbuthnot, *An Examination of Dr. Woodward's Account of the Deluge* (1697), quoted in Lester M. Beattie, *John Arbuthnot: Mathematician and Satirist* (Cambridge, 1935), p. 203. See also pp. 190-207.

147. Beattie, *Arbuthnot*, quoting letter Nicolson to Lhuyd, p. 206. Ray considered Burnet's theory to be "no more or better than a meer chimera or Romance"; quoted in Levine, *Dr. Woodward's Shield*, p. 25. For Newton's correspondence with Burnet see Richard S. Westfall, *Never at Rest: a Biography of Isaac Newton* (Cambridge, 1980) pp. 390-91.

148. Thomas Baker, *Reflections on Learning* (London, 1700), pp. 82-85. More observations and experiments were expected to "raise a Theory" (p. 84).

149. Some historians have contrasted the hostility to hypothesis presented in the *Principia* with the more favorable treatment in the *Optics*. J. F. McDonald distinguishes two varieties of hypothesis, one acceptable to Newton, the other not; John McDonald, "Properties and Causes: An Approach to the Problem of Hypothesis in the Scientific Methodology of Sir Isaac Newton," *Annals of Science*, 28 (1972), 227-28. See also I. B. Cohen, *Franklin and Newton* (Philadelphia, 1956), pp. 138-40, 179-82; A. C. Crombie, "Newton's Conception of Scientific Method," *Bull. of the Inst. of Physics*, 8 (1957), 350-62; Robert Palter, "Newton and the Inductive Method," in *Annus Mirabilis*, pp. 244-57; R. M. Blake, "Isaac Newton and the Hypothetico-Deductive Method," in Madden, *Theories of Scientific Method*, pp. 119-43.

150. For contrasts between Newton and Hooke, Boyle and Huygens see 'Espinasse, *Hooke*, pp. 29-31; McDonald, "Properties and Causes," 220-23; Zev Bechler, "Newton's 1672 Optical Controversies: A Study in the Grammar of Scientific Dissent," in ed. Y. Elkana, *The Interaction Between Science and Philosophy* (Jerusalem, 1974). Van Leeuwen, however, has stressed the similarity between Newton and the views of the Royal Society; *The Problem of Certainty*, pp. 90, 107-20. See also R. Westfall, "Uneasily Fitful Reflections on Fits of Easy Transmission," in Palter, *Annus Mirabilis*, pp. 96-97; R. Westfall, *Never at Rest*, pp. 240-51, 270-74, 447-52. For Newton and the corpuscularian hypothesis see A. R. Hall and M. B. Hall, "Newton's Theory of Matter," *Isis*, 51 (1960), 131-44. For a discussion of certainty which links Newton to Kepler, Galileo, and Descartes see E. A. Burtt, *The Metaphysical Foundations of*

Modern Physical Science (New York, 1927). See also R. Kargon, "Newton, Barrow and the Hypothetical Physics," *Centaurus*, II (1965), 46-56.

151. Quoted in Bechler, "Newton's 1672 Optical Controversies," pp. 118-19. Oldenburg omitted the "dogmatic" passage from the printed version; ibid., p. 119.

152. Ibid., pp. 122-24, 129-34. Newton thus appeared to be making claims of necessity and certitude which Hooke felt were too great. Bechler argues that Hooke never rejected Newton's hypothesis, that he regarded it as "ingenius," and that he was thoroughly capable of understanding it.

Hooke "wholly agreed with . . . the truth and curiosity of those observations" but could not "yet see any undeniable arguments to convince" him "of the certainty of the hypothesis"; quoted in ibid., p. 125. It was "not so certain as mathematical demonstrations"; quoted in ibid., p. 125, from *Isaac Newton, Correspondence,* ed. H. W. Turnbull (Cambridge, 1950), I, 113.

153. Hooke, *Posthumous Works,* p. 7.

154. *Isaac Newton's Papers and Letters on Natural Philosophy,* ed..I. B. Cohen (Cambridge, Mass., 1958), p. 2.

155. Ibid., p. 109. See also McDonald, "Properties and Causes," pp. 219-20; Bechler, "Newton's 1672 Optical Controversies," pp. 130-31.

156. *Newton's Papers and Letters,* ed. Cohen, p. 106.

157. Newton, *Mathematical Principles of Natural Philosophy,* ed. F. Cajori (Berkeley, 1934), p. 54. Translators are divided as to whether *fingo* should be rendered "feign" or "frame." McDonald, "Properties and Causes," p. 226.

158. Similar attitudes are expressed in his *Optics* (1704), which some scholars have viewed as more hypothetical than the *Principia.* The *Optics* however boldly proclaimed his "Design" was "Not to explain the Properties of Light by Hypothesis but to propose and prove them by Reason and Experiments"; Isaac Newton, *Optics* (New York: Dover, 1952), p. 6. An unpublished manuscript probably intended as an introduction suggests "The method of resolution consists in trying experiments and considering all the phaenomena of nature relating to the subject at hand and drawing the conclusion from them and examining the truth of those conclusions by new experiments . . . until you come to the general properties of things. . . . But if without deriving the properties of things from phaenomena you feign hypotheses . . . your system will be little better than a romance"; quoted in McDonald, "Properties and Causes," p. 230. See also J. E. McGuire, "Newton's Principles of Philosophy: An Intended Preface for the 1704 *Opticks* and a Related Draft Fragment," *Brit. J. for the Hist. of Science,* 5 (1970), 178-86; R. Westfall, *Never at Rest,* pp. 242-49. Westfall writes of Hooke as "highly gifted" but "more plausible than brilliant" (p. 243).

The "Queries" outlined Newton's notion of proper scientific methodology: "As in Mathematicks, so in natural philosophy, The Investigation of difficult things by the Method of Analysis, ought ever to precede the method of Composition. This Analysis consists in making Experiments and Observations, and in drawing general Conclusions from them by Induction, and admitting of no Objects against the Conclusions, but such as are taken from Experiments, or other certain Truths. For Hypotheses are not to be regarded in experimental Philosophy"; Newton, *Optics,* p. 404. In "Analysis," however, one proceeds "from Compounds to Ingredients and from Motions to the Forces producing them, and in general from Effects to their Causes, and from particular Causes to more general ones." Synthesis "consists in assuming the Causes discover'd and establish'd as Principles, and by them explaining the Phaenomena proceeding them, and proving the Explanations"; ibid. The "main business of Natural Philosophy is to argue from Phaenomena without feigning

Hypotheses, and to deduce Causes from Effects"; quoted in R. Westfall, *Never at Rest*, pp. 646-47.

In 1713 Newton wrote Cotes "Experimental philosophy proceeds only upon Phenomena and deduces general Propositions only from Induction"; quoted in Olyroyd, "Robert Hooke's Methodology of Science," p. 121n from J. Edelston, *The Correspondence of Sir Isaac Newton and Professor Cotes* (London, 1850), p. 156. Hypothesis, he told Cotes, was "here used by me to signifie only such a proposition as is not a phenomenon or deduced from any phenomena but assumed or supposed without any experimental proof"; quoted in McDonald, "Properties and Causes," p. 227. Whatever his practice, Newton consistently expressed a Baconian antagonism to hypothesis. Late in life he reiterated "In experimental philosophy we are to look upon propositions inferred by general induction from phenomena as accurately or very nearly true, not withstanding any contrary hypotheses that may be imagined, till such time as other phenomena occur, by which they may either be made more accurate, or liable to exceptions. . . . This rule we must follow, that the argument of induction may not be evaded by hypotheses"; quoted in R. Westfall, *Never at Rest*, p. 801. See also John Losee, *An Historical Introduction to the Philosophy of Science* (Oxford, 1980), pp. 81-90; N. R. Hanson, "Hypotheses Fingo," in *The Methodological Heritage of Newton* , ed. R. E. Butts and J. N. Davis (Oxford, 1970), pp. 14-33. Hanson suggests that hypotheses for Newton might involve explanation (p. 15). He discusses the variety of uses of the term hypothesis. See also Paul K. Feyerabend, "Classical Empiricism," in ibid., pp. 150-62.

159. Frank Manuel, *A Portrait of Isaac Newton* (Harvard, 1968); Westfall, *Never at Rest*, p. 179. *Newton's Papers and Letters*, ed. Cohen, p. 2.

160. Thomas Kuhn has argued that Newton was almost alone in bridging the classical physical sciences and the newer experimental sciences. "Mathematical vs. Experimental Traditions in the Development of Physical Science," *J. Interdisciplinary History*, 7 (1976), 1-31.

161. J. E. McGuire, "Force, Active Principles and Newton's Invisible Realm," *Ambix*, 15 (1968), 154-208; J. E. McGuire and P. M. Rattansi, "Newton and the 'Pipes of Pan,' " *Notes and Records of the Royal Society*, 21 (1966), 108-43; P. M. Rattansi, "Newton's Alchemical Studies," *Science, Medicine and Society in the Renaissance*, 2 vols., ed. A. Debus (New York, 1972), II, 167-82; R. Westfall, "Newton and the Hermetic Tradition," in ibid., 183-92; Betty Jo T. Dobbs, *The Foundations of Newton's Alchemy: The Hunting of the Greene Lyon* (Cambridge, 1975); J. E. McGuire, "Neoplatonism and Active Principles in Newton and the 'Corpus Hermeticum,' " in R. S. Westman and J. E. McGuire, *Hermeticism and the Scientific Revolution* (Los Angeles, 1977).

162. See W. R. Albury, "Halley's Ode on Newton's *Principia*," *J. Hist. Ideas*, 39 (1978), 24-43; Westfall, *Never at Rest*, p. 472. For the reservations of Huygens and Leibniz see ibid., p. 472-73.

163. "Systems of natural philosophy" should "be read more to know the hypothesis" than "to gain . . . a comprehensive, scientifical and satisfactory" knowledge of "the Works of Nature." Though nature could not be "brought into a science," one should concentrate on "rational experiments and observations" not "speculative systems." *John Locke on Education*, ed. Peter Gay (New York, 1964), p. 159.

164. John Locke, *The Conduct of the Understanding* (1706), Secs. 13, 25.

165. Locke, *Essay*, Bk. IV, Chapt. XII, Sec. 12. Locke, *Conduct*, Sec. 25. Thus one must not be "too forwardly possessed with the opinion, or expectation of knowledge, where it is not to be had; or by ways that it will not attain it: that we should not

take doubtful systems of complete sciences, nor unintelligible notions for scientifical demonstrations," (Locke, *Essay*, Bk. IV, Chapt. XII, Sec. 12).

166. Locke, *Essay*, Bk. II, Chapt. I, Sec. 10; Bk. IV, Chapt. XII, Sec. 13. Locke's position is restated in the context of medicine. "General theories" were often merely "waking dreams" which passed as "unquestionable truths." The proponents of these "began at the wrong end," with their fancies rather than with the phenomena of disease. If one built on a good history of disease, hypotheses might prove useful, but even then they must be considered aids to the physician, not "philosophical truths." Letter, Locke to Molyneux, 1692-93, in John W. Yolton, *The Locke Reader* (Cambridge, 1977), p. 101.

167. Locke, *Essay*, Bk. IV, Chapt. XVI, Sec. 12.

168. Yolton, *Locke Reader*, p. 102; *Essay*, Bk. II, Chapt. VIII, Secs. 1-2, 7-23. At another point, however, he refers to the corpuscular explanation as the most intelligible hypothesis; Gay, *John Locke on Education*, p. 159.

169. The Copernican hypothesis was not only the simplest but "also the likeliest to be true in itself"; Gay, *John Locke on Education*, p. 144.

170. Locke, *Conduct*, Secs. 43-44.

171. Gay, *John Locke on Education*, p. 160. See also G.A.J. Rogers, "Locke's *Essay* and Newton's *Principia*," *J. Hist. of Ideas*, 39 (1978), 217-37.

172. Gay, *John Locke on Education*, p. 160. With Newton, Locke used terms like "demonstration." Newton's propositions had been discovered with "truth and certitude." Rogers, "Locke's *Essay* and Newton's *Principia*," p. 225.

173. The mind was not a "smooth, clear and equal glass" which reflected truly, but "an enchanted glass, full of superstition and imposture"; "De Augmentis," *Works*, IV, 431.

174. Ibid., 431-33.

175. Ibid., 69.

176. Charleton, *Immortality*, pp. 52, 117; Glanvill, *Scepsis Scientifica*, Address to the Royal Society; Wilkins, *Discovery*, pp. 10, 26; Wilkins, *Natural Religion*, pp. 82, 106.

177. Glanvill, *Vanity of Dogmatizing*, p. 195. See also *Scepsis Scientifica*, pp. 170-71.

178. See Popkin, *The History of Scepticism*; Van Leeuwen, *The Problem of Certainty*.

179. Charleton, *Physiologia*, p. 5, and *Immortality*, pp. 116-17.

180. Hale, *Contemplations*, p. 161.

181. Boyle, *Some Considerations about the Reconcileableness of Reason and Religion* (London, 1675), pp. 64, 65, 86-88. See also Boyle, *Christian Virtuoso*, pp. 12-13.

182. Charleton, *Physiologia*, p. 5.

183. Isaac Barrow, "Of Industry in our Particular Callings as Scholars," in *Works*, I, 247.

184. Gay, *John Locke on Education*, pp. 155, 159.

185. See Margaret Osler, "Galileo, Motion and Essences," *Isis* (1973), 504-509; Margaret Osler, "John Locke and the Changing Ideal of Scientific Knowledge," *J. Hist. of Ideas*, 31 (1970), 3-16.

186. Hooke, *Micrographia*, Preface.

187. Sprat, *History of the Royal Society*, pp. 30-31, 105.

188. See Paolo Rossi, *Philosophy, Technology and the Arts*.

189. Wilkins, *Discovery*, pp. 113, 114. See also Sprat, *History of the Royal Society*, pp. 154-55; Glanvill, *Plus Ultra*, pp. 90-91.

190. See R. F. Jones, *Ancients and Moderns: A Study of the Rise of the Scientific Movement in 17th-Century England* (Berkeley, 1965).

191. Charleton, *Immortality*, p. 1.

192. Wilkins, *Discourse*, pp. 145-46, see also p. 150.

193. Charleton, *Immortality*, p. 3. See also *Physiologia*, p. 34.

194. [Joh]N. [Wilkin]S. and [Set]H. [War]D., *Vindiciae Academiarum* (Oxford, 1654), p. 2. Eugene Rice has suggested that the stance of intellectual liberty and freedom of judgment may owe something to Pierre Charron's tolerant skepticism, to skepticism more generally, and to Cicero's *De Academica; The Renaissance Idea of Wisdom* (Cambridge, Mass., 1958), pp. 188-90.

195. Sprat, *History of the Royal Society*, pp. 101-105. See also Glanvill, *Plus Ultra*, pp. 86-88.

196. However much admiration was expressed for any individual, there was a non-elitist thrust to the pre-Newtonian Royal Society. Its science tended to be co-operative, social and public rather than individualistic, contemplative or secretive. Mathematics and physical theory were beyond the comprehension of many members. The contribution of relatively unlearned men played an important role in that part of the Society's research program which was devoted to observing, recording natural data and the mechanical and manufacturing processes.

197. See M. B. Hall, "Science in the Early Royal Society," p. 65.

198. Sprat, *History of the Royal Society*, pp. 33-34.

199. Richard Baxter, a close observer of the Restoration intellectual scene, associated the modest stance of the Royal Society with its disclaimers to scientific certitude. *Reasons of the Christian Religion* (London, 1667), pp. 495-98. Baxter also associated this position with Cicero and the Academics, Sanchez, Glanvill, and Gassendi.

200. Glanvill, *Scepsis Scientifica*, p. 169; Glanvill, "The Usefulness of Real Philosophy to Religion," in *Essays*, p. 26.

201. Boyle, "Certain Physiological Essays," in *Works*, I, 306, 307. Criticism might be necessary but it must not be permitted to bring "disgrace or reproach" to the author; ibid., 312-13. See also Boyle, *Free Inquiry into the Vulgarly Received Notion of Nature* (London, 1686), Preface.

202. Charleton, *Immortality*, pp. 16, 19. See also *Physiologia*, p. 5.

203. Glanvill, "Usefulness," in *Essays*, p. 26. See also Sprat, *History of the Royal Society*, pp. 33-34, 56, 91, 92, 101, 104-105; Glanvill, *Plus Ultra*, pp. 86, 127-28, 147; Wilkins, *Discourse*, pp. 140, 145, 146, 153; Wilkins, *Natural Religion*, pp. 35-36.

204. See Zev Bechler, "Newton's Optical Controversies: A Study in the Grammar of Scientific Dissent," pp. 115-39. At times, however, both indicated that they wished to avoid conflict and Newton indicated "There is nothing wch I desire to avoyde in matters of philosophy more than contention." Quoted in Westfall, *Never at Rest*, pp. 273-74. Their long antipathy, however, may well have been responsible for Newton's reluctance to attend meetings of the Royal Society. Shortly after Hooke's death in 1703, Newton became president of the Society; ibid., p. 629.

205. Locke too noted that one "should not be too forwardly possessed with the opinion, or expectation of knowledge, where it is not to be had; or by ways that will not attain it: that we should not take doubtful systems for complete science, nor unintelligible notions for scientifical demonstrations." *Essay*, Bk. IV, Chapt. XII, Sec. 12.

206. Sprat, *History of the Royal Society*, p. 35. The same passage, however, is critical of Bacon's efforts at natural history. It seems unreasonable to insist, as some have recently done, either that Bacon provided the blueprint for the program and philosophy of the Society or that the philosophy of science which characterized its chief

members owed virtually nothing to Bacon. For the former see Margery Purver, *The Royal Society: Concept and Creation* (Cambridge, Mass., 1967); R. F. Jones, *Ancients and Moderns*; Charles Webster, *The Great Instauration: Science, Medicine and Reform 1626-1660* (London, 1975). For the latter see Van Leeuwen, *The Problem of Certainty*. For a more balanced view see M. B. Hall, "Science in the Early Royal Society," pp. 55-57; Michael Hunter, *Science and Society in Restoration England* (Cambridge, Eng., 1980), pp. 8-21; T. M. Brown, "The Rise of Baconianism in 17th-Century England: A Perspective on Science and Society during the Scientific Revolution," in *Science and History: Studies in Honor of Edward Rosen* (Wrocław, 1978), pp. 501-22.

207. Bacon, *Works*, VIII, 71. See also Aphorism 82, "I am building in the Human Understanding a true Model of the World, . . ." ibid., Aphorism 124.

208. Bacon's method was to be employed not only in natural philosophy but also in "the other sciences, logic, ethics, and politics"; ibid., Aphorism 126.

209. *Vindiciae Academiarum*, pp. 1-2, 39, 46; Charleton, *Immortality*, p. 8.

210. Quoted in John Hoyles, *The Waning of the Renaissance 1640-1740* (The Hague, 1971), p. 20.

211. *Vindiciae Academiarum*, pp. 3, 24, 25.

212. See Barbara Shapiro, *John Wilkins*, pp. 81-147; Brown, "Rise of Baconianism," pp. 501-22.

213. For a different approach see Arthur Quinn, *The Confidence of British Philosophers: An Essay in Historical Narrative* (Leiden, 1977).

214. Kuhn, "Mathematical versus Experimental Traditions in the Development of Physical Science," *The Essential Tension*, pp. 1-31.

215. For a different assessment of seventeenth-century opposition to natural science, see Michael Hunter, *Science and Society in Restoration England*, pp. 136-61; R. H. Syfret, "Some Early Reaction to the Royal Society," *Notes and Records of the Royal Society*, 7 (1950), pp. 207-58, and Syfret, "Some Early Critics of the Royal Society," ibid., 8 (1950), pp. 20-64.

216. Christian Huygens, "Memorandum for Colbert," *Nature and Nature's Laws: Documents of the Scientific Revolution*, ed. Marie Boas Hall (New York, 1970), pp. 226-227; Roger Hahn, *The Anatomy of a Scientific Institution: The Paris Academy of Sciences 1666-1803* (Berkeley, 1971), pp. 1-34. See also Popkin, *History of Scepticism*; J. S. Spink, *French Free Thought from Gassendi to Voltaire* (London, 1960); Robert Mandrou, *From Humanism to Science 1480-1700* (London, 1978); Paul Hazard, *The European Mind 1680-1715* (New York, 1963); Richard Watson, *The Downfall of Cartesianism 1673-1712* (The Hague, 1966); René Pintard, Les Problèmes de l'histoire du libertinage, notes et réflexions, *XVIIᵉ siècle*, 32 (1980), 131-62.

CHAPTER III: RELIGION

1. For a discussion of this controversy see Richard Westfall, *Science and Religion in 17th-Century England* (New Haven, 1964), pp. 221-28.

2. For the controversy concerning Puritanism and science, see *The Intellectual Revolution of the Seventeenth Century*, ed. T. Aston (London, 1974), articles by Christopher Hill, S. F. Mason, H. F. Kearney, T. K. Rabb, Barbara Shapiro, Lotte Mulligan, rpt. from *Past and Present*. See also R. K. Merton, *Science Technology and Science* (rpt. New York, 1970); D. Stimson, "Puritanism and the New Philosophy in 17th-Century England," *Bull. Inst. Hist. of Med.*, 3 (1935), 321-34; R. F. Jones, *Ancients and Moderns* (St. Louis, 1961); Christopher Hill, *Intellectual Origins of the English*

Revolution (Oxford, 1965); J. R. Jacob and M. C. Jacob, "Scientists and Society: The Saints Preserved," *J. of Eur. Studies*, 1 (1971), 87-92; Douglas Kemsley, "Religious Influences on the Rise of Modern Science," *Annals of Science*, 24 (1968), 199-226; Barbara Shapiro, "Debate, Science, Politics, and Religion," *Past and Present*, 66 (1975), 133-38; Lotte Mulligan, "Anglicanism, Latitudinarianism, and Science," *Annals of Science*, 30 (1973), 213-19; Charles Webster, *The Great Instauration* (London, 1975); T. K. Rabb, "Puritanism and the Rise of Experimental Science in England," *J. of World History*, 7 (1962); R. L. Greaves, "Puritanism and Science: The Anatomy of a Controversy," *J. Hist. Ideas*, 30 (1969), 346-60; J. R. Jacob and M. C. Jacob, "The Anglican Origins of Modern Science: The Metaphysical Foundations of the Whig Constitution," *Isis*, 71 (1980), 251-67; John Morgan, "Puritanism and Science: A Reinterpretation," *Historical Journal*, 22 (1979), 535-60.

For the problem of religion and science more generally, see Basil Willey, *The Seventeenth-Century Background* (London, 1934); E. A. Burtt, *The Metaphysical Foundations of Modern Science* (New York, 1924); P. H. Kocher, *Science and Religion in Elizabethan England* (San Marino, 1953); Westfall, *Science and Religion*; C. E. Raven, *Natural Religion and Christian Theology* (Cambridge, 1953); G. R. Cragg, *From Puritanism to the Age of Reason* (Cambridge, 1950); Barbara Shapiro, *John Wilkins, 1614-1672: An Intellectual Biography* (Berkeley, 1969); M. C. Jacob, *The Newtonians and the English Revolution* (Ithaca, 1976).

3. Erasmus-Luther, *Discourse on Free Will*, trans. and ed. E. G. Winter (New York, 1961), pp. 6, 7, 9-10.

4. R. H. Bainton, *Sebastian Castellio and the Toleration Controversy* (New York, 1931), p. 13. See also Richard Popkin, *The History of Scepticism from Erasmus to Descartes* (Assen, 1960).

5. Erasmus-Luther, *Discourse*, p. 103; see also pp. 101, 108. He also attacked Erasmus for employing the "Arguments of Lady Reason" in scriptural matters (p. 15).

6. Quoted in Bainton, *Castellio*, p. 33.

7. Erasmus could accept neither infallible Pope nor infallible Scripture. The inspired might be infallible, but there was no adequate means of determining who was truly inspired (*Discourse*, p. 36).

8. The Jesuits argued that since one could not arrive at infallibly true articles of faith from Scripture, or could not use rational procedure and evidence to justify statements of religious truth, it was necessary to accept the tradition of the Church and its dogma as faith (Popkin, *Scepticism*, pp. 70, 73, 79-80). See also G. H. Tavard, *Holy Writ and Holy Church* (London, 1959).

9. See Bainton, *Castellio*; H. F. Hirsch, "Castellio's *De Arte Dubitandi* and the Problem of Religious Liberty," in Bruno Becher, ed., *Autour de Michel Servet et Sebastien Castellion* (Haarlam, 1953); J. Lindebloom, "La Place de Castellion dans l'histoire de l'esprit," in Becher, *Servet et Castellion*.

10. William Haller, *The Rise of Puritanism* (New York, 1957), pp. 195-99; M. J. Tooley, "Political Thought and the Theory and Practice of Toleration," *New Cambridge Modern History* (Cambridge, 1968), III, 485.

11. *De Veritate* was translated into English by Simon Patrick in 1680. See also Donald Kelley, *Foundations of Modern Historical Scholarship* (New York, 1970), pp. 151-52; H. R. Trevor-Roper, "Clarendon," *Times Literary Supp.* (Jan. 10, 1975), pp. 31-33.

12. Quoted in John Booty, *John Jewel as Apologist of the Church of England* (Ithaca, 1963), p. 137; W. M. Southgate, *John Jewel and the Problem of Doctrinal Authority*

(Cambridge, Mass., 1962); Arthur B. Ferguson, *Clio Unbound: Perception of the Social and Cultural Past in Renaissance England* (Durham, N.C., 1979), pp. 129-224.

13. Quoted in Southgate, *Jewel*, pp. 145-46.

14. Southgate, *Jewel*, pp. 119-20, 182-83; Booty, *Jewel*, p. 82.

15. "The Laws of Ecclesiastical Polity," in *The Works of Richard Hooker*, ed. J. Keble, 3 vols. (New York, 1888); Peter Munz, *The Place of Hooker in the History of Thought* (London, 1952).

16. *The Works of Francis Bacon*, eds. J. Spedding, R. Ellis, D. Heath (London, 1875), V, 111-17. See also "Certain Considerations Touching the Better Pacification and Edification of the Church of England," in *Works*; "An Advertisement Touching the Controversies of the Church of England," in *Works*, VIII, 86-87; W. K. Jordan, *The Development of Religious Toleration in England* (London, 1932-40), IV, 463-64, 466, 469.

17. See B. H. G. Wormald, *Clarendon: Politics, Historiography, and Religion* (Cambridge, 1964); K. Weber, *Lucius Cary, Viscount Falkland* (New York, 1940); W. K. Jordan, *Toleration*, II, *passim*; Gerald Cragg, *Freedom and Authority: A Study of English Thought in the Early 17th Century* (Philadelphia, 1975), pp. 245-77.

18. Quoted in Cragg, *Freedom and Authority*. See also Wormald, *Clarendon*, pp. 250-55. Hales suggested schisms were derived from "matter of fact," "matter of opinion," or ambition (John Hales, *A Tract Concerning Schisme and Schismaticks* [London, 1642], p. 2).

19. *Discourse of the Infallibility of the Church of Rome* (London, 1651), pp. 242, 243, 245.

20. *The Religion of Protestants* (Oxford, 1638), pp. 31-32, 33-34. See Robert R. Orr, *Reason and Authority: The Thought of William Chillingworth* (Oxford, 1967); Henry Van Leeuwen, *The Problem of Certainty in English Thought, 1630-1690* (The Hague, 1963), pp. 15-32.

21. Chillingworth, *The Religion of Protestants*, p. 38.

22. Ibid., pp. 34, 36. See also Orr, *Chillingworth*, pp. 81-83, 94.

23. Henry More, "An Antidote against Atheisme" (1653) in G. G. Patrides, *The Cambridge Platonists* (Cambridge, Mass., 1969), pp. 216-17; Walter Charleton, *The Immortality of the Human Soul* (London, 1657), Preface, pp. 163, 186; John Wilkins, *Of the Principles and Duties of Natural Religion* (London, 1675); Sir Charles Wolseley, *The Unreasonableness of Atheism* (London, 1669); Thomas Tenison, *The Creed of Mr. Hobbes Examined* (London, 1707); Richard Bentley, *A Confutation of Atheism* (London, 1697). See Westfall, *Science and Religion*, pp. 106-45; John Redwood, *Reason, Ridicule, and Religion* (Cambridge, Mass., 1976), pp. 29-69.

24. Quoted in John Hoyle, *The Waning of the Renaissance 1640-1740: Studies in the Thought of Henry More, John Norris, and Isaac Watts* (The Hague, 1971), p. 71.

25. Seth Ward, *A Philosophical Essay Toward an Eviction of the Being and Attributes of God* (Oxford, 1652), Preface to the Reader.

26. Wilkins, *Natural Religion*, pp. 91-92; John Tillotson, *The Wisdom of Being Religious* (London, 1664), p. 20; John Ray, *The Wisdom of God Manifested in the Works of Creation* (London, 1691).

27. Charleton, *Immortality of the Soul*, pp. 61-63; see also p. 186.

28. Wilkins, *Natural Religion*, pp. 3-4; see also p. 82. See also Wilkins, *Essay Towards a Real Character and a Philosophical Language* (London, 1668), pp. 195-96.

29. Wilkins, *Natural Religion*, pp. 5-11.

30. Tillotson, *Wisdom*, pp. 20, 30-32.

31. Wilkins, *Natural Religion*, pp. 7-8.

32. Ibid., pp. 9-10.
33. Tillotson, *Wisdom*, pp. 30-34.
34. See John Locke, *An Essay Concerning Human Understanding* (1690).
35. Wilkins, *Natural Religion*; Ward, *Philosophical Essay*; Walter Charleton, *The Darkness of Atheism Dispelled by the Light of Nature* (London, 1652); Joseph Glanvill, *Philosophia Pia* (London, 1671); William Bates, *Considerations of the Existence of God and the Human Soul* (London, 1676); Samuel Clarke, *Demonstration of the Being and Attributes of God* (London, 1707); William Derham, *Physico-Theology: Or a Demonstration of the Being and Attributes of God* (London, 1714).
36. Wilkins, *Natural Religion*, p. 134.
37. Ibid., pp. 82, 83, 134-39.
38. John Smith, "Discourse Demonstrating the Immortality of the Soul," in *Selected Discourses* (London, 1660); Charleton, *Immortality of the Human Soul*; Henry More, *An Antidote against Atheism* (London, 1655); Henry More, *The Immortality of the Human Soul* (London, 1659); Wilkins, *Natural Religion*; Seth Ward, *A Philosophical Essay*.
39. For a discussion of hedonistic and utilitarian ethics, see Ernest Albee, *A History of English Utilitarianism* (New York, 1962), pp. 14, 19-62. See also Westfall, *Science and Religion*; Richard Schlatter, *The Social Ideas of Religious Leaders, 1660-1688* (New York, 1940); J. McAdoo, *The Structure of Caroline Moral Theology* (London, 1949).
40. Wilkins, *Natural Religion*, pp. 96, 157, 159-60, 190-91, 229, 285, 295. See also Tillotson, *Wisdom of Being Religious*; John Ray, *Persuasive to a Holy Life* (London, 1700), and *Wisdom of God*.
41. Wilkins, *Natural Religion*, pp. 50-51. The 1693 ed. of his *Ecclesiastes* contained a new section on persuasion. It suggested that in proving something from Reason (as opposed to Revelation) that one might persuade by "Equity" and/or "Necessity." The latter was divided into "Duty" and "Interest," that is, the "advantage accruing to our selves by it" (p. 28). This popular handbook for preachers inculcated the calculation of advantage. Wilkins believed that interest and duty would coincide. See also *Natural Religion*, pp. 176ff., 231-38.
42. See John Evelyn, *The History of Religion*, 2 vols. (London, 1850); Edward Stillingfleet, *Origines Sacrae* (London, 1666).
43. Charleton, *Immortality*, p. 82.
44. John Yolton, *John Locke and the Way of Ideas* (Oxford, 1956), pp. 27-48.
45. More, "Antidote against Atheism" (1653), in Patrides, *Cambridge Platonists*, pp. 222-26.
46. See John Tillotson, ed., *The Works of Isaac Barrow* (1683-87), III, 104; Sir Matthew Hale, *The Primitive Origination of Mankind* (London, 1677), pp. 22-24; Benjamin Whichcote, *Select Sermons* (London, 1698), pp. 9, 17-20; Charleton, *Immortality*, pp. 92-93, 118, 129-30, 135, 234-35; Samuel Parker, *A Free and Impartial Censure of the Platonicke Philosophie* (London, 1666), pp. 55-57; Boyle, *A Discourse of Things above Reason* (London, 1681), pp. 34-35, 84-85.
47. Wilkins, *Natural Religion*, p. 44.
48. Ibid., pp. 56, 57; see also pp. 47-51.
49. Ibid., pp. 59, 61.
50. Ibid., p. 71.
51. Ray, *Wisdom of God*, Preface to the Reader. See also Nehemiah Grew, *Cosmologia Sacra* (London, 1701).
52. Ward, *Philosophical Essay*, p. 20.
53. Barrow, *Works*, III, 104.

54. See John Locke, *Reasonableness of Christianity* (London, 1696).

55. Charleton, *Darkness of Atheism*, p. 111; Ray, *Wisdom of God*, p. 47.

56. Robert Hooke, *Micrographia* (London, 1665); Nehemiah Grew, *The Anatomy of Plants* (London, 1682); Wilkins, *Natural Religion*, p. 80; Marjorie Nicholson, *Mountain Gloom and Mountain Glory: The Development of the Aesthetics of the Infinite* (Ithaca, 1959). See also Westfall, *Science and Religion*, pp. 49-69.

57. John Wilkins, "A Discourse Concerning a New Planet," in *Mathematical and Philosophical Works* (London, 1708), p. 248.

58. Wilkins, *Discovery*, in *Mathematical and Philosophical Works*, pp. 98-99. See also his *Sermons Preached upon Several Occasions*, p. 72.

59. For a discussion of Providence and natural law, see Westfall, *Science and Religion*, pp. 70-105.

60. Wilkins, *Natural Religion*, pp. 65-66; Hale, *Primitive Origination of Mankind*, passim.

61. Wilkins, *Natural Religion*, p. 64. Tillotson called the Roman Catholic position on the infallibility of tradition an hypothesis; *The Rule of Faith* (London, 1666), pp. 18-19.

62. Robert Boyle, *Some Considerations Touching the Usefulness* (Oxford, 1664), pp. 46-47.

63. John Locke, "The Reasonableness of Christianity," in *Locke on Politics, Religion and Education*, ed. Maurice Cranston (New York, 1965), p. 217.

64. Edward Fowler, *The Principles and Practices of Certain Moderate Divines* (London, 1670), p. 119; see also pp. 66, 75.

65. Quoted in Westfall, *Science and Religion*, p. 45. The emphasis placed on the two books varied. The dissenter Richard Baxter felt nature was a "Hard Book" which few could understand. It was therefore safer to rely more heavily on Scripture; *The Reasons of the Christian Religion* (London, 1667), p. 193.

66. *The Truth of the Christian Religion* (London, 1680), p. 21; see also pp. 55-56.

67. Evelyn, *History of Religion*, p. 393.

68. Ibid., p. 392. See also Joseph Glanvill, *Seasonable Defense of Reason in the Affairs of Religion* (London, 1670), pp. 9-10.

69. Stillingfleet, *Origines Sacrae*, pp. 110-12.

70. Ibid., pp. 229, 230, 231, 232.

71. Ibid., pp. 232, 233-34.

72. Ibid., pp. 235, 237.

73. Ibid., pp. 237-40. See R. T. Carroll, *The Common Sense Philosophy of Bishop Edward Stillingfleet, 1635-1699* (The Hague, 1975); Richard Popkin, "The Philosophy of Bishop Stillingfleet," *J. of Hist. of Phil.*, 9 (1971), pp. 303-19.

74. Wolseley, *The Unreasonableness of Atheism Made Manifest* (3rd ed. London, 1675), pp. 124-26. See also his *The Reasonableness of Scripture Belief* (London, 1672); William Bates, *The Divinity of the Christian Religion Proved by the Evidence of Reason and Divine Revelation* (London, 1677), pp. 104-10. The dissenter Bates stressed man's corruption more than most natural theologians. See also Richard Baxter, *Reasons of the Christian Religion*, pp. 259ff.; Gilbert Burnet, *Four Discourses* (London, 1694).

75. Hale, *Primitive Origination*, pp. 57, 129. For a similar approach, see Samuel Parker, *A Demonstration of the Law of Nature and of the Christian Religion* (London, 1681), dedicated to Ralph Bathurst. The proof of Scripture was based on the evidence of matter of fact, from evidence so good "that if we our selves had been Eye-Witnesses of it, we could scarce have had a greater assurance of its truth and reality" (Preface, xxvii, xxix). Scriptural precepts were easily proved "beyond all doubt" by

"certain Revelation and experimental Proof." The evidence of matter of fact and faith, though historical in nature, were as "strong and convictive" as Mathematical Demonstration (p. 176). See also p. 179. Parker and Bathurst were both members of the Royal Society.

76. Barrow, *Works*, II, 30-40.

77. Ibid., II, 19, 20, 23, 28.

78. Ibid., I, 452.

79. Ibid. Barrow noted that the term "belief" had two accepted definitions, one popular, the other "more restrained and artificial." The first, which he associated with the Aristotelian Topics, consisted of any strong opinion, without regard for the means of producing it. The second, that of scholars, distinguished persuasion or belief from assent derived from sense or rational inference, and limited it to assent based on "authority," that is, the "dictate or testimony of some person asserting, relating, or attesting to the truth of any matter propounded" (I, 449). Barrow described this position, stressing the means of making an authority credible. He preferred the popular or vulgar usage since it permitted all kinds of reason and evidence, not just credible testimony (I, 450).

80. Ibid., I, 450, 451.

81. Robert Boyle, *The Christian Virtuoso* (London, 1690), p. 56.

82. Ibid., pp. 57-58.

83. Ibid., p. 59.

84. Ibid., p. 71.

85. Robert Boyle, *Some Considerations about the Reconcileableness of Reason and Religion* (London, 1675), pp. 91-95.

86. Boyle, *The Christian Virtuoso*, p. 72.

87. Ibid., pp. 73-74.

88. Ibid., p. 81.

89. Ibid. See also *Some Considerations about the Reconcileableness of Reason and Religion*, p. 93.

90. Locke, "Reasonableness of Christianity," pp. 272, 278, 279.

91. Ibid., pp. 266-67.

92. Locke, *Essay Concerning Human Understanding*, IV, 18.

93. See Westfall, *Science and Religion*, pp. 182-92; J. T. Moore, "Locke's Analysis of Language and Assent to Scripture," *J. Hist. Ideas*, 37 (1976), 707-14; Richard Ashcraft, "Faith and Knowledge in Locke's Philosophy," in John Yolton, ed., *John Locke: Problems and Perspectives* (London, 1969).

By the end of the century, John Toland, employing the epistemology outlined in Locke's *Essay*, argued that Christianity was an entirely "Rational and Intelligible Religion," that there was nothing "mysterious or Above Reason in the Gospel," and that he would hold "nothing as an Article of my Religion, but what the highest Evidence forc'd me to embrace"; *Christianity Not Mysterious* (London, 1696), Preface. See pages 1-17 for his treatment of self-evidence, demonstration, certitude, proof of matter of fact, the grounds of persuasion, the nature of ideas, and the use of evidence. Yolton suggests that Toland's stress on clarity and distinctness as the criteria for certainty went beyond Locke. See John Yolton, *John Locke and the Way of Ideas*, p. 125; see also pp. 118-26. John Biddle and Margaret Jacob have recently suggested that Locke's *Reasonableness of Christianity* was an answer to Toland's *Christianity Not Mysterious*, rather than vice versa. See John Biddle, "Locke's Critique of Innate Principles and Toland's Deism," *J. Hist. Ideas*, 37 (1976), 411-22; Jacob, *The Newtonians and the English Revolution, 1689-1730* (Ithaca, 1976), pp. 214-16.

For Toland, Scripture could be accepted *only* to the extent that it conformed to accepted models of rational proof (*Christianity Not Mysterious*, p. 37). Many latitudinarians, including Locke, were outraged with Toland's deism. By the end of the century, John Wallis, Edward Stillingfleet, and others campaigned to show the rationality of belief in the mysterious and incomprehensible doctrines of Christianity and to show that reason might be employed to support belief in things above reason.

94. Edward Stillingfleet, *A Rational Account of the Grounds of the Protestant Religion* (London, 1665), pp. 204, 206-207.

95. Edward Stillingfleet, *A Discourse on the Nature and Grounds of the Certitude of Faith* (London, 1688), pp. 16-17, 36, 50.

96. For Locke's 1661 consideration of the question of infallibility and its relation both to Roman Catholic polemics, and the *Essay on Human Understanding*, see John Biddle, "John Locke's Essay on Infallibility: Introduction, Text and Translation," *J. of Church and State*, 19 (1977), 301-28.

97. See Shapiro, *Wilkins*, pp. 154, 156, 163-64, 175, 293, 296, 297; L. G. Locke, *John Tillotson: A Study in 17th-Century Literature* (Copenhagen, 1954). The pulpit at St. Lawrence Jewry, which Wilkins and Tillotson shared, was well known for its latitudinarianism. Anon., "Cabbala, or an Impartial Account of the Nonconformists' Private Designs," in *Somers Tracts* (London, 1812), VII, 580. Wilkins, Tillotson, Stillingfleet, Outram, and Patrick often discussed scientific and theological issues.

98. Tillotson, *The Rule of Faith* (London, 1666). I have cited from the 3rd ed. (1688), p. 98. The work was appropriately dedicated to Stillingfleet.

99. Ibid., pp. 20, 45, 47, 57, 84, 87, 102, 114-17. See also Sir Charles Wolseley, *The Reasonableness of Scripture* (London, 1672), pp. 422, 426; Evelyn, *The True Religion*; Thomas Tenison, *Of the Incurable Skepticism of the Church of Rome* (London, 1688); Gilbert Burnet, *The Infallibility of the Church of Rome Examined and Confuted* (London, 1680). Roman Catholic Sir Kenelm Digby criticized Puritan and Anglican approaches to Scripture. He noted the Anglican tendency both to emphasize human fallibility and venerate the authority of the early Church fathers; *A Discourse Concerning Infallibility in Religion* (Paris, 1652).

100. Walter Pope, *The Life of Seth Ward, Bishop of Salisbury*, ed. J. B. Banborough (Oxford, 1691), p. 46. The members of the Great Tew circle were in many respects the forerunners of this tradition.

101. Thomas Wood, *English Casuistical Divinity in the Seventeenth Century* (London, 1952).

102. Ibid., pp. 68-74, 78-79. See also McAdoo, *Structure of Caroline Moral Theology; The Whole Duty of Man*, pp. 3-8. Their concern for natural theology led most latitudinarians to consider God more in terms of goodness, mercy, and love than those who remained in the Calvinist mold. They found the doctrine of absolute reprobation distasteful and preferred to believe that it was in man's power to cooperate with God's Grace. See S. P., *A Brief Account of the New Sect of Latitude Men* (London, 1662), p. 9; Fowler, *Principles and Practices*, pp. 176, 193, 333. Glanvill suggests their unhappiness with the doctrine of an arbitrarily awarded free grace was linked to their moralism. Joseph Glanvill, *Essays on Several Important Subjects in Philosophy and Religion* (London, 1676), Essay VII, pp. 21, 37ff.; Wilkins, *Natural Religion*, pp. 82-83, 138-39, 203-204. For Locke's rejection of Calvinism, see "Reasonableness of Christianity," pp. 207, 208-12.

103. See John Tulloch, *Rational Theology and Christian Philosophy in the 17th Century*, 2 vols. (London, 1874); E. A. George, *Seventeenth-Century Men of Latitude* (London, 1909); Willey, *Seventeenth-Century Background*; N. Sykes, *From Sheldon to Secker: Aspects*

of Church History, 1660-1768 (Cambridge, 1959); G. R. Cragg, *From Puritanism to the Age of Reason*; Hoyle, *The Waning of the Renaissance*.

104. See Thomas Hanzo, *Latitude and Restoration Criticism* (Copenhagen, 1961), pp. 24, 26, 30-31.

105. S. P., *New Sect of Latitude Men*, p. 24. See also Parker, *Censure of the Platonicke Philosophy*.

106. Joseph Glanvill, *Catholic Charity Recommended* (London, 1669), p. 18; [Charles Blount], *Religio Laici* (London, 1683), p. 78; Edward Fowler, *Principles and Practices*, p. 18. Sir William Petty also identified religion with good works, neighborly love, and charity (*Discourses* [London, 1674], pp. 4-5). See also Anon., *The Conformists' Sayings* (London, 1690); Glanvill, "Anti-Fanatical Religion and Free Philosophy," in *Essays*, pp. 24-25, and *The Way of Happiness* (London, 1670); George Berkeley, *Historical Applications and Occasional Meditations* (London, 1667); Fowler, *Principles and Practices*, p. 18; Locke, *Reasonableness of Christianity*, pp. 226-28.

107. Wilkins, *Sermons Preached upon Several Occasions*, p. 47; see also p. 15. See also Locke, "Reasonableness of Christianity," p. 228.

108. Glanvill, *Catholic Charity*, p. 31; see also pp. 18, 19; Simon Patrick, *A Parable of a Pilgrim* (London, 1670), pp. 180-81; Barrow, *Works*, I, 395.

109. See Patrick, *Parable of a Pilgrim*, p. 422; Anon., *The Way of Peace* (London, 1682), p. 3; Wilkins, *Sermons Preached upon Several Occasions*, pp. 400, 407-408; Charleton, *The Darkness of Atheism*, Preface; Boyle, *Some Considerations on the Reconcileableness of Reason and Religion*, pp. 28, 29, 44.

110. Fowler, *Principles and Practices*, p. xl.

111. Grotius, *The Truth of the Christian Religion*, p. 81; Edward Stillingfleet, *Irenicum* (London, 1662), pp. 2-3; Glanvill, *Catholic Charity*, pp. 21-22; Charles Blount, "A Just Vindication," in *Miscellaneous Works*, p. 2; Anon., *The Way to Peace*; Anon., *The Conformists' Sayings*, p. 43, quoting Barrow.

112. Wilkins, *Sermons Preached upon Several Occasions*, pp. 400, 407, 408. See also *Bishop Wilkins' Character of the Best Christian* (Dublin, 1759), p. 5.

113. Glanvill, *Catholic Charity*, p. 19. See also Gilbert Burnet, *Four Discourses*, p. 59; Anon., *The Way of Peace*, p. 41; Locke, "Reasonableness of Christianity," p. 230.

114. Glanvill, *Catholic Charity*, pp. 18, 31. Glanvill, *Essays*, Essay II, p. 31. See also his *The Vanity of Dogmatizing* (London, 1661); *Philosophia Pia* (London, 1671); Jackson Cope, *Joseph Glanvill: Anglican Apologist* (St. Louis, 1956).

115. Glanvill, *Catholic Charity*, p. 33; Fowler, *Principles and Practices*, p. 308.

116. John Smtih, "The True Way," in *Select Discourses*, pp. 11-12. See also Patrick, *Parable of a Pilgrim*, p. 442; Blount, *Religio Laici*, p. 89. Fowler associates "moral certainty" and "Opinion" with the latitudinarians (*Principles and Practices*, pp. 61-64).

117. See Fowler, *Principles and Practices*, p. 339; *The Gentleman's Companion* (London, 1672), pp. 42-43.

118. Sykes, *Sheldon to Secker*, p. 142; Fowler, *Principles and Practices*, pp. 299, 302.

119. Herbert Croft, *The Naked Truth* (London, 1675). I have cited the 1680 ed., p. 6.

120. Fowler, *Principles and Practices*, pp. 296, 347; Stillingfleet, *Irenicum*, Preface; Charleton, *Darkness of Atheism*, Dedicatory Preface, pp. 16, 66; Glanvill, "Anti-Fanatical Religion and Free Philosophy," *Essays*, pp. 12-13, and *Plus Ultra, Or the Progress and Advancement of Knowledge* (London, 1668), p. 159; Gilbert Burnet, *Four Discourses*, pp. 58-59; Evelyn, *The True Religion*, pp. 442-43.

121. Wilkins, *Sermons upon Several Occasions*, pp. 77, 88, 89; *Natural Religion*, p.

205; Sheridan, *Rise*, p. 83; Croft, *The Naked Truth*, p. 5; Patrick, *Parable of a Pilgrim*, p. 415.

122. *The Conformists' Sayings*, p. 11, quoting Wilkins. See also Stillingfleet, *Irenicum*, Preface, p. 27; S. P., *New Sect of Latitude Men*, p. 13.

123. For the evolution of Locke's views, see Biddle, *J. of Church and State*, 19 (1977), 301-28.

124. Fowler, *Principles and Practices*, pp. 8, 10, 33; see also pp. 17, 21, 36, 325-31, 334-35; Blount, *Religio Laici*, p. 16; Glanvill, *The Zealous and Impartial Protestant* (London, 1678), pp. 11, 26. *The Conformists' Sayings* clearly indicates the Anglican pedigree. See also McAdoo, *Structure of Caroline Moral Theology*.

125. Wilkins was said to have established a "club for comprehensions"; Anthony Wood, *Athenae Oxoniensis*, ed. Phillip Bliss, XIV (London, 1813-20), 512-13. The first major effort to modify the Act of Uniformity occurred in 1667-68. Wilkins and Sir Matthew Hale were active. Latitudinarian efforts were denounced by Archbishop Sheldon as the work of "treacherous Divines"; Samuel Parker, *History of His Own Time* (London, 1728), p. 36; see also pp. 37-49. Berkeley, *Historical Applications*, pp. 7, 61, 92-93. Another effort, spearheaded by Tillotson and Stillingfleet, was mounted in 1675, and still another in 1680. About 1680, Stillingfleet changed his mind about the desirability of comprehension. Glanvill, a continuing spokesman for comprehension, addressed Parliament in 1678. See Glanvill, *The Zealous and Impartial Protestant*. Robert Moray and Gilbert Burnet worked on a comprehension scheme for Scotland in 1668. In 1689, Tillotson, Lloyd, Patrick, and Tenison again attempted, and again failed, to broaden the church. Isaac Newton was the author of "Irenicum, or Ecclesiastical Polity Tending to Peace"; Frank E. Manuel, *Isaac Newton, Historian* (Cambridge, Mass., 1963), p. 14. For comprehension efforts, see A. H. Wood, *Church Unity Without Uniformity* (London, 1963); Sykes, *From Sheldon to Secker*, pp. 68-104; Shapiro, *Wilkins*, pp. 170-84; Roger Thomas, "Comprehension and Indulgence," in *From Uniformity to Unity*, eds. G. F. Nutall and O. Chadwick (London, 1962); Walter Simon, "Comprehension in the Age of Charles II," *Church History*, 30 (1972).

126. Pope, *Life of Seth Ward*, p. 29; Shapiro, *Wilkins*; Shapiro, "Latitudinarianism and Science in 17th-Century England," *Past and Present*, 40 (1968), 164.

127. For Petty see *The Petty-Southwell Correspondence, 1676-1687*, ed. Marquis of Lansdowne (London, 1928), pp. 9-10; Emil Strauss, *Sir William Petty* (London, 1954), p. 21. For Bathurst see Thomas Warton, *Life and Literary Remains of Ralph Bathurst* (London, 1761), pp. 180-81; Anthony Wood, *The Life and Times of Anthony Wood*, ed. A. Clark (Oxford, 1891-1900), I, 365. For Goddard see M. B. Rex, *University Representation in England, 1604-1698* (London, 1954), pp. 186-87. For Boyle see J. C. Crowther, *Founders of British Science* (London, 1960), p. 79. J. P. Wood, ed., *Funeral Sermons by Eminent English Divines, 1650-1760* (London, 1831), pp. 290, 291-92. See Mitchell S. Fisher, *Robert Boyle, Devout Naturalist* (Philadelphia, 1945); J. R. Jacob, *Robert Boyle and the English Revolution* (New York, 1977). John Dury's *The Plain Way to Peace and Unity in Matters of Religion* was written at Boyle's urging. Boyle requested that Sir Peter Pett write a similar tract in 1660; C. E. Whiting, *Studies in English Puritanism from Restoration to the Revolution, 1660-1688* (London, 1932), p. 482.

128. Gilbert Burnet, *History of My Own Times*, ed. O. Airy (Oxford, 1897-1900), I, 332-33. S. P. associates Cambridge latitudinarianism with the New Philosophy (*Brief Account*, p. 3.)

129. Seth Ward, though a natural theologian, became a persecuting bishop. John

Wallis was a Presbyterian who ended his life as a latitudinarian. For a more complete discussion, see Shapiro, *Past and Present*, 40 (1968).

130. Lloyd and Stillingfleet assisted in Wilkins's *Essay Towards a Real Character.* See A. Tindal Hart, *William Lloyd, 1627-1717* (London, 1952). Tillotson, Wilkins's protégé and son-in-law, was a member of the Royal Society. His sermons exhibit familiarity with and approval of the new science. Stillingfleet greatly admired Boyle. See Boyle, *Works* (1772), VI, 462. He made use of Boyle's natural philosophy in his 1662 *Origines Sacrae*, and of Newtonian science in his 1697 revision. See M. Jacob, *The Newtonians*, p. 31. Sir Matthew Hale and the duke of Buckingham were also latitudinarians with scientific interests.

131. S. P., *Brief Account*, p. 500; see also p. 508. Robert South, who was unsympathetic to the latitudinarians, also made the connection. See Henry Oldenburg, *Correspondence*, eds. A. R. Hall and M. B. Hall (Madison, 1968), VI, 129.

132. Sprat, *History of the Royal Society*, pp. 34-35.

133. Ibid. See also pp. 92, 101, 104-105.

134. Wilkins, *Natural Religion*, pp. 35-36; *Discovery*, Preface to the Reader; Glanvill, *Plus Ultra*, pp. 127-28, 147; Boyle, *The Christian Virtuoso*, p. 103; see also pp. 7, 13, 50, 52-53. Berkeley, *Historical Applications*, pp. 123-24.

135. Glanvill, *Plus Ultra*, p. 149.

136. Glanvill, *Essays*, Essay IV, p. 27.

137. Sprat, *History of the Royal Society*, pp. 53-54, 427. Sprat had been a student at Wadham during Wilkins's mastership.

138. Ibid., p. 53.

139. Ibid., pp. 55-56.

140. Wilkins, *Sermons Preached upon Several Occasions*, p. 414.

141. Wilkins, *Discourse*, pp. 145, 153, 122. See also Boyle, *Christian Virtuoso*, and *Some Considerations*, p. 44.

142. Quoted in H. G. Lyons, *The Royal Society* (Cambridge, 1944), pp. 42-44.

143. Wilkins, *Discourse*, p. 146.

144. Ibid., p. 140.

145. Glanvill, *Plus Ultra*, p. 147.

146. Sprat, *History of the Royal Society*, pp. 91, 34, 56. See also C. R. Weld, *A History of the Royal Society* (London, 1848), I, 218.

CHAPTER IV: HISTORY

1. George Huppert, *The Idea of Perfect History: Historical Erudition and Historical Philosophy in Renaissance France* (Urbana, 1970); Donald Kelley, *Foundations of Modern Historical Scholarship: Language, Law, and History in the French Renaissance* (New York, 1970); Nancy S. Streuver, *The Language of History in the Renaissance: Rhetorical Consciousness in Florentine Humanism* (Princeton, 1970); Myron Gilmore, "The Renaissance Condition of the Lessons of History," and "Fides et Eruditio: Erasmus and the Study of History," in *Humanists and Jurists: Six Studies in the Renaissance* (Cambridge, Mass., 1966); William Bouwsma, "Three Types of Historiography in Post-Renaissance Italy," *History and Theory*, 4 (1965), 303-14; F. J. Levy, *Tudor Historical Thought* (San Marino, 1967); Felix Gilbert, *Machiavelli and Guicciardini: Politics and History in Sixteenth-Century Florence* (Princeton, 1965); George Nadel, "Philosophy of History Before Historicism," *History and Theory*, 2 (1964), 291-315; Donald Wilcox, *The Development of Florentine Humanist Historiography in the Fifteenth*

Century (Cambridge, Mass., 1967); Eric Cochrane, *Historians and Historiography in the Italian Renaissance* (Chicago, 1981).

2. Frank Fussner, however, has suggested a link between scientific and historical thought. See *The Historical Revolution: English Historical Writing and Thought, 1580-1640* (London, 1962). See also Julian H. Franklin, *Jean Bodin and the Sixteenth-Century Revolution in the Methodology of Law and History* (New York, 1963); G. Wylie Sypher, "Similarities Between the Scientific and the Historical Revolutions at the End of the Renaissance," *J. Hist. Ideas*, 26 (1965), 353-68; Eric Cochrane, "Science and Humanism in the Italian Renaissance," *Amer. Hist. Rev.*, 81 (1976), 1039-57; Joan Gadol, "The Unity of the Renaissance: Humanism, Natural Science, and Art," in *From the Renaissance to the Counter-Reformation: Essays in Honor of Garrett Mattingly*, ed. Charles H. Carter (New York, 1965), pp. 29-55; Karen Reeds, "Renaissance Humanism and Botany," *Annals of Science*, 33 (1976), 519-43; Eugenio Garin, *Science and Civic Life in the Renaissance*, trans. P. Munz (New York, 1969); Paul L. Rose, *The Italian Renaissance of Mathematics: Studies on Humanists and Mathematics from Petrarch to Galileo* (Geneva, 1975); Barbara Shapiro, "History and Natural History in Sixteenth- and Seventeenth-Century England: An Essay on the Relationship Between Humanism and Science," in *English Scientific Virtuosi in the 16th and 17th Centuries* (Los Angeles, 1979).

3. Bruni's *History of Florence* provides an excellent example. See Denys Hay, *Annalists and Historians: Western Historiography from the VIIIth to the XVIIIth Centuries* (London, 1977), pp. 96-98.

4. Gilbert, *Machiavelli and Guicciardini*; William Bouwsma, *Venice and the Defense of Republican Liberty: Renaissance Values in the Age of the Counter-Reformation* (Berkeley, 1968).

5. Cochrane, "Science and Humanism," *Amer. Hist. Rev.*, 1039-79. Sarpi corresponded with Galileo on scientific matters. See also Fulgenzio Micanzio's prefatory "Life" of Sarpi, in Paolo Sarpi, *The History of the Council of Trent*, trans. Nathaniel Brent (London, 1676), pp. xxv, xxix, xl, li; see John Lievsay, *Venetian Phoenix: Paolo Sarpi and Some of His English Friends (1606-1700)* (Lawrence, Kan., 1973), pp. 89, 92-94, 138, 157, 167; William J. Bouwsma, *Venice and the Defense of Republican Liberty*.

6. See Beatrice R. Reynolds, "Latin Historiography: A Survey, 1400-1600," *Studies in the Renaissance*, 2 (1955), 16, 17.

7. Arnaldo Momigliano, *Studies in Historiography* (New York, 1966), p. 6; Reynolds, "Latin Historiography," pp. 10-11, 12. See also Eduard Fueter, *Histoire de l'historiographie moderne*, trans. Emile Jeanmaire (Paris, 1914); Denys Hay, "Flavio Biondo and the Middle Ages," *Proceedings of the British Academy*, 45 (1959), 97-128.

Momigliano has noted that the terms "historian" and "antiquarian" were used interchangeably, although antiquarian works were often omitted from sixteenth- and seventeenth-century discussions of the *artes historicae* (*Studies in Historiography*, pp. 6-7; see also pp. 217-19).

8. See Beatrice R. Reynolds, "Shifting Currents in Historical Criticism," *J. Hist. Ideas*, 14 (1953), 471-92.

9. Ibid., pp. 485-86. Patrizzi, who wrote on geometry as well as history, suggested that the subject matter of history be broadened to include histories of the earth. He not only suggested eliminating rhetorical and philosophical authority from the writing of history but indicated that the historian should analyze the causes of the events described. History should include the acts of private as well as public men. Geography, topography, food supply, the public revenue and the strength and mode of governing states were added to the traditional list of appropriate historical

topics. Cochrane, *Historians and Historiography*, pp. 482-83. See Hugh G. Dick, "Thomas Blundeville's *The True Order and Methode of Wryting and Reading Hystories* (1574)," *Huntington Library Quarterly*, 3 (1939-40), 150; Giorgio Spini, "Historiography: The Art of History in the Italian Counter-Reformation," in Eric Cochrane, ed., *The Late Italian Renaissance, 1525-1630* (London, 1970), pp. 103-104.

10. Thomas Blundeville, *The True Order and Methode of Wryting and Reading Hystories* (London, 1574). Only portions of their work were translated by Blundeville. Spini has distinguished two sixteenth-century anti-Ciceronian movements. The first, extending from Patrizzi to Campanella, emphasized the truth of history, and tended to merge natural and civil history. The second was political history in the naturalistic, inductive mode of Machiavelli and Guicciardini. He includes Aconcio, Bruto, Sarpi, Davila, and Ducci in the latter group; "Historiography," pp. 105, 112-14, 116-20; 125, 129. See also William Bouwsma, "Three Types of Historiography in Post-Renaissance Italy," *History and Theory*, 4 (1964-65), 303-14.

11. Eric Cochrane, "The Transition from Renaissance to Baroque: The Case of Italian History," *History and Theory*, 19 (1980), 21-38; Cochrane, *Historians and Historiography*, pp. 479-93.

12. See Gerald Strauss, "Topographical-Historical Method in Sixteenth-Century German Scholarship," *Studies in the Renaissance*, 5 (1958), 87-101.

13. Several scholars investigating the beginnings of modern anthropology have emphasized the significance of this tradition: see Margaret Hodgen, *Early Anthropology in the Sixteenth and Seventeenth Centuries* (Philadelphia, 1964); J. H. Elliott, *The Old World and the New, 1492-1650* (Cambridge, 1972); John Howland Rowe, "Ethnography and Ethnology in the Sixteenth Century," *The Kroeber Anthropological Society Papers*, No. 30 (Spring 1964), pp. 1-19; Howard F. Cline, "The *Relaciones Geográficas* of the Spanish Indies, 1577-1586," *Hispanic Am. Hist. Rev.*, 44 (1964), 341-74. For a mid-fifteenth-century humanist's combination of topography, ethnography, and history, see Robert Tate, "Italian Humanism and Spanish Historiography of the 15th Century," *Bull. of the John Rylands Library*, 34 (1951-52), 137-65. Tate, too, notes the influence of Strabo and Ptolemy (pp. 142, 152-53). See also François de Dainville, *La Géographie des humanistes* (Paris, 1940); Francisco Esteve Barba, *Historiografía indiana* (Madrid, 1964); Geoffrey Atkinson, *Les Relations de voyages du XVIIᵉ siècle* (Paris, 1920).

14. José de Acosta, *The Naturall and Morall Historie of the East and West Indies*, trans. Edward Grimstone (London, 1604), p. 327.

15. "The Author's Advertisement to the Reader," ibid., and pp. 33, 44, 77ff., 99, 496. See also Rowe, "Ethnography and Ethnology," p. 19; Elliott, *The Old World and the New*, pp. 34-35.

Dominican theologian Melchor Cano (1509?-1560) discussed the foundations of historical knowledge in the course of an inquiry into the sources of theology. He concluded that while one could not, sacred authors apart, take the statements of a single author or authority as certain, one could accept such statements as probable under certain circumstances. Belief should depend on the credit of the author and the number who concur in the statement. See Franklin, *Bodin*, pp. 103-15.

16. Valla, however, insisted on the alliance between rhetoric and history. See Kelley, *Foundations of Modern Historical Scholarship*, p. 33; Linda Janik, "Lorenzo Valla: The Primacy of Rhetoric and the De-Moralization of History," *History and Theory*, 12 (1973), 389-404. For Valla, rhetoric included philology. For the development of French historical thought, see Pocock, *The Ancient Constitution and the*

Feudal Law; Kelley, *Foundations of Modern Historical Scholarship*; Huppert, *Idea of Perfect History*; Franklin, *Bodin*.

17. Bodin separated history from natural history, but included climate, geography, and all human activities for which reliable sources could be found. La Popelinière took a similar position. For Bodin's influence in England, see Leonard Dean, "Bodin's *Methodus* in England Before 1625," *Studies in Philology*, 39 (1942), 160-66.

18. See Huppert, *Idea of Perfect History*, pp. 24, 31, 34, 50, 62-63.

19. Kelley, *Foundations of Modern Historical Scholarship*, pp. 215-38. See also G. Wylie Sypher, "La Popelinière's *Histoire de France*: A Case of Historical Objectivity and Religious Censorship," *J. Hist. Ideas*, 24 (1963), 41-53; Sypher, "Similarities," pp. 353-68; Donald R. Kelley, "History as a Calling: The Case of La Popelinière," in *Renaissance Studies in Honor of Hans Baron*, eds. Anthony Molho and John A. Tedeschi (Florence, 1971), pp. 773-89; Myriam Yardeni, "La Conception de l'histoire dans l'oeuvre de La Popelinière," *Revue d'histoire moderne et contemporaine*, 11 (1964), 109-26.

20. See Richard H. Popkin, *The History of Scepticism from Erasmus to Descartes*, rev. ed. (Assen, 1964); Craig Brush, *Montaigne and Bayle: Variations on the Theme of Skepticism* (The Hague, 1966); Franklin, *Bodin*, passim.

21. Lucien Levy-Bruhl, "The Cartesian Spirit and History," trans. Mary Morris, in *Philosophy and History: Essays Presented to Ernst Cassirer*, eds. Raymond Klibansky and H. J. Paton (Oxford, 1936), pp. 192-95; Huppert, *Idea of Perfect History*, pp. 168, 180, 181.

There has been relatively little investigation of historical thought between Pasquier and Bayle. Huppert has suggested that the decline began about 1600 when skepticism and revived religious orthodoxy threatened critical history. He has also suggested that historical writing and antiquarian erudition became separated about this time (pp. 166, 171-80). See also Paul Hazard, *The European Mind, 1680-1715*, trans. J. Lewis May (New Haven, 1953); Phyllis Leffler, *L'histoire raisonnée: A Study of French Historiography, 1660-1720*, Ph.D. dissertation, Ohio State University, 1971.

22. Josephine de Boer, "Men's Literary Circles in Paris, 1610-1660," *PMLA*, 53 (1938), 731-32, 734, 772; J. S. Spink, *French Free-Thought from Gassendi to Voltaire* (New York, 1960).

23. For comparison of English and French historians, see Pocock, *The Ancient Constitution and the Feudal Law*; Donald R. Kelley, "History, English Law, and the Renaissance," *Past and Present*, 65 (Nov. 1974), 24-51.

24. Levy, *Tudor Historical Thought*; Fussner, *Historical Revolution*; Herbert Butterfield, *The Englishman and His History* (Cambridge, 1944); Herschel Baker, *The Race of Time: Three Lectures on Renaissance Historiography* (Toronto, 1967); Leonard Dean, *Tudor Theories of History Writing* (Ann Arbor, 1947); Levi Fox, ed., *English Historical Scholarship in the Sixteenth and Seventeenth Centuries* (Oxford, 1956); J. R. Hale, ed., *The Evolution of British Historiography from Bacon to Namier* (London, 1967); F. Smith Fussner, *Tudor History and the Historians* (New York, 1970); Arthur B. Ferguson, *Clio Unbound: Perception of the Social and Cultural Past in Renaissance England* (Durham, N.C., 1979); David Douglas, *English Scholars, 1660-1730* (London, 1951).

25. James Spedding. ed., *The Works of Francis Bacon*, 14 vols. (London, 1857-74), IV, 293ff.; V, 503, 505; see also IV, 251-63. See Fussner, *Historical Revolution*, pp. 150-90.

26. Thomas Hobbes, *Leviathan*, ed. M. Oakeshott (New York, 1962), p. 69.

27. Braithwaite, *The Scholler's Medley* (London, 1614), pp. 44-47, 65.

28. Bacon, however, added ecclesiastical history and the history of learning.

29. Bacon, *Works*, V, 131; see also IV, 28. See Leonard F. Dean, "Sir Francis Bacon's Theory of Civil History-Writing," *ELH*, 8 (1941), 161-83. Natural history also included medicine, ethnology, sleep, diet, aging, music, vision, and the appetites. See Bacon, *Works*, IV, 251-63, 293-99; V, 506. For Bacon's classification in the context of the Renaissance encyclopedists, see Vergil Whitaker, "Francis Bacon's Intellectual Milieu," in *Essential Articles for the Study of Francis Bacon*, ed. B. Vicars (Archon, Conn., 1968), pp. 28-39.

30. Bacon, *Works*, IV, 311.

31. See Bacon's discussion of the requirements for a "History of Celestial Bodies," ibid., V, 510ff. See also Robert Hooke, *Lectures and Collections* (London, 1678), pp. 22-24, and his *Lectures de Potentia Restitutiva: Or, Of Spring* (London, 1678), pp. 36ff. (These were published together as *Lectiones Culterianae* [London, 1679].)

32. Heylyn, "A Generall Introduction," *Cosmographie . . . of the Whole World* (London, 1652), p. 20. Heylyn's *Cosmographie* was the most popular work of this type for fifty years. There were six editions before 1700. H. M. Wallis, "Geographie better than Divinitie: Maps, Globes and Geography in the Days of Samuel Pepys," in *The Compleat Plattmaker*, ed. N. Thrower (Los Angeles, 1978), p. 2. See also Heylyn, *Microcosmos, Or a Little Description of the Whole World* (Oxford, 1621); Robert Fage, *A Description of the Whole World* (London, 1658); John Newton, *Cosmographia* (London, 1679); Edmund Bohun, *A Geographical Dictionary* (London, 1688). But see Sprat, *History of the Royal Society*, p. 325.

33. Moses Pitt, *The English Atlas*, I (Oxford, 1680-83), 4. Hooke was deeply involved with Pitt's *Atlas*.

34. Thomas Burnet, *The Theory of the Earth*, I (London, 1684-90), 96; John Ray, *Three Physico-Theological Discourses*, (3rd ed. London, 1713), p. 5. See also William Whiston, *A New Theory of the Earth* (London, 1696), p. 32; John Edwards, *Brief Remarks Upon Mr. Whiston's New Theory of the Earth* (London, 1697), pp. 2, 26-27.

35. Cecil Schneer, "The Rise of Historical Geology in the Seventeenth Century," *Isis*, 45 (1954), 256-68; Robert Hooke, *The Posthumous Works of Robert Hooke*, ed. Richard Waller (London, 1705), p. 335; see also pp. 334, 410. Hooke, *Micrographia*, Preface.

36. T. C. Kendrick, *British Antiquity* (London, 1950), pp. 48-49, 56, 63; Richard Brathwaite, *The Scholler's Medley*. An expanded version appeared in 1638 as *A Survey of History*.

37. See Kendrick, *British Antiquity*, pp. 144-48; Fussner, *Historical Revolution*, pp. 230-52; Levy, *Tudor Historical Thought*, pp. 144, 154-55; Stuart Piggott, "William Camden and the *Britannia*," *Proceedings of the British Academy*, 37 (1951), 202.

38. *Britannia: Or, A Geographical Description of . . . England, Scotland, and Ireland* (London, 1673), Preface. See also John Seller, *The History of England* (London, 1696); *A Perambulation of Kent: Containing the Description, Historie, and Customes of That Shyre* (London, 1576). An expanded version appeared in 1596. Richard Carew, *The Survey of Cornwall*, ed. F. E. Halliday (London, 1953); John Norden, *Speculum Britanniae* (London, 1593); William Burton, *The Description of Leicester Shire* (London, 1622). Sampson Erdeswicke's *A Survey of Staffordshire* remained unpublished for many years. See also Sir William Dugdale, *The Antiquities of Warwickshire* (London, 1656); Robert Thoroton, *The Antiquities of Nottinghamshire* (London, 1677); Robert Plot, *The Natural History of Oxfordshire* (London, 1677), and *The Natural History of Stafford-shire* (Oxford, 1686). Thoroton excluded a description of Nottinghamshire only because Gervaise Pigot had already begun one. Joshua Childrey excluded antiquities from

his *Britannia Baconica* (London, 1660) because they had been " 'copiously handled' " by Camden, Dugdale, and Lambarde, among others (sig. B2^r). Plot's volumes dealt primarily with natural history, but also included material on antiquities. He limited himself to "things," omitting "both 'persons' and 'actions' "; *Stafford-shire*, p. 392. See also Charles Leigh, *The Natural History of Lancashire* (Oxford, 1700); Edward Lluyd, *A Design of a British Dictionary, Historical and Geographical with an Essay entituled Archaelogia Britannica: a Natural History of Wales* (Oxford, 1695).

39. For Stow, see Levy, *Tudor Historical Thought*, p. 163; Fussner, *Historical Revolution*, pp. 215, 221, 223, 227, 228. See also the anonymous *Chorographia: Or, A Survey of Newcastle Upon Tine* (1649), in *The Harleian Miscellany*, III (1744-46), 256-73; William Somner, *The Antiquities of Canterbury* (London, 1640). Nathaniel Crouch [Richard Burton], *Historical Remarques* (London, 1681), deals with the ancient and present state of London and Westminster.

40. Quoted in Fussner, *Tudor History*, pp. 283-84. Hakluyt thought of his labors as "the sweet historie of Cosmographie." Geography and Chronology were the "Sunne and the Moone, the right eye and the left of all history."

41. See, for example, William Dampier, *A New Voyage Round the World* (London, 1697), dedicated to the president of the Royal Society, which exhibited the familiar mixture of environmental description and ethnography. See also his *Voyages and Descriptions* (London, 1699).

42. *The Correspondence of Henry Oldenburg*, eds. Marie Boas Hall and A. Rupert Hall (Madison, 1963-), VII, 569.

43. *Philosophical Transactions* (1665-67), I-II, 186-89; Robert Boyle, *General Heads for the Natural History of a Country . . . for the Use of Travellers and Navigators* (London, 1692). See also John Woodward, *Brief Instructions for Making Observations in All Parts of the World* (London, 1696); Sir William Petty, "The Method of Enquiring into the State of Any Country," in *The Petty Papers: Some Unpublished Writings of Sir William Petty*, ed. Marquis of Lansdowne, 2 vols. (London, 1927), I, 175-78, and "Quaeries concerning . . . Pensilvania," II, 116-19. John Dury felt there should be a natural history for every nation.

The fact that some members of the Royal Society also engaged in translation efforts again suggests that we are dealing with a European, rather than a peculiarly English, enterprise. See Charles de Rochefort, *The History of the Caribby-Islands*, trans. John Davies (London, 1666); Johannes Scheffer, *The History of Lapland*, trans. Acton Cremer (Oxford, 1674); Johann Grueber, *China and France* (London, 1676); Jeronymo Lobo, *A Short Relation of the River Nile*, trans. Sir Peter Wyche (London, 1669). Samuel Sorbière, *Relation d'un voyage en Angleterre* (1663). See also Ira O. Wade, *Intellectual Origins of the Enlightenment* (Princeton, N.J., 1970), pp. 361-91; G. Atkinson, *Les Relations de voyage et l'évolution des idées* (Paris, 1928); G. Atkinson, *The Extraordinary Voyage in French Literature 1700-1720* (Paris, 1922); G. Atkinson, *Les Relations de voyages du xviie siècle* (Paris, 1920).

44. See Gerard Boate, *Ireland's Natural History* (London, 1652); Sir John Doddridge, *The History of the Ancient and Moderne Estate of the Principality of Wales* (London, 1630); Sir Robert Atkyns, *The Ancient and Present State of Gloucestershire* (London, 1712); Edward Chamberlayne, *Angliae Notitia, Or the Present State of England*, Pt. 1 (London, 1669), Pt. 2 (1671); Samuel Collins, *The Present State of Russia* (London, 1671); [Sir William Petty], *The Fourth Part of the Present State of England* (London, 1683).

Defoe's *A Tour Through the Whole Island of Britain* was "A Description of 'The Present State' of England" (London, 1927), pp. 1-3. Here again physical description

301

is combined with that of customs, manners and speech. See also John Robinson, *Account of Sweden* (London, 1694); Bernard Connor, *The History of Poland . . . [Its] Ancient and Present State* (London, 1695); Connor, a physician member of the Royal Society, was also the author of *Dissertationes medico-physicae* (Oxford, 1695).

Graunt defended his work as "Natural History"; Peter Buck, "17th-Century Political Arithmetic: Civil Strife and Vital Statistics," *Isis*, 68 (1977), p. 82. See also Charles Webster, *The Great Instauration* (London, 1975), pp. 420-80. For a discussion of the relationship between the Royal Society and travel literature, see Ray Franz, *The English Traveller and the Movement of Ideas 1660-1732*, 2 vols. (Lincoln, Neb., 1932), pp. 15-71. Churchill's "Rules for Travellers" (1704) included items on climate, religion, language, trade, antiquities, government, laws, etc.; ibid., pp. 23-24.

45. John Ray, *Observations Topographical Moral and Physiological; Made in a Journey* (London, 1673), Preface. The travel book was very similar. See John Norden, *England. An Intended Guyde for English Travailers* (London, 1625); Edmund Warcupp, comp. and trans., *Italy, in Its Original Glory, Ruine and Revival, Being an Exact Survey . . . and History* (London, 1660); Peter Heylyn, *A Survey of the Estate of France* (London, 1656). For non-European countries, see Richard Knolles, *General Historie of the Turks* (London, 1603); Sir Paul Rycaut, *The History of the Turkish Empire* (London, 1680). See also Andrew Moore, *A Compendius History of the Turks* (London, 1660); John Ray, comp., *A Collection of Curious Travels and Voyages*, 2 vols. in 1 (London, 1693); John Fryer, *A New Account of East-India and Persia* (London, 1698). For the American colonies, see John W. Shirley, ed., *Thomas Harriot: Renaissance Scientist* (Oxford, 1974), pp. 18-19, 42-46; Joseph and Nesta Ewan, *John Banister and His Natural History of Virginia, 1678-1692* (Urbana, Ill., 1970), pp. 73, 81, 84. Beverley's *History and Present State of Virginia* borrowed heavily from Banister, but gave greater emphasis to civil matters (p. 121). Sir Ferdinando Gorges, "A Description of New-England," *America Painted to the Life* (London, 1658-59). See also Richard Blome, *A Description of the Island of Jamaica* (London, 1672), rev. and exp. as *The Present State of His Majesty's Isles and Territories in America* (London, 1687).

46. S. L. Goldberg, "Sir John Hayward, 'Politic' Historian," *Rev. of Eng. Studies*, N.S., 6 (1955), 233-44; Levy, *Tudor Historical Thought*, pp. 252, 291. See also H. R. Trevor-Roper, *Queen Elizabeth's First Historian: William Camden and the Beginnings of English 'Civil History'* (London, 1971).

47. Fussner, *Historical Revolution*, pp. 151, 245, 247; Edmund Bolton, *Hypercritica* (1618), in *Critical Essays of the 17th Century*, ed. J. E. Spingarn (Oxford, 1908), I, 100; Edward Hyde, Lord Clarendon, *History of the Rebellion*, ed. W. D. Macray (Oxford, 1888), III, 232.

48. Bacon, *Works*, IV, 304. For Bacon's classifications, see pp. 302-14; L. F. Dean, "Sir Francis Bacon's Theory of Civil History Writing," *ELH*, 8 (1941), 161-83. For classification more generally, see Fussner, *Historical Revolution*, pp. 150-90; Degory Wheare, *The Method and Order of Reading . . . Histories* (London, 1685). See also G. H. Nadel, "History as Psychology in Francis Bacon's Theory of History," in Vicars, *Essential Articles for the Study of Bacon*, pp. 236-52.

49. Bacon, *Works*, IV, 307.

50. See Wheare, *Method and Order of Histories*, p. 15.

51. Bacon, *Works*, IV, 308.

52. Ibid., p. 302.

53. Ibid.

54. Ibid., p. 303.

55. Quoted in Joseph Frank, *The Beginnings of the English Newspaper, 1620-1660* (Cambridge, 1961), p. 7.

56. Bacon, *Works*, IV, 304.

57. John Selden, *Titles of Honor* (London, 1631), Preface.

58. John Evelyn, *History of the Late Imposters* (London, 1669), Preface.

59. Daniel Defoe, *A General History of the Pyrates*, ed. M. Schonhorn (London, 1972), Preface.

60. James Howell, *Lustra Ludovico, Or the Life of the . . . King of France* (London, 1646), Dedicatory Epistle.

61. James Howell, *Londinopolis: An Historical Discourse* (London, 1657).

62. See Ferguson, *Clio Unbound, passim.*

63. See e.g., Thomas Browne, John Aubrey, Edward Lhwyd, Robert Plot, and John Ray.

64. Inigo Jones, *The Most Notable Antiquity of Great Britain . . . Stone-Heng* (London, 1655); Walter Charleton, *Chorea Gigantum; Or, The Most Famous Antiquity of Great Britain . . . Stone-Heng* (London, 1663). In the late seventeenth century, Aubrey, Lhwyd, Woodward, and Ray continued to discuss Stonehenge; Joseph Levine, *Dr. Woodward's Shield: History, Science, and Satire in Augustan England* (Berkeley, 1977), pp. 73-74.

65. Schneer, "Rise of Historical Geology," pp. 261-62, 264. See also M.C.W. Hunter, "The Royal Society and the Origins of British Archaeology," *Antiquity*, 65 (1971), 113-22, 187-92.

66. Levy, *Tudor Historical Thought*, p. 146.

67. Sir William Temple, *An Introduction to the History of England* (London, 1695). Pope and Bolingbroke were also critical of antiquarianism; Douglas, *English Scholars*, pp. 18, 356, 360, 366. See also Isaac Kramnick, "Introduction to Lord Bolingbroke," *Historical Writings* (Chicago, 1971), pp. xi-liii. Bolingbroke's essay of 1720 provided rules to test historical facts:

> An historical fact contains nothing that contradicts general experience, and our own observation, had already the appearance of probability; and if it be supported by the testimony of proper witnesses, it acquires all the appearances of truth; that is, it becomes really probable in the highest degree. . . . The degree of assent, which we give to history, may be settled, in proportion to the number, characters, and circumstances of the original witnesses (p. xxxvii).

Bolingbroke expressed the need for critical stance, but refused a complete skepticism (pp. 55-57, 67).

68. See W. H. Greenleaf, *Order, Empiricism, and Politics: Two Traditions of English Political Thought, 1500-1700* (London, 1964), pp. 207, 216-19; Stuart Clark, "Bacon's *Henry VII*: A Case-Study in the Science of Man," *History and Theory*, 13 (1974), 97-118.

69. A fourth group, however, felt "science" had nothing to do with facts or probability and sought demonstrative certainty. This group was typically uninterested in history.

70. Acosta, *Naturall and Morall History*, p. 99.

71. Clarendon, *History of the Rebellion*, p. 254. See also Sir Charles Firth, "Clarendon's *History of the Rebellion*," *EHR*, 19 (1904), 456-65.

72. Gilbert Burnet, *The Memoires of the Lives of the Hamiltons* (London, 1677). Those "fittest" to write history were those like Caesar, Commines, Guicciardini, de Thou, and Davila who had been "Actors." Those with access to the cabinets of great ministers and public records were second-best. Burnet placed Sarpi, Sleiden, and

Grotius in this category. For the increase in the use of documents see Fussner, *Historical Revolution*, pp. 32-37, 60-91.

73. John Rushworth, *Historicall Collections* (London, 1682), Preface. See also White Kennett, *A Compleat History of England* (London, 1706), Preface.

74. Bacon, *Works*, IV, 305.

75. White Kennett, *A Compleat History*, I, Preface. See also T[homas] F[rankland], *The Annals of King James and King Charles the First* (London, 1681). Lord Bolingbroke felt that contemporary sources were to be preferred, but he recognized that they might be biased (Bolingbroke, *Historical Writings*, p. 56).

76. Fussner, *Historical Revolution*, pp. 236-48.

77. Sir Charles Firth, *Essays Historical and Literary* (Oxford, 1938), p. 175; Burnet, *Memoires of the Hamiltons*.

78. John Evelyn, *Sylva, Or a Discourse of Forest-Trees* (London, 1664), Preface; John Ray's Preface to his translation of Francis Willughby's, *The Ornithology of Francis Willughby* (London, 1678); Ray, *Observations*, Preface; Edward Tyson, *Orang-Outang* (London, 1699), Preface; Carew, *Survey of Cornwall*, p. 109; Wyche, Epistle Dedicatory to his translation of Lobo, *River Nile*; Plot, *Oxford-shire*, Preface; Connor, *History of Poland*, Preface; George Gardiner, *A Description of the New World* (London, 1651), Prefatory Epistle; John Rowland, Epistle Dedicatory to his revision of Edward Topsell, *The History of Four-Footed Beasts and Serpents* (London, 1658).

79. Gilbert Burnet, *Reflections on Mr. Varilla's History* (London, 1686), pp. 10-11.

80. Robert Brady *A Complete History of England* (London, 1685), Dedicatory Letter. Brady was physician to Charles II and James II.

81. Willughby, *Ornithology*, Preface; Plot, *Oxford-shire*, Preface.

82. Fussner, *Historical Revolution*, pp. 32-36, 60-84.

83. Howell, *Londinopolis*, Advertisement to the Reader.

84. See Anthony Wood, *Athenae Oxoniensis* (London, 1691), I, Preface; Dugdale, *Warwickshire*, Preface.

85. Quoted in Fussner, *Historical Revolution*, p. 259.

86. "Life of Camden," *Britannia* (1695 ed.).

87. Kennett, *A Compleat History*, Preface. See also Bacon, *Works*, IV, 304; Brady, *History of England*, Preface; Lloyd, *Memorials*, Preface.

88. Edward Stillingfleet, *Origines Sacrae*, Preface, p. iii.

89. John Milton, *The History of England* (London, 1670), p. 3.

90. Ibid. See also Sir Charles Firth, "Milton as an Historian," *Essays Historical and Literary* (Oxford, 1938); French Fogle, "Milton as Historian," in *Milton and Clarendon* (Los Angeles, 1965).

91. Thomas Sprat, *History of the Royal Society*, eds. Jackson I. Cope and H. W. Jones (St. Louis, 1958), pp. 214-15; see also p. 90.

92. William Nelson, *Fact or Fiction: The Dilemma of the Renaissance Storyteller* (Cambridge, 1973), quoting Blundeville. See also *Harleian Miscellany*, VIII (1602), 1.

93. See Gilmore, *Humanists and Jurists*, pp. 95-96; Dean, *Tudor Theories of History Writing*, pp. 5-6; Levy, *Tudor Historical Thought*, pp. 244, 291, 293; Fussner, *Historical Revolution*, p. 236.

94. Kennett, *Compleat History*, I, Preface. Camden seemed to come closest to the ideal. For an assessment of Camden's impartiality, see Wallace MacCaffrey, Intro. to Camden's *The History of . . . Princess Elizabeth* (Chicago, 1970), pp. xxxi-xxxii.

95. Rushworth, *Collections*, Preface.

96. Harold D. Hazeltine, "Selden as a Legal Historian," *Harvard Law Rev.*, 24 (1910), 110.

97. See Annabel M. Patterson, *Marvell and the Civic Crown* (Princeton, 1968), pp. 228-29.

98. White Kennett, *Life of William Somner* (London, 1693), p. 97.

99. Burnet, *Memoires of the Hamiltons*, Preface.

100. Bolton, "Hypercritica," in Spingarn, *Critical Essays*, I, 91; see also pp. 91-93.

101. Ibid. See also Stillingfleet, *Origines Sacrae*, p. xviii; Rushworth, *Collections*, Preface; Peter Heylyn, *The History of the Sabbath* (London, 1636), Preface.

102. Sprat, *History of the Royal Society*, p. 322. John Wallis described his *Defense of the Royal Society* not as a history, but as a "Chancery Bill for Discovery," admitting openly that he was making a Case (Preface).

103. If anything, historians, in the interest of avoiding bias, left too much to the judgment of the reader, who was confronted by complex and often conflicting testimony. The result, therefore, was frequently the painstaking collection of undigested material. The works on the "Reading and Writing" of history (e.g., Bolton's and Wheare's) also suggest that the distinction between reading and writing history had not yet been clearly made.

104. John Selden, *History of Tithes* (London, 1818), p. xiii.

105. David Douglas, *English Scholars, 1660-1730* (London, 1951), p. 281.

106. Fussner, *Historical Revolution*, pp. 199, 203, 292n. See also Edward Ayscue, *A Historie Contayning the Warres, Treaties, Marriages, and Other Occurents betweene England and Scotland* (London, 1607), p. 1; Heylyn, *Cosmographie*, Bk. IV, Pt. II (p. 95); Charleton, *Chorea Gigantum*, Preface; Braithwaite, *Scholler's Medley*, pp. 78, 84.

107. From *Opera Omnia*, 3 vols. in 6 (London, 1726), III, 96, quoted in Fussner, *Historical Revolution*, p. 300.

108. Ibid., pp. 101-102, 199-204, 236 and n.; Ernest A. Strathmann, *Sir Walter Raleigh: A Study in Elizabethan Skepticism* (New York, 1951), pp. 240-53.

109. Hazeltine, "Selden," XXIV, 110.

110. Charleton, *Chorea Gigantum*, Preface, pp. 55, 57.

111. Kennett, *A Compleat History*, Preface.

112. T[heophilus] G[ale], *The Court of the Gentiles* (Oxford, 1668), Preface.

113. Ibid., p. 3.

114. Fussner suggests that there was an *entente cordiale*, but never quite an alliance between science and antiquarianism (*Historical Revolution*, p. 104). See also Fussner, *Tudor History*, pp. 240-43; Schneer, "Rise of Historical Geology," pp. 256-68; Levine, *Dr. Woodward's Shield*, pp. 118-19, 128. Nehemiah Grew's catalog of antiquities and rarities included coins, Roman urns, and mosaics which had been contributed by John Aubrey, George Ent, and Abraham Hill (*Musaeum Regalis Societatis* [London, 1681], pp. 380-82). Halley contributed an article on the discovery of a Roman urn to the *Philosophical Transactions*, Thrower, *The Compleat Plattmaker*, p. 208. Excavations required for the rebuilding of London after the Great Fire stimulated an interest in Roman antiquities. Christopher Wren, Edward Stillingfleet, and John Woodward were among the many stimulated by Roman finds; Levine, *Dr. Woodward's Shield*, pp. 136ff.; see also pp. 3, 22.

115. We know relatively little of overlapping patterns of patronage. The names of the earl of Northumberland in the 16th century, Lord Brooke and Sir Henry Savile in the early 17th, and Lord Somers at the end of the period may suggest a pattern of support for scientific, historical, and humanistic scholarship. Joseph Williamson was both president of the Royal Society and the founder of a Queens College lectureship in Anglo-Saxon studies.

116. Sprat noted: "Of all the Labors of Men, Wit, and Industry, I Scarce know any, that can be more useful to the World, than Civil History: if it were written, with that sincerity and majesty, as it ought to be as a faithful Idea of Human Actions"; *History of the Royal Society*, p. 43. Like many others, Sprat felt that the English, though they "can already show many industrious, and worthy pieces in this kind," still lacked an adequate history.

117. Linda Van Norden, "The Elizabethan College of Antiquaries," Dissertation, UCLA, 1946, pp. 304, 334, 412. See also Joan Evans, *A History of the Society of Antiquaries* (Oxford, 1956).

118. We can see the cooperative spirit emerging as early as Leland among the historians. It was continued by Harrison, Camden, the Society of Antiquaries, and the collective revisers of the *Britannia*. For later collaborations see Douglas, *English Scholars*, pp. 36-38, 47.

Sprat envisaged a collaborative history of the English civil wars: "There lay now ready in Bank, the most memorable Actions; a Subject of as great Dignity, and Variety, as ever pass'd under any Man's hands." Such a work would give

a full view of the miseries, that attended rebellion. There are only therefore wanting, for the finishing of so brave an undertaking, the united endeavors of some public mind, who are conversant both in Letters and Business: and if it were appointed to be the labor of one or two men to compose it, and of such an Assembly, to revise and correct, it might certainly challenge all the Writings of past, or present Times.

History of the Royal Society, p. 44.

119. *Britannia: Or a Geographical Description of England, Scotland, and Ireland* (London, 1673), Preface. See also John Seller, *The History of England* (London, 1696). Blome and Seller authored several historical and geographical works. See also Michael Hunter, *John Aubrey and the Realm of Learning* (New York, 1975), pp. 70-71.

Bishop Gibson's scholarly team, which worked on what is often considered a straightforward historical enterprise, included a number of scholars connected with the Royal Society, e.g., Pepys, Aubrey, Evelyn, Ray and Lhwyd. See Piggott, "William Camden," pp. 210-11; Douglas, *English Scholars*, p. 28.

120. Gareth Bennett, *White Kennett, 1660-1728* (London, 1957), pp. 158-77.

121. Thomas Kuhn, "Mathematical versus Experimental Tradition in the Development of Physical Science," in *The Essential Tension: Selected Studies in Scientific Tradition and Change* (Chicago, 1977).

122. William Lloyd, *Historical Account of Church Government* (London, 1677); Edward Stillingfleet, *Origines Britannicae* (London, 1685); Gilbert Burnet, *History of the Reformation of the Church of England* (London, 1681); Douglas, *English Scholars*, pp. 198-99.

123. Ferguson, *Clio Unbound*, pp. 129-224.

124. For Bacon, church history was divided into ecclesiastical history, the history of prophesy, and the history of divine judgments or Providence.

125. Joseph Preston, "English Ecclesiastical History and the Problem of Bias, 1559-1740," *J. Hist. Ideas*, 32 (1971), 207.

126. Firth, *Essays*, p. 185.

127. Ibid., p. 180.

128. Stillingfleet, *Origines Britannicae*, Preface, p. xxii.

129. Douglas, *English Scholars*, pp. 28, 211 (William Lloyd, Edward Stillingfleet, and Gilbert Burnet).

130. Seth Ward, *A Philosophical Essay*. I cite the 4th ed. (1667), pp. 84-85, 87-88, 90. Scripture is described as having interwoven elements of doctrine and history.

131. Ibid., pp. 99-101, 102.

132. Ibid., pp. 107ff., 117.

133. Stillingfleet, *Origines Sacrae*.

134. John Tillotson, *The Rule of Faith*, p. 98. See also Richard Baxter, *The Reasons of the Christian Religion* (London, 1667), pp. 307-11; Samuel Parker, *A Demonstration of the Divine Authority* (London, 1681). Parker was a member of the Royal Society.

135. Joseph Addison, "Of the Christian Religion," in *Works*, I, 420.

135. John Locke, "Reasonableness of Christianity," in *Locke on Politics, Religion and Education*, ed. M. Cranston (New York, 1965), p. 208.

While this approach to Scripture was linked to philosophical currents, it made English thinkers unsympathetic to Richard Simon's biblical criticism. The defense of the truth and accuracy of scriptural events was as much a part of Protestant polemic as Simon's notion that change and alteration of the text was linked to the Roman Catholic defense of tradition and the denial of the sole authority of Scripture. See Paul Hazard, *The European Mind: 1680-1715* (New York, 1963), p. 190. Religious commitment thus played a role in determining which intellectual and scholarly currents might be employed or rejected.

For a similar approach, see Bolingbroke, *Historical Writings*, pp. 73-77. He argues that, though the clergy—Protestant and Roman Catholic—have damaged Christianity with their disputes, they must recognize that "history alone can furnish the proper truths, that the religion they teach is of God" (p. 73). The foundation of the "whole system" was "clear and unquestionable historical authority" (p. 76).

137. See Glanvill, *Plus Ultra*, p. 141.

138. Hale sent the manuscript to Wilkins and Tillotson in 1667.

139. See Roy Porter, *The Making of Modern Geology* (Cambridge, 1977), pp. 63-90; Joseph Levine, *Dr. Woodward's Shield*; John Redwood, *Reason, Ridicule, and Religion: The Age of the Enlightenment in England, 1660-1750* (Cambridge, Mass., 1966), pp. 113-16.

140. See Thomas Hearne, *Ductor Historicus* (London, 1698), pp. 18-19.

141. A. Grafton, "Joseph Scaliger and Historical Chronology," *History and Theory*, 14 (1975), 156-85; Frank Manuel, *Isaac Newton, Historian* (Cambridge, 1963), pp. 41-43, 48, 49, 172; Margaret C. Jacob, *The Newtonians and the English Revolution* (Ithaca, 1976).

142. Jean Le Clerc, *Compendium of Universal History* (London, 1696), p. 4.

143. Joseph Addison, *Spectator*, No. 420.

144. Fussner, *Historical Revolution, passim*; Christopher Hill, *Intellectual Origins of the English Revolution* (Oxford, 1965); Ferguson, *Clio Unbound*; Huppert, *The Idea of Perfect History*; Joseph Levine, "Ancients, Moderns, and History: The Continuity of English Historical Writing," in *Studies in Change and Revolution*, ed. P. J. Korshin (Menston, Yorks, 1972), pp. 43-75; Joseph Preston, "Was There an Historical Revolution?" *J. Hist. Ideas*, 38 (1977), 353-64.

CHAPTER V: LAW

1. Some Renaissance humanists expressed hostility toward Bartolist post-glossators who remained disinterested in reviving the purity of ancient Roman law or the elegancies of classical Latin.

2. Valla and Biondo were notaries.

3. Deny Hay, *The Italian Renaissance in its Historical Background* (Cambridge, 1966); Jerrold Seigel, *Rhetoric and Philosophy in Renaissance Humanism* (Princeton, 1968); Myron Gilmore, *Humanists and Jurists: Six Studies in the Renaissance* (Cambridge, Mass., 1963); Julian Franklin, *Jean Bodin and the 16th Century Revolution in the Methodology of Law and History* (New York, 1963); Donald Kelley, *Foundations of Modern Historical Scholarship: Language, Law and History in the French Renaissance* (New York, 1970); Donald Kelley, "Clio and the Lawyers: Forms of Historical Consciousness in Medieval Jurisprudence," *Medievalia et Humanistica*, New Ser. 5 (1974), 25-49; George Huppert, "The Renaissance Background of Historicism," *History and Theory*, 5 (1966), 48-60; George Huppert, *The Idea of Perfect History: Historical Erudition and Historical Philosophy in the French Renaissance* (Urbana, Ill., 1970); Levi Fox, ed., *English Historical Scholarship in the 16th and 17th Centuries* (London, 1956). See also William J. Bouwsma, "Lawyers and Early Modern Culture," *Am. Hist. Rev.*, 78 (1973), 303-327.

4. For the differences between French and English scholarship see J.G.A. Pocock, *The Ancient Constitution and the Feudal Law: English Historical Thought in the Seventeenth Century* (Cambridge, 1957); Donald Kelley, "History, English Law and the Renaissance," *Past and Present*, No. 65 (1974), 24-51. See also Christopher Brooks and Kevin Sharpe, "Debate History, English Law and the Renaissance," *Past and Present*, No. 72 (1976), 133-42; A. B. Ferguson, *Clio Unbound: Perceptions of the Social and Cultural Past in the English Renaissance* (Durham, N.C., 1979), pp. 225-311.

5. Over two thirds of the Society of Antiquaries were lawyers. See R. J. Schoeck, "The Elizabethan Society of Antiquaries and Men of the Law," *Notes and Queries*, 119 (1954), 417-21; Frank Fussner, *The Historical Revolution: English Historical Writing and Thought, 1580-1640* (New York, 1962), pp. 94-95; Wilfred R. Prest, *The Inns of Court under Elizabeth and the Early Stuarts* (London, 1972). The Society was dissolved c. 1605.

6. Lambarde's *Archaionomia* (1568) was built on Nowell's collection of Anglo-Saxon laws. Lambarde's *Archeion* (1635) is a study of past and present nature of the English courts., ed. C. H. McIlwain and P. L. Ward (Cambridge, Mass., 1957). Lambarde was a pioneer in the use of medieval legal records. His *Perambulation of Kent* (1574) was a model for Camden. Camden was made an honorary member of Gray's Inn. See Ferguson, *Clio Unbound*, 286-91; Kelley, "History, English Law and the Renaissance," pp. 34-37; Wilbur Dunkel, *William Lambarde: Elizabethan Jurist* (New Brunswick, 1965).

7. Richard Braithwaite, *The Scholler's Medley* (London, 1614); Richard Braithwaite, *A Survey of History* (London, 1638); see Schoeck, "Society of Antiquaries," p. 107; Pocock, *Ancient Constitution and the Common Law*, pp. 91-123.

8. See Fussner, *Historical Revolution*, pp. 272-86; H. D. Hazeltine, "Selden as a Legal Historian," *Harvard Law Rev.*, 47 (1932), 12-20.

9. He mentioned Judge Hales, Wadham Windham, Sir Thomas Jones, John Glynn and Hale; Roger North, *The Lives of the Norths*, ed. A. Jessopp, 3 vols. (London, 1890), I, 353.

10. Ibid., I, 353-55.

11. See Charles Gray, "Introduction" to Hale, *History of the Common Law* (Chicago, 1971); Pocock, *The Ancient Constitution and the Common Law*, pp. 162-81. See also "Reflections of the Lord Chief Justice Hales on Mr. Hobbes His Dialogue of the Law," printed in Holdsworth, *History of English Law*, V, 500-13. Thomas Hobbes, *A Dialogue Between a Philosopher and a Student of the Common Laws of England*, ed.

J. Cropsey (Chicago, 1971); J. H. Hexter, "Thomas Hobbes and the Law," *Cornell Law Rev.*, 65 (1980), 471-88; D.E.C. Yale, "Hobbes and Hale on Law, Legislation and the Sovereign," *Cambridge Law J.*, 31 (1972), 121-56. For Hale's interest in Gloucestershire antiquities see William Camden, *Britannia*, trans. and additions by Edmund Gibson (London, 1695). Sir Henry Chancy, sergeant-at-law, did a similar study of Hertfordshire antiquities.

12. Geoffrey Gilbert, *Treatise of the Court of the Exchequer* (London, 1758), IV, vi. See also his *The History and Practice of the Court of Common Pleas* (London, 1737); *The History and Practice of the Court of Chancery* (London, 1758); *An Historical View of the Court of Exchequer and the King's Revenue* (London, 1738). Gilbert died in 1726. Lord Chancellor Somers, whom Gilbert Burnet considered learned in philosophy and history, not only patronized but participated in antiquarian research. Edmund Gibson dedicated the 1695 edition of Camden's *Britannia* to Somers. Thomas Madox's *Formulare Englicanum* (1702), Thomas Rymer's *Foedora* (1704), Thomas Madox's *History and Antiquities of the Exchequer* (1711) and John Ayliffe's *Ancient and Present State of the University of Oxford* (1711) were dedicated to him as well. Robert M. Adams, "In Search of Baron Somers," in Perez Zagorin, *Culture and Politics: From Puritanism to the Enlightenment* (Berkeley, 1980), pp. 174, 175, 183, 197.

13. *The Analysis of the Law: Being a Scheme or Abstract of the Several Titles and Portions of the Law of England, Digested into Method* (London, 1713); *The History and Analysis of the Common Law of England* (London, 1713).

14. But see Paul Kocher, "Francis Bacon and the Science of Jurisprudence," *J. Hist. Ideas*, 18 (1957), 3-26.

15. See *The Works of Francis Bacon*, eds. J. Spedding, R. Ellis, and D. Heath (London, 1857), V, 105; see also Bacon's *Maxims of the Law* in ibid., VII, 320.

16. See Kocher, "Jurisprudence," *J. Hist. Ideas*, 3-26.

17. William Seagle, *Men of the Law* (New York, 1947), pp. 94, 95-110, 111.

18. Ian Hacking, *The Emergence of Probability* (New York, 1975), p. 88.

19. Howard Solomon, *Public Welfare, Science and Propaganda in Seventeenth-Century France: The Innovation of Théophraste Renaudot* (Princeton, 1972), pp. 62-63; Martha Ornstein, *The Role of Scientific Societies in the Seventeenth Century* (Chicago, 1938), pp. 74-76.

20. Christopher Hill, *Intellectual Origins of the English Revolution* (Oxford, 1965), pp. 100, 149, 174.

21. See Prest, *Inns of Court*, pp. 137-73.

22. Roger North, *A Discourse of the Study of Laws* (London, 1824), p. 9.

23. Thomas Sprat, *The History of the Royal Society*, ed. Jackson I. Cope and H. W. Jones (St. Louis, 1958), pp. 66, 144-45.

24. John Aubrey, *Brief Lives* (London, 1898), p. 322.

25. *Dictionary of National Biography*, eds. L. Stephen and S. Lee, XXVII, 399; Roger North, *The Life of Francis North, Lord Guildford* (London, 1742), p. 284.

26. E. Foss, *Biographia Juridica* (London, 1870), p. 301.

27. See Barbara Shapiro, "Law and Science in Seventeenth Century England," *Stanford Law Rev.*, 21 (1969), 738-39.

28. John Evelyn, *The Diary of John Evelyn*, ed. E. S. DeBeer (London, 1955), Jan. 23, 1682-83.

29. North, *The Life of . . . Lord Guildford*, pp. 13, 284.

30. Ibid., pp. 286-87, 292, 294-95. North helped Flamsteed obtain a good benefice so that he could more easily continue his scientific work.

31. Gilbert Burnet, *The Life and Death of Sir Matthew Hale* (London, 1682), pp.

15, 225. See also pp. 15-16, 27, 117-23. See also J. Williams, *Memoirs of the Life, Character and Writings of Sir Matthew Hale* (London, 1835), p. 243.

32. *Essay Touching the Gravitation of Fluid Bodies* (London, 1673); *Difficiles Nugae: Or Observations on the Toricellian Experiment* (London, 1674). Henry More's critique of the latter work resulted in Hale's *Observations Touching the Principles of Natural Motions, and Especially Touching Rarefaction and Condensation* (London, 1677). Francis North, a fellow judge, was also critical. See Francis Roger North, *The Lives of the Norths*, ed. A. Jessopp (London, 1890), I, 99, 383.

33. Hale, *Observations touching Natural Motions*, Preface. See also Hale, *Difficiles Nugae*, p. 6. See also Shapiro, "Law and Science," pp. 741-48.

34. Howard Berman, The Origins of Western Legal Science," *Harvard Law Rev.*, 90 (1977), 894-944; John P. Dawson, *A History of Lay Judges* (Cambridge, Mass., 1960), pp. 49, 52; Raoul Van Caenegen, "The Law of Evidence in the Twelfth Century," *Proceedings of the 2nd International Congress of Medieval Canon Law* (Vatican, 1965).
There is some dispute as to whether the rigid mechanical system was an early or a late development. Some have suggested that there was no adequate theory of evidence in the Justinian compilations and that the important developments were made by twelfth- and thirteenth-century canonists. Others suggested that the civil law went from a free to a bound theory of proof. See C. A. Morrison, "Some Features of the Roman and the English Law of Evidence," *Tulane Law Rev.*, 33 (1959), 483. Walter Ullmann argues that fourteenth-century post-glossators made significant contributions. He suggests that they advocated a free evaluation of proof and were not bound by rigid rules, which presumably were a later development. See Walter Ullmann, "Some Medieval Principles of Criminal Procedure," *Juridical Review*, 59 (1947), 1-28. See Mirjan Damaska, "The Death of Legal Torture," *Yale Law J.*, 87 (1978), 860-68.

35. J. H. Merryman, *The Civil Law Tradition* (Stanford, Calif., 1969), p. 126.

36. Mirjan Damaska, "Evidentiary Barriers to Conviction and Two Models of Criminal Procedure," *Univ. of Pa. Law Rev.*, 121 (1973), 515. See A. Esmein, *A History of Continental Criminal Procedure*, trans. J. Simpson (Boston, 1913); "La Preuve: Deuxième Partie; Moyen Age et Temps Modèrnes," *Recueils de la Société Jean Bodin pour l'Histoire Comparativée des Institutions*, XVII (Brussels, 1965).

37. See Dawson, *A History of Lay Judges*, pp. 68, 71, 87.

38. John Langbein, *Torture and the Law of Proof* (Chicago, 1977), pp. 59-60.

39. The Roman-canon system of proofs was not required for misdemeanors.

40. For a critique of Langbein see Damaska, "The Death of Legal Torture," pp. 860-83.

41. Theodore F. T. Plucknett, *A Concise History of the Common Law* (5th ed., Boston, 1956), p. 436.

42. See Dawson, *Lay Judges*; John Langbein, *Prosecuting Crime in the Renaissance* (Cambridge, Mass., 1974).

43. See Langbein, *Prosecuting Crime*, pp. 42-43; see Michael Dalton, *The Country Justice* (London, 1635).

44. Kilbourne cites Coke on presumption but does not note that Coke used these terms in connection with a jury trial not pretrial examination. See *Choice Presidents upon all Acts of Parliament* (London, 1715), p. 490.

45. Sir Edward Coke, *The First Part of the Institutes* (Philadelphia, 1853), p. 6.

46. Kilbourne, *Choice Presidents*, p. 490.

47. Sir Edward Coke, *The Third Part of the Institutes of the Laws of England* (Philadelphia, 1853), c. 104, p. 232.

48. English civilians were employed in the ecclesiastical and admiralty courts. See Brian Levack, *The Civil Lawyers in England 1603-1641* (Oxford, 1973).

49. One should not overestimate English satisfaction with juries. Awareness that juries might be packed, intimidated, or bribed or be partial to one party led to numerous sixteenth- and seventeenth-century efforts to solve these problems by legislative means.

50. John Wallis, *Institutio Logicae* (Oxford, 1687), p. 172 quoted in W. S. Howell, *Eighteenth Century British Logic and Rhetoric* (Princeton, 1971), p. 37.

51. Robert Boyle, *Some Considerations About the Reconcileableness of Reason in Religion*, in *The Works of Robert Boyle* (London, 1772), IV, 182. Boyle's statement is incorrect. There was no two-witness rule for murder in English law.

52. Robert Boyle, *The Christian Virtuoso* (1690) in ibid., V, 529. See also Edward Waterhouse, *Fortescue Illustratus* (London, 1663), p. 251.

53. Quoted in Henry Van Leeuwen, *The Problem of Certainty in English Thought 1630-1690* (The Hague, 1963), p. 135.

54. See *D.N.B.*, VII, 9.

55. Fussner, *The Historical Revolution*, pp. 277, 286.

56. Matthew Hale, *The Primitive Origination of Mankind* (London, 1677), p. 128.

57. Ibid., p. 129.

58. Ibid., p. 128.

59. Ibid., p. 130.

60. See Chapter III.

61. Quoted in Hacking, *Emergence of Probability*, p. 89.

62. Ibid., p. 90.

63. L. Jonathan Cohen, *The Probable and the Provable* (Oxford, 1977).

64. Sir Geoffrey Gilbert, *The Law of Evidence* (London, 1756).

65. Ibid., pp. 1-2. Gilbert was also the author of *An Abstract of John Locke's Essay on Human Understanding* (Dublin, 1752).

66. Ibid., pp. 2-3.

67. Ibid., p. 3.

68. Ibid., p. 4.

69. The idea of moral certainty and evidence so strong it "admits no doubt" appeared in *The Tryall of Viscount Stafford* (London, 1680-81), pp. 40-41, 186. See T. Waldman, "Origins of the Legal Doctrine of Reasonable Doubt," *J. Hist. Ideas*, 20 (1959), 299-316; Anthony Morano, "Historical Development of the Interrelationship of Unanimous Verdicts and Reasonable Doubt," *Valparaiso Univ. Law Rev.*, 10 (1976), 223-30; Gerald Abrams, *According to the Evidence* (New York, 1958), pp. 4, 194; A. Bucknell, *The Nature of Evidence* (London, 1953), p. 55. For the influence of Locke on Morgan's *Essays Upon the Law of Evidence* (1789), of Bentham on Best's *Principles of the Law of Evidence* and of Mill's *Logic* on Stephen's *Digest of Evidence* (1885), see J. S. Montrose, "Basic Concepts of the Law of Evidence," *Law Quarterly Rev.* (1954), pp. 527-55.

70. See Holdsworth, *History of English Law*, VI, 126-27; Waldman, "Reasonable Doubt," pp. 308-10.

71. J. Wigmore, *The Principles of Judicial Proof* (Boston, 1931), p. 35. Wigmore notes that the principles of proof are "the natural processes of the mind in dealing with evidential facts after they are admitted to the jury; while the rules of admissibility represent artificial legal rules"; ibid.

72. Ibid., pp. 5-6.

73. See Holdsworth, *History of English Law*, pp. 126, 127, 178; Waldman "Reasonable Doubt," pp. 308-10.

74. Sir Matthew Hale, *History and Analysis of the Common Law of England* (London, 1820), p. 348.

75. R. W. Baker, *The Hearsay Rule* (London, 1950) citing Bennett *v.* Hartford (1650). The hearsay rule dates from c. 1675-1690. J. H. Baker, "Criminal Courts and Procedure at Criminal Law 1550-1800," in J. S. Cockburn, *Crime in England 1550-1800* (Princeton, 1977), p. 39. In 1698 Judge Holt ruled, with some tentativeness, "In Case a Jury give a Verdict upon their own knowledge, they ought to tell the Court so, but the fairest way would be for such of the Jurors as had knowledge of the matter before they are sworn, to inform the Court of the thing, and be sworn as witnesses"; Holt, *Reports 1688-1710*, p. 404.

76. Vaughan, *Reports*, pp. 135, 149. The judge ruled jurors could not be fined since they might have access to evidence that the judge had not heard. See Thomas Green, "The Jury and the English Law of Homicide, 1200-1600," *Michigan Law Rev.*, 74 (1976), 414-99; Baker, "Criminal Courts and Procedure," pp. 15-48.

77. See Holdsworth, *History of English Law*, IX, 196, 204-209; J. H. Wigmore, "The Required Number of Witnesses," *Harvard Law Rev.*, 15 (1901), 83, 88-90.

78. Van Leeuwen, *The Problem of Certainty*, p. 32; John Wilkins, *Of the Principles and Duties of Natural Religion* (London, 1675), p. 132.

79. Sir Matthew Hale, *History of the Common Law*, ed. Charles Gray (Chicago, 1971), p. 164.

80. Ibid.

81. Ibid., p. 165. He contrasts this with the binding rules of the civil law which require two witnesses to prove every fact.

82. Sir Matthew Hale, *The History of the Pleas of the Crown* (London, 1736), p. 277.

83. Hale, *History of the Common Law*, p. 164.

84. Ibid.

85. Ibid.

86. Ibid. Chancery, which did not employ juries, too had to develop "rules of evidence" to discuss the various kinds of evidence and the reliability of witnesses; Alan Harding, *A Social History of English Law* (London, 1966), p. 128.

87. Coke, *The First Part of the Institutes*, 6a.

88. Waterhouse, *Fortescue Illustratus*, p. 259; *Ignoramus Vindicated* (London, 1681), pp. 4-5.

89. *The Perjured Phanaticke* (London, 1669), p. 31.

90. *The Tryal of Slingsby Bethal* (London, 1681), p. 5.

91. *The Tryal of Nathaniel Reading* (London, 1679), p. 53. See also *The Tryal of Thomas White* (London, 1679), p. 88.

92. *The Tryals and Condemnation of Robert Charnock* (London, 1696), p. 67. The testimony of accomplices, particularly those pardoned by the Crown, proved something of a problem. Over time it came to be assumed that a pardoned criminal was a legal witness but not necessarily a credible one. The testimony of Roman Catholics, which figured heavily in the Popish Plot trials, was legal but not necessarily credible. See John Kenyon, *The Popish Plot* (New York, 1972), p. 250; *The Tryall of Viscount Strafford* (London, 1680), pp. 70, 82; *The Tryal of Thomas White*, p. 70. The distinction between competent and credible witnesses is underlined in Leonard McNulty, *Rules of Evidence in Pleas of the Crown* (London, 1802), pp. 15-16. Competency was decided by the court, credibility by the jury.

Hale's distinction between legal and credible witnesses was brought to the attention of justices of the peace who tried minor offenses. See James Pye, *Summary of the Duties of the Justice of the Peace* (London, 1808), p. 31.

93. *The Tryal of Charles, Lord Bohun* (London, 1693), p. 44.

94. *The Tryal of Richard Langhorn* (London, 1679), pp. 28-29.

95. Ibid., pp. 29, 60, 62. See also *Tryal of Nathaniel Reading*, p. 133. Much of the case evidence for the seventeenth century comes from state trials for treason or related offenses because few other trials are adequately reported. The cases are often discounted because of the patent unfairness of many of the outcomes. Even taking the worst possible view—that the proceedings were only charades—the players would have been expressing the orthodox legal ideology of the day.

96. Quoted in Kenyon, *Popish Plot*, p. 161; see also p. 165.

97. William Cobbett, *State Trials* (1741), p. 767.

98. *Trial of Spencer Cowper* (London, 1699), p. 207.

99. Sir John Hawles, *The Englishman's Right* (London, 1680), p. 126.

100. Ibid., p. 51.

101. Ibid., pp. 52, 11.

102. North, *Lives of the Norths*, I, 203.

103. Ibid.

104. Ibid., I, 203-204.

105. See Sir James Astry, *The General Charge to all Grand Juries* (2nd ed., London, 1725), p. 23.

106. Hale, *Primitive Origination*, p. 130.

107. Isaac Barrow, *Works* (London, 1687), II, 114, 115, 124. Boyle noted "the testimony of several individuals was preferable not because their testimony was individually more credible but because it is thought reasonable to suppose that, though each testimony single be probable, yet a concurrence of such probabilities (which is reason to be attributed to the truth of what they jointly tend to prove), may well amount to a moral certainty, i.e., such a certainty as may warrant the judge to proceed to the sentence"; *Works*, IV, 182.

108. *The Tryal of John Giles* (London, 1681), p. 54.

109. *The Tryal of Henry Carr* (London, 1681), p. 22.

110. Ibid. See also *The Tryal of Hamden* (London, 1685), p. 45; *The Tryal of Ireland* (London, 1678), p. 70.

111. *The Tryal of Henry Carr*, p. 23.

112. Ibid., p. 25.

113. Ibid. In another case the judges instructed the jury to "consider seriously and weigh the circumstances and the probability of the things charged upon them." Kenyon, *Popish Plot*, p. 175 quoting *The Trial of Wakeman*. Even in the conduct of state trials, of all trials the most likely to be affected by bias and extraordinary procedure, there was an increasing effort to aid in the discovery of truth. See Sir James F. Stephen, *History of the Criminal Law of England*, 3 vols. (London, 1883), I, 358-459.

114. *Ignoramus Vindicated* (London, 1681), pp. 2, 9-10. See also Zachary Babington, *Advice to Grand Jurors in Cases of Blood* (London, 1677).

115. Hawles, *Englishman's Right*, p. 13.

116. Ibid., pp. 27, 28, 31, 33, 36, 42, 97-98.

117. Ibid., p. 125.

118. Ibid., p. 119. See also *Ignoramus Vindicated*, pp. 2, 9-11.

119. Hawles, *Englishman's Right*, p. 126.

120. Ibid., p. 127.

121. Ibid., p. 128.

122. Ibid., pp. 82, 86, 131, 146.

123. Ibid., pp. 131, 146.

124. The Act of 1547 required "two sufficient and lawful witnesses"; that of 1552 "two lawful accusers." See Geoffrey Elton, *The Tudor Constitution* (London, 1960), pp. 67-68, 72-76; Samuel Rezneck, "The Trial of Treason in Tudor England," in *Essays in History and Political Theory in Honor of C. H. McIlwain* (Cambridge, Mass., 1936), pp. 259-88.

125. Treason Act, 13 Car. 2 c.1. The new requirement, of course, helps to explain why the issue of credibility occurred so frequently in the Popish Plot trials.

126. Samuel Rezneck, "The Statuate of 1696: A Pioneer Measure in the Reform of Judicial Procedure in England," *Journal of Modern Hist.*, 2 (1930), 13. See also Walter Simon, "The Evolution of Treason," *Tulane Law Rev.*, 35 (1961), 669, 688, 697-98; L. M. Hill, "The Two Witness Rule in English Treason Trials: Some Comments on the Emergence of Procedural Law," *Am. J. of Legal History*, 12 (1968), 95-111.

127. 9 Will. 3, c. 35.

128. A. F. Havighurst suggests there was little to complain of Charles II's judges. See "The Judiciary and Politics in the Reigns of Charles II," *Law Quarterly Rev.*, 66 (1950), 62-78, 229-52; Havighurst, "James II and the Twelve Men in Scarlet," *Law Quarterly Rev.*, 69 (1953), 522. See also *The Triumph of Justice over Unjust Judges* (London, 1681).

129. See Holdsworth, *Some Makers of English Law* (London, 1938), pp. 144-45; J. Williams, *Memoirs of the Life, Character and Writings of Sir Matthew Hale* (1835), p. 85; *Triumph of Justices*, p. 35; Atkyns v. Holford Care, 86 *English Reports* (K. B., 1671), pp. 254, 256. For a hostile view of Hale see North, *Lives of the Norths*, 87-88. See also I, 27, 79-82, 83-84, 90-91, 94-101.

130. Quoted in Edmund Heward, *Matthew Hale* (London, 1972), 67.

131. Ibid., p. 68. For another view see North, *Lives of the Norths*, pp. 87-88.

132. North, *Lives of the Norths*, I, 164-65. A bill providing for permanent tenure was approved by both houses of Parliament in 1692 but the proposal did not become law until the Act of Settlement.

133. Barrow, *Works*, I, 277, 280, 282.

134. Hale, *Pleas of the Crown*.

135. He did not in a 1664 witchcraft case. See *A Tryal of Witches at the Assizes of Bury St. Edmunds* (London, 1682). See also Chapter VI.

136. Hawles, *Englishman's Right*, p. 14; see also p. 58.

137. Ibid., p. 39.

138. See Ibid., pp. 10-11, 49-50. The decision in Bushell's Case (1670) which ended the punishment of juries for their verdicts also deals with the relationship of judge and jury. Late seventeenth-century writers who emphasized the independence of juries tended to be suspicious of judges. They associated juries with English liberties and judges with despotic and arbitrary government. The political conflicts of the late seventeenth-century were therefore important in shaping contemporary views on judges and juries.

139. North, *Lives of the Norths*, I, 203.

140. Ibid., I, 204.

CHAPTER VI: WITCHCRAFT

1. Alan Macfarlane, *Witchcraft in Tudor and Stuart England* (London, 1979); Keith Thomas, *Religion and the Decline of Magic* (New York, 1979); Lawrence Stone, "Magic, Religion and Reason," *The Past and the Present* (Boston, 1981), pp. 154-74; Wayne Shumaker, *The Occult Sciences in the Renaissance* (Berkeley, 1972); C. L'Estrange Ewen, *Witch Hunters and Witch Trials* (London, 1929); H. R. Trevor-Roper, *The European Witch Craze of the 16th and 17th Centuries and Other Essays* (New York, 1967), pp. 90-192; Robert Mandrou, *Magistrats et sorciers en France au XVIIe siècle* (Paris, 1968); H. C. Erik Midelfort, *Witchhunting in Southwest Germany, 1562-1684* (Stanford, 1972); E. William Monter, *Witchcraft in France and Switzerland: The Borderlands during the Reformation* (Ithaca, 1976); Julio Baroja, *The World of Witches* (Chicago, 1964); E. W. Monter, "The Historiography of European Witchcraft: Progress and Prospects," *J. Interdisciplinary Hist.*, 2 (1977), 435-51; P. Boyer and S. Nussenbaum, *Salem Possessed: The Social Origins of Witchcraft* (Cambridge, Mass., 1974); Sanford Fox, *Science and Justice: The Massachusetts Witchcraft Trials* (Baltimore, 1968); Brian P. Levack, "The Great Scottish Witchhunt of 1661-62," *J. of British Studies*, 22 (1980), 90-108.

2. Thomas, *Religion and the Decline of Magic*, pp. 442-43.

3. Ibid., p. 575.

4. In 1604 the dual jurisdiction ended.

5. Alan Macfarlane, "Witchcraft in Tudor and Stuart Essex," in J. S. Cockburn, *Crime in England 1550-1800* (Princeton, 1977), pp. 73-74.

6. Reginald Scot, *The Discoverie of Witchcraft* (reprinted, London, 1964), p. 42; see also pp. 40-43.

7. Ibid., p. 34.

8. Ibid.

9. Ibid., p. 61.

10. Ibid., p. 63. For Scot's empirical and experimental bent see Sydney Anglo "Reginald Scot's *Discoverie of Witchcraft*: Skepticism and Sadduceeism," in *The Damned Art: Essays in The Literature of Witchcraft*, ed. Sydney Anglo (London 1977), pp. 106-40.

11. Peter Haining, ed., *The Witchcraft Papers* (London, 1974), pp. 83, 93, 98, 102. Most of Gifford's *Dialogue Concerning Witches and Witchcraftes* (1593) is included in Haining. See Alan Macfarlane, "A Tudor Anthropologist: George Gifford's *Discourse* and *Dialogue*," *The Damned Art*, pp. 140-55.

12. Ibid., pp. 82, 105.

13. Christina Hole, *Witchcraft in England* (London, 1966), pp. 166-68. The cases were tried at Leicester in 1616. See Wallace Notestein, *A History of Witchcraft in England* (London, 1911), pp. 138-43, citing *C.S.P.D. 1611-18*, p. 398; D. Harris Willson, *King James VI and I* (New York, 1956), pp. 308-12. Trevor-Roper has suggested that James was responsible for the 1604 statute; *European Witch-Craze*, pp. 142-43. But see Stuart Clark, "King James's *Daemonologie*: Witchcraft and Kingship," *The Damned Art*, pp. 156-81.

14. If the evidence from Essex can be taken to indicate the condition of England as a whole, the most dangerous period was 1570-1605. There were 503 indictments made at the Essex Assizes between 1560 and 1680. There were only 35 between 1620 and 1639. Many of the accused were found *Ignoramus* by the grand jury. Of the 140 tried, 129 were found guilty and 74 executed. Macfarlane, *Witchcraft in Tudor and Stuart England*, pp. 28, 57.

15. Francis Bacon, *The Advancement of Learning*, ed. G. W. Kitchin (London, 1915), p. 71.

16. Ibid. Narratives "which have a mixture with superstition" were not to be "mingled with" those which were "merely and sincerely natural."

17. Ibid.

18. Francis Bacon, "Parasceve," in *The Works of Francis Bacon*, eds. J. Spedding, R. Ellis and D. Heath (London, 1857), IV, p. 257.

19. Ibid., p. 255.

20. Ibid.

21. John Cotta, *The Trial of Witchcraft* (London, 1616), p. 4.

22. Ibid., p. 5. Coke had participated in drafting the 1604 statute.

23. Ibid., p. 29.

24. Ibid., pp. 80-81.

25. Ibid., pp. 83, 84, 85.

26. Ibid., p. 85.

27. Ibid.

28. Ibid., p. 98.

29. *The Mystery of Witchcraft* (London, 1617), p. 274. These included "notorious defamation," accusation by fellow witches, and the witch mark. Both his legal terminology and the fact that he permitted torture by the examining magistrate suggest the influence of Continental procedure; ibid., p. 276.

30. Ibid. The emphasis on confession and the two-witness rule again suggests Continental practice.

31. Their existence was proved by experience, confession, "the truth of historians and the many relations of the arraignment, and conviction . . ." and the laws of all nations; *Guide to Grand Jurymen* (London, 1627), pp. 89-90.

32. Ibid., p. 25.

33. Ibid., p. 23.

34. Ibid., p. 226.

35. Ibid., p. 31.

36. Ibid., p. 41.

37. Ibid., pp. 25, 42, 46, 53.

38. Ibid., p. 223. Conviction required clear proof of the diabolic compact.

39. Michael Dalton, *Countrey Justice* (London, 1635), p. 303. In murder, witchcraft and other secret offenses when "open and evident proofs are seldom to be had, there (it seemeth) halfe proofes; or probable presumptions are to be allowed, and are good causes of suspicion and are sufficient for the justice of the peace to committ the party so suspected" (p. 303).

40. Confession had to be made during arraignment or trial; ibid., pp. 278, 307.

41. [G. Dunscumbe], *Trials per Pais* (1665) (4th ed., London, 1702), p. 12.

42. Richard Bernard's *Guide to Grand Jurymen* was reissued with few changes in 1680 and 1686. John Brinsley's *A Discovery of the Impositions of Witches and Astrologers* (1680) is almost a reissue of Bernard. See Notestein, *Witchcraft*, p. 303n. Joseph Keble's *An Assistance to the Justices of the Peace* (1683) repeats material from Lambard, Bernard and Bolton but does not express the need for caution. It should be noted that justices of the peace dealt with what we might call "probable cause," not grounds sufficient for conviction. There was considerable disagreement in the late seventeenth century as to whether grand jurors were to present on the basis of presumptions or whether they required the same type of proofs as petty jurors.

43. Edward Fairfax, *A Discourse of Witchcraft* (1621) in *Miscellanies of the Philobiblon Society* (1858-59), V, 36.
44. Ibid., p. 126.
45. Thomas, *Religion and the Decline of Magic*, p. 444. This view, however, was rejected by the Westminster Assembly of Divines, which in 1645 insisted that the diabolic contract alone, "though no hurt insue" merited the death penalty.
46. Filmer's *An Advertisement to the Jury Men of England Touching Witches* (1653) was reprinted in 1679 and 1680 together with *The Freeholder's Grand Inquest*. I have cited from the 1680 edition, Preface. The first edition was occasioned by an execution in Kent (Preface).
47. Ibid., p. 304.
48. Ibid., p. 306.
49. Ibid., Preface.
50. Ibid., p. 312. Thomas Ady wrote in a similar vein though he attacked the "grand Errour" of "ascribing power to witches" which had led to "wrongful killing of the innocent under the name of witches." He deplored the fact that Scot, who had initially made such a "great impression" on magistrates and clergy, seemed to have been neglected of late. Ady addressed judges, sheriffs, and justices of the peace. He argued that Scripture did not support most witch belief. He attempted to refute James I, Thomas Cooper, William Perkins, John Caule, and George Gifford; *A Candle in the Dark*, (Oxford, 1656).
51. Thomas, *Religion and the Decline of Magic*, p. 458. Special commissions staffed largely by laymen seem to have been employed. The assizes resumed in the summer of 1646. Macfarlane does not find the lack of routine procedure to be an adequate explanation for the Hopkins episode.
52. Hopkins was attacked by John Gaule. Hopkins's reply, *The Discovery of Witches* (1647), denied charges of torture. Hopkins, however, did deny the accused sleep and employed leading questions of the "Have you stopped beating your wife?" variety. See Thomas, *Religion and the Decline of Magic*, p. 517; Haining, *The Witchcraft Papers*, pp. 177-85; Notestein, *Witchcraft*, pp. 188, 201.
53. Mandrou, *Magistrats et Sorciers*, p. 111.
54. Essex, a county with a particularly high incidence of witchcraft trials, is suggestive. Although there were about 500 prosecutions between 1560 and 1680, only 14 took place between 1660 and 1680. If one excludes the trials in which Hopkins participated, the last Essex execution took place in 1626. Grand jurors had become increasingly reluctant to indict. The last cases before Quarter Sessions and the Assize in Essex were 1664 and 1675 respectively. During the most active years, 1580-99, there were 195 indictments at the Assizes, some 13 percent of all criminal charges. Macfarlane, *Witchcraft in Tudor and Stuart England*, pp. 28, 51, 200. See also Macfarlane, "Witchcraft in Tudor and Stuart Essex," in *Crime in England*, ed. J. S. Cockburn (Princeton, 1977), pp. 72-89. Figures for the Home Circuit (1559-1736) indicate 513 accused, about 200 convicted, and 109 hanged; Thomas, *Religion and the Decline of Magic*, p. 450. Decline was less rapid on the western circuit. There were about 50 trials and 6 executions between 1670 and 1707. The last took place in Chester in 1675. The last execution in the Home Counties took place in 1660; Ewen, *Witch Hunting*, p. 43.
55. Thomas, *Religion and the Decline of Magic*, pp. 458-59, 459n., quoting *The Doctrine of Devils* (1676), p. 96.
56. Richard Baxter, *The Certainty of the World of Spirits* (London, 1691). Hale evidently discussed the nature of spirits with Baxter. Hale, however, did not accept

Henry More's views on spirit in nature. See J. Williams, *Memoirs of the Life, Character and Writing of Sir Matthew Hale* (London, 1835), pp. 251-52.

John Selden, Hale's mentor, more skeptical than Hale, nevertheless believed in enforcement of the law. "The law against witches does not prove there be any: but it punishes the malice of those People, that use such means to take away Men's Lives. If one should profess that by turning his Hat thrice, and crying Buz, he could take away a Man's life, though in truth he could do no such thing, yet this were a just law made by the State, that whosoever should turn his Hat thrice, and cry Buz, with an intention to take away a Man's Life, shall be put to death"; John Selden, *Table Talk* (London, 1860), pp. 164-65.

57. See *A Tryal of Witches at the Assizes held at Bury St. Edmunds, March 10, 1664* (London, 1682). Heward suggests that Hale also may have presided over a 1669 Lancashire witch trial; Edmund Heward, *Matthew Hale* (London, 1972), pp. 82-86. Dr. Browne indicated "I have ever believed, and do now know, that there are Witches; they that doubt of these, do not only deny them but Spirits; and are obliquely a sort . . . of Atheists"; *Religio Medici*, ed. J. J. Denomain (Cambridge, 1955), I, 40.

58. Gilbert Burnet, *The Life and Death of Sir Matthew Hale* (London, 1682), p. 85; see also p. 92.

59. See Hale, *Pleas of the Crown* (London, 1678); *History of the Pleas of the Crown* (London, 1737), pp. 276-77. See also *The Primitive Origination of Mankind* (London, 1677).

60. Hale, *History of the Common Law* (London, 1820), pp. 346, 353.

61. Hale, *History of the Pleas of the Crown*, p. 290.

62. It is not easy to determine what Hale thought to be correct judicial behavior in those instances where something was perceived to be amiss in the law. If on the one hand he argued in the dissent in Atkins *v.* Holford Chase, "I must argue as the Law is and not as I wish it" (*Ventris*, 22 and 23 Charles II), he preferred legal "amendment" by judges than reform by Parliament. See Barbara Shapiro, "Sir Francis Bacon and the Mid-Seventeenth Century Movement for Law Reform," *Am. J. of Legal Hist.*, 24 (1980), 359, 360.

63. Hale, *History of the Pleas of the Crown*, pp. 276-77.

64. In New England Hale was remembered as a "person, than whom no Man was more backward to condemn a Witch, without full evidence"; Samuel Drake, *Annals of Witchcraft in New England* (1967 reprint), p. xii. Hale's behavior continued to disturb Francis Hutchinson in 1712. He concluded Hale had made an error and that some blame should be placed on Browne, whose testimony, he thought, had turned things back in favor of the prosecution; *An Historical Essay Concerning Witchcraft* (London, 1718), p. 118. Browne had testified that the devil could make natural illnesses worse; Thomas, *Religion and the Decline of Magic*, p. 574n. For a defense of Hale see Richard Boulton, *The Possibility and Reality of Sorcery and Witchcraft Demonstrated* (London, 1712).

65. Jackson Cope, *Joseph Glanvill, Anglican Apologist* (St. Louis, 1956), p. 102, quoting a letter November 18, 1670, from Baxter to Glanvill.

66. Hutchinson, *An Historical Essay Concerning Witchcraft*, p. 6.

67. Ibid., pp. 43, 44, 46; Thomas, *Religion and the Decline of Magic*, p. 459.

68. Notestein, *Witchcraft*, pp. 320-28; Hole, *Witchcraft*, p. 196.

69. *The Impossibility of Witchcraft* (London, 1712); G. R., *The Belief of Witchcraft Vindicated* (London, 1712); *The Full and Impartial Account of the Discovery of Sorcery*

(London, 1712); *A Full Confutation of Witchcraft* (London, 1712); *The Case of the Hertfordshire Witchcraft Considered* (London, 1712).

70. *The Case of the Hertfordshire Witchcraft Considered*, p. 83; see also pp. 17, 33.

71. *The Impossibility of Witchcraft*, Preface.

72. Roger North, *The Lives of the Norths*, ed. A. Jessopp, 3 vols. (London, 1890), III, 130; see also I, 161-68. North handled the civil and Raymond the "crown side."

73. Ibid., III, 131. North felt the confessions to be the result of poverty, melancholy, and delusion.

74. Ibid., I, 168; see also III, 130-31.

75. Quoted in Thomas, *Religion and the Decline of Magic*, p. 462.

76. North, *Lives of the Norths*, I, 166-67, 169; III, 132.

77. *A Full Confutation*, p. 5.

78. Ibid., pp. 5, 47. The author contrasts country life with town life where there was "Freedom of Thought and Talk," ibid., p. 5.

79. Quoted in Thomas, *Religion and the Decline of Magic*, pp. 452-53.

80. Ibid., p. 473.

81. Ibid., p. 308.

82. Ewen in an early study suggested that during the worst period, between 1598-1607, 42 percent of those accused were executed. Eighty percent of those arraigned went free. *Witch Hunting and Witch Trials*, p. 31.

83. *Account of the Trial of Joan Butts* (London, 1682).

84. Hobbes rejected the idea of an incorporeal substance. See Henry More, *Antidote against Atheism* (London, 1655); *Immortality of the Soul* (London, 1659). For More, "that saying is not more true in politics, no Bishop no King: than this in Metaphysics, No Spirit, no God"; *Antidote against Atheism*, p. 142.

85. More's comments are included in Joseph Glanvill, *Saducismus Triumphatus: or a Full and Plain Evidence Concerning Witches and Apparitions* (2nd ed., London, 1682), pp. 9-10.

86. Ralph Cudworth, *The True Intellectual System of the World* (London, 1678), p. 702. Meric Casaubon also defended the existence of witches as a means of supporting religious belief. Unlike the Cambridge Platonists, however, he was hostile to the scientific movement and to the Royal Society. He was conversant with doctrines concerning certainty and belief. See *Of Credulity and Incredulity in Things Natural, Civil and Divine* (London, 1668); *A Treatise Proving Spirits, Witches, and Supernatural Operations* (London, 1672).

87. Glanvill's *Lux Orientalis* (1662) defended the Platonic doctrine of the preexistence of souls. For his defense of the Royal Society see *Plus Ultra: or the Progress and Advancement of Knowledge Since the Days of Aristotle* (London, 1668). His first work on witchcraft was *A Philosophical Endeavor towards the Defense of the being of Witches and Apparitions* (1666). It was reissued with some additions as *Some Philosophical Considerations Touching the Being of Witches and Witchcraft* (1667). He also wrote *A Blow at Modern Sadducism* (1668) and *Saducismus Triumphatus*, ed. Henry More (2nd ed., 1682). The last was reissued by More in 1688 with additional materials of his own. Glanvill's *Essays on Several Important Subjects in Philosophy and Religion* (1678) included "Against Modern Sadducism in the Matter of Witches and Apparitions." For a fuller account of Glanvill's views on witchcraft, religion, and natural science see Cope, *Glanvill*, passim; Moody E. Prior, "Joseph Glanvill, Witchcraft and 17th Century Science," *Modern Philology*, 30 (1932-33), 167-93.

88. Glanvill, *A Blow at Modern Sadducism*, pp. 5-6.

89. Glanvill, *Essays*, p. 17.

90. Glanvill, *A Blow at Modern Sadducism*, p. 60. Popular opinion might be ignored in matters of theory because reason, not sense, was the appropriate judge; ibid , p. 71.

91. Glanvill, *Essays*, p. 19.

92. Quoted in Cope, *Glanvill*, p. 102.

93. Glanvill, *Essays*, pp. 19-20.

94. Ibid., p. 11.

95. Glanvill, *A Blow at Modern Sadducism*, p. 6.

96. Glanvill, *Essays*, pp. 7-8.

97. Glanvill, *Saducismus Triumphatus*, Part II, pp. 10-11.

98. Glanvill, *A Blow at Modern Sadducism*, pp. 115-18.

99. Ibid., p. 95.

100. Cope, *Glanvill*, p. 102. Reports on trials were included.

101. Glanvill, *A Blow at Modern Sadducism*, Preface.

102. Ibid.

103. Prior, "Glanvill," p. 182n. R. Bovet's *Pandemoniam* (1684), a defense of witches and spirits, was dedicated to More. Bovet admired Glanvill and used much the same approach to evidence and proof. He admitted the difficulty of "prooving" a witch, stating that "it ought to be done with the greatest Caution and Tenderness Imaginable." Bovet indicated that many "openly and with great Zeal profess a disbelief of the Existence of Daemons and Witches" (pp. 59, 60, 62, 78).

104. Thomas Sprat, *History of the Royal Society*, ed. Jackson I. Cope and H. W. Jones (St. Louis, 1958), p. 339.

105. Ibid.

106. Ibid., pp. 340-41.

107. Samuel Pepys, *Diary*, ed. Henry B. Wheatley (London, 1946), II, 357.

108. Cave Beck thought it "might not be unphilosophical to acquaint you with the greatest and worst sect of Monsters among us which are witches" and offered to transmit a "Narrative" of a recent case obtained from a minister "of too much Prudence to be imposed upon and of approved Veracity not to deceive others" *The Correspondence of Henry Oldenburg*, eds. R. Hall and M. B. Hall (Madison, 1970), V, 15. His comments suggest a concern for appropriate, reliable evidence. Peter Nelson, a schoolmaster expressed the wish "(if this were not out of their way) to see something from the Royal Society about Spirits and Witches," noting "these are none of the most obvious things in Nature, so have they been discours'd of with ye least of clearness and satisfaction." While Glanvill was a "man of Excellent Learning" and "very elaborate upon these subjects, . . . he has many things not easily understood, and others no less hard to believe"; ibid., V, 23. John Aubrey, the antiquary and naturalist, and a member of the Society, also desired a serious investigation of psychic phenomena; John Aubrey, *Three Prose Works*, ed. J. Buchanan Brown (Fontwell, Sussex, 1972), p. xxx.

Several of the Royal Society's foreign correspondents also alluded to witchcraft about the time of Glanvill's first publication. One mentioned a case of possession in Cajors but wrote back again providing a naturalistic explanation; Oldenburg, *Correspondence*, VI, 335, 483. Another wished that the Roman Catholics "would choose to discuss witches, whether there are any and how they do what they do." He reported on several cases where the Parlement of Rouen had been "of good mind to condemn" the accused, only to be prevented by the Parlement of Paris. This turn of events had forced an inquiry into "whether there can be any witches." The "better advised" people, he wrote, "believe not"; ibid., VIII, 329.

109. Robert Boyle, "Of the Excellency and Grounds of the Corpuscular or Mechanical Philosophy," (1674), in ed. M. B. Hall, *Nature and Nature's Laws: Documents of the Scientific Revolution* (New York, 1970), pp. 312-13. See also Robert Hooke, *Lampas* (London, 1677), pp. 33-34.

110. Boyle, "Of the Excellency," in Hall, *Nature and Nature's Laws*, p. 316.

111. Robert Boyle, *Some Considerations about the Reconcileableness of Reason and Religion* (London, 1675), pp. 86-87.

112. Robert Boyle, *The Works of Robert Boyle* (London, 1772), ed. Thomas Birch, pp. ccxxi-ccxxii. His *Excellency of Theology* (1674) published together with his exposition of the mechanical philosophy allowed for the possibility of witches along with other noncorporeal agents; Boyle, *Works*, IV, 19.

113. In 1662 Glanvill, then a young man, sent Boyle his *Lux Orientalis*, a treatise on the pre-existence of souls, confident that Boyle's "free and enquiring genius" would be "no enemy to pre-existence"; Boyle, *Works*, VI, 630. See also ibid., III, 452; M. B. Hall, ed., *Robert Boyle on Natural Philosophy* (Bloomington, Indiana, 1966), pp. 57-80.

114. Boyle, *Works*, VI, 631.

115. Ibid., 632.

116. Ibid., 578.

117. Ibid., 58. Isaac Barrow was unwilling to suppose all accounts of witchcraft to be fictional for to do so would be to "charge the world with both extreme Vanity and Malignity." Quoted in Notestein, *Witchcraft*, p. 308.

118. Boyle, *Works*, VI, 58.

119. Ibid.

120. Ibid., 59.

121. Quoted in Aubrey, *Three Prose Works*, p. xxx.

122. John Wagstaffe, *The Question of Witchcraft Debated* (London, 1671), pp. 112, 113, 123-24, 146. (The first edition appeared in 1669.)

123. It was written in 1673.

124. John Webster, *The Displaying of Supposed Witchcraft*. Webster reminds the reader of Casaubon's distaste for experimental philosophy and the Royal Society, p. 4. For a somewhat different view, see T. H. Jobe, "The Devil in Restoration Science: The Glanvill-Webster Witchcraft Debate," *Isis* (1981), pp. 343-56.

125. Webster, *The Displaying of Supposed Witchcraft*, p. 5.

126. Ibid., p. 13.

127. Ibid., p. 14.

128. Ibid., p. 15.

129. Ibid., p. 17.

130. Ibid., pp. 20, 21.

131. Ibid., p. 39.

132. Ibid., p. 55.

133. Ibid.

134. Ibid., p. 57.

135. Ibid., p. 60.

136. Ibid.

137. Ibid., pp. 61, 62.

138. Ibid., p. 64.

139. Hobbes suggested that witches, like fairies, ghosts, and goblins, had no power except in the minds of the credulous. Thomas Hobbes, *Leviathan*, ed. Michael Oake-

shott (New York, 1962), pp. 26-27, 92. Sir William Petty suggested that Bedlam was the appropriate place for witches; *The Petty Papers*, II, 213.

140. Quoted in Thomas, *Religion and the Decline of Magic*, p. 579, from *Remarks upon a late Discourse of Free Thinking*.

141. Hutchinson, *An Historical Essay Concerning Witchcraft*, p. 134.

142. John Locke, *Some Thoughts on Education*, ed. Peter Gay (New York, 1964), p. 157.

143. Tenison, *The Creed of Mr. Hobbs Examined* (London, 1670), pp. 59-60.

144. *Spectator*, July 11, 1711, No. 117. Addison felt witchcraft was one of those areas "in which a Man should be neuter, without engaging his Assent to one side or the other. . . . When the Arguments press equally on both sides in Matters that are indifferent to us, the safest Method is to give ourselves to neither." On the one hand he had heard "relations . . . from all Parts of the world." "But when I consider that the ignorant and credulous Parts of the World abound most in these Relations, and that the Persons among us who are supposed to engage in such an infernal Commerce are People of a weak Understanding and crazed Imagination, and at the same time reflect upon the many Impostures and Delusions of this Nature, . . . I endeavor to suspend my Belief till I hear more certain accounts. . . ." Poor, aging women were "turned into" witches by neighbors and even began to believe themselves to be witches.

145. Dissenting circles maintained a belief in witchcraft longer than others. Thomas, *Religion and the Decline of Magic*, p. 487. See Richard Baxter, *Certainty of the World of Spirits* (1691). Daniel Defoe, also a dissenter, felt there was "Abundant Testimony both from Scripture and from Criminal Process of the Truth" of witchcraft. Defoe discussed both Webster and Glanvill; *The Review* (October 19, 1711), VIII, 363; see also pp. 94-95, 335, 362-63.

146. Continental belief emphasized the witches' sabbat, demonic possession, and was far more closely associated with heresy. English accusations centered on harm allegedly done to animals and humans. Continental accusations also affected a broader range of social groups.

147. See E. William Monter, "Inflation and Witchcraft: The Case of Jean Bodin," *Action and Conviction in Early Modern Europe*, ed. T. K. Rabb and J. E. Seigel (Princeton, 1969), 371-89; Christopher Baxter, "Jean Bodin's *De la Démonomanie des Sorciers*: The Logic of Persecution," in Anglo, *The Damned Art*, pp. 76-105. Although there were nine French editions of *Démonomanie* by 1604 and three Latin editions, the *Démonomanie* was not translated into English.

148. Quoted in review of S. Anglo (ed.), *The Damned Art* in *Renaissance and Reforme*, 16 (1980), 99, and Shumaker, *Occult Sciences in the Renaissance*, p. 66. See also Brian Easlea, *Witch-Hunting, Magic and the New Philosophy* (Brighton, Sussex, 1980).

149. *An Examen of Witches*, p. 212. There were editions in 1590, 1602, 1603, 1605, 1608, and 1611. My citations are to the 1929 English translation.

150. Ibid., pp. 212-22, 228-30, 232.

151. Mandrou, *Magistrats et Sorciers*, pp. 317, 326-27, 335.

152. *The Essential Montaigne*, ed. S. Hughes (New York, 1970), pp. 315-16. See also E. W. Monter, "Law, Medicine, and the Acceptance of Witchcraft, 1560-1580," in *European Witchcraft*, ed. E. W. Monter (New York, 1969), pp. 67-70. Monter feels that attempts to overthrow the system of witchcraft could only come from medicine or philosophy and that the necessary philosophical position, "mechanism buttressed by Cartesian doubt . . . lay in the future." Thus in the sixteenth century, medicine was the sole profession that "could so battle with witchcraft" (p. 70). For a mechanistic

Cartesian argument against witchcraft see Malebranche, "Recherche de la vérité" (1674), in ibid., pp. 121-26. Malebranche emphasized the roles of imagination and customary belief and noted the role of the parlements in the declining rates of prosecution. He nevertheless maintained "that Witches . . . could exist and that the demon sometimes exercises his malice upon men by special permission of a superior power" (p. 126). See also Gabriel Naudé, *Apologie pour les grande hommes accusé de magic* (1625); Ira Wade, *The Intellectual Origins of the French Enlightenment* (Princeton, N.J., 1970). pp. 188-92; J. S. Spink, *French Free-Thought from Gassendi to Voltaire* (New York, 1960); Easlea, *Witch-Hunting, Magic and the New Philosophy*. Easlea emphasizes changing social conditions particularly attitudes toward women.

153. In 1635 Mersenne and Peiresc were exchanging information on the subject of possession; Howard Solomon, *Public Welfare, Science, and Propaganda in Seventeenth Century France: The Innovations of Théophraste Renaudot* (Princeton, 1972), pp. 80-81. Gassendi attacked the occultism of Robert Flood in 1629. Renaudot's group discussed the Sabbat and the activities of the devil in 1637; Mandrou, *Magistrats et Sorciers*, p. 296. Mandrou notes the cultural cleavage between rural and urban areas and suggests that medical explanations became increasingly naturalistic.

154. "A Letter Against Witches," (1654), Monter, *European Witchcraft*, pp. 114-15. Monter suggests that Cyrano's ideas were derived from those of Montaigne; ibid., p. 113.

155. Mandrou, *Magistrats et Sorciers*, p. 342. Unfortunately Mandrou does not describe the new jurisprudence except to say that reputation or "ill fame" would no longer be accepted; ibid., p. 343.

156. Ibid., pp. 348-51; see also 108n.

157. Alfred Soman, "Les Procès de Sorcéllière au Parlement de Paris 1565-1640," *Annales*, 4 (1977), 790-814; "The Parlement of Paris and the Great Witch Hunt (1565-1640)," *Sixteenth Century Journal*, 9 (1978), 31-44; "Criminal Justice in Ancien-Régime France: The Parlement of Paris in the Sixteenth and Seventeenth Centuries," *Crime and Criminal Justice in Europe and Canada*, ed. L. A. Knafla (Calgary, 1980). Trevor-Roper also emphasizes the role of judicial procedure and rules of evidence, *European Witch Craze*, pp. 118-23.

158. The announcement of the decrees of 1670-72 emphasized that it would "establish the quality of proofs and witnesses" which could be employed; Monter, *European Witchcraft*, p. 139.

159. Monter indicates that the peak years were 1590-1660. *Witchcraft in France and Switzerland*, p. 36. See also Midelfort, *Witch Hunting in Southwest Germany*, pp. 6, 194. Trevor-Roper has emphasized the role of judicial torture, *The European Witch Craze*, pp. 118-19.

160. Midelfort, *Witch Hunting in Southwest Germany*, pp. 25, 192. Monter, *Witchcraft in France and Switzerland*, p. 163. See also *Etienne Delcambre*, "Witchcraft Trials in Lorraine: Psychology of the Judges," and "The Psychology of Lorraine Witchcraft Suspects," in Monter, *European Witchcraft*, pp. 85-95, 95-109.

161. In Scotland, a Roman law country, prosecutions lingered somewhat longer. Prosecution virtually ceased during the brief Cromwellian interlude when English standards seem to have been imposed. Considerable anger was expressed in Scotland when the English Parliament abolished witchcraft as a crime in 1736. See George F. Black, "A Calendar of Cases of Witchcraft in Scotland, 1510-1727," *Bull. of the N.Y. Public Library*, 41 (1937), 825-26, 832; Brian Levack, "The Great Scottish Witch-hunt of 1661-1662," *J. of Brit. Studies*, 22 (1980), 90-108. Levack indicates that the revival of prosecution was the responsiblity of the ruling elite which controlled the

judicial machinery. Decline occurred when judges and privy councillors became skeptical of the evidence presented to them. The council's prohibition of torture was also critical. Levack argues that George Mackenzie believed in the reality of witchcraft but exhibited a "legal skepticism." His moderation thus resulted from dissatisfaction of legal procedures. Of all crimes, witchcraft required " 'The clearest relevancy and the most convincing probation.' " *The Law and Custom in Matters Criminal* quoted in ibid., p. 107. For the decline in Guernsey and Jersey see G. R. Balleine, "Witchcraft in Jersey," Société jéraise, *Bulletin*, 13 (1939), 383-84; S. C. Curtis, "Trials for Witchcraft in Guernsey," Société guernaise, *Reports*, 13 (1937), 110.

162. See H. R. Trevor-Roper, *The European Witch Craze*, pp. 90-192.

CHAPTER VII: LANGUAGE, COMMUNICATION, AND LITERATURE

1. See Wilbur S. Howell, *Logic and Rhetoric in England: 1500-1700* (New York, 1961); W. G. Crane, *Wit and Rhetoric in the Renaissance* (New York, 1937); Bernard Weinberg, *A History of Literary Criticism in the Italian Renaissance*, 2 vols. (Chicago, 1961); Walter J. Ong, *Rhetoric, Romance, and Technology: Studies in the Interaction of Expression and Culture* (Ithaca, 1971); Thomas O. Sloan and Raymond Waddingston, eds., *The Rhetoric of Renaissance Poetry* (Berkeley, 1974); George Kennedy, *Classical Rhetoric and its Christian and Secular Tradition* (Charlotte, N.C., 1980).

2. Richard Rainolde, *A Booke Called the Foundation of Rhetoricke* (1563), quoted in Crane, *Wit and Rhetoric*, p. 68.

3. Crane, *Wit and Rhetoric*, pp. 1-8, 11, 62-68, 78; Rosemund Tuve, *Elizabethan and Metaphysical Imagery* (Chicago, 1947); Brian Vickers, *Francis Bacon and Renaissance Prose* (Cambridge, 1968), pp. 141-73.

4. Quoted in Howell, *Logic and Rhetoric*, p. 328. See also O. B. Hardison, "The Orator and the Poet: The Dilemma of Humanist Literature," *J. of Medieval and Renaissance Studies*, I (1971), 33-44.

5. Quoted in Marjorie H. Nicolson, *The Breaking of the Circle* (New York, 1960), p. 122.

6. Lisa Jardine, *Francis Bacon: Discovery and the Art of Discourse* (Cambridge, 1974), pp. 5, 26, 29-39; Howell, *Logic and Rhetoric*; Neal W. Gilbert, *Renaissance Concepts of Method* (New York, 1960), pp. 119-44; Thomas O. Sloan, "The Crossing of Rhetoric and Poetry in the English Renaissance," *Rhetoric of Renaissance Poetry*.

7. Howell, *Logic and Rhetoric*, pp. 146-281; Gilbert, *Renaissance Concepts of Method*, pp. 196-212, 221-27; Walter J. Ong, *Ramus: Method and the Decay of Dialogue* (Cambridge, Mass., 1958), *Ramus and the Talon Inventory* (Cambridge, Mass., 1958), and *Rhetoric, Romance, and Technology*, pp. 142-89; Perry Miller, *The New England Mind: The Seventeenth Century* (New York, 1939); Craig Walton, "Ramus and Bacon on Method," *J. Hist. Phil.*, 10 (1971), 289-302.

8. Recent scholarship suggests how intricately Bacon's philosophy and method were enmeshed with rhetoric, dialectic, and logic. Paoli Rossi has linked Bacon's reformed logic to the rhetorical outlook of the period, suggesting that he adopted rhetorical approaches to scientific inquiry; *Francis Bacon: From Magic to Science*, trans. S. Rabinovitch (Chicago, 1968). Lisa Jardine places him in the context of the changing tradition of sixteenth-century rhetoric and dialectic, suggesting that he subordinated rhetoric to dialectic, and that the *New Organon* was a new dialectic to be understood in the context of Agricola's and Ramus's related efforts; (*Francis Bacon:*

Discovery and the Art of Discourse). James Stephens suggests Bacon adopted something of a new Aristotelian stylistics at least for the learned; *Francis Bacon and the Style of Science* (Chicago, 1975). Howell has emphasized Bacon's approach to learned and popular communication; *Logic and Rhetoric*, p. 364-67. Karl Wallace has indicated Bacon's indebtedness to and concern with traditional rhetoric; "Bacon's Concept of Rhetoric," in *Historical Studies in Rhetoric and Rhetoricians*, ed. R. F. Howes (Ithaca, 1961), pp. 114-38, and *Francis Bacon on Communication and Rhetoric* (Chapel Hill, 1943). Brian Vickers notes the rhetorical and poetic aspects of Bacon's writing; *Francis Bacon and Renaissance Prose*. See also Robert Adolph, *The Rise of Modern Prose Style* (Cambridge, Mass., 1969), pp. 26-77; James Stephen, "Rhetorical Problems in Renaissance Science," *Philosophy and Rhetoric*, 8 (1975), 213-29.

9. Francis Bacon, "The New Organon," in *The Works of Francis Bacon*, eds. J. Spedding, R. Ellis, D. Heath (London, 1875), IV, 61. See also pp. 53-69.

10. Bacon, "De Augmentis Scientarum," *Works*, IV, 433-34.

11. Bacon, *The Advancement of Learning*, ed. G. W. Kitchin (London, 1915), p. 24.

12. Bacon, "Parasceve ad Historiam, Naturalem et Experimentalem," *Works*, IV, 254-55.

13. Bacon, *The Advancement of Learning*, p. 141. See also Bacon, *Works*, IV, 449.

14. Bacon, *The Advancement of Learning*, p. 34.

15. Ibid., p. 141. But see Bacon, *Works*, IV, 449.

16. See Vickers, *Francis Bacon and Renaissance Prose*, pp. 60-83.

17. Ibid., pp. 3, 153, 158.

18. Bacon, *Advancement of Learning*, p. 146. See also Bacon, *Works*, IV, 454-55. See K. Wallace, "Bacon's Concept of Rhetoric," pp. 117, 118, 122, 129, 130, 132; John L. Harrison, "Bacon's View of Rhetoric, Poetry and the Imagination," in *Essential Articles for the Study of Francis Bacon*, ed. Brian Vickers (Hamden, Conn., 1968), 253-71.

19. Bacon, *Advancement of Learning*, p. 24.

20. Vickers, *Bacon and Renaissance Prose*, p. 112n.

21. Howell, *Logic and Rhetoric*, pp. 279, 384-85.

22. Thomas Hobbes, *Leviathan*, ed. Michael Oakeshott (New York, 1962), p. 34. See also "On Speech and Sciences," *Man and Citizen*, ed. B. Gert (New York, 1972), pp. 37-71.

23. Hobbes, *Leviathan*, p. 36.

24. Ibid.; see also pp. 34, 40.

25. Ibid., p. 61.

26. Ibid.

27. Thomas Sprat, *History of the Royal Society*, eds. J. I. Cope and H. W. Jones (St. Louis, 1958), p. 62.

28. Ibid., p. 111.

29. Ibid., p. 112.

30. Ibid.

31. Ibid., p. 113.

32. *Statutes of the Royal Society*, Ch. V, Art. iv, quoted in R. F. Jones, "Science and English Prose Style, 1650-1675," in *Seventeenth-Century Prose*, ed. Stanley E. Fish (New York, 1971), p. 61. See Wilbur S. Howell, *Eighteenth-Century British Logic and Rhetoric* (Princeton, 1971), pp. 441-502.

33. Sprat, *History of the Royal Society*, p. 112.

34. John Wilkins, *Essay Towards a Real Character and a Philosophical Language* (London, 1668), Preface.

35. Ibid., pp. 17-18. Sprat and Wilkins viewed the pre-Restoration era as the worst.
36. Ibid., p. 319.
37. Samuel Parker, *A Free and Impartial Censure of the Platonic Philosophy* (2nd ed., Oxford, 1667), p. 75.
38. See R. F. Jones, "Science and English Prose Style," *passim*; Jackson I. Cope, *Joseph Glanvill, Anglican Apologist* (St. Louis, 1956), pp. 144-68.
39. Joseph Glanvill, *Philosophia Pia* (London, 1671), p. 73. See also pp. 90-94; *The Vanity of Dogmatizing* (London, 1661), pp. 151, 156-61; and *Essays on Several Important Subjects in Philosophy and Religion* (London, 1676), pp. 22, 25, 28.
40. Quoted in R. F. Jones, "Science and Language in England of the Mid-Seventeenth Century," in *Seventeenth-Century Prose*, p. 99, from *The Petty Papers* (London, 1927), I, 150-51. See also p. 149; *The Advice from W. P. to Mr. Samuel Hartlib* (London, 1647).
41. Jones, "Science and Language," p. 99, quoting *Petty-Southwell Correspondence: 1676-1687*.
42. William Petty, *Discourse Made Before the Royal Society* (London, 1674), Dedicatory Epistle.
43. Robert Hooke, *The Posthumous Works*, ed. Richard Waller (London, 1705), p. 63.
44. *The Works of Robert Boyle*, ed. T. Birch (London, 1772), IV, 365. Walter Charleton felt ambiguity was "one of the greatest impediments" to knowledge; A *Brief Discourse Concerning the Different Wits of Men* (London, 1669), p. 9. Neither Boyle nor Charleton was a consistent practitioner of the plain style. Barrow contrasted the clarity of mathematical definition with the "Obscurity, Perplexity and Confusion of the Notions and Inconstancy of the Words by which the Notions are signified"; *The Usefullness of Mathematical Learning* (London, 1734), pp. 54-55. The problem of "inconstancy," which afflicted all sciences except mathematics, resulted in uncertain conclusions.
45. Childrey, *Britannia Baconia*, Pref. See also Francis Glisson, *A Treatise of the Rickets* (London, 1651), Preface; Robert Plot, *The Natural History of Oxford-shire* (Oxford, 1676), p. 2.
46. Locke, *An Essay Concerning Human Understanding*, Bk. III, Ch. IX, Sec. 21; Ch. X, Sec. 2. Book III, "Of Words," concerns problems of language.
47. Ibid., Ch. IX, Secs. 3, 4.
48. Ibid., Secs. 5, 7.
49. Ibid., Secs. 4, 5.
50. Ibid., Sec. 11.
51. Ibid., Ch. X, Secs. 2, 14.
52. Ibid., Ch. XI, Sec. 3.
53. Ibid., Sec. 8.
54. Ibid., Sec. 9.
55. Ibid.
56. Ibid., Sec. 24.
57. Ibid.
58. Ibid., Secs. 10, 11.
59. Ibid., Sec. 26. Locke was attracted to the idea of dictionaries which would precisely define simple ideas. He felt, however, that "a dictionary of this sort, containing as it were, a natural history, requires too many hands as well as too much time, cost, pains, and sagacity ever to be hoped for." He was therefore willing to

settle for "definitions of the names of substances as explain the sense men use them in"; Bk. III, Ch. XI, Sec. 25.

60. Ibid., Ch. X, Sec. 34.

61. Ibid.

62. James Knowlson, *Universal Language Schemes in England and France: 1600-1800* (Toronto, 1975); Murray Cohen, *Sensible Words: Linguistic Practice in England, 1640-1785* (Baltimore, 1977); Michel Foucault, *The Order of Things: An Archaeology of the Human Sciences* (New York, 1970); Jonathan Cohen, "Of the Project of a Universal Character," *Mind*, 68 (1954), 49-63; Vivian Salmon, *The Works of Francis Lodowick: A Study of His Writings in the Intellectual Context of the 17th Century* (London, 1972); R. F. Jones, *The Triumph of the English Language* (Stanford, 1953).

63. Beck, *The Universal Character* (London, 1657); Wilkins, *Mercury, Or the Secret and Swift Messenger* (London, 1641).

64. See Barbara Shapiro, *John Wilkins, 1614-1672: An Intellectual Biography* (Berkeley, 1969), pp. 206-23.

65. *Advice from W. P.*, p. 5; Thomas Birch, *Life of the Honorable Robert Boyle* (London, 1744), p. 73.

66. Cohen, *Sensible Words*, p. 10.

67. Dalgarno, *Ars signorum* (London, 1661).

68. [Joh]N. [Wilkin]S. and [Set]H. [War]D., *Vindiciae academiarum* (Oxford, 1654), p. 21. See also pp. 22, 24-25. For a discussion of Leibniz, whose views exhibited some similarities with those of Ward, see Knowlson, *Universal Language Schemes*, pp. 107-11.

69. Charleton, *Immortality of the Soul*, pp. 45-46. See John Wallis, *Defense of the Royal Society*, p. 17.

70. Wilkins, *Essay Towards a Real Character*, Dedicatory Epistle.

71. Thomas Baker, *Reflections Upon Learning* (London, 1700), pp. 18-19; Wallis, *Defense of the Royal Society*, pp. 12, 17-18; Shapiro, *Wilkins*, pp. 220-21, 313-14; Knowlson, *Universal Language Schemes*, pp. 100-11; Vivian Salmon, "John Wilkins' *Essay* (1668): Critics and Continuators," *Historiographica Linguistica*, I (1974), 147-64.

72. Hooke, *A Description of Helioscopes* (London, 1676), p. 31. Hooke and Aubrey were among the most enthusiastic.

73. Ibid.

74. Robert Vaughn, *British Antiquities Revived* (Oxford, 1662), Dedicatory Preface.

75. Aylett Soammes, *Britannia Antiqua Illustrata* (London, 1676), Preface.

76. John Rushworth, *Historical Collections* (London, 1682), I, Preface.

77. Herschel Baker, *The Race of Time: Three Lectures on Renaissance Historiography* (Toronto, 1967), pp. 73-89. Even Milton noted "The offices of a rhetorician and an historian are as different as the arts which they profess" (quoted, p. 89). Self-conscious rhetorical history seems to have been more strongly established and perhaps lasted longer in France. Denys Hay, *Annalists and Historians: Western Historiography from the VIII to the XVIII Century* (London, 1977), pp. 142-43.

78. Baker, *The Race of Time*, pp. 81-82.

79. William Camden, *Britannia*, ed. E. Gibson (London, 1695), p. 53.

80. Sprat, *History of the Royal Society*, Advertisement to the Reader; René Rapin, *Instructions for History* (London, 1680), p. 53.

81. John Esquemeling, *Buccanneers of America* (London, 1684), Preface.

82. Charleton, *Wits of Men*, p. 225.

83. Rushworth, *Historical Collections*, I, Preface.

84. See Baker, *The Race of Time*, pp. 82-88.

85. Charleton, *Wits of Men*, p. 15; White Kennett, *A Compleat History of England* (London, 1706), Preface.

86. Plot, *Natural History of Oxford-shire*, p. 2.

87. Quoted in Joseph Levine, "Ancients, Moderns, and History: The Continuity of English Historical Writing in the Later 17th Century," in *Studies in Change and Revolution*, ed. Paul Korshin (1972), pp. 48, 50.

88. John Milton, *The History of England* (London, 1670), p. 3.

89. For a discussion of the relationship between historical narrative and anti-quarian erudition in Hume, Robertson and Gibbon, see Hay, *Annalists and Historians*, pp. 167-85.

90. Ed. J. M. Major (New York, 1969), pp. 126-27. Elyot wished the barbarities of Law French, which he found to be "void of all eloquence," to be replaced with good Latin or "doulce" French; see also pp. 120, 122, 123, 124.

91. For contrasting views, see R. J. Schoeck, "Rhetoric and Law in 16th-Century England," *Studies in Philology*, 50 (1953), 110-27; D. S. Bland, "Rhetoric and Law Studies in 16th-Century England," *Stud. in Philology*, 54 (1957), 498-508.

92. Fraunce, *Lawyers Logicke* (London, 1588); Wilfred Prest, *The Inns of Court Under Elizabeth I and the Early Stuarts: 1590-1640* (London, 1972), pp. 143, 145-46; Howell, *Logic and Rhetoric*, pp. 222-28, 391.

93. Hale, *Difficiles Nugae, Or Observations Touching the Torricellian Experiments* (London, 1674), Epistle to the Reader; Hale, *The Primitive Origination of Mankind* (London, 1677), pp. 262-65.

94. Gilbert Burnet, *The Life and Death of Sir Matthew Hale* (London, 1700), p. 65.

95. Ibid., pp. 65, 66.

96. Matthew Hale, *History and Analysis of the Common Law of England* (London, 1820), pp. xxvii, xxix.

97. *English Man's Right* (London, 1680), p. 127.

98. Ibid.

99. Quoted in Robert Adolph, *Rise of Modern Prose Style*, p. 203.

100. Richard West, *The Profitableness of Piety* (London, 1671), p. 23. The judges, however, would see through "Flourishes and Fallacies."

101. St. Augustine, *On Christian Doctrine*, ed. and trans. D. W. Robertson, Jr. (Indianapolis, 1958).

102. R. F. Jones, "The Attack on Pulpit Eloquence in the Restoration," in *The 17th Century: Studies in the History of English Thought and Literature from Bacon to Pope*, by R. F. Jones et al. (Stanford, 1951), pp. 110-42; George Williamson, "The Restoration Revolt Against Enthusiasm," in *Seventeenth-Century Contexts* (Chicago, 1969), pp. 202-40; C. F. Richardson, *English Preachers and Preaching: 1640-1670* (New York, 1928); Fraser Mitchell, *English Pulpit Oratory From Andrewes to Tillotson* (London, 1931); Rolf P. Lessenich, *Elements of Pulpit Oratory in Eighteenth-Century England 1660-1800* (Kölm, 1972); Adolph, *Modern Prose Style*, pp. 190-210. See also *Style, Rhetoric, and Rhythm: Essays by Morris W. Croll*, eds. J. Max Patrick et al. (Princeton, 1966).

103. Wilkins, *Ecclesiastes* (London, 1646), and *The Gift of Prayer* (London, 1651).

104. Wilkins, *Ecclesiastes*, p. 72. See also Shapiro, *Wilkins*, pp. 70-80.

105. Wilkins, *Ecclesiastes* (1660 ed.), Preface to the Reader, and 1646 ed., pp. 42-43, 49, 71.

106. Ibid. (1646 ed.), p. 71. See also Wilkins, *Gift of Prayer*, p. 48. Wilkins was more concerned with sectarian "excess" than with the silenced court preachers.

107. Wilkins, *Essay Towards a Real Character*, Preface.

108. Wilkins, *Gift of Prayer*, p. 48. *Ecclesiastes* was issued ten times in the seven-

teenth century, and twice in the early eighteenth century. Lessenich views this work as an early neo-classic *ars concionandi*; *Elements of Pulpit Oratory*, p. 2.

Ecclesiastes was also the title of Erasmus' last work, a treatise on preaching. Erasmus' work dealt with the history of preaching, permissible rhetorical devices, and the organization of classification of the preachers' sources.

109. Edward Stillingfleet, "A Sermon Preached at a Public Ordination," in *Works* (London, 1710), I, 366-67; A. T. Hart, *William Lloyd: 1627-1717* (London, 1952), p. 222. Robert Boyle and John Evelyn, both laymen, and Herbert Croft, a latitudinarian cleric, suggest that Scripture might provide the appropriate stylistic model for a plain, but moving style (Boyle, *Some Considerations Touching the Style of Holy Scripture* [London, 1661], Evelyn, *The History of Religion: A Rational Account of the True Religion*, 2 vols. [London, 1850], I, 359-60; Croft, *The Naked Truth* [London, 1680], p. 13).

For Glanvill, see *An Essay Concerning Preaching* (London, 1687) and *A Seasonable Defense of Preaching and the Plain Way of It* (London, 1673); Cope, *Glanvill*, pp. 144-66. See also James Arderne, *Directions Concerning the Matter and Style of Sermons* (London, 1671); Parker, *Free and Impartial Censure*, p. 61; Edward Fowler, *The Principles and Practices of Certain Moderate Divines* (London, 1670), pp. 41, 104, 105, 112, 116-17. Arderne, Glanvill, and Parker were members of the Royal Society.

110. Gilbert Burnet, *History of My Own Times*, ed. O. Airy, 2 vols. (Oxford, 1897-1900), I, 339. See Louis Locke, *John Tillotson: A Study in 17th-Century Literature* (Copenhagen, 1954).

111. Tillotson, "The Necessity of Repentence and Faith," in *Works*, VIII, 223. For the connection between latitudinarian religion and neo-classic sermon style see Lessenich, *Elements of Pulpit Oratory*, passim.

112. Burnet, *History of My Own Times*, I, 339. See also 340-41. The style of the Cambridge Platonists was considered obscure and overly allegorical; Parker, *Free and Impartial Censure*, pp. 69-72, 75.

113. Locke, *An Essay Concerning Human Understanding*, Bk. III, Ch. XI, Secs. 11, 15-18.

114. Sprat, *History of the Royal Society*, pp. 111-13.

115. "Ode to the Royal Society," prefixed to Sprat's *History of the Royal Society*. Sprat's "candid style" possessed "all the Beauties Nature can impart, And all the comely Dress without the paint of Art." See Robert Hinman, *Abraham Cowley's World of Order* (Cambridge, 1960).

116. Quoted in Boris Ford, *From Dryden to Johnson* (London, 1966), pp. 54, 56, 127.

117. E.M.W. Tillyard, *The Elizabethan World Picture* (New York, 1944); Basil Willey, *The Seventeenth-Century Background*; Herschel Baker, *The Wars of Truth* (Cambridge, Mass., 1952); Douglas Bush, *Science and English Poetry* (Oxford, 1950). These works tend to emphasize the hostility between poetry and science. But see also M. Nicolson, *The Breaking of the Circle*; H. H. Rhys, ed., *Seventeeth-Century Science and the Arts* (Princeton, 1961).

118. See K. G. Hamilton, *The Two Harmonies: Poetry and Prose in the 17th Century* (Oxford, 1963); Russell Fraser, *The War Against Poetry* (Princeton, 1970).

119. Earl Miner, *The Restoration Mode: From Milton to Dryden* (Princeton, 1974), p. 43. See also *The Metaphysical Mode from Donne to Cowley* (Princeton, 1969).

120. See Fraser, *War Against Poetry*, passim.

121. Bacon's views were typical of his generation, coinciding substantially with those of Sidney. See Bacon, *Advancement of Learning*, pp. 82-85. See also Hinman, *Cowley*, pp. 92-107.

122. Locke, *Essay Concerning Human Understanding*, Bk. III, Ch. XI, Sec. 26.

123. Locke, *Some Thoughts Concerning Education*, ed. Peter Gay (New York, 1964), p. 137.

124. Quoted in Ford, *From Dryden to Johnson*, p. 206.

125. Hobbes, *Leviathan*, p. 125.

126. Hobbes, "The answer to D'Avenant's Preface" (1650), in *Literary Criticism of 17th-Century England*, ed. E. W. Taylor (New York, 1967), p. 282.

127. Ibid., p. 286.

128. Ibid.; see also p. 185; *Leviathan*, p. 60.

129. Ibid., p. 287. See also Hinman, *Cowley*, pp. 107-34.

130. Sprat, *History of the Royal Society*, pp. 414, 416, 417.

131. Ibid., p. 416; see also p. 417.

132. Hinman, *Cowley*, pp. 5-6, 92-134, 147, 154, 179.

133. Miner, *Restoration Mode*, p. 87.

134. Quoted in Willey, *Seventeenth-Century Background*, p. 228.

135. See Williamson, *Seventeenth-Century Contexts*, pp. 272-88. Dryden also explored the problem of religious certainty. See Phillip Harth, *Contexts of Dryden's Thought* (Chicago, 1968).

136. Miner, *Restoration Mode*, pp. 291, 294, 297, 300, 349, 350.

137. See Boris Penrose, *Travel and Discovery in the Renaissance* (Cambridge, 1952); J. H. Parry, *The Age of Reconnaissance* (London, 1963); J. H. Elliott, *The Old World and the New: 1492-1650* (Cambridge, 1972). For the style of travel literature, see Ray Franz, *The English Traveller and the Movement of Ideas 1660-1732* (Lincoln, Neb., 1934), pp. 48, 54-56, 59.

138. Swift could assume that his readers were familiar with the language and format of ethnography, travel, and natural history. Gulliver thus insists he had provided "a faithful history," avoided "strange improbable tayles," and would "strictly adhere to the truth." His relation would include only "plain matter of fact in the simplist manner and style" because his aim was to inform, not amuse. He recommends legislation that travelers planning to publish travel reports must swear an oath that "all he intended to print was absolutely true to the best of his knowledge"; *Gulliver's Travels* (New York, 1960), p. 313. The descriptions of Lilliput adhere to the format of natural history and chorography. See also M. K. Starkman, *Swift's Satire on Learning in "A Tale of a Tub"* (Princeton, 1950); Marjorie Nicolson and Nora Mohler, "The Scientific Background of Swift's *Voyage to Laputa*," in Nicolson, *Science and Imagination* (rpt. Hamden, Conn., 1976), pp. 110-54.

139. The Houyhnhnms, who lacked concepts of opinion and plausible reason, would affirm or deny only what was certain. They thus avoided controversy, disputes, and false and dubious propositions; *Gulliver's Travels*, p. 288. For a discussion of certainty in a religious context, see P. Harth, *Swift and Anglican Rationalism* (London, 1961).

Travel literature and "moral history" lent itself to satire and social criticism. *A Voyage Around the World* (1691) purported to provide "the whole Description" of "all the Habitable and Inhabitable . . . described as plain as Ireland in Petty's Survey." It would tell no tale but only "true real matter of fact," and would include "all the vices, follies, customs, and connundrums of Mankind" (*Voyage*, Intro.). An entirely fictional creation, George Psalmanaazer's *Historical and Geographical Description of Formosa* (1704) convinced the English scholarly community into believing that a native author had described Formosa; Knowlson, *Universal Language Schemes*, p. 125.

The distinction between fact and fiction seemed simple enough to draw. Addison easily distinguished poets and fiction writers from "historians, natural Philosophers, Travellers [and] Geographers," on the grounds that the former borrowed the "materials from outward Objects," joining them "together at their pleasure," while the latter were "obliged to follow Nature more closely," and "describe visible Objects of a real existence." Yet Addison went on to blur the distinction, commenting that talented historians might, with more "Art than Veracity," create such an "admirable Picture" that the "Reader becomes a kind of Spectator, and feels himself all the Variety of Passions which are correspondent to the several Parts of the Relation." He also suggested that the theories and discoveries of the New Philosophy might engage the fancy as well as the Reason; *Spectator*, No. 420. See also No. 521.

140. Ian Watt, *The Rise of the Novel* (Berkeley, 1974). But see also Maximillian Novak, "Fiction and Society in the Early 18th Century," *England in the Restoration and Early 18th Century: Essays in Culture and Society*, ed. H. T. Swedenberg (Berkeley, 1972), pp. 51-70; Wayne Booth, *The Rhetoric of Fiction* (Chicago, 1961). Though there are disputes as to whether or not readers were intended to consider narrators reliable, it is safe to assume early eighteenth-century audiences were familiar with the conventions of the factual report. Whether these were employed sincerely or satirized, early modern novelists adopted current conventions about eyewitnesses and hearsay. They shaped public fascination with "matter of fact" into new literary genres. See also Leo Braudy, *Narrative Form in History and Fiction* (Princeton, 1970); Lennard Davis, "A Social History of Fact and Fiction: Authorial Disavowal in the Early English Novel," in *Literature and Society*, ed. Edward W. Said (Baltimore, 1980). Davis emphasizes the contribution of journalism. For early eighteenth-century French literature, see Geoffrey Atkinson, *Prelude to the Enlightenment: French Literature 1690-1740* (London, 1971), pp. 135, 176.

141. Daniel Defoe, *Robinson Crusoe* (New York, 1961), Preface.

142. Ian Watt, "Defoe as Novelist," in Ford, *From Dryden to Johnson*, p. 206.

143. *Moll Flanders* (New York, 1950), Author's Preface.

144. See Joseph Frank, *The Beginnings of the English Newspaper: 1620-1660* (Cambridge, 1961).

145. Ibid., p. 43.

146. Ibid., p. 214; see also pp. 40, 54, 68, 74, 76, 85, 122, 188, 214, 234, 300.

147. Ibid., p. 97; see also pp. 10, 29, 40.

148. Ibid., p. 85.

149. Ibid., p. 54; see also pp. 187, 188, 228-29.

150. They did not live up to their goals. Many were conceived as instruments of propaganda or reform.

151. Quoted in Lois Schwoerer, "Press and Parliament in the Revolution of 1689," *The Historical Journal*, 20 (1977), pp. 558-59.

CHAPTER VIII: CONCLUSION

1. For important exceptions see Christopher Hill, *Intellectual Origins of the English Revolution* (Oxford, 1965); Theodore K. Rabb, *The Struggle for Stability in Early Modern Europe* (New York, 1975).

2. Thomas Kuhn, "Mathematical versus Experimental Traditions in the Development of Physical Science," in *The Essential Tension: Selected Studies in Scientific Tradition and Change* (Chicago, 1977).

INDEX

Academia dei Lincei, 169
Académie française, 169
Academy of Sciences, 73
Acontio, Jacopo, 8, 77, 122, 298n
Acosta, José, 122-23, 140
Act of Uniformity, 111, 295n
Addison, Joseph, 157, 160, 221, 257, 322n, 331n
Ady, Thomas, 218, 317n, 318n
aesthetics, 92, 94
Agricola, Rudolph, 227, 230, 231, 325n
Alciato, Andreo, 163-64
allegory, 238, 254
amplification, 229, 232, 237, 256
"ancient constitution," 164, 166
ancients and moderns, 122-23
Andrewes, Lancelot, 252, 256
Anglicans, 78, 79, 95, 107, 110-11, 157; adiaphora 78, 108; church fathers, 293n; comprehension, 79, 101, 110-11; theologians, 74-75, 101. See also latitudinarians
annals, 139
anthropology, 128, 298n
antiquarian movement, 121, 127, 128-29, 131, 134, 135-39, 143-47, 152, 249, 299-301, 303n, 309n; and natural science, 136, 305n. See also history
aphorism, 234-35, 236, 239
appearance, 3, 9, 70
Aquinas, Thomas, 7, 8, 17. See also Thomism
Arbuthnot, John, 55, 277n
archeology, 136
Aristotelians, 6, 8, 68, 93, 218, 270; and Gassendi, 39; physics, 148; science, 7-8, 15; Topics, 292n. See also scholasticism

Aristotle, 6, 18, 22, 69, 78, 83, 88, 103, 139, 201, 230; dialectic, 230-31; philosophical discourse, 230, 236; rhetoric, 235; and virtuosi, 64
archives, 144
Ascham, Roger, 235
assent, 181; Barrow, 98, 292n; Boyle, 100; collective, 64; compelled, 6, 32, 33, 35, 41, 65, 72, 84, 156; Hale, 97; levels of, 27-37; More, 90; natural sciences, 21, 25; suspended, 21, 33, 116; Tillotson, 103; Wilkins, 85, 86; voluntary, 43. See also demonstration
astrology, 38, 277n
astronomy, 45, 69, 170, 278-79; and scripture, 159
atheism, 86, 95, 104, 106-107, 158, 318n; repudiation of, 83, 97; and witchcraft, 207, 210, 211, 212, 216, 319n
Atkyns, Sir Robert, 170
atomism, 7, 46-47, 83, 93, 107
Aubrey, John, 129, 136, 152, 153, 170, 217, 303n, 305n, 320n
authority, 10, 21, 27, 32, 106, 109, 114, 116, 213, 229; Barrow, 98, 292n; church fathers, 79, 80; humanists, 19; in the natural sciences, 17, 20, 64, 72, 113; rejection of, 113, 229; in religion, 74-75, 78, 79, 80, 105; in rhetoric, 38, 105, 229; scripture, 75; Tillotson, 103; Wilkins, 40
axioms, Bacon, 24, 27; civil, 125; historical, 138; metaphysical, 28, 81; natural sciences, 24, 25, 26, 27, 49, 51, 67, 115, 125

Bacon, Francis, 14, 15, 22, 38, 45, 59, 63, 68-69, 84, 138, 152, 169, 268-69, 270, 285n, 329n; ancients and mod-

Bacon, Francis (*cont.*)
  erns, 122-23; certitude, 38-39, 67,
  139-40; dialectic, 324-25n; "forms,"
  24, 25, 67; historical classification,
  125, 126, 128, 129, 131, 132, 133;
  historical thought and writing, 130,
  132, 134, 135, 137, 142, 144, 146,
  155, 165, 306n; and humanism, 18;
  hypothesis, 46, 67; *Idols*, 61-62, 63,
  66, 82, 146, 219, 233; influence of,
  66-69 (*see also* Baconianism); law,
  165, 168-69; language and style,
  233-34, 235-36, 242, 243, 260;
  mathematics, 68, 274n; natural history, 234, 286n; natural philosophy,
  9-10, 16, 18-19, 24, 46, 67, 324n;
  New Organon, 61, 63, 67; probability,
  67, 279n; religion, 79, 108; rhetoric,
  235, 236, 239; role of experience,
  70, 267; and Royal Society Research
  program, 10, 18-27, 47, 49, 66, 67,
  70, 286n; scientific communication,
  233-35, 236; and skepticism, 19,
  149, 273-74n; witchcraft, 200-201,
  213, 215, 316n
Baconianism, 9-10, 18-27, 35-36, 46,
  49, 66, 69, 154, 269, 286n; of Hooke,
  56, 280n; of Newton, 56
Baronius, 155
Barrow, Isaac, 24, 35, 187, 191, 321n;
  belief and faith, 98, 103, 291n; categories of knowledge, 35-36, 98-99;
  fallibility of human knowledge, 62-
  63; hypothesis, 49-50, 276n; language and style, 251-52; latitudinarianism, 112; philosophy of science,
  17, 25, 35-36
Bates, William, 291n
Bathurst, Ralph, 112, 292n
Baxter, Richard, 206, 208, 286n, 291n,
  317n
Bechler, Zev, 283n
belief, 4, 6, 10, 29, 30, 43, 74, 78, 103,
  117; Barrow, 98-99; 291n; Melchor
  Cano, 298n; Castellio, 76-77; Charleton, 31; Chillingworth, 30; Hale,
  34, 97-98; historical, 119, 156-58;
  Hooke, 35; rational, 158; religious,
  99, 271, 272, 393n; scientific, 35, 99;

scriptural, 156-58; Stillingfleet, 95,
  102. *See also* faith
Benthan, Jeremy, 182
Bentley, Richard, 220
de Bergerac, Cyrano, 223
Bernard, Richard, 203-204, 205, 211,
  316n
Beza, Theodore, 77
bias, eyewitness, 141; historical, 147-
  48, 149, 305n; juries, 176; reporting,
  228, 261-62, 264; rhetorical, 229-30
bias, 5, 6, 219, 227, 228, 256
Biddle, John, 292n
biography, 131-32. *See also* history
Biondo, Flavio, 121, 122, 128, 162
Blackstone, William, 182
Blasphemy Act, 190
Boate, Gerard, 129
Bodin, Jean, 123, 222, 223, 224, 299n,
  322n
Boguet, Henri, 222, 223, 224
Boileau-Despréaux, Nicholas, 260
Bolingbroke, Henry St. John, Viscount, 144, 303n, 304n, 307n
Bolton, Edmund, 165, 316n
book of nature, 94, 159, 271, 291n
Book of Scripture, 271. *See also* Scripture
botany, 122, 126
Boyle, Robert, 13, 24, 66, 67, 70, 104,
  107, 140, 167, 171, 179, 193, 213,
  218, 296n; categories of knowledge,
  31, 34, 99; corpuscular hypothesis,
  46-48, 88; experience, 99, 100; hypothesis, 46-47, 53-54, 56, 67, 281n;
  matters of fact, 99, l00; natural history, 129; natural philosophy, 17,
  20-21, 28, 30, 31, 34, 53-54, 62,
  276n; physical certainty, 30, 31;
  probability, 42, 52; religion, 99-100,
  112, 295n; Revelation, 99, 100; scientific discourse, 64, 239, 286n;
  senses, 22-23, 281n; universal character, 244; witnesses and testimony,
  100, 187, 274n, 313n; witchcraft,
  215-17, 220, 321n
Brady, Robert, 143
Brahe, Tycho, 44, 45, 51, 278n
Brathwaite, Richard, 125, 128, 165

Brooke, Fulke Greville, 1st Baron, 152
Browne, Thomas, 153, 207, 208, 318n
Burnet, Gilbert, 107, 113, 140, 141, 142, 143, 147, 155, 255, 295, 303n, 309n
Burnet, Thomas, 54-56, 127, 159, 282n
Bushell's Case, 183, 314n

Caesar, Julius, 157, 303n
Calvin, John, 77, 79
Calvinists, 76, 87, 293n
Cambridge Platonists, 83, 88, 106-107, 112, 319n, 329n
Cambridge, University of, 13, 112
Camden, William, 128, 129, 130, 131, 134, 136, 137, 150, 151, 153, 155, 247, 304n, 306n
Cano, Melchor, 123, 298n
Car, Nicholas, 235
Carew, Richard, 128
Carneades, 37, 276n
Cartesians, 52, 54, 68, 73; criticisms of, 25; and history, 124; hypothesis, 46, 56; physics, 45, 46, 56. See also Descartes, hypothesis
Casaubon, Meric, 218, 319n, 321n
Castellio, Sebastien, 76-77
casuistry, 37, 39, 69, 105, 106
causes, 70; analysis of, 32-33; Bacon, 24; explanation of, 17, 25, 26, 27, 32-33, 41, 47, 71, 139, 149, 150; Glanvill, 48; Hooke, 52; Locke, 42; Royal Society, 40. See also explanation, hypothesis
certainty, 3, 8-10, 16, 17, 28, 29-30, 139, 182, 213; Bacon, 14, 67; Chillingworth, 81; degrees of, 8, 123, 268, 271; Descartes, 14; Glanvill, 48; in history, 121; Huygens, 43; in law, 11, 168, 178-79, 180, 183, 189; in natural science, 25; latitudinarians, 114-15; Locke, 181-82; mathematical, 28, 85, 102; Newton, 56-57; physical, 30, 31, 32, 102, 122; in religion, 76; of Scripture, 156-57; Stillingfleet, 102; Tillotson, 30; Wilkins, 85. See also moral certainty, demonstration probability

Chancery, 178, 197, 312n
character, universal, see universal language and character
Charleton, Walker, 17, 39, 136, 140, 151, 152; atomism, 46; and Bacon, 67; common notions, 89, 90; hypothesis, 50, 281n; philosophy of science, 22, 23, 34-35, 62; poetry, 248; style, 326n; theory of knowledge, 22-23, 30-31, 62; universal language, 245
charity, religious, 80, 104-105, 110, 114
Charron, Pierre, 286n
Childrey, Joshua, 239, 300n
Chillingworth, William, 32, 40, 80-82, 103, 117, 140; categories of knowledge, 30; rule of faith controversy, 101; Scripture, 95
chorography, 122, 126-28, 130, 136-37, 271, 330n. See also topography, history, antiquarians
Christ, 88, 99
Christianity, 6, 27, 61, 256, 271; rationality of, 14, 74, 88, 94-101. See also Revelation, Scripture
chronology, 154, 158, 159
church fathers, 79, 80, 109, 283n
Cicero, 90, 120, 121, 125, 148, 235, 250, 286n
Ciceronians, 121
civil law, see law, Roman law
Clarendon, Edward Hyde, Earl of, 130, 132, 141, 170
classification, historical, 124, 125, 129, 131, 132, 133, 138; legal, 168, 172; philosophical, 244-45; scientific, 23, 24, 168, 172
clergy, 13, 27
Cohen, Jonathan, 277n
Coke, Sir Edward, 177-78, 251, 310n, 316n
common consent, 76, 89, 90-91, 94, 101, 106, 201, 202
common fame, 158, 174, 199, 204, 222. See also presumptions, legal
common notions, 89-90, 107. See also innate ideas
communication, 227-66; religious, 252-

communication (*cont.*)
55; philosophical and scientific, 232-45

confession, 174, 175, 194, 195, 197-99, 203, 204, 205, 209-10, 222, 225, 316n

conjecture, 3, 4, 11, 26, 47, 55, 56, 181; Boyle, 53, 281n; history, 149-51, 152; Hooke, 35, 51; natural philosophy, 25, 279n, 281-82n; on causes, 26, 46, 47, 71, 73; Ray, 282n; witchcraft, 200, 203

conscience, 105

consent, universal, 42. *See also* common consent

Cooper, Anthony Ashley, Earl of Shaftsbury, 170

Cooper, Thomas, 202-203

cooperation, intellectual, 5, 153-54; historical, 124, 306n; natural sciences, 64, 65, 66, 116

Copernican hypothesis, 22, 40, 44-45, 46, 50, 51, 60, 68, 158, 167, 278n, 279n. *See also* hypothesis

copia, 231, 235, 256

corpuscular hypothesis, 53, 60, 68. *See also* hypothesis

cosmography, 126, 128

Cotes, Roger, 284

Cotta, John, 200-202

Cotton, Robert, 143, 165

courts, 81, 178, 197. *See also* law, trials

Cowley, Abraham, 257, 260, 261

creation, 93, 127, 158, 159; Hale, 97, 98; Stillingfleet, 95, 96

credibility, 4, 277n; witnesses, 167, 168, 179, 180, 182, 183-88, 190; linked to frequency, 277n. *See also* testimony, witnesses

Cudsworth, Ralph, 112, 212

custom, 108, 149

customs, 122, 136; description of, 128, 129, 262

Dalgarno, George, 244

Dalton, Michael, 177, 204, 205, 316n

Daniel, Samuel, 130, 248

Davila, Enrico, 121, 298n, 303n

deism, 88, 293n

demonstration, 3, 5, 8, 27, 29, 31, 34-35, 36-38, 41, 182; impossible in law, 189; inappropriate in religion, 80, 83, 89, 97, 156, 157; mathematical, 16, 30 32, 44, 54, 72, 77, 84, 95, 96, 97, 118, 267n, 271, 276n. *See also* certainty

Descartes, René, 14, 15, 38, 46, 60, 64, 68-69, 96, 167, 212, 218, 282n; certain knowledge, 39, 140, 267; hypothesis, 45, 46, 280n; philosophical language, 244

description, 226, 262-63, 330n; chorographical, 128, 129, 130; geographical, 121; historical, 121, 128, 130; natural, 23, 122, 128, 130; social, 122, 128, 129, 130; language of, 12; Locke, 43. *See also* matters of fact

devil, 194, 195, 201, 204, 214, 218

dialectic, 6, 27, 38, 125, 228, 230, 256; Bacon, 324-25n; new, 236; and rhetoric, 230-32; scholastic, 242

dictionaries, 227, 238, 243, 244

Digby, Sir Kenelm, 293n

disciplines, compartmentalization of, 269; links among, 12-13

discourse, 232; historical, 246-50; legal, 250-52; philosophy and natural science, 115-16, 230, 232-45, 287n; popular, 228; religious, 116-17, 252-55; unified art of, 8, 231, 236, 239, 242. *See also* style

disputation, 242, 256

dissenters, 109, 110

documents, historical, 166, 249; legal, 166, 167, 176. *See also* history

dogmatism, 17, 41, 62, 68, 149, 253; among Cartesians, 39, 64; rejection by latitudinarians, 109, 110, 114, 116-17; rejection by natural scientists, 26-27, 65, 66, 68, 69, 72; in religion, 69, 76, 78, 80, 108, 112

Donne, John, 252, 256, 259

Douglas, David, 149

Drayton, Michael, 248

Drury, John, 169

Dryden, John, 252, 257, 258, 260, 261, 329n

Dugdale, William, 128-29

Dunscumbe, Giles, 204, 205

Echard, Laurence, 130
eloquence, 120, 230, 233, 243, 256-57, 273n; in history, 249; in law, 251, 252. *See also* rhetoric, discourse, style
Elyot, Sir Thomas, 250, 252, 328n
empiricism, 8, 9, 10, 15, 72, 270-71, 280n; and humanism, 269-70; and probability, 12, 38, 39
Enlightenment, 270-71
Ent, George, 305n
enthusiasm, religious, 83, 95, 109, 114, 156
epistemology, 13, 117, 119, 121, 154, 182, 261, 268. *See also* knowledge, certainty, moral certainty, demonstration, senses
Eramus, Desiderius, 75-76, 108, 122, 288
eternality of the world, 97, 159
ethics, 100-101, 104-105, 106; natural, 88-89, 132; Christian, 188
ethnography, 122
Evelyn, John, 95-96, 134, 142, 274n
evidence, 3, 8, 140, 197; credibility of, 180; concurring, 187; hearsay, 199; in law, 163, 171-72, 174-83, 187, 311n; Locke, 179; in matters of fact, 180; probable, 192; Wilkins, 85, 86; in witchcraft, 199, 214, 222, 316n. *See also* law, witnesses
experience, 6, 8, 9, 38, 70, 140, 229; Acosta, 123; Bacon, 18; Barrow, 36; Boyle, 21; communication of, 232; historical, 145; Hooker, 79; humanists, 70; lack of definition, 140; natural sciences, 15, 16, 19, 38; Tillotson, 30
experiment, 19, 26, 47, 70, 115, 281n; Boyle, 53; Hooke, 50; Huygens, 43; Locke, 42; Newton, 283n; Royal Society, 21; Wilkins, 40; Wren, 48
experimental science, 9, 15-73
explanation, Boyle, 52, 53; causal, 11, 17, 25, 26, 27, 41, 47, 71, 137, 139, 279n; historical, 123-24, 130, 131, 134, 137, 139, 149-154. *See also* causes, hypothesis, conjecture

fables, 123, 146, 147, 156, 200, 247
fact, 7, 9, 12, 33, 38, 71, 125; histori-cal, 11, 120, 135, 139, 271, 303; natural, 139; statements of, 227-28. *See also* matters of fact, history, natural history
Fairfax, Edward, 205
Falkland, Lucius Cary, 2d Viscount, 79, 80, 101, 103
fancy, 259, 260, 262
faith, 6, 74, 117, 154, 156, 158; Barrow, 98, 103; Chillingworth, 8, 30; Hale, 97-98; Stillingfleet, 102; Tillotson, 103. *See also* belief
fallibility, 40, 80, 113, 115, 116, 149; judgment, 108-109; of knowledge, 5, 53, 61-66, 72; in religion, 79; of the senses, 5, 22, 33, 62, 272
fictions, 4, 12, 121, 160, 216, 247, 257, 261, 262-64, 272, 331n; historical, 141, 150; hypothesis, 46, 47; mathematical, 44-45; poetic, 256-57
fideism, 76
figures of speech, 229, 231-32, 233, 236, 238. *See also* language, rhetoric, poetry
Filmer, Sir Robert, 205-206, 317n
Flamsteed, John, 171, 309n
Flood, 127, 158, 159, 282n
Foley, Paul, 166
Fontenelle, Bernard de, 73
Fortescue, Sir John, 8, 178
France, 72, 164; historians, 123-24; law, 173, 175; Reformation, 77; skepticism, 22, 23, 76, 149; witch-craft, 221-24
Fraunce, Abraham, 250
free will, 109
Fuller, Thomas, 132, 155
Fussner, Frank, 150, 161, 297n, 305n

Gale, Thomas, 151, 152
Galileo, 15, 38, 39, 40, 45-46, 66, 68, 69, 121, 158, 167, 218, 279n, 282n
Gassendi, Pierre, 39, 40, 46-47, 167, 277n, 286n, 323n
generalization, Barrow, 36; Boyle, 53; historical, 132, 138, 139; human be-havior, 132; legal, 168-69; natural sciences, 17, 24, 25, 26, 35, 36, 44, 53, 71, 97, 138, 281n. *See also* the-ory, axioms, maxims

general reader, 246, 247, 249, 250
gentlemen, ·13, 167
geography, 122, 126, 127, 128, 129,
    130, 153, 160, 170, 301n, 331n
geology, 5, 127, 128, 159
geometry, 46, 235, 236, 278n
Germany, 121, 122
Gibbon, Edward, 145, 249, 329n
Gibson, Edmund, 153, 154, 309n
Gifford, George, 199
Gilbert, Sir Geoffrey, 166, 167, 171,
    193, 309n, 311n; evidence, 180-82,
    183
Gilbert, William, 230, 232
Glanvill, Joseph, 17, 21, 32, 43, 67, 73,
    113, 158, 286n; axioms and theory,
    48, 49; Cambridge Platonists, 107;
    categories of knowledge, 31; dogma-
    tism, 41; enthusiasm, 109; grace,
    293n; hypothesis, 279-80n; language
    and style, 64, 255; latitudinarianism,
    113, 295n; moral certitude, 41; nat-
    ural history, 49; probability, 42; on
    religion and science, 113, 144; pro-
    pagandist of science, 113; scientific
    discourse, 116, 238; skepticism, 62;
    theory of knowledge, 23, 28, 116;
    witchcraft, 212-18, 220, 225, 319n,
    320n
God, 29, 194, 212; attributes, 87; exist-
    ence proved, 68, 83, 87, 88, 92-94,
    96, 99, 113, 220
Goddard Jonathan, 112
grace, 83, 87
grammar, 120, 227, 260
grand jury, 176, 177, 188-89, 316n; in
    witchcraft trials, 194, 195, 196, 203,
    204, 205, 211, 226. See also juries
Graunt, John, 130, 277n, 302n
gravitation, 52, 58, 60, 221
Great Tew Circle, 78, 79, 80, 293n
Gresham College, 170
Grew, Nathaniel, 20, 305n
Grotius, Hugo, 77-78, 82, 117, 169,
    303n; proof, 273n
Guicciardini, Francesco, 120, 130, 141,
    162, 298n, 303n

Hacking, Ian, 38, 277n
Hahn, Roger, 73

Hakluyt, Richard, 129, 262
Hale, Sir Matthew, 97, 309n, 318n;
    evidence, 180, 182, 276n; faith, 97-
    98; and Hobbes, 166, 172; language,
    251, 252; latitudinarianism, 111,
    296n; law, 97, 166, 168, 177, 180,
    182-83, 184-85,190,191, 251, 312n,
    318n; matters of fact, 98; natural
    science, 26, 171-73; probability, 93,
    184; Scripture, 93, 97, 158; varieties
    of knowledge, 34, 97-98; witchcraft
    trials, 206-208, 209, 314n, 318n; wit-
    nesses, 180-81, 184, 185-87
Hales, John, 80, 289n
Hall, Marie Boas, 280n
Halley, Edmund, 58, 305n
happiness, 36, 87, 89, 105
Harrison, William, 128
Hartlib, Samuel, 129, 169, 244
Harvey, William, 50, 218
Hawles, Sir John, 188-89, 191-92, 251-
    52
Hayward, Sir John, 130, 146
hearsay, 21, 123, 312n
heraldry, 127
Herbert, Lord of Cherbury, 89, 135,
    137, 146
hermeticism, 117, 196
Heylyn, Peter, 126-27, 305n
Hill, Abraham, 305n
Hill, Christopher, 74
historians, ancient, 146, 147, 248; Eng-
    lish, 124-62; French, 123-24, 140,
    164, 299n; German, 122; Italian,
    120-22, 140, 163; Spanish, 122
historical revelation, 161
history, 7, 9, 10-11, 13, 28, 31, 33, 71,
    119-62, 227-29, 268-69, 270-71,
    297n, 337; archives, 124; belief, 119,
    156-58; civil, 97, 123, 125, 126, 128,
    129, 130-33, 135, 137, 138, 139,
    140, 141, 143, 145-46, 155, 165, 213
    271, 298n, 306n; classification, 124,
    125, 129, 131, 132, 133, 138; con-
    temporary, 141-42, 158, 303n;
    county, 128, 136; discourse, 246-50;
    documents, 135, 136, 139, 142, 143,
    141-46, 150, 154, 155, 164, 166,
    167; ecclesiastical, 155-56, 159,
    306n; faith, 95, 96, 97; and fiction,

263-64; invented speech, 146, 147, 247; and law, 119, 163-67, 178-79, 180; lessons of, 121; and literature, 148; narration, 134, 136, 138, 143-45, 147-49; natural, 97, 120, 125, 126, 128-29, 130-31, 133, 137-39, 140, 142, 143, 145-46, 159, 165, 213, 272, 280n; and natural science, 119-21, 126, 136, 138, 148, 152, 154, 160-62, 246-47; "perfect," 123-24, 130-39, 142, 144, 150, 152, 271; and poetry, 247, 248, 260; "politic," 130, 131, 146; and probable knowledge and religion, 77, 119, 154-60, 271; and proofs of witchcraft, 213-15; research, 122, 135, 137; and rhetoric, 11, 119, 120-22, 130, 132, 146, 148, 151, 160, 163, 247-49, 298n, 327n; sources, 10, 121, 123, 124, 125, 133, 137-38, 142-44; terminology, 139; truth of, 120, 221; *See also* antiquarians, natural history, witnesses, testimony, belief, faith

Hobbes, Thomas, 39-40, 83-84, 87-88, 94, 125, 166, 172, 319n; denial of incorporeal substance, 221, 319n; language, 235-36, 242; poetry, 248, 259, 260

Holder, William, 244

Holinshed, Ralph, 128

Holt, Sir John, 191, 208, 312n

Hooke, Robert, 17, 24, 48, 53, 68, 72, 126, 140, 153, 167, 283n; and Bacon, 25, 35, 67, 280n; causal explanations, 25, 53; fallibility of the senses, 22-23; geology, 51, 127; hypothesis, 50-52, 56, 58, 67, 276n, 280n, 283n-84n; and Newton, 56-57, 65; philosophy of science, 25, 35, 50-52; probability, 41; rejection of dogmatism, 115-16; universal language, 246; scientific discourse, 238-39

Hooker, Richard, 78, 79, 82, 117

Hopkins, Matthew, 206, 317n

Hoskins, Sir John, 153, 170

Howell, James, 134

humanism, 15, 122, 162, 267, 269-70; dialectic, 230-31; and empiricism, 269-70; and history, 119, 132, 161;

and law, 250-51, 307n; and natural sciences, 13, 18, 19, 122, 136, 160-62, 269, 273n; and poetry, 256; Renaissance, 3, 6-9, 70, 119, 120, 161; and rhetoric, 230-31, 273n; term "humanist," 152, 269

humanities, 160-62

Hume, David, 89

humility, 62, 98, 116, 153, 154

Hutchinson, Francis, 209, 318n

Huygens, Christian, 73, 278n, 281n, 284n; hypothesis, 43, 281n; probability, 43-44

hypothesis, 3, 11, 33, 44-61, 114, 116, 146, 278-79n, 280n, 371; atomical, 68, 107, 151; Bacon, 46, 67; Boyle, 67; Charleton, 50, 281n; corpuscular, 281n; Descartes, 45, 46, 56, 280n; geological, 159; Glanvill, 62, 279-80n; Hale, 172; historical, 149-52, 151, 152; Hooke, 50-52, 56, 58, 67, 276n, 280n, 283n-84n; Huygens, 43, 281n; Locke, 42, 59-60, 284n, 285n; medical, 281n; mechanical, 280n; Newton, 54, 56-58, 151, 282n, 283n, 284n; and probability, 277n; Royal Society, 26-27, 47, 56, 60, 270n; scientific, 16, 17, 25, 26, 37, 41, 62, 66, 70, 71, 168; Stillingfleet, 97. *See also* Copernican hypothesis, conjecture

imagination, 9, 149, 213-14, 238, 239, 242, 257

impartiality, of grandjurors, 188, of historians, 142, 147-49, 150, 155, 192; of judges, 190-92; of natural scientists, 192. *See also* bias

"indices," 222. *See also* signs, presumption

indictment, 188, 189, 199, 204

induction, 25, 35, 36, 85, 283n, 284n

infallibility, in natural science, 64; in religion, 10, 78, 79, 80, 82, 101-104, 114, 117

innate ideas, 89-92, 101, 102, 106

Inns of Court, 13, 164, 170, 208

interest, calculations of, 88, 108, 290n

Interregnum, 104, 108, 110, 111-12, 253

intuition, 37
invective, 248

Jacob, Margaret, 292n
James I, 199-200, 315n, 317n
Jardine, Lisa, 324n
Jesuits, 76, 288n
Jewel, John, 79, 155
Jones, Inigo, 136, 151
journalism, 264, 265, 272. *See also* description, newspaper, matters of fact
judges, 11, 28, 81-82, 149, 167, 170, 173, 175, 179-80, 183, 184, 186-87, 190-93, 314n, 328n; impartiality, 147-48; Romano-canon, 174, 175, 176; witchcraft trials, 194-96, 198, 199, 205, 206-208, 209-11, 213, 218, 222-26. *See also* trials, law
judgment, 259, 260; historical, 133; juries, 177-78; suspension of, 86
jury, 11, 176, 177, 178, 181, 182, 183, 185-89, 192, 193, 194, 272, 310-12n, 314n; in witchcraft trials, 194, 196, 203, 205-208, 209, 210, 211, 225-26. *See also* trials, law, grand-jury
justices of the peace, 176, 177, 178; witchcraft cases, 194-96, 204, 205, 210, 211, 226, 316n

Kargon, Robert, 280n
Kennett, White, 151, 154, 155
Kepler, Johannes, 45, 46, 68, 278-79n, 282n
Keyling, John, 207
Kilbourne, Richard, 177, 310n
King, Gregory, 153
knowledge, 3, 5, 9, 10, 42, 43, 44, 47, 152; Barrow, 98; Boyle, 99; Castellio, 76; categories, 27-37, 81, 84-86, 97-98, 99, 103; changing conceptions, 267; Chillingworth, 81; demonstrable, 139, 272; fallibility of, 53, 61-66, 72; Hale, 97-98; probable, 139, 140, 152, 161; progressive nature of, 123; Tillotson, 85; Wilkins, 85-86. *See also* "science," moral certainty, demonstation, certainty, probability, reasonable doubt
Kuhn, Thomas, 73, 154, 271, 284n

Lambarde, William, 128, 164-65, 177, 306n, 316n
Langbein, John, 175
language, 8, 12, 227-66; ambiguity in, 229-30, 232, 236, 237-39, 256, 259, 261; clarity of, 232, 243, 247, 252; non-assertive, 64; ornamentation, 229, 231, 237-38, 239, 252, 256, 257; scientists, 65; universal language and character, 12, 227, 243-46. *See also* discourse, style
latitudinarianism, 10, 14, 75, 78, 104-11, 140, 255-56, 268, 271, 292n, 293n; discourse and style, 253-55, 255, 329n; Great Tew Circle, 80; hostility towards, 296n; moral certainty, 294n; moral righteousness, 94; and natural science, 104, 111-17, 295n; rationality of Scripture, 95. *See also* natural religion
Latin, 243
law, 9, 31, 33, 71, 153, 163-93, 227, 268, 270-71, 272; Anglo-Saxon, 166; canon law, 310n; civil (Roman) law, 123, 164, 173-76, 178, 184, 222, 250, 307, 311n; civil law influence on English witch trials, 197-98, 204; classification, 168; and history, 119, 163-67, 178-79, 180; language and discourse, 250-52, 256; natural law, 94, 291n; and natural science, 167-93; presumptions, 174, 175; rational science, 169; and rhetoric, 163, 164, 250-52; Roman-canonist procedure, 173-78, 310n; systematization, 168, 172. *See also* trials, judges, juries, lawyers, evidence, matters of fact, confession, torture, reasonable doubt, satisfied conscience
law, French, 251
lawyers, 13, 113, 134, 167, 169, 173, 178
legal profession, 13, 208, 211, 222, 250, 270
legends, 123, 146
Leibniz, Gottfried Wilhelm, 49, 181, 277n, 284n, 327n
Leland, John, 128, 153
Levack, Brian, 323n
Lhuyd, Edward, 55, 303n

libraries, 124, 125, 143, 165
Lister, Martin, 20, 23, 136
literature, 7, 9, 12, 119, 121, 137, 269, 272
Lloyd, William, 107, 113, 255, 295n
Locke, John, 13, 14, 15, 17, 63, 70, 72, 82, 94, 104, 167, 170, 179, 193, 255, 284n, 293n; belief, 100-101; categories of knowledge, 31-32, 37; dictionaries, 326n; empiricism, 268, 269; *Essay Concerning Human Understanding*, 101, 143; ethics, 100-101; evidence and testimony, 179, 183; hypothesis, 42, 59-60, 284n, 285n; innate ideas, 90, 91, 101, 102; language and communication, 239-42, 246, 251, 255, 256, 257, 286n; natural history, 59; natural religion, 88, 92; and Newton, 60, 285n; probable knowledge, 42-43, 59, 140; poetry, 259; reasonableness of Revelation, 94, 100-101; Royal Society, 59; Scripture as history, 158; theory, 59, 285n; theory of knowledge, 28, 31-32, 263, 284n; and Toland, 292-93n; toleration, 110-11; witchcraft, 221
logic, 4, 5, 6, 7, 9, 15, 37, 71, 120, 140, 227, 228, 230-31, 260, 261; ancient, 163; Aristotelian, 6, 227, 232, 239; Charleton, 34; inductive, 231, 277n; Leibniz, 181, 277n; and poetry, 256, 260; *Port Royal Logic*, 277n; scholastic, 8, 18, 27, 67, 127, 235, 242; and universal language, 245; Wallis, 34; Wilkins, 86. *See also* "science," demonstration
Lucian, 248
Luther, Martin, 75-76

Machiavelli, Niccolò, 120, 130, 141, 298n
Mackenzie, George, 324n
Magdeburg Centuries, 155
Malleus malificarum, 222
Mandrou, Robert, 223, 224, 323n
maps, 122, 128
Marvell, Andrew, 147
materialism, 83, 212, 221
mathematics, 8, 9, 16, 23, 27, 28, 31, 32, 44, 72, 170; Bacon, 68; Charle-

ton, 30, 34; and language, 239, 260; "mixed," 23-24, 32; proofs, 28, 35; Tillotson, 85; Wallis, 34; Wilkins, 31. *See also* demonstration
matter, 87-88, 194
matters of fact, 3, 12, 55, 71, 103, 104, 140, 152, 157, 192, 267, 271, 272, 330n; appropriate proofs, 28-29; Boyle, 100; communication of, 232, 237; Grotius, 77; Hale, 98; history, 119, 138, 143, 158, 164, 179; law, 163, 165, 176, 178; language of, 261; and literature, 261, 263-64, 330n, 331n; Locke, 42, 43; narrations of, 147; natural history and natural science, 19-22, 36, 71; reporting, 264-65; Scripture, 95, 157, 158, 291n; Stillingfleet, 95; Tillotson, 30, 85, 103; witchcraft cases, 194, 213, 214, 217, 219-20. *See also* history, natural history, witnesses, testimony
maxims, 97, 130; legal, 168-69; natural sciences, 234-35, 236. *See also* generalization, axioms
mechanical philosophy, 83, 107, 212, 215-16, 220
medicine, 30, 277n
Melanchthon, Phillip, 230, 231
Merrett, Christopher, 23
Mersenne, Marin, 46, 223, 244, 323n
Merton, Robert K., 74
metaphor, 236, 237, 238, 239, 253, 256
metaphysics, 24, 25-26, 47, 64, 114
Middlefort, Erik, 224
Milton, John, 146, 249, 327n
Miner, Earl, 258, 261
miracles, 93, 100, 103, 157
moderation, 104, 110, 112, 116
Momigliano, Arnaldo, 297n
Montaigne, Michel de, 22, 23, 61, 223-24, 274n, 323n
Monter, E. W., 224, 322n, 323n
moral certainty, 4, 10, 16, 17, 28, 31-33, 40, 55, 71, 103, 104, 118, 272; Boyle, 41, 313n; category of knowledge, 84; Chillingworth, 30, 81; Glanvill, 41; of God's existence, 92; Hooke, 35; in history, 139, 149, 151,

moral certainty (*cont.*)
161, 164; and hypothesis, 50; in law,
179, 180, 272, 311n, 313n; latitudinarians, 294n; link with probability,
277n; in natural science, 36, 37; in
religion, 78, 157; of Scripture, 94,
97; Stillingfleet, 96, 102; Tillotson,
30, 103; Wilkins, 40, 86. *See also* certainty
morality, 80, 104, 106, 107, 108
moral philosophy, 7, 120, 132, 138,
156, 269
Moray, Sir Robert, 142, 295n
More, Henry, 83, 90, 107, 112; witchcraft, 212-13, 215, 216, 218, 220,
225, 318n, 319n, 320n
More, Thomas, 130, 262
Moses, 96, 127, 156; as an historian,
96, 159. *See also* Scripture du Moulin, Peter, 216
myth, 146, 156

narration, 260-61; appropriate style,
234, 256; Bacon, 24, 200; Boyle, 53;
T. Burnet, 54-55; Glanvill, 49; historical, 121, 122, 133, 328n; matters
of fact, 263-65; natural history, 11,
19-21, 22, 23, 36, 47, 49, 54, 67,
122, 248, 262, 263, 280n, 302n, 323-
24, 330n; of travel and discovery,
228, 262-63; reliable, 331. *See also*
history, matters of fact
natural philosophy, 6, 9, 15-73, 133-
34, 138, 139, 227, 267; Aristotelian,
6, 7-8; and language, 232-45, 256;
and natural history, 233, 234. *See
also* philosophy, natural history
natural religion, 10, 14, 77-79, 81, 82-
89, 104, 107, 108, 113, 115, 117,
271, 272, 293n; harmony with revealed religion, 88, 94, 117
natural science, 3, 4, 7, 9-10, 13, 15-
73, 267-68, 277n; discourse, 232-45,
256; empiricism in, 119; and history,
10-11, 98; intellectual style of, 61-66,
72; and law, 167-93; model scientist,
66; and poetry, 242, 243, 257-59,
260; probabilistic, 71-72; and religion, 74-75; 104, 111-17. *See also*
Royal Society, experiment, natural
history

Nelson, Benjamin, 38-39
neoclassicism, 243, 247, 249, 260, 261,
270, 329n
neo-Platonism, 117, 196, 197, 212,
213, 225, 279n
newspaper, 12, 123, 228, 262, 264-65,
331n. *See also* matters of fact, reports
Newton, Isaac, 17, 24, 36, 66, 72, 167,
171, 221, 271, 282n, 284n, 286n;
chronological studies, 159; and
Hooke, 56-57, 65; hypothesis, 54,
56-58, 151, 282n, 283n, 284n; latitudinarianism, 112, 295n; and Locke,
60, 285n; mathematics, 35-36; philosophy of science, 56-58, 283n-84n;
poetry, 256
Nicolson, William, 55, 153-54
North, Francis, Lord Guildford, 166,
171, 185, 186, 193, 209-10, 309n,
319n
North, Roger, 192, 209
novel, 148, 228, 262, 263, 264, 331n
Nowell, Lawrence, 128

oaths, 183, 185, 186
observation, 29, 141, 267; first-hand,
121, 142, 144. *See also* witnesses, testimony, matters of fact
opinion, 3, 4, 6, 9, 15, 16, 27-29, 31,
33, 37, 42, 44, 67, 71, 74, 106, 109,
118, 140, 218, 231, 270, 272, 289n,
292n; Chillingworth, 30, 81; Cicero,
90; diversity of, 65, 66, 108, 109;
Hale, 97; historical, 147, 151; religious, 76, 77, 82, 104, 105, 108, 110,
113, 115; and rhetoric, 229; Wilkins,
31, 85, 86; zeal for, 108, 109
oratory, 147, 163, 228; Roman, 251
Oxford, University of, 68, 69, 83, 112,
113; science in, 17, 68, 69, 70, 111-
12

panegyric, 120, 147, 248
Parker, Samuel, 49, 113, 237-38, 280n,
281n, 292n
Pasquier, Étienne, 123
passion, 63, 82, 108, 148, 190, 229
Patrick, Simon, 113, 288n, 293n, 295n
patronage, 305n, 306n
Pepys, Samuel, 215
perjury, 176, 186

Perkins, William, 205-206, 317n
Pett, Sir Peter, 295n
Petty, Sir William, 112, 129, 238, 244, 277n, 321n, 322n
philology, 121, 122, 123, 125
philosophy, 3, 5, 6, 8, 9, 12, 228; Aristotelian, 8; civil, 139; empirical, 18, 229, 277n; intellectual style, 82; intellectual liberty, 64, 115; and language, 232-45, 256; scholastic, 6, 7, 60, 78, 80-81, 84, 96, 102, 120, 148, 233, 234, 238; and "science," 269; of science, 15-73. See also moral philosophy, natural philosophy, knowledge, "science"
physicians, 13, 197; and witchcraft, 201, 204, 208, 216, 221, 223
physics, 15; Aristotelian, 44; Bacon, 24; Boyle, 34; Cartesian, 45, 46, 56. See also natural science, natural philosophy
physiology, 126
Pigot, Gervaise, 300n
Pitt, Moses, 127
Plato, 7, 258
plausibility, 140, 151, 163, 164, 178, 229, 230. See also probability
Plot, Robert, 129, 142, 152, 248
poetry, 9, 12, 120, 147, 160, 228, 231, 243, 247, 248, 256, 257-61, 263; and history, 144, 146, 247; and natural science, 242, 243, 257-59, 260, 329n, and rhetoric, 119, 120, 228-29. See also style, language
Polybius, 120, 123, 125, 130, 146, 248
Popish Plot, 185, 188, 192, 314n
popularization, 144, 250; preaching, 228, 231, 252-55, 280n, 328n
predestination, 87, 109
prediction, 54
prejudice, 63, 82, 108, 115, 229
presumptions, in law, 171, 174, 175, 176-77, 316; in withcraft trials, 195, 198, 202, 203, 204, 205-206, 222, 316n
prima facie case, 204
probabilism, 276n, in casuistry, 105, 180
probability, 3-6, 8, 9, 10, 15, 16, 28, 31, 33, 37-44, 47, 140, 201, 213, 267, 268, 270, 271, 272; Bacon, 67,

279n; changing meaning of, 189; Jonathan Cohen, 277n; concurrence of probabilities, 41, 179, 313n; degrees of, 181; Hacking, 38, 277n; Hale, 97, 184; in history, 151; Hooke, 41; Huygens, 43-44; and hypothesis, 277n; in law, 11, 168, 178, 180, 181-82, 184, 187, 189, 313n, 316n; Leibniz, 181; Locke, 37, 42-43, 59, 140; mathematical, 38, 181, 193n, 277n; in the natural sciences, 16, 17, 25, 26, 71; Newton, 60; in religion, 80; and rhetoric, 190, 229-30, 231; Tillotson, 102; Wilkins, 31, 33, 34, 40, 42, 85, 86, 278n. See also certainty, moral certainty
progress, 63-64, 153
proof, 8; from effects of nature, 89, 92-94; legal, 173-76, 180, 182, 187, 188-89, 190, 310n; of witchcraft, 194, 197-99, 205-206, 208-209, 212, 213, 217-18, 316n, 320n. See also witnesses, evidence, testimony, matters of fact, reasonable doubt
prose style, see style
Protestant-Roman Catholic controversy, 10, 57, 80, 81, 82, 95, 101-104, 122, 155, 307n
Protestantism, 14, 61, 157, 252
Providence, 87, 91, 92-93, 94, 110, 131, 154, 292, 306
psychology, 132, 139
Ptolemaic hypothesis, 44, 97
Ptolemy, 122, 298n.
Pufendorf, Sammuel, 169
Puritans, 14, 74, 79-80, 83, 109, 253; science, 287n; preaching, 252-53; Ramism, 231
Puttenham, George, 229
Pyrhonnism, see skepticism

quantification, 23
Quintillian, 241

Raleigh, Sir Walter, 150, 152
Ramism, 80, 231, 232, 250, 251, 252-53
Ramus, Peter, 8, 227, 231, 325n
rationalism, 270
rational religion, see natural religion
Ray, John, 24, 55, 107, 127, 130, 142,

Ray, John (*cont.*)
152, 167, 171, 217, 282n, 303n; latitudinarianism, 112; natural sciences, 17, 20; proofs of God's existence, 92-94
Raymond, Thomas, 209-10
reason, 8, 44, 53, 79, in evaluation of sense data. *See also* natural theology, demonstration, logic
reasonable doubt, beyond, 11, 31, 71, 118, 157, 180, 311n; Boyle, 53; Hale, 97; in law, 168, 180-82, 190; in natural science, 33, 37, 43, 53, 62; in religion, 84, 103; Tillotson, 103; Wilkins, 85-86. *See also* moral certainty
reasonable man, 16, 31, 34, 35, 37, 66, 71, 77, 98, 118, 202, 209; in religion, 81, 84
Reformation, 27, 75-78, 105, 155
religion, 9, 14, 31, 71, 74-118, 156, 227, 268; and history, 77, 154-59, 119, 271; and natural science, 74-75, 82, 111-17, 287n, 288n; and rhetoric, 252-55. *See also* natural religion, faith, belief, Protestant-Roman Catholic controversy, latitudinarians
Renaissance, 119, 162, 270
Renaudot, Theophrastes, 223
report, 29, 133, 140, 142, 143, 148, 179; faithful, 157; of fact, 262-63, 264-65. *See also* matters of fact, history, testimony, witnesses, observation
Restoration, 111
Resurrection, 103
Revelation, 10, 88, 96, 99, 100; Locke, 100-101. *See also* Scripture, Protestant-Catholic controversy
Revolution of 1688, 110, 131
rhetoric, 3, 5, 6, 8, 9, 12, 15, 37, 67, 71, 106, 146, 220, 227-30, 268, 269; ancient, 163; authority, 38, 105, 229; Bacon, 324n, 325n; changes in, 119, 120, 261; Ciceronian, 227, 232, 250, 251; and dialectic, 230-32; and history, 11, 119, 120, 122, 130, 132, 146, 148, 151, 152, 160, 163, 247-49, 298n, 327; Hobbes, 235; humanist, 120, 233; and law, 163, 164, 250-

52; Locke, 242; and logic, 230-31, 232, 239, 242; and philosophy, 7, 273n; and natural science, 232-45, 324n, 325n; and poetry, 119, 120, 228-29; preaching, 252-55, probability, 189, Ramist, 251; Renaissance revival of, 233; scientific discourse, 230-45. *See also* style, discourse, probability, Ramism
Robinson, Thomas, 55
romance, 221, 254, 263, 282n, 284n
Roman Catholicism, claims to infallibility, 78, 79, 80, 82, 117; probabilism, 105. *See also* Protestant-Roman Catholic controversy, Scripture
Rooke, Laurence, 68
Ross, Alexander, 236
Rossi, Paolo, 38, 324n
Royal College of Physicians, 170
Royal Society, 8, 9, 17, 37, 38-41, 49, 52, 59, 62, 65, 113, 122, 127, 129, 213, 215, 301n, 306n; and Academy of Sciences, 73; anti-elitism, 64, 73, 286n; antiquarians, 127, 128, 153-55; assent, 64; and Baconianism, 16, 18-27, 66-70, 286n; epistemology, 104; and history 156; hostility to dogmatism, 65; hypothesis, 47, 56, 60, 279n; language, 12, 251, 261, 265; and law, 170-71; "Ode to The Royal Society," 260; *Philosophical Transactions*, 263; and religion, 112, 115; research and program, 9, 16, 18-27, 43, 67, 286n; scientific discourse, 236-38, 239; and Wadham College, 68; and Wilkins, 112; witchcraft, 215-16, 218, 221-22, 320n. *See also* natural sciences, natural philosophy, Bacon
rule of faith controversy, *see* Protestant-Roman Catholic controversy, Roman Catholics, Scripture
Rushworth, John, 141, 144, 147, 248

St. Augustine, 252
Sallust, 157
Salvation, 87
Sarpi, Paolo, 121, 141, 155, 162, 297n, 303n
"satisfied conscience," 186, 187, 189-

90. *See also* moral certainty, reasonable doubt
Savile, Sir Henry, 152
Scaliger, Joseph, 159
Schneer, Cecil, 127
scholasticism, 6, 7, 60, 78, 84, 120, 148, 230, 233, 234, 238; critique of, 80-81, 96, 102. *See also* Aristotelians
Scot, Reginald, 198-99, 218, 317n
Scroggs, Judge, 185, 190, 192
"science," 3, 4, 5, 8, 9, 15, 27-28, 29, 33, 74, 77, 139, 267, 269; Glanvill, 41, 48; Hale, 97. *See also* knowledge, demonstration, certainty, natural philosophy, natural sciences
scientific revolution, 13, 14
scientism, 73
Scripture, 10, 11, 75, 78, 79, 94-95, 256, 291n, 307n; Castellio, 377; certainty of, 95, 156-57, 158; Chillingworth, 81; Sir Kenelm Digby, 293n; and geology, 127; and history, 155-58; as history, 95, 103; interpretation, 75-76, 79; latitudinarians, 107; Locke, 100-101; Stillingfleet, 103; stylistic model, 239, 253, 329n; Tillotson, 103; Wilkins, 157, 158, 159; and witchcraft, 207, 218; Wolseley, 97. *See also* Revelation, Moses, Protestant-Roman Catholic controversy
sects, religious, 82-83, 117, 254
Seigel, Jerrold, 273n
Selden, John, 134, 147, 149, 150, 165, 169, 318n
senses, 28, 37, 44, 124; Bacon, 24, 61; Barrow, 98, 99; Boyle, 20-21, 53, 281n; fallibility of, 5, 22, 33, 62, 72; Gilbert, 181; Grotius, 77; Hale, 97, 98, 172, 180; Hooke, 35; in natural science, 18-27; Newton, 35; Stillingfleet, 96; Wilkins, 40, 90-91
Servetus, Michael, 77
Seton, John, 231
Sheldon, Gilbert, 295n
Sidney, Algernon, 185
Sidney, Sir Philip, 127, 144, 229, 248, 252, 256, 264, 329n
signs, 38, 111, 175, 277n. *See also* presumptions, probability
Silvius, Aeneas, 122

similitudes, 229, 234, 239
Simon, Richard, 307n
skepticism, 5, 22, 23, 34, 39, 61, 63, 74, 76, 78, 149, 267, 272, 274n, 286n; academic, 76; ancient, 7, 124; avoidance of, 66, 114; Bacon, 19, 149, 173n, 274n; Glanvill, 62; constructive, 62; in England, 61, 124; in France, 22, 23, 76, 124, 149; and history, 124, 299n; religious, 104; Royal Society, 26; and scientific method, 21; Wilkins, 86
Smith, John, 106
Society of Antiquaries, 128, 136, 152-53, 164, 165, 308n
Socinianism, 111
Soman, Alfred, 224
Somers, John, Lord, 170, 309n
soul, immortality of, 68, 83, 87-88
South, Robert, 269n
Spain, 122
Spectator, The, 263-64
Speed, John, 128
Spelman, Sir Henry, 150, 165
Spencer, Edmund, 229, 252, 258, 259, 264
Spinoza, Benedict, 212
spirit, existence defended, 206-207, 220. *See also* witchcraft, soul
Sprat, Thomas, 17, 43, 59, 73, 170, 273n; on alliance of religion and science, 113, 114; and Bacon, 66, 67; causal explanation, 26-27; history, 148, 306n; *History of the Royal Society,* 19, 24-25; hypothesis, 47; language and style, 236, 237, 241-42, 246, 247, 252, 256-67, 326n; latitudinarianism, 107, 113; poetry, 259-61; probability, 40-41; and Royal Society, 113, 274n; scientific discourse, 116; scientific generalization, 26; scientific method, 21; style, 329n; and Wilkins, 296n; witches and apparitions, 215
Stephen, Sir James, 193
Stephens, James, 325n
Stillingfleet, Edward, 88, 101, 107, 113, 140, 157, 255, 293n, 305n; and Boyle, 296n; categories of knowledge, 95-96; defense of Protestant-

Stillingfleet, Edward (*cont.*)
ism, 102, 155; ecclesiastical history, 155-56; faith, 96; and latitudinarians, 111, 295n; natural philosophy, 96; reasonable doubt, 157
Stow, John, 129, 134
Strabo, 122, 298n
style, 230-31; clarity of, 247, 254, 255, 260-61; Cambridge Platonists, 329n; historical, 121, 122; latitudinarian, 107, 329n; oratorical, 121; plain, 12, 107, 230, 233, 238, 239, 247-49, 252-56, 262, 265, 326n; preaching, 252-55; prose, 107, 227, 255-56; scientific, 236-39; Senecan, 235. *See also* discourse, language, poetry
substance, 194; immaterial, 68, 88, 107, 197, 212, 319n; material, 87-88
survey, 121
suspicion, 177, 178, 199. *See also* presumptions, signs
Swift, Jonathan, 262-63, 330n
Sydenham, Thomas, 281n
syllogism, 8, 230
system making, 17; hostility toward, 65, 68, 72, 73

Tacitus, 120, 125
Tatler, The, 263, 264
Taylor, Jeremy, 105
Telesio, Bernardino, 8
Temple, Sir William, 144, 249
Tenison, Thomas, 111, 221, 295n
testimony, 21, 32, 140, 193, 271; Barrow, 98, 99; Boyle, 21; conflicting, 142, 188-89; concurring, 187; credible, 33, 145, 186; Grotius, 95; Hale, 98; historical, 10, 142; in law, 171, 174, 177, 179, 186, 272, 312n; and moral certainty, 32; in natural science, 21-22; Scripture, 95; Stillingfleet, 95-96; Tillotson, 30, 103; Wilkins, 31, 40, 86; in witchcraft trials, 196, 201, 202, 204, 211, 214. *See also* witnesses, credibility, reports, natural history
theology, 13, 27, 170. *See also* natural religion
theory, 48, 282n; Boyle, 34, 53; T. Burnet, 54-56; Charleton, 34;

corpuscular, 46; in history, 150; Hooke, 50-52; Locke, 285n; in natural science, 25, 27, 46, 47-48, 55, 71-72; Newton, 57. *See also* axioms, generalization, hypothesis.
Thomas, Keith, 206
Thomism, 84, 88, 105
Thoroton, Robert, 129, 300n
Tillotson, John, 82, 101, 107, 113, 117, 140; categories of knowledge, 30-31, 85; comprehension, 295n; controversy, 102-103, 157, 291n; and Hale, 189; harmony of natural and revealed religion, 88; historical faith, 157; latitudinarianism, 107, 111; style, 254-55, 286n; rational theology, 87, 88-89, 106; Scripture, 157; and Wilkins, 293n
Toland, John, 292-93n
toleration, religious, 10, 77, 111
topography, 122, 126, 128, 130, 165, 298n. *See also* history, natural history, chorography
torture, 174, 175, 177, 178, 198, 222
tradition, 78, 79, 80, 158, 288n, 291n; oral, 95, 101, 103, 157
treason, 186, 313, 314n
Trevor-Roper H. R., 315n, 323n
trials, 173-76, 184; Popish Plot, 185-87, 188, 192. *See also* juries, judges
Trinity, 96
tropes, 231, 233, 236, 238
Tyson, Edward, 142

Ullmann, Walter, 310n
universal language and character, 12, 227, 243-46
utility, in religion, 105; of knowledge, 18, 19

Valla, Lorenzo, 123, 162, 273n, 298n
Van Leeuwen, Henry, 27, 282n
verisimilitude, 147, 189, 230, 259, 261, 262, 272
Vickers, Brian, 325n
Virgil, Polydore, 125
"virtuoso," term, 273n
Vives, Juan Luis, 8
voyages, history and description, 129,

130; imaginary, 262-63; narratives, 262-63

Wadham College, Oxford University, scientific group, 17, 68, 69, 70, 111-12
Wagstaffe, John, 217-18
Wallace, Karl, 325n
Wallis, John, 17, 24, 68, 70, 178-79, 293n, 295n, 296n; hypothesis, 49; language, 245; philosophy of science, 34
Ward, Seth, 17, 24, 68, 70, 104, 156, 295n, 327n; historical faith, 156-57; natural theology, 83-84; Scripture, 156-57; theories of knowledge, 28; universal character and language, 245
Watt, Ian, 263
Weber, Max, 74
Webster, John, 216-20, 321n
Westfall, R. S., 283n
Westman, Robert, 278n
Whichcote, Benjamin, 107
Whiston, William, 55, 56, 159, 282n
Wigmore, J., 182, 193, 311n
Wilkins, John, 13, 28, 32, 70, 104, 115, 140, 193, 213, 276n, 326n; categories of knowledge, 31-32, 85-86; Copernican hypothesis, 40, 46, 68, 90, 158; on diversity of opinion, 108; *Ecclesiastes*, 290n; and Galileo, 40; and Hale, 171, 172, 189; and Tillotson, 102-103; natural science, 17, 33-34; natural theology, 83, 84-87, 93, 106; probability, 31, 33, 34, 40, 42, 85, 86, 278n; reasonable doubt, 85-86; on religion and science, 113; religious discourse and style, 246, 254-55, 328n; scientific discourse, 237; Scripture, 157, 158, 159; scientific classification, 23, 172; senses, 22-23, 90-91; and Sprat, 296n; testimony, 183-84; and Tillotson, 102-103; Wadham College, Oxford; 111-12; universal charater and language, 234-46, 254, 255

Willis, Thomas, 23
Willughby, Francis, 23, 112, 142
Wilson, Thomas, 250
Winthrop, John, 129
wit, 259, 260
witchcraft, 11, 88, 178, 194-226, 314n-22n; Bacon, 200-201, 213, 215; 316n; Boyle, 215-17, 220, 321n; continental, 224-25, 326; diabolic compact, 195, 203, 215, 317n; decline, 194, 196, 197, 198-200, 203, 205, 206, 211, 221-26, 322n; dissenters, 322n; in France, 221-24, 320n, 323n; Glanvill, 212-18, 220, 225, 319n, 320n; Hale, 206-208, 209, 314n, 318n; More, 212-13, 215-16, 218, 220, 225, 318n-20n; Royal Society, 215-16, 218, 221-22, 320n; use of civil law language, 197, 198, 203, 204
witnesses, 14, 119, 145; authentic, 180; Boyle, 179; credible, 141, 167, 168, 183-88, 190; eye and ear, 100, 123, 141, 142, 144, 145, 156, 158, 180, 213, 214, 219-20, 264-65, 291n; history, 164, 167; law, 11, 167, 168, 163-80, 190, 193, 272, 312n, 313n; Locke, 143; and moral certitude, 33; multiple, 187; Scripture, 95, 291n; witchcraft trials, 198, 201, 204, 213, 214, 217-18, 219-20, 222. *See also,* testimony, credibility, matters of fact.
Wolseley, Sir Charles, 31, 97
Wood, Anthony, 132
Woodward, John, 55, 282n, 303n, 305n
Wren, Christopher, 17, 24, 48, 68, 72, 153, 275n-76n, 305n
Wyche, Sir Cyril, 170

Yolton, John, 90, 292n

zeal, 109
zoology, 126
Zwinglianism, 76

LIBRARY OF CONGRESS CATALOGING IN PUBLICATION DATA

Shapiro, Barbara J.
Probability and certainty in seventeenth-century England.
Includes bibliographical references and index.
1. England—Intellectual life—17th century.
2. Knowledge, Theory of—History—17th century. I. Title.
II. Title: Probability and certainty in 17th-century England.
DA380.S53 1983   001.2   82-61385

ISBN 0-691-05379-0   ISBN 0-691-10146-9 (lim. pbk. ed.)